Understanding
terrorism

Understanding terrorism

Psychosocial Roots,

Consequences,

and Interventions

Edited by
Fathali M. Moghaddam
and Anthony J. Marsella

American Psychological Association, Washington, DC

First Printing June 2003
Second Printing June 2004
Third Printing September 2005

Published by
American Psychological Association
750 First Street, NE
Washington, DC 20002
www.apa.org

To order
APA Order Department
P.O. Box 92984
Washington, DC 20090-2984
Tel: (800) 374-2721; Direct: (202) 336-5510
Fax: (202) 336-5502; TDD/TTY: (202) 336-6123
Online: www.apa.org/books/
Email: order@apa.org

In the U.K., Europe, Africa, and the Middle East, copies may be ordered from
American Psychological Association
3 Henrietta Street
Covent Garden, London
WC2E 8LU England

Typeset in Goudy by Stephen McDougal, Mechanicsville, MD

Printer: United Book Press, Baltimore, MD
Cover Designer: Michael Hentges Design, Alexandria, VA
Technical/Production Editor: Jennifer L. Zale

The opinions and statements published are the responsibility of the authors, and such opinions and statements do not necessarily represent the policies of the American Psychological Association.

Library of Congress Cataloging-in-Publication Data

Understanding terrorism : psychosocial roots, consequences, and interventions / edited by Fathali M. Moghaddam and Anthony J. Marsella— 1st ed.
  p. cm.
 Includes bibliographical references and index.
 ISBN 1-59147-032-3 (alk. paper)
  1. Terrorism—Psychological aspects. 2. Terrorists—Psychology. 3. Social conflict—Psychological aspects. 4. Victims of terrorism—Psychology. 5. Psychic trauma.
6. Terrorism—Prevention. I. Title: Terrorism : psychosocial roots, consequences, and interventions. II. Moghaddam, Fathali M. III. Marsella, Anthony J.
 HV6431.U35 2003
 303.6'25—dc21   2003009643

British Library Cataloguing-in-Publication Data
A CIP record is available from the British Library.

Printed in the United States of America

This volume is dedicated to the September 11, 2001, victims of terrorism. We join the world in saluting your courage and in sharing the pain suffered by your family and friends. Your death will not be in vain but will serve as part of a foundation on which enduring world peace will be built.

CONTENTS

CONTRIBUTORS

Naji Abi-Hashem, PhD, Meier Clinics and Venture International, Seattle, WA

Albert Bandura, PhD, Department of Psychology, Stanford University, Stanford, CA

Laura Barbanel, EdD, School of Education, Brooklyn College, City University of New York, Brooklyn

Yael Danieli, PhD, private practice and Group Project for Holocaust Survivors and Their Children, New York

Patrick H. DeLeon, PhD, Past President, American Psychological Association, Washington, DC

Thomas F. Ditzler, PhD, Department of Psychiatry, Tripler Army Medical Center; Center of Excellence in Disaster Management and Humanitarian Assistance, Honolulu, HI

Brian Engdahl, PhD, Department of Veterans Affairs Medical Center, Minneapolis, MN

Brien Hallett, PhD, Matsunaga Institute for Peace, University of Hawaii, Honolulu

Rom Harré, DLitt, Linacre College, Oxford University, Oxford, England; Department of Psychology, Georgetown University and American University, Washington DC

Ronald F. Levant, EdD, ABPP, Center for Psychological Studies, Nova Southeastern University, Ft. Lauderdale, FL

Katherine R. Long, BA, Department of Psychology, Bates College, Lewiston, ME

Winnifred Louis, PhD, Department of Psychology, Queensland University, Queensland, Australia

Anthony J. Marsella, PhD, Department of Psychology, University of Hawaii, Honolulu

Fathali M. Moghaddam, PhD, Department of Psychology, Georgetown University, Washington, DC

William E. Schlenger, PhD, Research Triangle Institute, Research Triangle Park, NC; Department of Psychiatry and Behavioral Sciences, Duke University Medical Center, Durham, NC

Ervin Staub, PhD, Department of Psychology, University of Massachusetts at Amherst

Donald M. Taylor, PhD, Department of Psychology, McGill University, Montreal, Quebec, Canada

Richard V. Wagner, PhD, Department of Psychology, Bates College, Lewiston, ME

Michael G. Wessells, PhD, Department of Psychology, Randolph-Macon College; Christian Children's Fund, Macon, VA

PREFACE

The purpose of this volume is to provide a critical assessment of the psychological origins and consequences of *international terrorism*: violence in which the perpetrators or their targets cross international borders and whose intentions and consequences are international or global. The tragic events of September 11, 2001, as well as the multitude of other terrorist attacks in recent years, have demonstrated that the world community can no longer ignore the growing risks and consequences of terrorism. The roots of terrorism are complex and reside in historical, political, economic, social, and psychological factors. Of all of these, psychosocial factors have been among the least studied and the least understood, but arguably the most important.

Whereas it is clear that a comprehensive understanding of international terrorism is best grasped from a multidisciplinary and multicultural perspective, the psychosocial component is a fundamental one that requires more thorough articulation and discussion. After all, a terrorist act is intended to alter psychological states in target populations through terror. However, even when a terrorist act is carried out by a lone individual, the motivation can be understood only through a psychosocial approach that accepts a basic idea: The human psyche owes fundamentally important parts of its characteristics to the larger context in which it exists.

Soon after the tragedy of September 11, we accepted the invitation of the American Psychological Association to edit a volume on terrorism that would represent part of the psychology community's contribution to the understanding of this form of violence. We invited leading scholars in the area to prepare critical, brief, but substantive chapters that could be resources for broadening knowledge and implementing psychosocial action agendas. We encouraged them to write in a style that would be accessible to undergraduate students. The contributors have succeeded in providing lucid and stimulating assessments from a variety of viewpoints representing contemporary psychology.

We set out to produce a volume that is both accessible and academically rigorous; one that would serve to nurture further interest and stimulate research in the psychosocial aspects of terrorism. According to a recent survey of book publishers by *Newsweek* magazine, this volume may be one of more than 150 books on terrorism and related topics that are being published in the wake of September 11 ("The Last Word," 2002, p. 56). Several of these books represent firsthand accounts by family members, emergency personnel, and media figures and emphasize the human-interest dimension. Another category consists of books that are explicitly concerned with political issues; for example, they analyze the political reasons behind the September 11 attack and the response to it. A third category, to which the present volume belongs, consists of scholarly books that are readable by the general public but are of special interest to students, teachers, and researchers.

ACKNOWLEDGMENTS

We express our deep appreciation to the chapter authors, who met stringent deadlines for submission of work and rigorous demands for quality in the content of their chapters. It has been an honor to work with you.

This volume was the brainchild of Dr. Gary VandenBos, Executive Director of Publishing and Communications at the American Psychological Association (APA). Following the September 11, 2001, tragedy, Gary immediately recognized the urgent need for psychology to address the complex challenges of understanding and preventing terrorism. He saw that research and practicing psychologists have invaluable contributions to make in this complex arena, but there are few resources that can be used for graduate and undergraduate coursework that include a broad spectrum of psychology's scientific knowledge and practices.

We also extend our deep gratitude and respect to the many other APA Books staff members and freelancers who brought this volume to successful fruition, including Elizabeth Bulatao, Lansing Hays, Ed Meidenbauer, Anne Woodworth, Jennifer Zale, and Ida Audeh.

Lastly, we express our deep affection and regard for our spouses, Maryam and Joy Ann, who once again offered both patience and understanding as the book devoured time and intruded into family life. We are hopeful that the volume will justify your caring and support by providing a substantive contribution.

Understanding terrorism

INTRODUCTION

FATHALI M. MOGHADDAM AND ANTHONY J. MARSELLA

This volume focuses on the psychosocial dimension of terrorism. The term *psychosocial* refers to the close and interactive relationship between the human psyche and the diverse social contexts in which we live. Although these chapters are diverse in their content and perspectives, they share a common commitment to the importance of understanding cultural variations in worldviews and orientations. This commitment is neither an apology for nor an endorsement of the actions of any nation or group in the aftermath of September 11; rather, it is a recognition that unless we understand the perspectives of different cultures around the world, we, as individual human beings and as societies, will be limited and constrained in our ability to live successfully in a global community. Peace, our common goal, can only prevail through an increased understanding of the psychological complexities in which human beings—driven and characterized by diverse motivations, attitudes, and perceptions—come to endorse and prefer certain behaviors over others.

All cultures have theories (even if only implicit) of human behavior and of the linkages between behavior and the constructed world in which people live. This constructed world is both shaped and sustained through the socialization process that merges each of us in interlocking institutions that include the family, community, school, and the realms of politics, commerce, and religion. Ultimately, it is through change in this institutional matrix that the human psyche itself can be changed and reshaped toward broader and less ethnocentric views of reality—a reality that can accommodate and tolerate diversity, uncertainty, and trust. Terrorism may be contained but never defeated as long as there are real or perceived threats and injustices that foster widespread hatred and revenge. There may be small and large military successes, but eventually there must be a coming to grips with the strengths and weaknesses of the human psyche and the cultural milieu in which it is fostered.

Although this volume emphasizes the current international terrorism challenge associated with fundamentalist forms of Islam and with certain Middle Eastern cultural and historical traditions, clearly this is not the only context in which terrorism flourishes. More than 68 low-intensity wars are going on in the world today, and many different cultural and ethnic groups are involved in these deadly struggles, including Northern Ireland (i.e., Catholics vs. Protestants), Sri Lanka (Buddhists vs. Hindus), Aceh Indonesia (Christians vs. Muslims), and tribal Rwanda–Congo (i.e., Tutsi vs. Hutu). There is also a great need to study and understand terrorist acts by single individuals (e.g., the Unabomber) and domestic terrorists (e.g., Oklahoma City bombing), because they too constitute a major challenge to national security. Lastly, much to our national dismay, the international media have often pointed out that in the eyes of some nations and people, the United States is a terrorist nation, one that has used military and diplomatic pressures to ensure corporate expansion and control, particularly in the realm of an "axis of oil."

The present volume is divided into three major sections, moving from broad conceptual discussions about collective life, to more specific discussions about psychological processes, to practical issues of coping with terrorism. The first part explores the wider social context of terrorism, with particular emphasis on the pervasive nature of terrorism in past human behavior, the manufacturing of the meaning of terrorism in contemporary Western societies, and the cultural conditions in which terrorism is more likely to arise. The main theme of the second part is psychological processes associated with terrorism. The chapters in the final part are more applied, focusing on the role of psychology and psychologists in helping populations cope with terrorism.

There are thematic similarities and differences across chapters in their approach to understanding and defining terrorism. Hallett (chap. 2) sees terrorism as simply an ordinary crime by another name, but Abi-Hashem (chap. 3) argues that what is defined as terrorism is a matter of perspective. Using social constructionist language, Harré (chap. 4) seems to agree with Abi-Hashem by proposing that it is not the action that gets a person labeled as a terrorist but the interpretation of the action as an act of terrorism. In some ways similar is Ditzler's (chap. 9) argument that terrorism is characterized by its impact. A common theme in chapters by Bandura (chap. 6); Staub (chap.

7); Wagner and Long (chap. 10); Danieli, Engdahl, and Schlenger (chap. 11); and Levant, Barbanel, and DeLeon (chap. 13) is the crippling psychological consequences of terrorism on noncombatants. For these authors, the targeting of noncombatants is a key defining feature of terrorism. Finally, in exploring the meaning of terrorism, several authors give more importance to the antecedent conditions. For example, Moghaddam (chap. 5) gives importance to cultural prerequisites, and Taylor and Louis (chap. 8) highlight the powerlessness and marginalized nature of terrorist groups. Thus, on the basic question of "what is terrorism?" the contributors adopt approaches with elements that are both similar and dissimilar.

Part I, Foundations and Context, includes chapter 1 by Anthony J. Marsella, a cross-cultural psychologist, who provides some basic background and issues that must be understood in the study of terrorism. Marsella challenges readers to question the conventional wisdom and to broaden their viewpoints by accepting an element of Cartesian doubt rather than insisting that our quest is one for absolute certainty, that most elusive of phenomena. In chapter 2, Brien Hallett, a political scientist and peace scholar, raises some vexing questions about the nature and definition of terrorism. Hallett rejects the view of terrorists as soldiers, and he argues that terrorists, and not their environments, create terror. However, he also acknowledges that certain environmental conditions make terrorism possible. It is noteworthy that some sections of Hallett's recent book, *The Lost Art of Declaring War*, have been distributed to the members of the United States Senate. In chapter 3, Naji Abi-Hashem, a psychologist in private practice and of Middle Eastern descent, provides a broad psychopolitical analysis of peace and war in the Middle East, with a strong emphasis on understanding the worldview and orientation of Islamic cultures in this explosive region. Dr. Abi-Hashem uses his grasp of the cultural complexities of the Middle East to explore some misperceptions by outsiders about the region. Rom Harré, the author of chapter 4, is a social psychologist who shares an appointment between Oxford University and Georgetown University, and he is a leading scholar in postmodernism. Harré raises some fundamental issues about how we can become prisoners of the very words that we choose to use in talking about terrorism. His semantic and syntaxic analysis, clearly influenced by Wittgenstein, illuminates one of the many challenges we face: determining which words and which meanings shall be used to speak of terrorism. Chapter 5, by Fathali M. Mogahaddam, a cultural psychologist of Eastern origin, explores the cultural preconditions that support potential terrorist groups. Like Hallett, Moghaddam accepts that terrorism is not causally determined by environmental conditions but that certain conditions make terrorism more probable. Among the 10 preconditions Moghaddam identifies, he proposes that isolation of the potential terrorist group from the rest of society and a particular belief system toward societal change may serve as catalysts for the emergence of terrorists.

Part II, Psychosocial Context, opens with chapter 6 by Albert Bandura, one of the founders of social behaviorism. He uses the language of this framework to provide a fascinating analysis of the origins and prevention of terrorism. Building on his seminal publications in the area of learning and behavior, Bandura offers a schematic representation that illuminates how terrorism arises and can be contained and prevented. Chapter 7 offers a scholarly presentation on the roots of ethnopolitical violence and aggression. Written by Ervin Staub, a social psychologist who is one of the foremost experts on violence and aggression, this chapter addresses both the origins and prevention of intergroup hostility. Staub has conducted extensive fieldwork in Rwanda, where he and his coworkers have been engaged in the application of social psychological principles to the rebuilding of this new nation.

In the same section, in chapter 8, Donald M. Taylor and Winnifred Louis, social psychologists working in Canada and Australia, explore one of the most important yet vexing challenges of our times: the quest for identity. What emerges from their writing is the critical importance of human identity in a world that continuously challenges cultural and historical roots and traditions. Under such circumstances, identity becomes a primary need, something to be nurtured and defended against a threatening world. Chapter 9, written by Thomas F. Ditzler, a clinical psychologist who is active in training military health professionals, takes the reader on a journey into the nature of the malevolent mind, highlighting some of the origins and consequences of destruction and war. In many respects, this is the most "psychological" of all the chapters in its orientation and analysis of terrorism.

Chapter 10 addresses the potential of peace psychology for understanding and ameliorating terrorism. This chapter, written by Richard V. Wagner, editor of the *Journal of Peace Psychology*, and Katherine R. Long, of Bates College, offers alternatives to military intervention and war that are rooted in increased international understanding, mutual or shared interests and concerns, and the wisdom that ultimately violence begets violence. How can we de-escalate situations that bring cultures, nations, and peoples into conflict? This is a very difficult question for victims of terrorism to confront, but in the long term this challenge must be taken up.

In Part III, Consequences of Terrorism, three internationally known experts in trauma—Yael Danieli, a private practitioner in clinical psychology and an international activist at the United Nations; Brian Engdahl, a clinical psychologist working with the Veterans Administration; and William E. Schlenger, a research psychologist at the Research Triangle Institute and a leader in Vietnam-era posttraumatic stress disorder studies—discuss the complexities of coping with trauma. Their vast clinical and research experience makes chapter 11 a feast of theory, research, and practice on trauma. Chapter 12 is penned by Michael G. Wessells, perhaps the most visible psychologist involved in refugee and internally displaced person care in the world today. Every war, every conflict, every terrorist act brings with it casualties and victims who are uprooted and who are compelled to search for security, often in strange and distant lands. Dr. Wessells brings forth the human face of these survivors who live daily amid peril and pain. In chapter 13, Ronald F. Levant, a clinical psychologist and an active member of the American Psychological Association (APA) committee on terrorism; Laura Barbanel, a researcher at the City University of New York; and Patrick H. DeLeon, a former APA president and one of psychology's best-known professionals, invoke the concept of resiliency as a counter to the problems of terrorism and trauma. Resiliency has become a popular concept in psychology, in part because of its positive implications. The threat of terrorism may not be eliminated, but its effects can definitely be dealt with if we can better understand the resources that are available to us.

I

FOUNDATIONS
AND CONTEXT

1

REFLECTIONS ON INTERNATIONAL TERRORISM: ISSUES, CONCEPTS, AND DIRECTIONS

ANTHONY J. MARSELLA

While nothing is easier than to denounce the evildoer, nothing is harder than to understand him.

—Fyodor Mihailovich Dostoevsky, *The Possessed*

This chapter is intended to provide an overview of international terrorism—its definitional problems, its conceptual issues, and its psychosocial foundations. The psychosocial approach adopted in this chapter (and in the volume as a whole) is one that takes into consideration the familiar topics of motivation, cognition, group behavior, violence, and the pursuit of peace within a context that acknowledges the complex psychological, situational, and social determinants of international terrorism. This chapter asserts that the deeper roots of terrorism are located within complex historical and cultural contexts that are often centuries old. This approach does not mean that terrorism is justified but rather that understanding its origins and sustaining influences cannot be achieved by demonizing specific individuals or cultures. In today's global community, international terrorism occurs in a milieu of competing and conflicting religious, economic, cultural, psychological, and historical worldviews and ideologies. This environment is further complicated by omnipresent military, political, and legal pressures and counterpressures. Thus, it is important to try to understand individual and collective terrorist behavior in context.

Today's world is a global community whose complex individual and national interdependencies challenge the skills and imaginations of governments. Dr. Max Manwaring of the Strategic Studies Institute of the U.S. Army War College posited four characteristics that define the new economic and political order facing our global community:

First, the world has seen and will continue to see a wide range of ambiguous and uncomfortable threats in the "gray area" between war and peace. These threats and challenges are the consequences of root cause pressures and problems perpetrated and/or exploited by a variety of internal and international political actors. They are manifested by transnational illegal drug trafficking, organized crime, corruption, terrorism, warlordism, insurgency, civil war, regional wars, humanitarian problems such as large-scale refugee flows and famine, and the horrors of ethnic cleansing.

Second, as a consequence, there is a need to redefine "enemy," "power," and "victory." The enemy is no longer a recognizable military entity or an industrial capability to make traditional war. The enemy now becomes "violence," and the causes of violence. Power is not simply combat firepower directed at a traditional enemy's military formation or industrial complex. Power is multi-level and combined political, psychological, moral, informational, economic, societal, military, police, and civil bureaucratic activity that can be brought to bear appropriately on the causes as well as the perpetrators of violence.

Third, these ambiguities intrude on the "comfortable" vision of war in which the assumed center of gravity has been enemy military formations and the physical capability to conduct war. Clausewitz reminds us, however, that "in countries subject to domestic strife . . . and popular uprisings, the [center of gravity] is the personalities of the leaders and public opinion. It is against these that our energies should be directed." Thus, in contemporary intra-national conflict, the primary center of gravity changes from a familiar military concept to an ambiguous and uncomfortable political-economic-psychological-security paradigm.

Fourth, the conflictual means to secure, maintain, and enhance interests abroad have become multi-dimensional, multi-lateral, and multi-organizational. Conflict is no longer a military to military confrontation. Conflict now involves entire populations. Conflict now involves a large number of national civilian and military agencies, other national civilian organizations, international organizations, nongovernmental organizations, and subnational indigenous actors involved in dealing in one way or another with complex threats to security, peace, and well-being. (Manwaring, 2001, p. 1)

What is at stake for many nations and subcultural groups is identity, meaning, status, wealth, power, and (above all) survival. Survival has become the justification for immediate action, even if the actions are setting new precedents in international relations, diplomacy, and the conduct of war. The emphasis on survival compels us to rethink our basic assumptions about the nature of human collective life. Today, the quest for identity, meaning, status, wealth, and power has merged with the need for survival, creating a contemporary situation unique in cause and consequence. For example, "survival" is used by both the Palestinians and the Israelis as justification for their struggle, and the result is a seemingly endless conflict.

In the so-called "war on terrorism," we stand on the brink of widespread global war and violence, testing yet again our national resolve, resiliency, and wisdom. Do we have the wisdom to transcend the passions of the moment in favor of greater national and global security in the future? The governments of the United States, Great Britain, and Israel hold that terrorism can be defeated through vigilance, counterterrorism, and the elimination of terrorist resources. However, I believe that these actions alone, potent though they may be, can never be sufficient to stem the tide of terrorism, which springs from human discontent with and resentment of inequality and indifference and from widespread beliefs that violence is justified in the face of oppression and insult. This belief that the end justifies the means has become commonplace in business, government, and war. Now we are facing it as a global community. We must combine any military actions with economic, cultural, and diplomatic activities directed toward establishing hope, opportunity, and social justice.

In the present chapter I discuss the deeper historical and cultural roots of international terrorism and our failure to understand how these roots in turn are determining our current military and political policies and actions. I note how the very pressures for social change brought on by globalization constitute serious threats around the globe and how this is being ignored by Western powers in favor of temporary fiscal gain. The anger occurring is directed toward Westernization, with its emphasis on consumerism, exploitation, and profit. Western emphases on individualism, materialism, consumerism, change, and competition are in conflict with traditional cultural values that emphasize collectivism, spirituality, stability, fixed roles, and cooperation.

In this chapter, I also cite the Israeli–Palestinian conflict as a continuing and perhaps never-ending source of global discord. It is out of control on all sides, and countries throughout the world are being drawn into its violence and hate. Religious fanatics see in this conflict the fulfillment of biblical prophecy. This clash cannot be solved by the West's reflexive pro-Israeli sentiment and action, no matter how deep the roots of this support may be because of cultural and intellectual similarities. Disproportionate support inflames hate, and although it may bring Israel closer to the West, it deepens the West's divide with many other parts of the world. It is only a matter of time before terrorists decide to move beyond Israel to attack Jews and Israel's supporters throughout the globe. This is the reality we face.

The terrorist attacks on New York City and Washington, DC, on September 11, 2001, are an expression of the reality we face, and this chapter pursues its specific roots, impact, and determinants. The destruction and trauma of that day are not the result of one man's hate; Osama bin Laden managed to tap into widespread fear, hate, and anger toward the United States by using basic "fundamentalist" and "authoritarian" psychology principles. He preached revenge, and was successful in recruiting followers because he linked Western injustices and Western errors of arrogance, overconfidence, and ethnocentrism to numerous abuses of Islam.

I posit that terrorist groups have existed throughout history and that the minds of people who willingly embrace violence and seek to coerce others for political and social ends may have certain shared characteristics, including a commitment to a set of beliefs that offers certainty and a psychological immunity to reason, negotiation, and empathy.

IN PURSUIT OF CONTEXT

When, where, and why did it begin, this idea, this force, this act called "terrorism," this form of violence that seeks to influence, coerce, threaten, or destroy a people, a government, a nation, or perhaps even a civilization? Over the past several centuries, terrorism has killed, injured, or permanently brutalized countless human beings. It has left many people bewildered by its nature, its capacity to control minds, and its ability to survive across time and place. Governments, scholars, and military officials are locked in debate over its definition. Terrorism is simultaneously criminal, political, economic, social, psychological, and moral in origin and consequence. Terrorists target innocent victims who are unknowingly caught in the inner turmoil of minds that nurture and proclaim hate, anger, and violence and that claim injustice, indignity, and abuse. Terrorists cross borders and disrupt a world drawn ever closer and interdependent. Their acts are simultaneously rooted in distant history and in the passions of the moment. They are coldly calculated and precisely planned and yet reflexively and impulsively acted out in rage and fury.

What are the psychosocial roots of terrorism? Are the seeds to be found in troubled and perverted minds that seek anarchy and chaos for the sheer delight of it? Or are they to be found in the minds of those so driven by revenge and hatred that they are blind to reason and morality? Are its seeds to be found in the desperate and urgent cries for freedom from state oppression such as those that occurred in Joseph Stalin's Soviet Union or Mao Tsetung's China? Are they to be found in the struggle to throw off domination and exploitation by foreign colonial powers, as was the case in British-ruled Palestine and French-ruled Algeria? Are they to be found in the equally intense and desperate cries for recognition and attention by those who consider themselves to be "voices crying in the wilderness," voices that claim to be the saviors of a world mired in wickedness and evil, a world turning from

"God," such as those voices found in fundamentalist religious groups like the Aum Shinrikyo in Japan or the *Wahhabi* Islamists of the Middle East?

DEFINING *TERRORISM*: AN ENDLESS DEBATE

One person's terrorist is another person's freedom fighter. Some Palestinians suffering under Israeli oppression view Osama bin Laden or members of such groups as Hizballah, Hamas, and al-Qaeda to be freedom fighters, martyrs, revolutionaries, and guerillas; however, Israel and the United States regard them as terrorists. Taylor (1988) stated,

> The fact is, of course, that there is a vast amount of hypocrisy on the subject of political terrorism. We all righteously condemn it—except where we ourselves or friends of ours are engaging in it. Then we ignore it, or gloss over it, or attach to it tags like "liberation" or "defense of the free world" or national honor to make it seem like something other than what it is. (Taylor, 1988, p. 3)

There are scores of definitions of *terrorism* (e.g., Miller & File, 2001; Whittaker, 2001). Miller and File noted four problems associated with efforts to define *terrorism* today: (a) There have been historical changes in the definition, (b) media and states have been inconsistent in their use of the term, (c) there are multiple definitions across agencies even within a single country such as the United States, and (d) there is international disagreement on the definition of the term (2001, p. 13). They observed that all contemporary "terrorist" organizations "liken themselves to armies or instruments of liberation or defense" (Miller & File, 2001, p. 13).

Carr (2002) defined *terrorism* as "the contemporary name given to, and the modern permutation of, warfare deliberately waged against civilizations with the purpose of destroying their will to support either their leaders or policies that the agents of such violence find objectionable" (p. 6). The Federal Bureau of Investigation defines *terrorism* as "[t]he unlawful use of force or violence against persons or property to intimidate or coerce a government, civilian population, or any segment thereof, in furtherance of political or social objectives" (Whittaker, 2001, p. 3). In his book on the legal control of terrorism, Han (1993) discussed the extraordinary complexities of defining *terrorism* without considering context, motives, and consequences. The law fails us because motives, intent, choice, responsibility, and circumstance all become involved with the meaning of *terrorism*.

The U.S. Department of State defines *terrorism* as it is defined in Title 22 of the United States Code, Section 2656f(d): It is "premeditated, politically motivated violence perpetrated against noncombatant targets by subnational groups or clandestine agents, usually intended to influence an audience" (Reich, 1990/1998, p. 262). The term *international terrorism* means terrorism involving citizens or the territory of more than one country. The term *terrorist group* means any group that practices, or that has significant subgroups that practice, international terrorism.

The numerous definitions of *terrorism* converge around certain points: *Terrorism* is broadly viewed as (a) the use of force or violence (b) by individuals or groups (c) that is directed toward civilian populations (d) and intended to instill fear (e) as a means of coercing individuals or groups to change their political or social positions. Yet, without specific historical and cultural context, all definitions are subject to debate. This is why a psychosocial perspective becomes so important: It locates the behavior within the larger context in which we live.

Whittaker (2001) and Reich (1990/1998) have discussed in detail the nuances and complexities of defining *terrorism* and even the impossibility of achieving a suitable definition. The task is further complicated by the variety of patterns of terrorism, including (a) political terrorism, (b) separatist terrorism, (c) religious terrorism, and (d) pathological terrorism (e.g., Miller & File, 2001; Post, 2002a, 2002b; Reich, 1990/1998). Terrorist motives are numerous and varied and may be related to destruction of the social and political order (anarchy), divinely sanctioned violence (God's will), revenge, economic and financial gain, racial or cultural supremacy, state-sponsored terrorism, and political and national collapse (revolutionary and liberation).

CATEGORIZATION AND CLASSIFICATION
OF TERRORISM PATTERNS

Many efforts have been made to categorize different types of terrorism on the basis of the terrorists' motives (e.g., religious, political), goals (e.g., instilling fear, destruction), and methods (e.g., bombs, weapons of mass destruction). One of the most comprehensive efforts has been made by Post (2002a, 2002b). Post proposed that political terrorism can be divided into *substate terrorism* (e.g., groups not necessarily linked with a national government), *state-supported terrorism* (e.g., Libya, North Korea, Sudan), and *state or regime terrorism* (e.g., use of a state's resources, such as its police and military, against its own citizens). He suggested that substate terrorism comprises the most varied and diverse terrorist groups, including (a) leftist social revolutionaries (e.g., *Sendero Luminoso* of Peru), (b) rightist groups (e.g., neo-Nazis), (c) nationalist separatist groups (e.g., the IRA in Ireland, the ETA in Basque), (d) religious extremist groups, and (e) single-issue groups (e.g., anti-abortion groups, environmental groups). He divided the religious extremist groups into fundamentalist groups (al-Qaeda) and new religion groups (*Aum Shinrikyo*). Post went on to differentiate the kinds of weapons or methods each of these groups is likely to use because of their intentions or goals. He also posited that there is criminal terrorism and pathological terrorism. An emerging problem is that political terrorism and criminal terrorism are now fusing into one, as evidenced by the situation in Colombia, where revolutionaries and cocaine smugglers become mutual supporters. This is also true in Afghanistan, where money from heroin sales is used to support groups such as al-Qaeda.

Post's (2002a, 2002b) discussion of these varied terrorist groups is one of the most illuminating presentations on this very complex topic. However, critics have suggested that Post is ignoring another spectrum of terrorism because of his own ethnocentric and context-dependent biases. For example, Montiel and Anuar (2002) argue that there are other forms of terrorism, including *global-structural violence* and U.S.-legitimated acts of terror. They allege that the United States is responsible for a hegemonic globalization equal to terrorism because it continues to perpetuate American global domination over developing countries by fostering material inequities and cultural domination and exploitation. Montiel and Anuar contend that the United States encourages extensive global poverty and that this poverty engenders hopelessness and resentment that leads to terrorism. They further propose that the United States is among the world's state sponsors of terrorism because they have supported rightist groups that have undermined legitimate governments in South and Central America and even in the Middle East. They also claim that Israel started the terrorist group Hamas to undermine the PLO, and yet today labels it a *terrorist group* because it engages in violence against Israel. In these instances, the definition of *terrorism* is expanded from "direct acts of violence" to "political actions that seem to encourage or sanction violent behavior."

In yet another critique of Post's (2002a, 2002b) typology, Langholtz (2002) noted that there is a need to include "capability" in considering distinctions among the various groups proposed by Post. Further, Langholtz argued that motives overlap across the various groups, so there may be complex motivational patterns. Both Post and Langholtz agree that there are many different terrorist psychology patterns and that more needs to be done to clarify and evaluate our knowledge of these patterns and their various risk parameters. Nevertheless, the Post typology represents a useful starting point for understanding the complex spectrum of terrorism patterns that must be addressed in today's world.

In her excellent chapter on the logic of terrorism, Crenshaw (1998) raised a number of interesting questions about the intentions and behaviors of terrorists. She asked: "Why is terrorism attractive to some opponents of the state but unattractive to others?" (p. 10). Clearly it is possible to be very discontent with government, even to the point of public protest and condemnations, without resorting to violence and destruction directed against the State. This is what happened as American citizens became disenchanted with America's involvement with the Vietnam War, especially following the display of police brutality in suppressing protest at the 1968 Democratic

Party Convention in Chicago and the Kent State shootings. Protests became endemic, and protesters were beaten by police in the name of public safety and in support of government policy in Vietnam. Groups such as the Weathermen Underground Organizations emerged during the Vietnam War period (1969–1974) and were responsible for more than 19 bombings (Nash, 1998). Members of the Weatherman Underground consisted of former members of the Students for a Democratic Society. However, most people, despite their discontent with government war policy, did not become terrorists seeking to harm or kill innocent citizens to achieve their political ends.

There are thousands of terrorist groups in the world today. The following is a list of some of the more active terrorist groups.

- Abu Nidal Organization (Middle East)
- Abu Sayyaf Group (Philippines)
- Aum Shinriykyo (Japan)
- Basque Fatherland and Liberty (Spain)
- HAMAS (Islamic Resistance Movement; Palestine)
- Hizballah (Party of God; Lebanon)
- Gama'a al-Islamiyya (Islamic group; Egypt)
- Japanese Red Army (Japan)
- Kahane Chai (Jewish group; Israel/United States)
- Kurdistan Workers' Party (Turkey)
- Liberation Tigers of Tamil Elam (Sri Lanka)
- Mujahedin-e Khalq Organization (Iran)
- Palestine Islamic Jihad-Shaqaqi Faction (Palestine)
- Palestine Liberation Front-Abu Abbas Faction (Palestine)
- Popular Front for the Liberation of Palestine (Palestine)
- Popular Front for the Liberation of Palestine—General Command (Palestine)
- al-Qaeda (Afghanistan/Sudan/Saudi Arabia)
- Revolutionary Armed Forces of Colombia (Colombia)
- Shining Path (Peru)

TERRORIST METHODS

The methods available to terrorists for executing their operations are numerous and varied. Most terrorist acts in the past have been by bombing, and this has certainly been the case in Israel where Palestinian "suicidal" bombers called *"martyrs"* have chosen to strap bombs to their body and to explode them in crowded settings in Israel/Palestine. Other methods of terrorists include kidnapping and hostage taking (e.g., Abu Sayyaf in the Philippines), assassinations of political figures (e.g., the Israeli government in West Bank and Gaza), cyberterrorism (e.g., efforts to create computer viruses or to destroy files of security agencies and governments), bioterrorism (e.g., use of bacteria, viruses, and various germs—popular agents include anthrax, bubonic plague, and smallpox—to infect civilians such as occurred in China and Korea by Japanese forces in the 1930s and Saddam Hussein's poisoning of Kurdish people in Northern Iraq), nuclear terrorism (e.g., use of nuclear bombs or dirty bombs that make use of radioactive material), and chemical terrorism (e.g., the use of sarin gas as occurred with the Aum Shinryko cult in Japan). Recently, there has been concern about agro-terrorism, in which food supplies would be destroyed through genetic engineering or bacterial infections. Terrorists do not usually meet or face armies in the field in open armed contact; the methods used are mostly surreptitious and the targets are civilian. The intention is not only destruction, but also instilling fear and terror in a population. Ultimately, target availability, risk, impact, and fiscal costs are also prime determinants of the method used.

A BRIEF CHRONOLOGY OF TERRORISM: PLAYING WITH WORDS

Exhibit 1.1 provides a brief history of terrorism, with special reference to the many possible patterns of terrorism that have existed through the years if one chooses to define terrorism broadly. Detailed histories of terrorism can be found in Anderson and Sloan (1995), Laquer (2001), and Nash (1998).

WILL TERRORISM CONTINUE?

International terrorism probably will continue well into the 21st century, because many of the root causes of terrorism are not being addressed as much as they should be by developed and developing nations. Among the conditions that encourage terrorism are the following:

1. *Global poverty.* Poverty destroys the human spirit and erodes reason. Wealthy nations are considered by some to be the source of poverty, and anger and hate are kindled because of the disparities.
2. *Racism.* Much of the world considers the inequities in the distribution of wealth and power to be the source of racism. For example, many Arabs and Muslims feel that the West is very biased against them and does not give them respect and compassion. The disproportionate support of Israel by the U.S. government validates and amplifies this conclusion.
3. *Oppression.* Throughout the world, oppression of minority groups and subnational groups continues on a wide scale (e.g.,

EXHIBIT 1.1
A Brief Historical Chronology of Terrorism: Some Important Dates

Date or time period	Description	Type of terrorism
200 B.C.E.	Imperial Rome uses destruction (punitive war) to control populations and states it has conquered. There is brutalization of populations, servitude, and torture in the name of bringing order to the empire.	State-sponsored terrorism under guise of war
63–72 C.E.	Radical Jewish assassins (*Sicarii* in Latin), called *Zealots*, known for their fervent commitment to the Torah, kill Roman soldiers and suspected Jewish collaborators in an attempt to drive Rome from ancient Palestine.	Liberation terrorism
1000–1200	A group called *assassins* emerges among Shiite Muslims; they murder Muslim leaders whom they accuse of responsibility for corrupting Islam; the assassins resent the passing of Islamic leadership from Mohammad's family to others.	Terroristic assassinations
1789–1799	The French Revolution (1789–1799) brings Maximilien de Robespierre (1758–1794) to power as an enemy of the French monarchy and an advocate of democratic reforms. He urges the guillotine execution of King Louis XVI and later eliminates members of both moderate and extremist political factions, instituting a "Reign of Terror." He is subsequently overthrown from his position as President of the National Convention; he and 99 of his supporters are beheaded by the very instrument with which he terrorized the people of France.	State-sponsored terrorism
1879–??	An ideological group in Russia called *Narodnaya Volya* (The People's Will) is formed to bring about revolution and the downfall of the Czarist state. They assassinate Czarist officials and others in their efforts.	The beginning of modern terrorism
September 6, 1901	President William McKinley is shot in Buffalo, New York, by Leon Czolgosz, an anarchist. McKinley dies from the wounds on September 14, 1901.	Anarchy terrorism
June 28, 1914	Serbian nationalists, belonging to a group known as the Serbian Black Hand Society, led by Gavrilo Princip, assassinate Francis Ferdinand, Archduke of Austria, and his wife, in Sarajevo, Bosnia. The assassination ignites World War I.	Political terrorism

continues

EXHIBIT 1.1
(Continued)

September 1–3, 1923	In the wake of the great Tokyo-Yokohama earthquake, Emperor Hirohito of Japan commands his special private organization (the Black Dragon Society) to round up 4,000 Koreans and behead them. The Koreans are blamed for the earthquake. Hirohito also uses the occasion to murder some political critics.	State-sponsored terrorism under the guise of protecting national security; Criminal and political terrorism
	The Black Dragon Society was founded in the 1890s by Mitsuru Toyama as a criminal terrorist organization. It has been succeeded in modern times by the *Yakuza*.	
December 1, 1934	Joseph Stalin executes 117 members of a Stalin-contrived plot to purge and destroy undesirables (e.g., gypsies, kulaks, nomads). During Stalin's reign, tens of millions of Soviet citizens are killed, imprisoned, and tortured.	Psychopathological terrorism—terrorism combined with sociopathic character of political leader
1936–1945	Nazi Germany begins the eradication of all Jews through mass executions at various concentration camps. More than six million Jews are killed in what has come to be known as the Holocaust.	Genocidal terrorism
December 21, 1988	Pan Am Flight 103 is destroyed by a bomb over Lockerbie, Scotland, killing 259 people in the air and 11 on the ground; a Libyan terrorist is convicted of the crime.	Modern-day state-sponsored international terrorism
February 26, 1993	The World Trade Center is damaged from a car bomb planted in its underground garage by Islamic terrorists who are followers of Omar Abd al-Rahman. Six people die and more than 1,000 people are injured.	International substate terrorism
March 20, 1995	The religious and political cult, Aum Shinri Kyo (Supreme Truth), under the leadership of Shoko Asahara, attempts to poison the Tokyo subway passengers using sarin gas; 12 die and 5,500 are injured.	Religious extremist terrorism
September 11, 2001	Civilian airplanes are flown into the World Trade Center and the Pentagon in an attack attributed to al-Qaeda; almost 3,000 people are killed.	International substate terrorism

Note. The material in this exhibit was drawn from Carr (2002), Laquer (2001), Nash (1998), and Reich (1998).

Chechnya, Palestine, Indonesia, China). Because the governments in power are so strong and are unwilling or unable to work out an accommodation, terrorism emerges as an option for fighting oppression. The resistance to oppression offers some groups a sense of hope and empowerment. They may be destroyed by the oppressing nation but they will at least call attention to their plight and exact some revenge for their treatment.

4. *Israel.* No matter the justification for Israel's actions, its continued antagonism toward the Palestinians fuels anger, hate, and discontent on a global basis. Jews and Jewish symbols will be attacked across the world even if the Israelis can stop the suicide bombers at home. This continuing struggle is the most serious flash point for a possible global conflagration that could involve the use of weapons of mass destruction. It remains a wellspring of terrorism on both sides.

5. *Unstable nations.* Many nations (e.g., Afghanistan and Sierra Leone) exist in a chronic state of instability in which the governmental infrastructure is broken down or destroyed. These nations can no longer provide their citizenry with basic security (e.g., housing, food, medical care). Physical security is often threatened by domestic or international groups seeking to take control of the nation. Under these conditions war and violence become a way of life, and terrorism emerges as a response to the instability and chaos. Nation-building will be a major challenge of this century. Failure to meet this challenge can result in the emergence of internal terrorism as a form of rebellion and revolt. It can also spur international terrorism.

6. *Rogue nations.* President George W. Bush's designation of some nations as constituting an "axis of evil" was a poor choice of words for the pursuit of peace, and these words are now being used by some nations to describe the United States and Great Britain. Nevertheless, certain nations that greatly resist cooperation with others can foster terrorism within their borders or can nurture it in other countries. Because Cuba, Iraq, Iran, Lebanon, Libya, North Korea, and Syria are often cited by the U.S. State Department as source nations for international terrorism, it is clear that efforts must be made to defuse the economic and political conditions that lead to such a designation. This does not mean that war is the answer. Rather, diplomacy and economic development must be combined with new levels of mutual respect and support.

As the threat of terrorism has become more apparent, we have witnessed in the last decade a dramatic increase in the number of books and journal articles concerned with biographies of terrorist groups and individuals as well as psychosocial analyses of related topics such as ethnopolitical war, trauma, security, religion, defense and counterterrorism, and medical and mental health services. Even more than in books and journals, the Internet has today given rise to thousands of Web sites devoted to terrorism and terrorists, many of which provide substantive psychosocial information (e.g., Terrorism Research Center, www.terrorism.com; www.hatemonitor.org; www.stratfor.com; www.brookings.org; www. State.gov/www/global/terrorism; www.paknews.com). For an interesting and overwhelming experience, type in the terms *terrorism*, *psychology*, and *terrorist* in your search engine entry box (e.g., www.google.com), and within seconds you will get thousands of hits.

Some of the recent prescient books that address various aspects of psychology related to terrorism include Pearlstein's (1991) *The Mind of the Political Terrorist*, Reich's (1990/1998) *The Origins of Terrorism*, and Billington's (1980) *Fire in the Minds of Men: Origins of Revolutionary Faith*. Rapoport's (2001) *Inside Terrorist Organizations* and Whittaker's (2001) *The Terrorism Reader* provide an excellent introduction to the history, structure, and dynamics of terrorist organizations. Christie, Wagner, and Winter (2001) introduced the urgent need for peace psychology in the global community. We have in-depth biographical studies of terrorists such as Osama bin Laden (e.g., Bodansky, 2001) and of terrorist groups such as Aum Shinrikyo (e.g., Lifton, 2000; Williams, 2002). Jay Lifton's (2000) psychological analysis of the Aum Shinryko cult in Japan, *Destroying the World to Save It*, is an exceptionally good inquiry into the foundation and dynamics of blind belief and commitment. A growing number of universities are now developing special programs in international violence, disasters, and humanitarian assistance; most notable among these programs is the Solomon Asch Center at the University of Pennsylvania.

TOWARD UNDERSTANDING THE COMPLEX, MULTIPLE, AND INTERACTIVE PSYCHOLOGICAL DETERMINANTS OF TERRORISM

When psychology's relevance for understanding terrorism is examined, a sizable literature emerges with regard to possible explanatory concepts that are rooted within major personality and social psychology views of human nature (see Exhibit 1.2). Many of these explanatory concepts remain the theoretical assumptions of well-known figures, and they would obviously benefit from specific empirical studies of terrorists; however, at this point, they

EXHIBIT 1.2
Psychology's Relevance for Understanding Terrorism

Theorist	Application of theory to understanding terrorism
Sigmund Freud	Freud's classical assumption that aggression and violence toward authority figures and symbols represents a basic and primitive part of the human psyche presents an interesting hypothesis for understanding terrorism. Could it be that terrorism is, in part at least, an effort to discharge primitive impulses directed toward authority? Eros and Thanatos—the life and death instincts—represent yet other Freudian concepts that may be at play in understanding terrorism. Here we have the struggle between impulses toward life and destruction. Perhaps the most useful Freudian contribution for understanding terrorism resides in his concept of defense mechanisms. In this instance, we need to explore whether terrorists may be inclined to use a spectrum of ego defenses such as scapegoating, projection, denial, rationalization, and repression in their daily lives. These defenses may shape and guide the psychology of hate and violence that is directed toward various target groups.
Alfred Adler	Adler believed that there is an inherent human impulse directed toward superiority or mastery that can become distorted through faulty development. This impulse becomes transformed into the pursuit of superiority through power, supremacy, dominance, and control. According to Adler, the superiority impulse often emerges in response to feelings of inferiority. Thus, it may be useful to study whether terrorist attacks represent a response to perceived inferiority that then leads to efforts to obtain superiority by means of nonsocial or antisocial behaviors, including violence and aggression.
Erich Fromm	Fromm believed that many people cannot deal with the uncertainties and ambiguities of life and therefore turn to blind commitment to authority figures as a means of feeling secure. They pursue absolute conformity to escape from the freedom that they find intolerable. The conformity also provides a firm sense of identity and meaning. They no longer have to think for themselves or make decisions within the context of ill-defined circumstances. By accepting authority, one no longer has to accept individual responsibility for one's actions. Much of Fromm's work has interesting implications for understanding terrorism—especially his articulation of the pathologies that can emerge from the denial of basic human needs for identity, transcendence, a frame of reference, relatedness, and rootedness (Fromm, 1973). When denied through oppression, pathologies of behavior can emerge, including hate, hoarding, and exploitation of others.

continues

EXHIBIT 1.2
(Continued)

Rollo May	A major existential theorist, Rollo May emphasized the pursuit of meaning and purpose as a basic human impulse. But, as is the case for other theorists, May held that the presence of life contexts in which opportunity is denied and hopelessness abounds can lead to distortions in one's humanity, including anger, frustration, and violence. This can create a false sense of meaning and purpose in which there is a felt sense of direction that evidences itself in destructive acts toward people and governments perceived to be denying hope and opportunity.
Albert Bandura	Bandura's contributions toward understanding terrorism are presented in chapter 6 of this volume. Many of Bandura's concepts of modeling, imitation, and the pursuit of self-efficacy are relevant for understanding terrorism. Terrorists may pursue personal control through their actions. Through modeling and imitation, terrorism becomes an acceptable mode for dealing with problems and for establishing goals.
Joseph Berke	Joseph Berke's contributions to understanding terrorism reside in his penetrating analysis of envy and jealously as motives for behavior, especially angry behavior. He noted that people can become so consumed by envy and jealously that they engage in pathological responses. Jealously and envy, he stated, are primitive, survival-based emotions, and in the case of terrorism, the rage that emerges from them can be linked to a perceived struggle for survival. In these cases, resentment reaches intense levels and easily justifies the behavior in the mind of the perpetrator. There are obvious reasons for jealousy and envy among terrorists, given the lack of power that often characterizes their lives. These emotions can result in intense hate, anger, resentment, and a willingness to seek revenge—blind revenge. Terrorists reason that "we are poor, and the U.S. is rich; the U.S. is rich because it exploits us; let's fight against the U.S." (Berke, 1988, p. 252).
B. F. Skinner	Skinner's elementary principles of behavioral shaping and modification suggest that terrorist acts may often be low-risk behaviors with high payoffs (i.e., reinforcement). Consider the possibility that many terrorist acts are successful and pose minimal survival risks to the terrorists. In that case, although some acts may fail, those that succeed provide sufficient reinforcement to promote future acts. Skinnerian schedules of reinforcement (e.g., variable ratio) can be explored for their predictive value.

continues

EXHIBIT 1.2
(Continued)

Theorist	Application of theory to understanding terrorism
Psychopathologists	There are numerous opinions about the relationship between psychopathology and terrorism (e.g., Reich, 1998). For example, it would be easy to conclude that individuals who kill others intentionally are sociopaths or pathological narcissists. Their willingness to use violence without remorse certainly suggests that the possibility that they have mental disorders should be considered. But what is important here is the fact that terrorist acts are often done in response to a higher calling, such as religion or liberation. This justifies the behavior in the mind of the terrorist. The act is conscious, intentional, and done with little or no remorse. More research is needed regarding pathological problems with alienation, anomie, and social detachment and isolation. Many terrorists can obviously separate their actions from the destruction caused by those actions, including the death of innocent people. Pathological obedience, conformity, and dehumanization of others need to be explored. Pathological levels of anger and the inability to control violent impulses also emerge as interesting hypotheses. And, of course, there is also the possibility of reasonable suspicions escalating into a full-blown paranoia replete with its delusions, especially the belief that one is called by God to engage in certain violent acts. Although these disorders and dysfunctions may not be experienced by all terrorists, they may be by some, and in those cases they may constitute the basis for terrorist actions.
Social psychologists	There is considerable research in social psychology that is relevant for understanding terrorism. For example, research on ethnocentrism, dehumanization, obedience, prejudice, group psychology, conformity, and hatred of outgroups constitutes a substantive source of knowledge for understanding terrorism. Although some of this may be biased by Western cultural assumptions and methods, there is still much that can offer hypotheses about terrorism. For example, there is the challenge of understanding different world views and life styles and the challenge of negotiating tensions that arise from perceived differences in human behavior. Within the field of social psychology, numerous studies of conformity, altruism, deception, and trust have been conducted, all of which have implications for understanding terrorism. Topics such as communication and social influence also can serve as entry points for studying terrorism. A quick review of any social psychology text will generate a list of variables that can be used to understand and explain terrorism and the terrorist (e.g., violence/aggression, attribution, stereotypes, group dynamics, social facilitation, social cognition). Many of the chapters in the present volume make extensive use of our knowledge of social psychology and address some of the concepts cited here.

continues

EXHIBIT 1.2
(Continued)

Other personality theorists	Personality researchers have studied a score of constructs that are relevant for our understanding of terrorism. For example, authoritarianism, fascism, fanaticism, religiosity, moral behavior, and intolerance of ambiguity all have implications for the "true believer" syndrome—that is, that the terrorist is willing to destroy lives for his or her cause. It is possible that forces of rapid social change, often replete with disrespect for traditional ways of life, can create a psychology that is intolerant of other viewpoints. That which is foreign is considered a threat to existing world views. From this there emerges a willingness to blindly follow charismatic leaders who offer simplistic but seemingly logical answers that readily appeal to the mind seeking to reduce stress and tension.

constitute a good beginning for generating hypotheses regarding motivational/ goal patterns that may engender and sustain terrorism.

Yet another view on the determinants of terrorism that must be considered has been presented by Hedges (2003). Hedges is not a major psychological theorist. However, in his 2003 book he has raised the possibility that—for all sides—war may be an addiction that releases us from the humdrum of daily life and gives us a new sense of meaning and purpose. It becomes an elixir rooted in a new sense of purpose that is perceived to be noble and just. Hedges, a military veteran, stated,

> I learned early on that war forms its own culture. The rush of battle is a potent and often lethal addiction, for war is a drug, one I ingested for many years. It is peddled by mythmakers—historians, war correspondents, filmmakers, novelists, and the state—all of whom endow it with qualities it often does possess: excitement, exoticism, power, chances to rise above our stations in life, and a bizarre and fantastic universe that has a grotesque and dark beauty. It dominates culture, distorts memory, corrupts language, and infects everything around it, even humor which becomes preoccupied with the grim perversities of smut and death. . . . War exposes the capacity for evil that lurks not far below the surface within all of us. . . . The enduring attraction of war is this: Even with its destruction and carnage it can give us what we long for in life. It can give us purpose, meaning, a reason for living. Only when we are in the midst of conflict does the shallowness and vapidness of much of our lives become apparent. . . . And war is an enticing elixir. It gives us resolve, a cause, it allows us to be noble. (2003, p. 3)

Hedges's (2003) views about the addictive nature of war raise many possibilities for understanding terrorist and counterterrorist military action. Because human beings are constantly engaged in meaning-making in their

ISSUES, CONCEPTS, AND DIRECTIONS 27

lives, war presents an easy opportunity for profound and sudden shifts in personal and collective meaning. Amid the boredom of daily life, war emerges as a positive counter—an "elixir" for individuals and for nations seeking meaning.

Early classical psychological studies of authoritarianism, dogmatism, tolerance of ambiguity, prejudice, trust, alienation, conformity, and other personal predispositions and inclinations can still provide a firm conceptual and empirical foundation for contemporary efforts (e.g., Adorno, Frenkel-Brunswik, Levinson, & Sanford, 1950; Allport, 1954; Fromm, 1941; Hoffer, 1951, Milgram, 1963). Through the years, psychosocial knowledge of topics of violence, intergroup relations, and belief have been refined and expanded to cross-cultural levels. Insights into the mind of the terrorist and the origin of terrorist organizations are also provided by studies of the various defense mechanisms that are so basic in our studies of the human psyche, particularly the ego defense mechanisms of projection, denial, repression, displacement, rationalization, and reaction formation.

Yet missing from most of these early efforts has been extensive psychosocial coverage of terrorism itself and of the cultures that nurture and sustain it. This is especially true for Middle-Eastern and Arab cultures. The average person in the West knows little about Arab and Islamic cultures and the psyches they engender. Although this is changing as a result of September 11, much remains to be done. What are the Arab/Islamic concepts of personhood, honor, envy, empathy, jealousy, love, malice, evil, peace, greed, and revenge? National and religious psyches mimic those of individuals and become the defining zeitgeist for a time and for a culture (Berke, 1988). We now have a growing knowledge of Islam and its practices but still need to know much more about this vast religion that has a membership of more than one billion people.

There are resources on Arab psychology (e.g., Ahmed & Gielen, 1998) and Islamic psychology (e.g., www.crescentlife.com). In fact, there is much in Western psychological theory and the empirical field to be mined, but little has been done thus far (see Bandura, chap. 6, this volume). Indeed, contemporary social psychological theory has immediate relevance because of its knowledge base in social conflict theory, identity theory, group dynamics, interpersonal relations, and the study of human values. However, not until September 11, 2001, did psychologists display a sudden and dramatic increase in interest and writing about terrorism and terrorists. This is likely to continue for four reasons: (a) Terrorism is now considered an important and timely topic for exploration and understanding, (b) terrorism will continue despite recent successes in attenuating its fiscal and military foundations, (c) psychology has much to contribute to our understanding and prevention of terrorism, and (d) government leaders and decision makers want and need psychological input. A score of books on terrorism and related topics by and for psychologists are appearing (e.g., La Greca, Silverman, Vernberg,

& Roberts, 2002; Pyszcynski, Solomon, & Greenberg, 2002). Clay (2002) provides a summary of the many roles and activities that psychologists have played in the wake of September 11, especially with regard to the management of trauma. Clearly psychology—as a science and as a profession—has a major role to play in our understanding and response to terrorism.

ROOTS OF HATRED AND RESENTMENT: HISTORY AND CULTURAL CONFLICT

The September 11, 2001, attack on the United States was an act of terrorism—a crime of untoward proportion—an undeclared war by nonstate actors (subnationals) scattered across a number of countries and sharing a common hatred, contempt, and resentment toward the United States because of their perception of the United States as a hegemonic military, political, economic, and cultural power with a long history of injustice and abuse of Islam. To add further to the complexity of our present situation, the terrorists who committed this act may have possessed weapons of mass destruction. Weapons of mass destruction have been used by governments (including the United States, Israeli, and North Korean governments) as a deterrent to war and as a means of threatening other nations to accede to their wishes. In the hands of terrorist groups bent on destroying American society, these weapons create another unpredictable element.

For the United States and for other Western nations, the challenge of international terrorism is unique and bewildering. Whom do we fight against? What strategies or tactics should be used? The war with terrorism is unlike wars of the past. In World War II, the struggle was among nations. This was followed by wars of revolution against colonial oppression (e.g., Kenya, India, Algeria, Vietnam). Then the world entered a period of wars of identity—wars fought against civilians often by civilians with genocidal overtones (e.g., Bosnia, Rwanda), and these wars are still being fought. Now, we are faced with new struggles in which nations are concerned with terrorism and related crimes in their many forms (e.g., kidnappings, bombings, cyberterrorism).

For the terrorists, their hatred, contempt, and resentment are fueled, in part, by their perceptions of the massive, dislocating societal changes and questionable political and economic policies they feel the United States is imposing on the non-Western world through the forces of globalization (i.e., the forced interdependency created by telecommunications, transnational capital flow, the mass media, transportation, and the work of agencies such as the World Trade Organization, the International Monetary Fund, and the World Bank). Most of all, there appears to be a resentment of the United States for its efforts to impose its commercial interests on others. The terrorists resent even as they envy, and the outcome of this collision in emotional ambivalence is hatred, anger, and fury.

Pressures From Change and Westernization

Across the globe, voices are being raised against the United States and what it represents and symbolizes. Many see the United States as being indifferent to the world's suffering. Many feel that it contributes to the political suppression of the poor. In a world increasingly being torn between the forces of globalization and the forces of localism, the United States is often seen as insensitive to global cultural diversity and to the importance of local identity. The mass techno-commercial society emerging from American culture and penetrating the rest of the world is considered a real and tangible threat to traditional cultural identities and ways of life.

Non-Western cultures and nations often express ambivalence: They believe that they must join the global march toward capitalism, democratization, and individualism or be left behind, and yet they feel a simultaneous pull to preserve lifestyles that are familiar and that provide a strong attachment to history. The "push" and "pull" create unbearable tensions. Even if they favor the push toward change, they are powerless to act. It is easier to be disillusioned. Zakaria (2001) noted that Arab nations are disillusioned with the West:

> Young men [in Arab countries] . . . leave their traditional villages to find work. They arrive in noisy crowded cities like Cairo, Beirut, and Damascus. . . . In their new world they see great disparities of wealth and the disorienting effects of modernization; most unsettlingly, they see women unveiled and in public places, taking buses, eating in cafes, and working along side them. . . . Arabs feel they are under siege from the modern world and the United States symbolizes this world. (Zakaria, 2001, pp. 32, 36)

However, it is more than this collision of cultures over time—it is the very nature of the content of the cultures that must also be included in the equation of violence. In the name of commercial interests and expanding profits, the United States, through its popular cultural icons that have assumed a global omnipresence (e.g., Coca Cola, McDonalds, popular music, Levis), is perceived to be an "invader" threatening the survival of other cultures. Many of these cultures are simply unprepared or unable to resist because of existing power structures. Thus, these nations are faced with the challenge either of joining the global "commodification" of life replete with secularism and unbridled liberties or of becoming an anachronism, out of step with the demands of the times (e.g., Mittleman, 2000). Fareed Zakaria, an editor of *Newsweek Magazine*, noted that "Bin Laden and his fellow fanatics are products of failed societies that breed their anger." "America," he claimed, "needs a plan that will defeat terror, but also reform the Arab world" (Zakaria, 2001, p. 22). Easier said than done.

Challenges to Ethnic Identity

The materialistic culture of the West is a threat to Islamic spiritual values and religion-based practices. Modernization is change, but change does not mean progress. Furthermore, modernization has come to mean Westernization or Americanization, with all this means and implies for undermining Muslim daily life. American popular culture favors a culture of individualism, materialism, change, and competition, whereas many non-Western cultures favor a cultural ethos of collectivism, spirituality–religion, stasis–stability, and sharing. Here, the threat to identity becomes a crucial part of the equation for violence. Cultural identity is the crucible in which human survival and human purpose become yoked to promote a sense of well-being, meaning, and cohesion (e.g., Cote & Levine, 2002; Rothman, 1997; Volkan, 1997; see also various issues of *Identity: The International Journal of Theory and Research*). For members of traditional societies who define their identity and self in terms of ethnic and historical group membership (i.e., a sociocentric self), the offenses of the West are not impersonal events but rather direct personal attacks that inflame individual passions, giving rise to fantasies of revenge fueled by resentment and self-righteousness. This lethal combination has been the source of violence throughout history. Within this context, judgment becomes impaired and innocent citizens of other lands come to be seen as willful and intentional agents of cultural destruction. The process is intensified by Islamic terrorist leaders' claims of American hypocrisy, pointing out that whereas the United States claims virtue, it is, in fact, selfish, ethnocentric, and satanic. This has especially been true of Osama bin Laden (Bodansky, 2001). The cycle of hate is intensified by the demonizing of individuals and cultures on both sides of the struggle.

The Arab and Islamic world was at certain points in history (e.g., the early Middle Ages, the late 19th century) among the dominant civilizations of the world. In medieval times, Arab culture was the source of advances in math, physics, and astronomy and also of beautiful architecture, poetry, and art. It had conquered Spain, Portugal, and Sicily, and much of central Europe was at one point under Muslim control and influence. Until the early 20th century, the Ottoman empire was among the top military and colonial powers in the world. Then it collapsed, and the search for blame turned not to its own limitations, but to the Western colonial powers (Holmes, 1992). Although Westerners may give Arab culture and Islamic potency little attention or respect, much of the Arab world maintains heroic images of a powerful political and military past, and these two strengths are merged with religion in the *madrassas* (i.e., fundamentalist religious schools).

Contemporary Arab–Islamic societies have continued to intertwine the secular and the religious (although this is certainly less true for Turkey), but they are finding it hard to compete and survive in a world where other societies are outpacing them in science, industrial production, and social organization. Once again, they are victims of history. Unfortunately, there appears to be little willingness among Arab leaders to address the difficulties of mixing the secular and religious worlds. What is easy is to project blame onto the West. One psychological consequence of this situation is a feeling of inferiority that is hidden beneath layers of projected anger, hate, and envy toward the West. Under these conditions of fear, uncertainty, doubt, and failure, fundamentalism can rear its ugly head and offer an alternative: blind belief in religious dogma issued by demagogues who pander to simplistic solutions for complex problems.

Israeli–Palestinian Conflict

To these problems must be added the perennial problem of the Middle East, the conflict between Israel and Palestine. Here the psychology required for understanding terrorism is also complex. The reflexive American response has always been to side with Israel, even when Israel's military responses in the West Bank, Gaza, and other Palestinian population centers have clearly served to inflame hatred and to escalate this age-old conflict to new levels of brutality and violence. Jewish religious heritage and cultural traditions are more closely tied to American Christian roots than are Islamic and Arab traditions; there is also the issue of familiarity and respect for Jewish contributions to American history. Jews have made enormous contributions to American and European scientific, cultural, and professional progress. Furthermore, there are more Jews in America than Arabs, and Jews occupy more positions of power and influence in the economic, social, and political arenas. The issue of Jewish political influence and power in the United States is undeniable. Israel also is seen as the only democracy in the Middle East, and this offers America a chance to endorse this way of life in a region in which dictators thrive and abound.

The demographic situation in Israel and the Palestinian states (West Bank/Gaza) is considered by Israelis to be a problem, and thus may be the trigger for many Israeli actions. According to *Newsweek* (April 1, 2002), there are currently 3,191,000 Palestinians in the West Bank and Gaza. By 2050 this population is estimated to grow to 12,000,000. There are 1,131,000 Palestinians in Israel and 2,560,000 Palestinians in Jordan. The situation is clear: Whereas Israel's Jewish population is creeping along in growth (6,040,000 in 2000), aided by immigration from Russia, the Palestinian population is growing rapidly. The average age of the Palestinians in the West Bank and Gaza is 17, and the average monthly wage is $360. There is an unemployment rate of 38% and an average household size of 6. Life expectancy is 72, and the number of children born per female is 6.1. These facts are not escaping Israel's government and people, and they may be feeding, in part, the brutal treatment of Palestinians in these areas. Israel is not likely to yield its hundreds of settlements in Gaza and the West Bank, even though they are recognized as illegal by international law and the world community. Under these conditions, dehumanization can occur on both sides as the world has witnessed, and for Israel, the moral position it enjoyed because of the Holocaust is rapidly being lost.

For Muslim and Arab communities, the United States's disproportional support of Israel cannot be rationalized with the previous arguments. The United States clearly supports Israel and does not support the Palestinian cause, even though the latter is also justified. The Israeli rejection of United Nations (UN) Security Council Resolution of September 23, 2002, requesting that Israel withdraw its troops immediately from the vicinity of Yassir Arafat's compound and to stop bombing it constitutes yet another example of Israel's failure to comply with UN resolutions. In this instance, the United States abstained rather than vetoing the resolution because it was seeking support for an invasion of Iraq. However, it has become patently clear that whereas the United States argues that Iraq's failure to comply with UN resolutions justifies invasion, Israel's failure to comply will have little or no consequence for Israel as far as the United States is concerned. Double standard? Of course, and this only escalates the hate and the paranoia. I maintain that there must be both a State of Israel and a Palestinian state. The actions of both parties threaten regional and global peace and stability.

Thus, the scene is set for an American encounter with international terrorism that is rooted in deep and passionate hatred and resentment that can be traced both to history and to present circumstances. It is not only the offenses of American culture and militaristic presence in the Middle East, especially Saudi Arabia (land of the prophet Mohammad) but the virtually total support of the enemies of Islam. America may well defeat bin Laden and al-Qaeda, but we must recognize that others will follow. This is true because the enemy is more than a group of terrorists, it is the conditions that spawn and nurture them, and these, unfortunately, are not being addressed.

Root Causes of Terrorism

What the root causes of terrorism are continues to remain a subject of great debate. Yet, without identifying and addressing its root causes, terrorism is likely to continue to pose a major risk. The United States chose to respond to the shocking September 11 attack by al-Qaeda with a strong military response against the Taliban in Afghanistan because of al-Qaeda's entrenched position. This response was strongly endorsed and supported by Congressional votes of 420 to 1 in the House and 98 to 0 in the Senate (Moerk, 2002). The United States and many other nations also launched a massive global intelligence effort, which was needed to destroy al-Qaeda's broad fiscal and manpower resources. These efforts have not proven to be successful. At the time of this writing, Afghanistan remains a dangerous war zone outside of Kabul, and the news media have often pointed out that much of the rehabilitation money promised to the nascent government in Kabul in the heady post-Taliban days has failed to materialize. Further, the destruction of the al-Qaeda organization does not address the numerous other terrorist groups that may rise up in response to American use of military forces.

Military responses to terrorism will never be sufficient to contain the problem of terrorism because they do not address the root conditions that spawn it. A military retaliation to terrorism is too late, no matter how successful it may be. There must be a response to prevent its emergence and its growth and development as an appealing option. The roots of terrorism are complex, and our response to it must be complex if terrorism is to be contained and ultimately stopped. Consider this situation: In every Arab nation, 50% of the population is below the age of 25 years. This is a demographic time-bomb because the demands for employment and opportunity that will emerge as these young people age can lead only to great frustration, anger, and resentment toward what the Western world has come to represent to them (Zakaria, 2001, 2003).

This problem is exacerbated by the fact that with the possible exception of Turkey and Jordan, Arab nations are governed by strong, centralized regimes that offer little opportunity for change. Further, as Zakaria (2001, 2003) points out, many Muslims perceive that the West has little respect for their cultural and religious traditions. Further, they see the United States as arrogant, belligerent, and hegemonic. They feel that their heritage is denigrated and insulted by Westerners who know little of Middle Eastern history. This is a dangerous combination: population explosion among youth, high rates of unemployment, repressive regimes, and contempt and anger toward the West because of perceived current and historical circumstances.

Perhaps it is useful to think of terrorism within an ecological context in which the conditions that give rise to it and those that precipitate, exacerbate, and maintain it exist in a reciprocal relationship., Both the terrorists and target nations may be creating a unique dynamic that leads to violence. Consider the sources of rage that exist among certain nations and particularly among certain Islamic fundamentalist groups. To this, add the frustrating life circumstances of poverty, deprivation, social injustice, identity conflicts, and shame. Now add in the West, which is perceived as unanimously supporting a globalization that brings inequities and abuses in developing countries and is seen as a malevolent group of nations bent on controlling the world political and economic system.

Smith (2002), in an exposition of the United States's slow decline into unilateral isolationism, noted that the United States is becoming an international pariah. He contended that we have abused our power for selfish aims and have failed to understand and to empathize with the consequences of our actions. Smith cited Samuel Huntington's comments denouncing the United States as a "rogue superpower" that is out of step with the rest of the world. Huntington stated,

> At a 1997 Harvard conference, scholars reported the elites of countries comprising at least two-thirds of the world's people . . . see the United States as the single greatest threat to their societies. They do not regard the United States as a military threat but as a menace to their integrity, autonomy, prosperity, and freedom of action. They view the United States as intrusive, interventionist, exploitative, hegemonic, hypocritical, and applying double standards, engaging in what they label "financial imperialism" and "intellectual colonialism," with a foreign policy driven overwhelmingly by domestic politics. (Huntington, 1999, quoted in Smith, 2002, p. 256)

Clearly, the United States is caught in an unenviable position whereby the pursuit of its political, cultural, and economic interests is creating conflicts with much of the world, especially certain Arab–Islamic countries. A destructive ecology is emerging in which the perceived problems of both sides generate a destructive cycle (see Exhibit 1.3).

What then are the root causes of Islamic terrorism? Some would say that there is poverty around the globe, but most people in poverty do not become terrorists. They argue that it is flaws in the character of individuals, and they assign disorders such as "narcissism" and "sociopathy." This can certainly be the case for some, but it cannot be the answer in all cases of terrorism. We must go beyond indictments of villainous individuals bent on satisfying evil impulses for their own sake. We can destroy villains, but we cannot stop terrorism, because its roots are deep and complex. They reside in the past and in the present; they reside in anger but also in envy; they reside in religion but also in economics, politics, and culture; they reside in global inequality, racism, poverty, and ignorance—especially ethnocentric bias and ignorance; they reside in the rapidly changing dynamics of the emerging world of global interdependence which seems to be pointing toward a uniform and mass society with little respect or tolerance for the past.

This section is not intended to justify international Islamic fundamentalist terrorism, but rather to call attention to how individual and group terrorists might justify their actions. The United States is and has been a beacon for hundreds of millions of people throughout the world because of its commitment to freedom and democracy and the opportunities it has to offer. In a world filled with oppression, the United States has stood for opportunity, choice, and liberty. However, we must not allow these strengths of American society to obscure the simultaneous acts of commercial exploitation of developing countries, the abuses of labor, and the destruction of traditional ways of life.

EXHIBIT 1.3
Perceptions and Goals of Anti-American Terrorism

Perception of United States by Terrorist Groups ⟷	Motives/Goals of Anti-American Terrorism
Hegemonic globalization leader	Revenge (history)
Critical of Islam	Cultural security
Engages in name-calling (i.e., "axis of evil")	Religious justification
	Political ideology
	Cost-effective/low risk
Exports popular culture	Increase power
Failed to join world community (e.g., Kyoto Treaty, International World Court)	Acquire media status
	Unite the Islamic community
	Pride/self-respect, jealously, envy
Has self-righteous attitude regarding corruption and human rights yet violates its own principles	Instill fear, anxiety, and chaos
	Create public opinion against the U.S.
Has reflexive impulse to use war in self-interests	Reduce U.S. influence around the world
Appeals to economic interests of nations above principle (e.g., Turkey)	Increase support and economic power
Major dealer of military arms	Instill new meaning and pride for Islamic cause
Cultural/economic imperialist	Undermine European/U.S. relations
Provides disproportionate support to Israel	Destroy modern national state system
Supports dictatorial regimes in American self-interest	Unmask U.S. motives
Hypocritical	Reveal U.S. is hypocritical
Source of global poverty	Decrease U.S. ties to Israel
Supports corrupt Arab regimes	

Note. Items are not listed in any particular order. There are numerous elements in the ecological equation, and they do not necessarily correspond to one another in a specific or direct relationship (e.g., perception of the United States as a "hegemonic globalization leader" leads to the desire to "unite Islamic community" [*Umah*]). Nevertheless, there is some value in recognizing that terrorism does not occur in a contextual vacuum. The formation, precipitation, exacerbation, and maintenance of terrorist acts occur in response to complex and dynamic historical and contemporary forces and events. If there are evil people, there are circumstances and contexts that have spawned them and that encourage their growth.

Americans must now consider the realities of life in a global community in which we are the most powerful nation, but we must remember that we are not the only nation. Michael Lerner (2001) wrote the following in an editorial titled "Healing After Terror":

A central problem here is that most Americans have never been exposed to the notion that we live in one world system that is inextricably interconnected. Don't blame Americans that every inch of education we've received has encouraged us to think of ourselves as different, better, unique and special, and "not like them." . . . Nothing in our schooling helps us understand that several hundred years of colonialism and imperialism were not done so that Western societies could educate the natives, but so that the West could enrich itself at the expense of the rest of the world. (p. 8)

The roots of hatred and resentment may reside in history and culture, but their precipative causes reside in the contemporary events that trigger long-festering wounds and burdens. The response to the precipitating events often serves to exacerbate and maintain the problem. This is what is happening in the current Israeli–Palestinian crisis, which is bringing the entire world to the brink of disaster, and why it must be halted and solved. Figure 1.1 displays these dynamics.

Formative causes, such as collective memories of humiliation and defeat, become magnified within a culture that values and prizes the past and that seeks to limit rapid social changes because of their dislocating impacts, especially changes in the power structure. These root causes have not been addressed by any of the players in the struggle, including the UN, the United States, the Arab and Islamic world, or Israel. This is simply poor leadership, and it highlights the great need for nations to elect and support informed thinkers whose vision and ethics can move beyond situational and immediate responses to building long-term security for the world.

What then follows are precipitating causes or events that set things off, causes that are used to justify century-old struggles. Thus, the cycle continues with new responses simply adding to the accumulated problems such that all the players are locked into nonnegotiable positions. Blame is assigned easily, the conflict escalates and acquires increasing complexity, and solutions become more elusive. War becomes the only option in the minds of many.

The United States, the UN, the Palestinians, and the Israelis are caught in a causal matrix that has obscured the differences between the various causes and their effects. We are confusing history with the present; we are confusing things that set off the struggle with things that are keeping it going. We need to clarify and to disentangle the web of connections between the past and the present. Israel may be buying moments of relief for the present with its horrendous attacks on the Palestinians, but it is destroying the possibility of peace for the future. The memories of the oppression of the Palestinians in the West Bank and Gaza will be kept alive for generations in oral histories, myths, and legends, and one day these will become a new source for terrorist attacks. Similarly, the Palestinians are discharging momentary passions of revenge, but they are closing doors for a solution in the future. The simple fact of the matter is that the national security of any country is now intimately tied to common global security; struggles for local security must con-

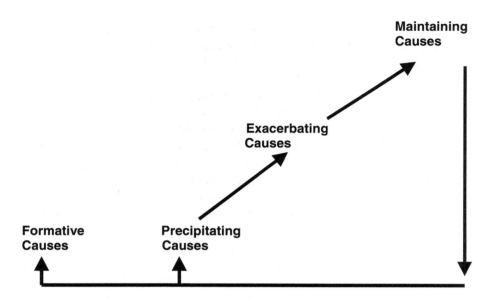

Figure 1.1. Progressive and interactive causality model. In this model, causality is seen as a dynamic process in which formative causes are set off by precipitating causes that, in turn, can become exacerbating and maintaining causes. These, in turn, can lead to new formative and precipitating causes. Rather than seeing causality as a simple linear process, this model argues that we must be aware of the complex and interactive natures of causes when attempting to understand a problem. Causes are often confused because they belong to different categories as a result of time progression. One must avoid confusing formative causes with causes that have precipitated a problem and those that further excite it and keep it festering. Understanding causality in its more dynamic perspective can improve interventions and preventions because of increased causal specificity.

sider the broader implications for international peace (Stephenson, 2002). Terrorism thrives on a fodder of hate both sides are generating by their indifference to each other. We need to remember the old adage: When you go forward for revenge, dig two graves.

Terrorism is a criminal act. It can be nothing else. This does not mean, however, that its definition is not subject to considerable debate (see chap. 2, this volume). Terrorism is an act of violence against an existing legal order. It is directed toward civilians for the purpose of inducing fear, dread, and terror. What if the existing "legal" order has been imposed by force and not by democratic choice? What if the existing legal order is oppressive? What if the existing legal order stands in direct contradiction to one's religious and political beliefs? What if the existing legal order does not provide for democratic change? Is terrorism then justified? We must be careful here, for what seems like a moral absolute can too easily conceal the conditions that spawn terrorism.

We must ask whether terrorism is ever justified, and if so, under what conditions. If the rule of law is to be followed, changes in the existing legal

38   ANTHONY J. MARSELLA

order must be sought through legitimate methods, and if these are not available (e.g., Saudi Arabia), the only legal or appropriate option may be the use of nonviolent civil disobedience. One must, however, be prepared to accept the consequences of nonviolent protest, which could be imprisonment or death. Gandhi (1869–1948) concluded that nonviolence was the only path available to him in his efforts to liberate India from colonial British rule. Ultimately, he was successful in his efforts; but subsequent struggles between Muslims and Hindus were not amenable to the same method and continue to this day. How do we judge success? What would Gandhi propose today given the tensions between India and Pakistan? How would he address the internal tensions that continue to exist because of poverty and corruption?

Is it right for Americans and for others across the world to conclude that the al-Qaeda leadership, supporters, and agents are criminal terrorists? The answer is an unequivocal yes. They meet all of the necessary criteria: (a) They have engaged in a premeditated attack on innocent people; (b) they have attempted to influence American foreign policy by intimidation; (c) they have violated international law and the laws of war; (d) they have instilled fear and insecurity in national and global populations; and (e) they have intentionally attempted to destroy an existing domestic political, social, and economic order.

Questions abound, however. Is there something psychologists can do—as scientists, professionals, and human beings—to encourage a de-escalation of tensions and to restore a sense of security to the world? The United States has committed itself to the total destruction of al-Qaeda and other international terrorist groups, but the question must be asked whether there are nonmilitary means to promote a halt to terrorism and to promote peace. Or, has the threshold been crossed and are we now headed toward unstoppable and enduring global warfare?

SEPTEMBER 11, 2001

The tragic events of September 11, 2001, have brought a new American awareness of the implications of terrorism for daily life. Never before had Americans been the target of such a destructive attack, in their own land, by a well-funded and globally organized terrorist organization. The September 11 attack had achieved its purpose: to create a global psychological state of fear, uncertainty, and terror. It also served the purpose of humiliating the United States in the eyes of many around the world and of showing its vulnerability.

Osama bin Laden had accused the United States for crimes against Islam and Muslims. He gave voice to the rage and anger of many in the Muslim community for the perceived indignities the West had committed against them. Although governments of Muslim nations condemned the September

11 attacks, many of the people cheered the destruction. My metacommunication analysis of Osama bin Laden's public statements against the United States reveals the following:

1. God is on our side.
2. Our (Islamic) cause is just.
3. We (Muslims) have been abused and insulted for too long. You must remove your troops from our holy sites and stop your many wars against Islamic people (Iraq, Chechnya, Palestine).
4. We (al-Qaeda and other militant terrorist groups) speak for the poor and oppressed of the world.
5. It is time for you (the United States) to suffer as we have suffered.
6. The culture you have created and forced upon the world is antithetical to an Islamic way of life because of its materialism, hypocrisies, abuses of power, and privilege.
7. History has spoken—even President Bush said this was a continuation of the struggles and violence of the eleventh century Crusades. We won in the past and we will win again.

The interactive forces of history provide little respite from the complexity of issues and questions that surround terrorism and its definition. Samuel Huntington, in his well-known article "The Clash of Civilizations" (1993), argued that it is the very contrast among civilizations—the varying constructions of reality—that are at the heart of current struggles. He suggested that the nature of current local and global pressures is pushing ethnocultural and national groups toward a new cultural consciousness in which differences are exaggerated for the purpose of establishing identity (see also Volkan, 1997). The result is an increased sense of conflict and strain between in-group and out-group members. Wars of identity are now the norm, and the variations in Islamic, Asian, African, and Western identities are fertile ground for extremism. We cannot force uniformity on a world that considers this uniformity to be colonialism in new clothing—identity is an essential human need, and threats to identity are threats to our being and survival.

FANATICS, EXTREMISTS, AND TERRORISTS

It is impossible to clarify the nature and meaning of *terrorism* without encountering critical questions about the differences between the label *terrorists* and several other terms that have often been used depending on one's political persuasion, including *fanatics, extremists, zealots,* and *true believers. Zealot* is one of the most ancient terms and is derived from the 66–73 C.E. period. Today, the term has come to mean anyone who pursues a cause or belief with such intensity and devotion that they become *fanatics*, individuals responding with unbridled extremes of emotion and determination. However, years ago in ancient Palestine, the Zealots were Jews who rebelled against Roman laws and governance. They assassinated Romans as well as the Jews who supported them in an effort to obtain freedom from oppression.

The True Believer

In his classic volume, *The True Believer* (1951), Eric Hoffer pointed out the importance of belief for the human mind and the problems that arise when uncertainty in belief cannot be tolerated. He stated:

> It is doubtful whether the fanatic who deserts his holy cause or is suddenly left without one can ever adjust himself to an autonomous individual existence. . . . An individual existence, even when purposeful, seems to him trivial, futile, and sinful. To live without an ardent dedication to is to be adrift and abandoned. He sees in tolerance a sign of weakness, frivolity, and ignorance. . . . He hungers for the deep assurance which comes with total surrender—with the wholehearted clinging to a creed and cause. What matters is not the contents of the cause but the total dedication and communion with a congregation. He is ever ready to join in a holy crusade against his former holy cause, but it must be a genuine crusade—uncompromising, intolerant, proclaiming the one and only truth. (Hoffer, 1951, p. 90)

Belief provides meaning and purpose—it reduces uncertainty and facilitates adaptation and adjustment. It offers "deep assurance" and "communion" with others. However, we must acknowledge that some belief systems are dangerous and pathological for a person, group, or nation; indeed, there are well-known psychiatric disorders that are rooted in *delusion*, or beliefs that are idiosyncratic and bizarre. At some point beliefs and actions may actually become relatively enduring and permanent and assume the quality of a personality or character. For example, the famous studies of the authoritarian personality conducted by Adorno, Frenkel-Brunswik, Levinson, and Sanford (1950) concluded that a constellation of personality qualities and dispositions existed (especially in Nazi Germany) that coalesced around blind and unquestioned belief in authority.

Some of the qualities included blind belief and commitment to authority, intolerance of ambiguity or uncertainty, ethnocentrism, commitment to tradition, resistance to change, hate, anger, extremism, fanaticism, ideological simplicity, dehumanization of outsiders, obedience and control, and the presumption of moral justification. Although these studies generated much criticism in certain academic circles because of methodological issues and their endorsement of a "personality type or character," the constellation they proposed does fit present-day observations about terrorist groups, but it does not include cultural contexts and settings as contributing determinants.

Of special significance in this syndrome is the inability to tolerate doubt and uncertainty. The fundamental premise of science is that doubt and uncertainty must be not only tolerated but promoted because that is the basis of inquiry and change:

> The process of "asserting" yet "refuting" . . . captures the essential force behind human progress through the ages. It is an adaptive dialectic that enriches and extends our human possibilities and potential. Even as we reach a hard-won conclusion, doubt emerges to move us toward yet other possibilities. Unlike other beings whose behavior is fixed by reliance upon instinct and reflex, human beings have the capacity for reflective thought. We can reach a conclusion in one moment and modify it a moment later. . . . There is within our nature an imperative to question, and to order our answers in increasingly complex systems of beliefs designed to reduce our uncertainties and to increase our sense of control and mastery of the world. This is a reflexive and automatic response. So too is our inclination to doubt. Yet, because of the discomfort associated with doubt, it often requires greater effort to question the very beliefs we hold with comfort and contentment. . . . Thus, the human mind . . . constructs an elaborate and ritualized [set of] beliefs and/or practices . . . that provide us with a sense of certainty, comfort, and significance from the vicissitudes of life's experiences. But it is at this point that we must doubt the very beliefs we hold so dearly. (Marsella, 1999, pp. 41–42)

For the terrorist and other "true believers," blind commitment to political, economic, religious, or philosophical beliefs comforts the mind by eliminating or reducing the uncertainty. It is the blind commitment that offers the comfort of knowing one is "right." Within a culturally constructed reality, a person's beliefs can become so firmly entrenched they can even provide a sense of righteousness and messianic fervor. The possibility of their relativity is never considered. When beliefs become linked to the meaning of life itself, the conviction becomes even more rigid. Taggart (1994) stated:

> [O]ur belief systems are . . . the basis for our existence; they are symbol systems that enable us to derive meaning from a chaos of stimuli and instincts and to decode the mystery of our existence. Our separate core beliefs, whether secular or religious, anchor us in the dizzying vastness of the great unknown we call reality. (p. 20)

The classic research studies by Stanley Milgram (1963) on blind obedience and Philip Zimbardo (1969) and Herbert Kelman (1973) on dehumanization also are important starting points for studies of contemporary terrorism. The participants in the Milgram study gave increasingly higher levels of what they thought was an electric current to the study's confederates when asked to do so. What happens to the human conscience under pressures from authority? Are we witnessing this in the United States as the media bombard us with persuasive rhetoric from authority figures? Do torchlight parades come next? Is this what is happening in those Islamic fundamentalist schools that promote "martyrdom"?

Motivations

What motivates terrorism? What is the psychosocial wellspring of terrorism? When we consider the human psyche and the daily life that gives rise to it, we find that there is no single motive. Consider revenge: If a Palestinian is killed by Israeli troops, the anger, hate, grief, and sorrow experienced by family members could easily combine to push one of them to becoming a suicidal–homicidal bomber. These motives might be sufficient for some, but for others, the prestige of joining a larger terrorist group, combined with the promise of financial incentives, could be the governing force. As the Crusades and the Protestant–Catholic brutalities in Europe remind us, religion itself could be added to the calculus of motivations by suggesting that killing others for the sake of God is justifiable.

Yet another motive might simply be the unquestioned reality that the killing of certain groups of people is acceptable because it is validated in ancient history and is kept alive through legends of past wrongs. Consider here the tragedies of the Kosovo. On June 28, 1389, Christian Serbs fought a decisive battle with Ottoman Turks in Kosovo. The legend of this battle was kept alive for centuries. Newborn Serbian sons allegedly are held above their father's head with the cry, "One more avenger for Kosovo." Centuries later, Serbian leaders invoked the earlier defeat as justification for the killing of Muslims; after all, this was the heart of the Serbian nation before the Ottoman Turkish occupation. This is an example of how a group's collective memory of events that occurred six centuries earlier is used to justify the brutal killing of another group (in this case, Kosovo Muslims). How many examples do we need before we become aware of the pernicious and destructive powers of vilifying others across history?

In the case of the September 11 terrorists, media accounts of their final hours indicate that there was formal indoctrination regarding their suicidal–homicidal acts. The suicide terrorists were carefully recruited after rigorous observation of their commitment, and once selected, they were given incentives that included both the rewards of heaven and the rewards of revenge for the victimization of Muslims. "You will live forever as a martyr—you will live in paradise—you will live forever in the hearts and minds of our people." As the training process continues, it becomes increasingly difficult for the new recruit to change his mind because this would be a major loss of face for him. According to Volkan (1997), young Islamic suicidal–homicidal recruits are told to read Qur'anic verses: "Think not of those who are slain in God's way as dead. Nay, they live, finding their sustenance in the presence of their Lord" (Volkan, 1997, p. 165). This combination of psychological motive and external incentive (i.e., fame, financial reward, tradition, immortality, honor, martyrdom) constitutes strong reasons for their actions.

The September 11 bombers were given the following express instructions for their last night:

> *Steel the will:* "Remind yourself that in this night you will face many challenges. But you have to face them 100% . . . . Obey God, his Messenger, and don't fight with yourself when you become weak. . . . Stand fast. God will stand with those who stand fast."
>
> *Invoke religion:* "You should pray, you should fast. You should ask God for guidance, you should ask God's help . . . . Continue to pray throughout the night. Continue to recite the Qur'an."
>
> *See purity of purpose:* "Purify your heart and clean it of all earthly matters. The time of fun and waste has gone. The time of judgment has arrived. Hence we need to utilize those few hours to ask God for forgiveness. You have to be convinced that those few hours that are left in your life are very few."
>
> *Be optimistic:* " From this point on you will begin to live the happy life, the infinite paradise. Be optimistic! The Prophet was always optimistic. . . . You will be entering paradise. You will be entering the happiest, everlasting life."
>
> *Crave death:* "Everybody hates death and fears death. But only those believers who know the life after death, and the reward of death, will be the ones seeking death."
>
> (From "Keep Faith," 2001, p. A5; the headings in italics are my addition)

The motives are many and complex: revenge, anger, paradise, status, respect, life everlasting.

Group Process and Influence

Volkan (1997) offered a psychodynamic perspective on the role of groups in influencing terrorist behavior. He argued that terrorist groups may provide the security of the family by subjugating individuality to the group identity. A protective cocoon is created that offers shelter from a hostile world.

> Individuals perceive the group as seeking to satisfy the same vital needs they themselves want to satisfy. This congruity makes them idealize, identify with, and love the group. They suspend their critical faculties, falsely inflating the group's values. Humility and subjection replaces insight, so the many who operate with the same object of love are tied libidinally to it and to one another. (Volkan, 1997, p. 27)

In his superb book, *Bloodlines*, Volkan (1997) offered a rich and detailed analysis of terrorism around the world. Islamic terrorism, in particular, is made even stronger within the group by the common commitment to Islam as the one and only true religion. Islam offers a highly codified and ritualized way of life that links individual identity with group identity. This can be used by terrorist groups to ensure absolute conformity and obedience. A common bond (Islam) for a common purpose (One God). In the case of Osama bin Laden's brand of Islam, Wahabbism (the most fundamentalist form of Islam), the beliefs are few, straightforward, certain, and nonnegotiable. Tie this to hatred of the United States for the many reasons that have been articulated, and the result is a dangerous fundamentalist army of true believers.

CONSEQUENCES OF TERRORISM

International terrorism presents many concerns for the United States and the world. These concerns involve psychology as a profession and a science and present it with an opportunity to make a contribution to our nation and the world. Among the growing concerns are the following:

1. Domestic security (e.g., Homeland Security Act) may limit constitutional freedoms.
2. Economic costs of the war on terrorism may be exorbitant, especially when combined with international wars and nation re-rebuilding.
3. Political and diplomatic costs will also be high because in the push for the destruction of terrorism, our national image might be tarnished. Depending on how the war is conducted, we might be seen as warlike and racist.
4. An international court must be convened to address the legal aspects of the struggle, and this may actually end up indicting the United States and Great Britain.
5. Globalization will be challenged as an agent of Western domination and exploitation. Western symbols and values will be challenged and will be at risk.
6. Support for the UN will be at risk. For many, the UN is seen as an agent of the West, and international respect for the UN will continue to decrease in the face of its powerlessness to attenuate conflict and to rebuild nations (e.g., Shawcross, 1998).
7. The national psyche will be increasingly characterized by fear, uncertainty, and anger. Feelings of optimism will be diminished. This will affect economic and governmental activities.

CONCLUSION

In previous articles (Marsella, 1998, 2000), I suggested that psychology must expand its horizons to meet the emerging political, environmental, social, and cultural challenges of the 21st century:

If psychology is to survive and grow as a profession and academic discipline, it is essential for it to be responsive to the changing world in which we live. Unlike the world of the last few decades, today's world requires psychology to acknowledge the global context of our times, including the increased interdependency of our individual and collective lives. Today, events and forces in distant lands and cultures—once considered inconsequential and unimportant—have a daily impact upon our lives. Under these circumstances, psychology needs both to reconsider its training and research priorities, assumptions, methods, and ethics with a new vision, vigor, and commitment, and to respond to the emerging international challenges of overpopulation, poverty, environmental desecration, cultural disintegration, ethnopolitical warfare, and urbanization. (Marsella, 2000, p. 1)

There is a need to study terrorism, but there is also a need to study peace. This can be done through the development of linked institutes at universities across the country. Whenever possible the institutes should be multidisciplinary, multisectoral, and multicultural. Given the billions that are being spent for national defense, it is reasonable to expect that minimal funds could be expended to support academic and scholarly inquiry in the area of peace. Never before in history has there been a greater need for psychosocial studies of the conditions that give birth to terrorism and also to peace.

History still remains the best predictor of future action. We need to increase the study of terrorism and peace through the study of human history. What are the lessons learned from the past? But, we must not become so wedded to history that the forces of the moment are ignored. There were many warning signs prior to September 11. Why did we not respond, and what are we doing now to promote peace?

We need to increase the cross-cultural study of the psychological and behavioral determinants of terrorism, and we need, especially, to encourage the study of different non-Western and indigenous psychologies. The unfortunate fact is that Americans are not well-informed about the cultures and ways of life of other people across the globe, and when we are, our views are often tainted by ethnocentrism. Is this the fault of our education system? Is it the fault of a popular culture that seems oblivious to its implications? Is it the result of too much power and too much comfort without a commensurate sense of social responsibility? Psychology's extensive interests in aggression, violence, identity, conformity, obedience, dehumanization, intergroup conflict, prejudice, and so forth should be examined and applied within other cultural contexts.

We need to increase fieldwork in psychology in the developing nations and to make case studies of nation building, poverty, peace keeping, and citizen empowerment. We must begin to address the major social problems facing our global community and to recognize that office practice is insufficient. The world is now our client, and psychologists must think in new ways, including internationalizing our psychology curriculum and developing a new generation of psychologists prepared and motivated to live within the passions of their times and to make a difference by contributing to an improved understanding of people from other cultures and lands.

2

DISHONEST CRIMES, DISHONEST LANGUAGE: AN ARGUMENT ABOUT TERRORISM

BRIEN HALLETT

The most salient fact about the word *terrorism* is that it establishes a superfluous, redundant, unnecessary category. Every terrorist incident, after all, is essentially a common crime—the crime of arson, kidnapping, murder, or the like. As a result, no need exists to establish a new category, a new type. Any terrorist incident can be fully prosecuted under one or another of the existing criminal statues. Just to muddy the waters further, every victim of the common crimes of arson, kidnapping, murder, or the like has been terrorized, whether the perpetrator claims to be a terrorist or not. Furthermore, the terror felt by the direct victims radiates out to the larger community and influences others and affects their sense of security as well as social and political policies. Hence, logically, no distinction exists between common criminal incidents and so-called terrorist incidents. A murder by the local mafia gang is essentially the same as a murder by the local terrorist cell. Murder, in the final analysis, is murder.

However, if "terrorism" is little more than a difference searching for a distinction, an ordinary crime by another name, the terrorists do not see it that way. They do not think they are criminals committing crimes. Rather, adopting the language of war, they see themselves as "freedom fighters," "soldiers" on the front lines of some "war" against oppression and injustice. Yet again, whatever the terrorists' self-understanding, in reality, their language is dishonest. They possess none of the characteristics of soldiers but all of the characteristics of common criminals. According to the Geneva Convention, a "soldier" is one who meets the following four conditions: "(a) that of being commanded by a person responsible for his subordinates; (b) that of having a fixed distinctive sign recognizable at a distance; (c) that of carrying arms openly; (d) that of conducting their operations in accordance with the laws and customs of war" (Geneva Convention (I) for the Amelioration of the Condition of the Wounded and Sick in Armed Forces in the Field (1949), Article 13 (2)). As is true in any criminal organization, a terrorist might be "commanded by a person responsible for his subordinates," but terrorists fail to meet the other conditions. More important terrorists do resemble common criminals both in the crimes they commit and in the secret, clandestine nature of their lives.

However, terrorists do differ from common criminals in two respects: First, with few exceptions, terrorists' crimes are much more spectacular than ordinary crimes of the same type. Second, terrorists say that their crimes are not motivated by any self-interests but, rather, are committed solely in the interests of others, the oppressed. Thus, what distinguishes terrorist incidents from common criminal incidents is, first, the public relations or theatrical aspect of the crime and, second, the presumption on the part of the perpetrators of a self-sacrificing motivation. To say the same thing in different words, the terror generated by common crimes is largely an unintended consequence of those crimes, which are committed for other self-serving reasons. Terrorists reverse the equation. They commit their crimes specifically for the terror they generate. Moreover, because their crimes are not self-interested, only the most theatrical setting and effects serve the terrorists' public relations aim.

What all this head-spinning dissonance adds up to, I would suggest, is the inexplicable character of terrorist crimes. To be sure, no crime can be justified. By definition, arson, kidnapping, murder, and the like are ethically repugnant. Although not justified, common crimes are easily understood and explained. The explanation in every case is instrumental. The crime serves the perceived self-interest of the perpetrator, whose greed or lust or vengeance is thus satisfied. Whenever a crime does not serve the perpetrator's perceived self-interest, it becomes, literally, inexplicable.

Terrorism is just such an inexplicable crime. Both the exaggerated, theatrical character of the crime itself and the terrorists' claim that they have committed the crime for the benefit of others create a mystifying confusion between self-interested crime and self-sacrificing love: One of the characteristics of love is a willingness on the part of the lover to sacrifice his or her interests for those of the beloved. Terrorists see themselves in this self-sacrificing role. Yet, is there any other word besides *perverse* to describe a lover who commits not just crimes but spectacularly theatrical crimes for his beloved? Is this not the language of the abuser? "I hit you because I love you." "I kidnap, murder, and destroy buildings because I love you." Like all abusers, terrorists wish people to believe that their crimes are acts of self-sacrificing love, when, in reality, they are unjustified perversions, the delusional self-interest of the terrorists masquerading as self-sacrifice.

Put simply, whenever criminals portray themselves as self-sacrificing martyrs for a cause, confusion and cognitive dissonance are the only possible results. Significantly, the September 11 terrorists left no note explaining why they hijacked the planes, turned them into bombs, and murdered thousands. What, after all, could they have written to explain such horrors? Would anything they could have said make us understand their crimes?

In a most curious way, therefore, common criminals are basically honest, whereas terrorists are basically dishonest. Common criminals honestly acknowledge that they are motivated by simple greed. They also honestly understand that what they are doing is wrong. This self-understanding means that they attempt to accomplish their crimes as surreptitiously as possible, so as to avoid detection and arrest. The publicity generated by spectacularly theatrical crimes, they understand, is not in their best interests. When caught, their self-understanding also leads them to deny that they perpetrated the crime, which they honestly acknowledge was heinous. The unity and simplicity of their self-serving, self-interested motivation and self-understanding is reflected in the unity and simplicity of people's reaction to them: They are crooks; lock them up and throw away the key.

Terrorists, in contrast, are dishonest about their motives, which are mixed. In their public manifestos, they claim that they are motivated by the need to remedy some great political or social injustice. In private conversations, however, they reveal that they are really socially isolated "true believers,"[1] lashing out against an irredeemably corrupt world that can be saved only by destroying it. On account of their mixed motivations, terrorists do not admit that their crimes are wrong; indeed, they think that their crimes are not crimes but, instead, are fully justified by the absolute corruption of the world, on the one hand, and the absolute purity of their own motivation, on the other hand. This mixed motivation produces a bizarre situation: In the first place, when arrested, their confused self-understanding leads them either to proudly plead guilty to their crimes, because they are not crimes in their eyes, or to praise the crimes as righteous blows against oppression but to plead that they did not take part in the incidents with which they are charged. In the second place, the crimes themselves are perpetrated in the most spectacular and theatrical manner possible, so as to

---

[1]Eric Hoffer's (1951) *The True Believer* is still the best book on this topic.

produce maximum publicity for the cause espoused in their public manifestos. The desire for maximum publicity, however, only illustrates the confusion under which these dishonest criminals labor: The publicity is, the terrorists believe, good for their publicly espoused cause; it is, however, not good for the terrorists themselves, as any honest criminal would tell them, because it draws attention to them and pressures authorities to arrest and prosecute them.

In fine, the simple, honest, self-serving, self-interested greed that normally explains criminal behavior does not explain terrorists' behavior. Rather, the mixed motivation and self-understanding of terrorists produces cognitive dissonance both in their own minds and in the minds of all who observe them. Being inexplicable, the void is filled by a venerable, Machiavellian theory for gaining political power: The terrorists, so the theory goes, seize the "weapon of the weak" to wage an "asymmetric war" against the oppression and injustices of the powerful. The terrorists, the theory continues, do not commit crimes; rather, their spectacularly theatrical "operations" give a "voice to the voiceless." Indeed, the rhetoric of the theory of terrorism is seductive. However, what this theory really does is to create a false impression through a dishonest language. It leverages the mixed motivation and confused self-understanding of the terrorists so as to shift the locus of their self-interest from the individual criminal to an imagined collective, "the oppressed."

Willfully blinded and confused by this shift, the terrorists are unable to see the self-defeating nature of their tactics. From the perspective of nonterrorists, the primary ethical and political error made by terrorists is that they have chosen the least effective means for conducting their conflict and achieving their publicly espoused goal.

ETHICS OF TERRORISM: EVALUATING ENDS AND MEANS

Gandhi characterized his struggles for justice with the Sanskrit word *satyagraha*, which translates as an insistence upon, searching, or struggling for truth. By extension, the person who engages in *satyagraha* by insisting upon truth is a *satyagrahi*. The two Sanskrit terms are useful because they provide terms that contrast directly with terrorism and terrorist.

Building upon this terminological contrast, the initial difference between a *satyagrahi* and a terrorist is that the *satyargahi* engages his opponent both openly and directly; the terrorist, secretly and indirectly. The *satyagrahi*, therefore, is much more like a soldier than is a terrorist. Indeed, the *satyagrahi* meets all but one of the conditions of the Geneva Conventions for a soldier. The *satyagrahi* does not carry any arms, openly or otherwise. More specifically, the *satyagrahi* begins by engaging the opponent in direct negotiations over a well-articulated grievance. When these fail, the *satyagrahi*, then and only then, engages the opponent in direct action—a march, a boycott, a sit-in, or the like[2]—the purpose of which is to rekindle the failed negotiations so as to achieve a settlement of the grievance. Crucially, any casualties that may result from the direct action are from among the *satyagrahi* and not from among their opponents. In contrast, terrorists denigrate negotiations and, instead, issue manifestos, which they follow up with attacks involving the destruction of property, people, or both. Such attacks, however, are not for the purpose of rekindling negotiation so as to resolve some grievance; rather, they are for the purpose of gaining media attention for their "cause," giving a "voice to the voiceless," as the cliché has it. Crucially, any casualties that may result from the attacks are usually not from among the terrorists, but rather from among people whom nonterrorists consider to be innocent bystanders. Should any terrorists become casualties, their death or injury most frequently results either from a mistake—the bomb they are carrying explodes too early—or from a breech in their secrecy that has allowed the police to discover their plot.

The only exception to this is an incident involving a suicide bomber. This horrible exception only exacerbates the cognitive dissonance, however. On the one hand, a suicide bombing is simply an act of murder, usually multiple murders. Yet, on the other hand, it is even more inexplicable than other types of terrorist incidents precisely because of the accompanying and accomplishing suicide. The self-understanding of the terrorist as being motivated by a self-sacrificing love for the oppressed is seemingly reinforced and confirmed by a very real self-sacrifice. In consequence, the terrorist is now labeled by his sympathizers as a *martyr*. However, true martyrs are not criminals. Martyrs die for their beliefs at the hands of others. They do not murder others for their beliefs. Again, like *satyagrahi*, the only blood on the hands of martyrs is their own. Suicide bombers must also account for the blood of the multiple victims of their murderous death, a death that greatly increases the theatrical quality of their dishonest crime.

The second difference between the *satyagrahi* and the terrorist is that terrorists fight on one front only, whereas the *satyagrahi* fights on two fronts simultaneously. That is, both terrorists and Gandhi and his spiritual heirs fight against some specific injustice: colonial or dictatorial rule, racial segregation, foreign domination and oppression, and the like. These are the mediagenic battles, the ones that one reads about in newspapers and sees on television. For terrorists, this is the one and only battle. As soon as they have made headlines, their battle is over. They recede into the shadows to plot their next headline-grabbing event. In contrast, for Gandhi and his heirs, this is a secondary, less important, front. More important, if hidden from the media, are the battles where they fought against their own supporters, who,

---

[2]In his classic study of strategic nonviolence, Gene Sharp (1973) analyzed nearly 200 protest techniques. For an overview of the 20th century history of nonviolence, see Ackerman and Kruegler (1994).

either in their enthusiasm or their frustration, cried out for more justice faster. Justice is not a quantity, however; it is a quality. It cannot come faster or slower; it can come only when opponents join together in a more perfect community. Thus, the *satyagrahi*, unlike the terrorist, knows that whatever the passions and conflicts of the moment might be, both sides to the dispute ultimately must live in harmony with each other. And so, whenever emotions of revenge, retaliation, or retribution arose among their followers, Gandhi and his spiritual heirs swung into action, closed down the protest that had allowed emotion to outpace common sense, and began the process of retraining and reindoctrinating their followers, unlike terrorists who feed precisely upon these raw emotions.[3]

The third difference between the *satyagrahi* and the terrorist grows out of the second. For, the *satyagrahi's* knowledge that they and their opponents must live together in harmony after their conflict has ended, as all conflicts must, means that the *satyagrahi* cares as much for the means used as for the end sought. In contrast, the terrorists, not caring for future harmony but only the cause of the moment, believe that their end justifies their means. This observation brings one to the heart of the ethics of terrorism. The ethics of terrorism turn upon an evaluation of the ends sought and the means employed. For terrorists, the absolute value of the end—the justice of the cause found in their public manifestos and for which they say they are murdering—fully justifies any means whatsoever. For the *satyagrahi*, the overarching value of their end—that they and their opponents will live together in peace after the grievance has been resolved—justifies only a limited number of means.[4]

More formally, the evaluation of ends and means is framed by two reciprocal, contingent propositions:

1. When the end sought truly justifies the means chosen, the act is just and, therefore, by definition, not terrorism.
2. When the end sought does not justify the means chosen, the act is unjust and, therefore, by definition, an act of terrorism.

For example, consider two contrasting cases: If voting is a right guaranteed by the Constitution to all adult Americans and if registration is a justifiable prerequisite for voting, then is walking to the place of registration—either singly or in a group—either illegal or unjust? In contrast, if a small subset of the Basque people, appealing to the right of self-determination, wish to establish an independent Basque nation-state, then are assassination, car bombings, bank robberies, and extortion either legal or just means to achieve this

---

[3]The classic example of shutting down a campaign at the moment of its greatest success is Gandhi's 1930 Salt March (see Weber, 1997).

[4]For the mature expression of Martin Luther King, Jr.'s (1967) thinking, see his *Where Do We Go From Here: Chaos or Community?* For Gandhi, the best source is still the *Bhagavad Gita*, especially chapter 11. For a secular or "strategic" view, see Burrows (1996).

independence? Under Franco's dictatorship? Under the post-Franco Spanish democracy? Those who answer "no" to both cases will not characterize a voter registration march as terrorism, but they will characterize the *Euskadi Ta Askatasuna* (Fatherland and Liberty; ETA) campaign as terrorism. The opposite is of course also true; those who answer "yes" to both cases will characterize a voter registration march as terrorism or, at least, as illegal, and ETA's campaign as just, if not legal.

EVALUATING ENDS AND MEANS: EXPLANATION VS. JUSTIFICATION

As with any moral judgment, the myriad factors and circumstances of the two categories render the analysis extremely complex and difficult. Fortunately, though, resolving the extreme complexity of these or any other specific cases is very much beyond the scope of this chapter. What is within the scope, however, is the oft-neglected distinction between justification and explanation, an important distinction already noted above which, not incidentally, allows one to explore further the relationship between ends and means.

If the quicksands of fanatical extremism explain how terrorists and their enabling sympathizers can both explain and justify terrorism to themselves, it does not do the same for third-party observers. For, unlike "true believers," third-party observers usually possess a relatively high tolerance for uncertainty and ambiguity in their world. Recognizing the existence of uncertainty, non-"true believers" have a perspective that rejects any and all horrors in the means used to attain their desired ends. They draw the line when the horror is too horrible. They are, therefore, able to understand, first, that the end (always) justifies the means only in a trivial and formal manner. Cognizant of this formal trap, they are, then, able to establish criteria for evaluating the moral acceptability of the means used with respect to the ends sought. That is, they understand that the end never justifies all the means, only some means—it justifies only those means that are (a) proportional, (b) discriminating, and (c) well-intentioned. However, because acts of terror are, by definition, neither proportional, discriminating, nor well-intentioned, the public "justifications" for acts of terror neither explain nor justify such acts for non-"true believers."

In fine, the twisted logic of terrorists and other "true believers," based, as it is, on tortured tautologies, leads inevitably to immorality, if not to terrorism. Convinced of the absolute truth of their cause, "true believers" cannot imagine that the most horrible means are not fully justified. They cannot imagine that they too could follow the examples of Gandhi, King, Aquino, the East Europeans, Mandela, and others. These *satyagrahi* all understand that justice is elusive and, hence, that only well-intentioned, discriminate, and proportional protests can draw it out of their opponents. Terrorists, lacking this understanding, are unable to imagine the alternative to their theatrical crimes. This is the terrorists' ultimate sin, a lack of imagination.

COGNITIVE DISSONANCE OF TERRORISM SCHOLARSHIP

When one turns from terrorists to those who study terrorists, the sources of the cognitive dissonance change. For terrorists, it is the incongruence between their public explanation and their private explanation as "true believers" that generates extreme dissonance in their minds and ours. For those who study terrorism, it is the misclassification of the phenomenon. Instead of classifying terrorism as a species of crime, they have too often classified it as a species of "war," which is to be located under the genus of "political violence." For example, one of the leading journals in the field is entitled *Journal of Terrorism and Political Violence*. This error is natural enough for anyone who spends much time reading what terrorists write. That is, the misclassification has, no doubt, arisen because in their public manifestos, terrorists always allege that they are "soldiers" "waging war" in the service of some higher political or social cause. Although this portrayal is flattering to the terrorists, cognitive dissonance, not clarity and coherence, is the only result that one can expect from privileging the terrorists' self-understanding and dishonest language.

The problem is that terrorists are not waging a "war"; they are committing crimes. Thus, the true genus for their activities is "crime," which, in turn, needs to be broken down into the species of "arson," "kidnapping," "murder," and the like, before identifying the subspecies of "theatrical arson," "theatrical kidnapping," "theatrical murder," and the like, should one so desire this further division of the phenomenon. Be this as it may, having misclassified terrorism as "war," terrorism experts have had to acknowledge that terrorism is not really "war"; rather, it is somewhat like a photographic negative of "war." That is, under the genus of "political violence," terrorism experts have discovered at least two species: "real" or "positive" war, which is "positive" in the sense that it is the legitimate or lawful exercise of "political violence," and "unreal" or "negative" war, which is the photographic "negative" of "real" war in the sense that it is the illegitimate or unlawful use of "political violence." In summary, if "war" is the positive image of "political violence," then terrorism is its negative image.

Take, for example, a 1985 pamphlet from RAND by Brian M. Jenkins, a well-known expert on terrorism. Entitled *International Terrorism: The Other World War*, it illustrates both how old the association of terrorism with war is and how dissonance naturally arises whenever the self-image of the terrorists is taken at face value. Jenkins began with the testimony of terrorists and others:

"The Third World War has started," the notorious terrorist Carlos told his hostages in Vienna in 1975. A French soldier in Beirut, a survivor of the suicide terrorist bombing that killed 58 of his comrades, made a similar observation: "Our 58 comrades are perhaps the first, deaths of the Third World War." Unlike the wars of the past, this war did not begin with one identifiable event. Indeed, no one can say for certain when or where it began. (1985, p. 1)

Terrorists claim to be not criminals, but soldiers at war who are therefore privileged to break ordinary laws. (1985, p. 3)

A page later, however, Jenkins correctly refuted the terrorists' claim to be soldiers waging a war:

All terrorist acts are crimes. . . . The purpose is political. . . . Terrorism differs from ordinary crime in its political purpose and in its primary objective. . . . Terrorism is not synonymous with guerrilla warfare or any other kind of war . . . (1985, p. 4)

Terrorists, it appears, are not "soldiers" after all; in reality, they are criminals, albeit criminals with a "political purpose." Because this "political purpose" is based upon a claim made by the terrorists themselves, its validity is suspect. For the moment, I pass over these suspicions to evaluate further why terrorism is not "war," not even "guerrilla war." Although "not synonymous with guerrilla warfare," according to Jenkins, modern terrorism yet derives from modern theories of guerrilla warfare:

Present-day terrorism derives largely from twentieth century theories of guerrilla warfare, for which Mao Zedong deserves the most credit, although his paramount concern for winning the support of the masses would probably have made him reject the tactics of contemporary terrorism . . . [5]

Mao suggested that guerrillas must aim for and depend upon the political mobilization of people who are mere bystanders in a conventional military conflict. Mao thus introduced a relationship between military action and the attitude and response of the audience. This added a new dimension to armed conflict: Instead of gauging success primarily in terms of the physical effect that military action had on the enemy, strategists could now say that the effect a violent action has on the people watching may be independent of, and may equal or even exceed in importance the actual physical damage inflicted on the foe. Terrorism is that proposition pursued to its most violent extreme, though terrorists have not been very good at explaining it. (1985, p. 8)

What is most peculiar about the passage is not its claim for a Maoist origin for modern terrorism but rather the last clause. That is, although terrorists

---

[5]The final clause is important. Although Jenkins did not explain which excesses of contemporary terrorism Mao would reject, his point is that "political violence" has its limits. At some point, the means (tactics) chosen become so disproportionate, indiscriminate, and ill-intentioned that they revolt the oppressed masses and turn them against the terrorists.

can recite supposedly explanatory theories of terror, according to Jenkins, they have yet to justify their acts of terror; most especially, they have yet to either explain or justify how their terrorism will achieve their publicly declared goals:

> In recent years, terrorists have turned out thousands of pages of manifestos, manuals, assessments, directives, claims, communiqués, commentaries, critiques, and self-criticisms, but they have yet to articulate a clear and convincing theory to explain just how laying a bomb here or pulling a trigger there relates to the achievement of their objectives. (1985, p. 8)

In other words, terrorists have a well developed theory for the Machiavellian or instrumental use of terror, but they lack even the rudiments of a theory for the effective achievement of political and social goals.[6] In contrast, Gandhi and his followers possess a proven theory for the effective achievement of political and social goals, precisely because they do not possess (indeed, they reject) all Machiavellian and instrumental theories of terror. But I digress.

The suspicion creeps in that the experts have spent too much time reading the "thousands of pages of manifestos, manuals, assessments, directives, claims, communiqués, commentaries, critiques, and self-criticisms" and not enough time reflecting upon the fact that terrorists are simply criminals, who, as "true believers" possess a more grandiose self-justification than most criminals.

The cognitive dissonance in expert analyses of terrorism becomes more acute when the experts attempt to define terrorism. For example, Jenkins cannot decide whether "Terrorism is the use of criminal violence to force a government to change its course of action" (1985, p. v, also p. 2) or whether "Terrorism is theater [it is aimed at the people watching]" (1985, p. 9). In terms of simple logic, no need exists to define terrorism at all. All acts of terror are already crimes, as both Jenkins and I have already noted above. The dissonance is not reduced by reference to more official definitions of terrorism. For example, the FBI's definition reads, "Terrorism: 'The Unlawful Use of Force against Persons or Property to Intimidate or Coerce a Government, the Civilian Population, or Segment Thereof, in the Furtherance of Political or Social Objectives'" (28 C.F.R. section 0.85), whereas the congressional definition, found in the law establishing the State Department's Annual Country Reports on Terrorism, is, "The term 'terrorism' means premeditated, politically motivated violence perpetrated against noncombatant

---

[6]One of the better books on the continual failure of terrorists to reach their publicly stated goals is Calb Carr (2002), *The Lessons of Terror: A History of Warfare Against Civilians, Why It Has Always Failed and Why It Will Fail Again.*

targets by sub-national groups or clandestine agents" (Title 22 USC, Chapter 38, Sec. 2656f (d) (2)).[7]

Of the three, the FBI definition is the more narrowly drawn, because it limits terrorism to "the unlawful use of force," whereas the "politically motivated violence" of the congressional definition could encompass almost anything. Strangely, however, neither definition is based upon the rock hard fact that "All terrorist acts are crimes." Instead, both are based on an effort to distinguish terrorism from war, terrorism being viewed as an antiwar or as a nonwar or, in some sense, as the photographic negative of war. That is, in order to transform both definitions into definitions of war, all that has to be done is to change one negative in the definition to a positive. Hence, the FBI's definition is almost a paraphrase of a definition of war, "*War*: The *Lawful* Use of Force against Persons or Property to Intimidate or Coerce a Government, the Civilian Population, or Segment Thereof, in the Furtherance of Political or Social Objectives," whereas the congressional definition is virtually a paraphrase of a definition of international war, "The term '*international war*' means premeditated, politically motivated violence perpetrated against *combatant* targets by *national* groups or clandestine agents." The same inversion is possible with the first of Jenkins's definitions, "*War* is the use of *non-criminal (lawful?)* violence to force a government to change its course of action."

Terrorism is not an illegitimate war, however. Jenkins is surely right on three crucial points: (a) that terrorism is theatre, (b) that it not "synonymous with guerrilla warfare or any other kind of war," and (c) that "all terrorist acts are crimes." This being the case, then terrorism has nothing to do with war and everything to do with crime and theatre. Or, to cite Jenkins summarizing Mao again, war gauges "success primarily in terms of the physical effect that military action had on the enemy," whereas terrorists gauge success by "the effect a violent action has on the people watching. . . . " War deals with physical facts on the ground; terrorism deals with theatrical displays in the media.

Thus, instead of regarding terrorists as having political purposes and engaging in "political violence," a more factual and realistic conception is that they are criminals engaged in theatrical crimes. What distinguishes terrorists from other, more easily understood criminals, as Jenkins argued, is the theatrical quality of their crimes. Instead of seeking to hide their crimes from detection, terrorists actively seek to commit the crimes that bring them the most publicity, precisely because they are self-regarding, self-deluding, "true believers" turned criminals. Hence, a better definition of terrorism is that it

---

[7]No internationally recognized definition of *terrorism* exists. The United Nations is currently trying to develop one, in the wake of the attacks on New York City and Washington, DC, of September 11. Instead of a single definition, the international community has negotiated a number of conventions, each of which deals with a specific crime: hijacking airliners, attacking diplomats, and so on (located at http://untreaty.un.org/English/Terrorism.asp).

is a theatrical crime against persons or property. Developing the conception further, a terrorist is one who places greater value on affect than on effect, one who wishes to affect a real or imagined problem at the expense of effecting it so as to resolve it. Hence, again, the theatricality of terrorism and the polar contrast with Gandhi and his many followers.

THINKING ABOUT THEATRICAL CRIMES

Theatrical crimes confront one with three great, perplexing problems: (a) trying to understand the pain and trauma of the victims, (b) trying to understand the motivations of the theatrical criminals, and (c) trying to understand the relationship between terrorists, terrorism, and their social milieu: What conditions enable terrorism and terrorists more than others? The relationship between terrorists and their environment is critical, most especially for combating this type of crime. Because of its importance, I shall devote the next section, "Enabling Terrorism: The Social Milieu," to analyzing this relationship.

With respect to the first problem cited above, one simply cannot understand the pain and trauma of the victims. As with any crime, the victims are innocent; they are people who are truly caught in the wrong place at the wrong time. The word that describes their situation is tragedy. Furthermore, theirs is a wrenching tragedy over which one can only grieve, passing through the stages of shock, denial, anger, bargaining, guilt, depression, loneliness, acceptance, and (finally, one prays) hope. Arresting the perpetrators and bringing them to trial is all well and good; it should be done. But it does little to ease and nothing to erase the grief and suffering for the victims.

With respect to the second problem, the terrorists' motivations, the terrorists' press releases say that their terror is motivated by some palpable injustice, by oppression. But can one accept the self-justification of criminals? After all, crimes committed with the greatest sincerity are still crimes. Sincerity does little to reduce individual responsibility and culpability for a crime. Indeed, as argued above, the palpable injustice alleged cannot justify the terrorists because the means chosen were disproportionate, indiscriminate, and ill-intentioned. One can go further, however. The oppression alleged also cannot explain the terrorists's acts because neither the injustice nor the oppression "caused," "created," or was their "source." The simple truth is that terrorists, and terrorists alone, "cause" or "create" terrorism. They, and not their environment, are the "source" of their terrorism.

That no causal relation exists between oppression and terrorism is demonstrated by the simple fact that every day, hundreds of millions of people all around the world suffer from unimaginable oppression and injustice. Yet, terrorists number in the hundreds, perhaps, the thousands, only. If political and social injustices "caused" or "created" terrorism, if they were the "source" of terrorism, then this "cause" would "create" millions, not hundreds, of terrorists. A "cause" that produces such a small effect is clearly not a "cause" at all. To make the same argument in a different way, many say that oppression, by blocking other avenues of expression, leads to "political violence." However, this was not true for Gandhi, Martin Luther King, Jr., or the leaders of the Eastern European overthrow of Soviet rule in 1988–1989. In too many cases to count, people have effected permanent change in their countries without turning to crime and terrorism. To say that there is "no alternative" to "political violence" is only to acknowledge an immense lack of political imagination. With patience and imagination, another way always exists. Patience stretching to decades is the key, as Lech Walesa, Vàclav Havel, and the other leaders of the "Velvet Revolutions" in Eastern Europe during the 1980s have well demonstrated.

However, this is to look at the issue from a purely negative perspective. Turn the question around and ask why more of the oppressed of the world do not turn to theatrical crimes of terror. The simplest answer is that most people do the right thing most of the time. Even in the face of the greatest oppression and injustices, the vast, overwhelming majority of people continue to follow the simple dictates of the golden rule. They continue to respect the sanctity of life and dignity of all, even that of their oppressors. In a word, most people value their integrity more than terrorist do. Surprisingly, perhaps, this includes the vast majority of common criminals, who almost never think of participating in the senseless atrocities of terrorism. To do so would seldom serve their own selfish interests. Consequently, only a small fraction of mankind is ever tempted to become terrorists. With these thoughts in mind, a more detailed analysis of terror, terrorism, the agents of terror, and terrorists is needed.

Terror

Psychologically, *terror* is a state of intense fear. As such, terror may arise anywhere at anytime from anything. Small children are terrified of the dark, even shadows. In a criminal sense, however *terror* is the fear generated by the use of unjustified physical or psychological means. The gap between psychological and criminal terror means that not all terror is criminal. For example, when the physical or psychological means used are justified because they are (a) proportionate, (b) discriminate, and (c) well-intentioned, then any feelings of terror are not criminal, but psychological alone. Hence, dentists and surgeons use means that frighten many, but any "terror" induced in their patients is proportionate, discriminate, and well-intentioned. In addition, their "acts of terror" are for the benefit of the patients, and not solely for their own benefit. Dentists and surgeons therefore are not "terrorists."

Terrorism

Terrorism, as defined in the introduction to this chapter, is a theatrical crime against persons or property. Crucially, this theatrical crime provides no tangible, instrumental benefit to the perpetrators, only symbolic or "psychological" satisfaction. More fully, terrorism is a particularly brutal and senseless type of theatre or cinema because the actual victims are not the target; rather, they are theatrical props sacrificed so as to produce the maximum horror and fear among the audience, among the target population. As Osama bin Laden has explained, "The September 11 attacks were not [directed] at women and children. The real targets were America's icons of military and economic power" (Mir, 2001, p. 3). Thus, the object of the attack is to influence those who witness it, either firsthand or in the media; the object is not to influence, or even punish, those directly attacked. As a secondary matter, the attack is also designed to produce a sense of awe at the power and cleverness of the terrorists among the terrorists themselves and their enabling group.

Because the primary purpose of the attack is to garner the maximum media coverage possible, these theatrical criminals strive to create the most striking visual effects possible. When compared to guns, knives, or poisons, the most striking visual effects are produced by explosives. The explosion itself is very striking, and the ruins created by the explosion are equally effective. News photographs of both the initial explosion and of the ruins are a permanent record, a constant reminder, of the horror for the target population. Indeed, the ruins alone intimidate all who see them or view photographs of them. The superior cinematographic effect of explosions, therefore, explains why more than 80% of terrorist acts involve explosions (Federal Bureau of Investigation, 1999, p. 41).

Mapping the Agents of Terror

I say "agents of terror" because not all those who both use terror and are criminals should qualify as terrorists, both "terror" and "agents of terror" being a larger set than the set of terrorists. The agents of terror, then, may be classified by their motivation. Their motivation is mixed, to be sure, but it ranges from the purely theatrical to the fully instrumental. More concretely, the most theatrical terrorists are apocalyptic or messianic terrorists who are motivated by a desire "to save the world by destroying it." At the other extreme, the most instrumental terrorists are simple honest criminals who have no greater pretensions than self-interested greed. Somewhere in the middle are those terrorists who do possess some political motive, or at least say they do. When laid out on an axis, this schema produces six different types, as is depicted in Figure 2.1.

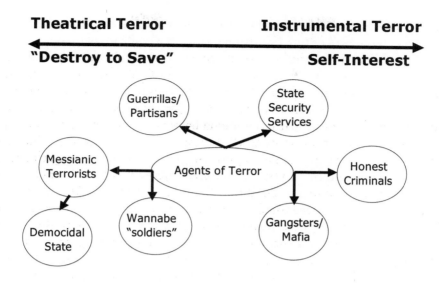

Theatrical Terror ← "Destroy to Save"   **Instrumental Terror** → Self-Interest

Guerrillas/Partisans

State Security Services

Messianic Terrorists

Agents of Terror

Honest Criminals

Democidal State

Wannabe "soldiers"

Gangsters/Mafia

Figure 2.1. Six agents of terror.

1. Messianic terrorists usually cloak their true motivation under some social, religious, or political grievance or injustice, but their true motive is the apocalyptic belief that the world is so corrupt that they must destroy it to save it. Messianic terrorists come in all sizes, shapes, and apocalyptic forms. Examples are Aum Shinrikyo, Timothy McVeigh, Ted Kaczynski, and most recently Osama bin Laden. They may also become democidal[8] if they can gain control of a State, as was the case with Hitler, Pol Pot's Khmer Rouge, the Hutu Rwandans, and the like.

2. Wannabe "soldiers" (a.k.a. "freedom fighters") are usually not messianic. Instead, they use terror for some specific absolutized political goal (e.g., independence). Although they never engage in open combat, only in secret operations, they assert they are "soldiers" fighting for some political cause or injustice. Again, unlike real soldiers, they feel "authorized" to violate all laws to support themselves through common crime (drugs, extortion, kidnapping, bank robbery, etc.) Examples of wannabe "soldiers" are the Irish Republican Army, Ulster Defense Force, ETA, and Fuerzas Armadas Revolutionaries de Colombia.

---

[8]*Democide* is a term developed by R. J. Rummel (1992) to aggregate genocide and mass murder committed by governments against their own people. The term is needed to cover cases such as the Cambodian killing fields, which was not a case of genocide. It is further needed to dramatize the fact that several times the number of people have died during the 20th century at the hands of their own governments than in all the wars of a very bloody century.

3. Gangsters and the mafia use terror to maintain control of their businesses or turf. Sometimes gangs or a mafia invoke a political cover for their criminal activities. More often, gangs and mafia are just in it for the loot. Examples of this "political" type of gang are Foday Sanko's Revolutionary United Front in Sierra Leone, Charles Taylor's forces in Liberia, or Khun Sa's old Shan Liberation Army in Burma.

4. Honest criminals produce terror as an "unintended" consequence of their crimes. They are self-interested and are not motivated by politics or a sense of injustice.

5. State security services can be either messianic or brutally instrumental depending on their circumstances. If they are messianic, then, like messianic terrorists, they are very likely to become democidal, as happened in Nazi Germany and Pol Pot's Cambodia. If they are instrumental, then they are simply brutal. That is, they use terror and torture to maintain state power, as in the Argentine and Chilean "Dirty Wars."

6. Guerrillas and partisans are not usually messianic, although Mao's Chinese People's Army is one exception. They are, instead, political and use terror for some specific absolutized political goal (e.g., independence). With respect to terrorism, the situation is complex. Those guerrillas who do engage in open combat are clearly soldiers under the Geneva Convention (I), cited above. However, those who do not engage in open combat, but, instead, engage in Agit-Prop and other forms of terror are not soldiers, but terrorists. Because an individual can be reassigned from a combat unit to an Agit-Prop unit and back, it can be confusing to determine who is a terrorist and who is not. In addition, sabotage may be considered an act of terrorism by the enemy, although it may on occasion be a legitimate military activity. Examples include the French Maquis and Soviet and Yugoslav partisans in World War II and the Viet Cong.

Terrorists

The criminal character of gangsters, the mafia, and honest criminals is undisputed. State security services are better characterized as torturers or assassins, not as terrorists. Their acts of terror usually lack the mediagenic theatricality of true terrorism. Putting these agents of terror aside, despite vast areas of ambiguity, the label *terrorist* is best reserved for one of three general types: (a) guerrillas and partisans, (b) wannabe "soldiers" (or "freedom fighters"), and (c) messianic terrorists. Generally, terrorists are "true believers" whose acts of terror are, first, crimes and, second, theater (i.e., committed for their media value and not for any substantive instrumental value). Accordingly, a terrorist is an alienated, socially isolated, but often charismatic, criminal engaged in theatrical crimes.

ENABLING TERRORISM: THE SOCIAL MILIEU

Although theatrical criminals or terrorists are extremely few in number and socially isolated, they do not operate in a vacuum. Like other criminals, they are enabled or disabled by the social and political conditions around them. Or, to begin on a more positive note, humans are social animals. As a result, everything they do is influenced by their social environment. Humans are also self-conscious individuals, and, as such, they are autonomous moral agents. As a result, they must take responsibility for their decisions and actions. Out of the dynamic interaction of the social milieu with its individual members and of the individual members with their social milieu comes the decisions and actions that produce mankind's collective history and each individual's biography. As a result of this dynamic interaction, one cannot say that the terrorists' social milieu "creates" him. To do so is to deny the terrorist his individuality, his moral agency. Like all criminals, only terrorists can "create" terrorists. Terrorists do this through the personal decisions that they make and action that they take. That said, one must immediately recognize that some social milieus are more favorable to the creation of terrorists than others. In the paragraph that follows, I identify these social factors as (a) enabling leadership, (b) enabling history, and (c) enabling sympathizers. For now, however, I simply note that three general conditions also appear to be influential: (a) a youth bulge, (b) poverty and gross injustice, and (c) a culture of disrespect and intolerance.

Not to belabor the obvious, societies or groups with relative prosperity and a culture of respect and tolerance tend to have low rates of crime, in general, and to disable terrorists, in particular. In contrast, societies or groups with high levels of poverty, injustice, and a culture of disrespect toward "outsiders" (however defined by the society or group), intolerance, and hatred tend to have high rates of crime, in general, and to enable terrorists, in particular. For example, the last 40 years or so of terrorism in Northern Ireland was all but guaranteed by the palpable discrimination against Catholics by the Protestants in Northern Ireland. Fueled by poverty and a long-cultivated sense of disrespect and hatred in both communities for the other, the Irish Republican Army, on the one side, and the Ulster Defense forces, on the other side, soon hijacked the Gandhian civil rights movement of the 1960's, turning peaceful protests into a campaign of assassination, bombings, bank robberies, and a scramble to monopolize the drug trade. Economic development and social justice are essential tonics for both crime and terrorism. Still, societies with high levels of prosperity, tolerance, and a respect for human dignity harbor terrorists and are not immune from terrorism. The United States, Timothy McVeigh, and Ted Kaczynski come to mind. Likewise, other societies with great intolerance and little respect for human dignity escape terrorist incidents. Eastern Europe during the 1980s as it threw off the Soviet yoke comes to mind.

A third general condition enabling crime, including terrorism, occurs whenever a population is experiencing a youth bulge. A *youth bulge* is a demographic phenomenon that occurs whenever the 15–24-year-old age cohort reaches or exceeds 20% of a population, thereby throwing off the symmetry of a normal age pyramid (Fuller & Pitts, 1990). Unless some means can be found to dissipate the youth bulge and return the population to a more normal age distribution, all indicators of social tension, including crime, will predictably rise significantly. Mexico has succeeded in managing its youth bulge through illegal immigration to the United States. The United States was somewhat less successful in managing its last youth bulge during the late 1960s and early 1970s. The current upsurge in social turmoil, including terrorism, in Islamic countries is not surprising in light of the large youth bulges that these countries are experiencing now.[9] In general, then, societies experiencing youth bulges predictably experience significant increases in social tension, including increased rates of crime and terrorism.

In addition to these three general conditions that enable terrorism, three more specific factors greatly facilitate or inhibit an individual in choosing to become a terrorist: history, leadership, and presence or absence of sympathizers. An enabling history teaches that "power grows out of the barrel of a gun" and that a resort to terror is "honorable." This is especially true in cultures of vengeance. A dis-enabling history does the opposite. One of the sadder examples of an enabling history is W. B. Yeats's (1983) poem, *Easter, 1916*, commemorating the fallen "heroes" of the Easter Rebellion in Ireland:

> For England may keep faith
> For all that is done and said.
> We know their dream; enough
> To know they dreamed and are dead;
> And what if excess of love
> Bewildered them till they died?
> I write it out in verse—
> MacDonagh and MacBride
> And Connolly and Pearse
> Now and in time to be,
> Wherever green is worn,
> Are changed, changed utterly:
> A terrible beauty is born. (p. 182)

---

[9]A convenient source is the United Nations Population Division's World Population Prospects, Population Database. Either "Panel 2" (http://esa.un.org/unpp/index.asp?panel=2) or the "Country profile" (http://esa.un.org/unpp/index.asp?panel=3) will provide the percentage of population between the ages of 15 and 24.

An enabling leadership promotes intolerance and hatred in pursuit of some absolutized goal, either the messianic goal of "saving the world by destroying it" or some political end, such as independence, that is said to justify all means. A dis-enabling leadership does the opposite, as Gandhi and King illustrate. Enabling sympathizers accept, even if they do not encourage, both the acts of terror and the theatrical criminals who commit them as in some sense justified. Minimally, enabling sympathizers are silent and do nothing either to condemn or thwart the terrorists. Dis-enabling sympathizers do the opposite. To paraphrase Mao, enabling sympathizers are the water in which the terrorists swim. A small subgroup of youth within the enabling sympathizers, what might be called "wannabe" terrorists, form the pool from which terrorists can be recruited easily.

In terms of the social milieu that enables terrorists, the obvious strategy is to turn the sympathizers from enabling into dis-enabling, to drain away the social water in which the terrorists swim. This goal cannot be accomplished by arresting or otherwise removing enabling sympathizers. Indeed, arresting or displacing enabling sympathizers, experience shows, only increases their sympathy for the terrorists, fear of false arrest or removal to concentration camps now being added to the list of their grievances. However, if enabling sympathizers cannot be arrested, what is to be done to turn them into dis-enabling sympathizers? This is the point at which politics and social policy often become crucial to ending episodes of terrorism. The grievances that cause them to sympathize and accept the theatrical criminals must be identified and remedied. These grievances are often, but not always, some injustice.

Ideally, one would live in a society without either terrorists or terrorism. Such a society would possess (a) a dis-enabling leadership, (b) a dis-enabling history, and (c) an absence of sympathizers as well as grievances. Such an ideal society would also be characterized by a normal age profile, relative prosperity and justice, and a culture of respect and tolerance. More realistically, in a society with terrorists and terrorism, the first line of defense is good police work. As a second line of defense, however, one must dis-enable both the general and the more specific social factors that enable terrorists.

3

PEACE AND WAR IN THE MIDDLE EAST: A PSYCHOPOLITICAL AND SOCIOCULTURAL PERSPECTIVE

NAJI ABI-HASHEM

The situation in the Middle East has been intense, highly complicated, and profoundly disheartening. Many observers seriously wonder whether an authentic peace is still possible or whether the region is destined to remain in a state of turmoil, bloody conflict, and tragedy.

The question on the minds of millions of concerned people worldwide is whether the peace movement in the Middle East is completely dead, or whether there is some hope for a reasonable accord and long-term tranquility. That hope (*amal*) may be an illusion or mere fantasy, but without it, life can be truly unbearable (cf. Abi-Hashem, 2001b).

In the Middle East, several issues are so complex and explosive that any one of them could trigger a large-scale war. The Middle East is geographically vast and is known for its rich cultures, beauty, and natural resources. It is the birthplace of many civilizations and major world religions. Despite its oil wealth, however, many Middle Eastern countries are economically stagnant (Barakat, 1993; Crossette, 2002) or suffer from sociopolitical instability either because of external interference or internal disintegration. Obviously, these conditions cause deep suffering and damage the cultural fabric, rich heritage, and friendly nature of the region.

Historically, there have been several levels of disputes (Abi-Hashem, 2001a):

1. Land (either conquered, possessed, or gained). The new inhabitants are fighting to claim it, and the indigenous inhabitants are fighting to keep it.

2. Oil ("black gold"). The Middle East's vast oil resources are the source of great tension between the countries that have them and those that need them. The desire to control oil was a hidden psychopolitical motive behind the last Gulf War.

3. Water (essential source of livelihood). Water resources are becoming increasingly scarce in the Middle East (like elsewhere in the world), so much so that the desire to control water may very well trigger the next war in the region. Parched countries might fight over running rivers and fresh lakes; countries that have water might be tempted to cut its flow to downstream countries and might insist on keeping all of it.

4. Cultural and religious heritage versus sociopolitical freedom. During the last few decades, there has been a constant tension in many parts of the Middle East between the forces of traditionalism and those of modernism. These opposing trends and conflicting polarities are becoming increasingly pronounced as manifested by the rise of radical and fundamentalist groups on one side and the secular and materialist groups on the other.

All of these factors are dynamically interrelated as they affect and shape the psychosocial and ethnopolitical conditions in the Middle East. They have tremendous implications for the stability of the region as a whole.

This chapter attempts to examine the nature of terrorism and to clarify some misunderstandings about Arabs, Muslims, and other Middle Easterners. The chapter reviews the historical and religious backgrounds of the crises in the Middle East and analyzes the geopolitical dynamics in the area. The reasons that many groups are angry with the West in general and with the United States in particular are explored. The chapter also discusses the rise of fundamentalism and militancy and the complicated question of Israel versus the Palestinians. A word of encouragement is provided to psychologists to consider volunteering time overseas to help serve people in troubled areas, where a little care usually goes a long way and the personal rewards are great. In addition, psychologists are encouraged to be active in their local communities and governments and policymakers are encouraged to restore high ethics and compassion into the political process and, thus, contribute to a better and more genuine world peace.

TERMS AND DEFINITIONS

Terrorism is a difficult term to define. The more one tries to define it, the more complex and obscure it becomes. There is no clear understanding or complete agreement on what constitutes a *terrorist*, either. The *terrorism* label implies a wide range of qualities and characteristics; it readily evokes negative feelings, biased attitudes, and stereotypical reactions. However, according to Greenstock, the chairman of the UN Security Council's committee on terrorism, "it might be easier to define terrorist acts rather than terrorism generally" (as quoted in Roberts, 2002, ¶ 6).

To some degree, what constitutes "terrorism" is a matter of perspective. Although there are some international guidelines and principles for defining or denouncing sociopolitical violence, the broad range of violent activities has not yet been comprehensively analyzed and conceptualized. The definition of the term *terrorism* is determined largely by the party or group making the judgment. In the Middle East, for example, most Israelis accuse most Palestinian groups and activists of being terrorists because they are resisting Israeli policy of mistreatment and occupation in the West Bank and Gaza Strip. In the minds of most Palestinians and some Arabs-Muslims, however, the Israeli government and military also behave like an organized terrorist group. This type of definition refers to a state-sponsored terrorism. Roberts (2002) observed that

> Governments had varying degrees of involvement in supporting terrorism, almost invariably at arm's length so as to be deniable. The causes espoused by terrorists encompassed not just revolutionary socialism and nationalism, but also religious doctrines rejecting the whole notion of a pluralist world of states. ("Varieties of terrorism" section, ¶ 1)

However defined, terrorism can take many shapes and forms and can be either spontaneous and impulsive or carefully planned and calculated. Bombings, shootings, kidnapping, torturing, hijackings, brutal killing, and assassinations are examples of such acts. Some experts believe that terrorism is not a mere random or blind act of violence but rather is intentional in that it is almost always conducted and delivered with a strategy behind it. Terrorism includes but is not limited to a deliberate use of violence against civilians as a target, mainly without warning.

In Arabic the closest word for *terrorism* is *irhaab*, whereas *terror* could be translated as *ro'ob* (horror). *Terror* is similar but not quite identical to *terrorism*, although the two are sometimes used interchangeably. "Conventionally, the term [terrorism] applies to the acts of revolutionaries or nationalists who challenge governments, while terror refers to government actions to crush resistance. In practice the distinction between terrorism and terror is not always clear" (Crenshaw, 2002, p. 1). At one time or another, extremists on the far right and the far left as well as governments and underground organizations seem to resort to the use of some forms of terrorism. Many secretive and repressed groups occasionally resort to horrifying acts, readily available to them, in order to press their cause.

Israeli leaders and Jewish media constantly label certain Palestinian, Arab, or Muslim groups as terrorists. However, these "terrorists" call themselves *munadiloon* or *mujahidoon*, which means, individuals who strive, struggle, or embrace jihad toward a noble and just cause. Previously, Israel used to refer to them as *trouble-makers* or *destroyers*. More recently, Israel calls any form of resistance simply *terrorism*. On the other hand, in some Palestinian, Arab, and Muslim circles and media, Israel itself is labeled as a *terrorist state*. For example, Israel calls its army the *Israeli Defense Forces* (IDF), whereas some Arab and Muslim media refer to it as the *Occupying Israeli Army*. These mutually contrary labels have been part of a long history of a war of words, since the inception of Israel.

All being said, it is important to keep in mind that those sharp labels and terminologies are not the only language used or adopted in the whole Middle East, including inside Israel. There are plenty of moderate communities and good-willed people everywhere (politically, culturally, and religiously) who genuinely desire to find an end to the chronic dispute and live together in peace. There have been examples of that model already on many small scales. Many Arab and Muslim thinkers, groups, regimes, and media agencies, previously antagonistic and more sympathetic with hard-liners, have been reevaluating their positions and softening their political rhetoric. So far, it seems that the makers of global and world politics, the race to be superpower in the region, the territorial and geopolitical greed, the radical wings within each party are preventing any meaningful settlement or coexistence on the actual ground.

The phenomenon of terrorism is as old as the beginning of hostility and conflict among nations and peoples. Jenkins (1974, as quoted in Hoffman 1998) explained that terrorist acts are often deliberately spectacular, designed to rattle and influence a wide audience, beyond the victims of the violence itself. The point is to use the psychological impact of violence or of the threat of horror to effect political change. Similarly, Crenshaw (2002) defined *terrorism* as the use or threat of violence that may be limited in its physical destructiveness but is high in its psychological impact.

Thus, the definition of *terrorism* depends on one's perspective and position on issues like politics, society, culture, religion, and the dynamics of regional tension and world powers. The majority of people would consider terrorists to be radicals, lawless, separatists, fundamentalists, revolutionists, inhumane, extremists, rageful fanatics, cold-blooded killers, evil-doers, barbarians, sociopathic murderers, fascists, and destroyers of civilization. A minority within the population would probably consider terrorists to be freedom fighters, determined activists, legitimate resistance fighters, strugglers against oppression, pure nationalists, social reformers, defenders of a supreme cause, and executors of divine missions (as guided by spiritual or political inspirations).

In the minds of oppressed, traumatized, and hopeless young Palestinians, the case is clear. Revengeful fighting is necessary and is held as a heroic act (Steele, 2002a). Their passions are such that they prefer death and martyrdom to life under occupation. From a psychiatric and existential point of view, they are becoming suicidal patients, acting out their impulses and desperation on behalf of oppressed people. Some suicide bombers are basically civilians, not trained soldiers or militants, who have decided to carry out such missions secretly, even without telling their own families or friends. They refer to these bombings as "martyrdom operations" and not as "suicide missions," as the Western media portray them.

Terrorists usually upgrade their methods as the heat of conflict intensifies. For example, the radicals on the Palestinian side started their activities by attacking Israeli checkpoints and posts from a distance, then attacking tanks and soldiers at close range. More recently, they have been sneaking into settlements, shops, and public squares and blowing themselves up. Hamas, once opposed to Israel's existence, altered its position to oppose Israel's occupation (i.e., West Bank [including East Jerusalem] and Gaza Strip). "Hamas once had a policy of attacking only Israeli military and government targets, but after a militant Jewish settler attacked Palestinians praying at a mosque in Hebron in 1994, killing 29 people and injuring 60, Hamas leaders began targeting Israeli civilians" ("Radical Islamic Group," 2002, p. A14).

Radicals who resort to violence usually see themselves as the real victims and feel they are merely defending themselves. Thus, in the heat of the passion, trying to determine who is the victim or abused and who is the victimizer or abuser becomes a heated battle in itself. At times, some radical groups take the form of a cult when all members become indoctrinated and their cause is justified on the ground of ideology, economics, ethnicity, politics, or spirituality (or a combination of these). When these factors are present, coupled with an impulsive, zealous, or antisocial types of personalities, then the outcome will invariably result in some form of terrorism. Normally, those who conduct or participate in horrifying acts have been psychologically abused, traumatized, or victimized in one way or another. At the very least, they have witnessed severe harm and injustice done to their people, their land, or their ideals, matters they hold very dear and sacred. Therefore, they feel obligated to respond forcefully regardless of the obstacle or price.

Finally, "there may be a form of action called terrorism, but the labeling of individuals and movements as 'terrorist' will remain complicated and highly political" (Roberts, 2002, "Varieties of terrorism" section, ¶ 6). Some states quickly label any violent act as *terrorism*. Other states or groups see these brutal and violent acts as a legitimate "response to real grievances, and thereby insinuating that it was justified" (¶ 6). Others are reluctant to condemn any terroristic activities unless the real causes of terrorism are addressed. Therefore, any internationally agreed upon definition will serve only as a helpful guideline for discussion, description, or decision but not as an ultimate definition. There is an element about terrorism that is quite abstract, and perhaps it will remain so for a long time to come.

COMMON MISUNDERSTANDINGS AND MISCONCEPTIONS

Western media tend to spread misunderstandings and misconceptions regarding the Arab world and the Middle East. Such misconceptions are often due to inaccurate impressions or sociocultural stereotypes; at times, they can be misleading and even dangerous. Some of these misconceptions include the following (Abi-Hashem, 1992):

1. All Arabs are Muslims. In fact, not all Arabs are Muslims, nor are all Muslims Arabs. Although the majority of Arabs are Muslims, there are significant Christian communities in the region, in some countries more than others. Moreover, there are the Druze in Lebanon, Israel/Palestine, and Syria; they are mostly a mystic sociocultural group characterized by strong ethnic and communal bonds. The Druze's belief system is considered an offshoot of Islam, but it incorporates elements of Judaism, Islam, and Christianity along with some Eastern religious philosophy. The Alawites, who are loosely connected to the Shiite Muslims, are mostly found in Syria; despite their minority status, they have dominated the political system. Large Jewish communities were well established in the region before all the wars and migrations. Christians and Jews were present in the Arabian peninsula centuries before Islam. Some Christian, Jewish, and other nontheistic groups in the Arabian peninsula gradually converted to Islam either because of economic conditions, for social acceptance, or simply under religious pressure. Since then, Islam has become one of the major religions and political powers in the world whose adherents exceed one billion, roughly four-fifths of whom are non-Arab.

Most people in the Middle East live in social harmony and integration regardless of their background. However, depending on the area and the political climate, tension among various groups may arise. Presently, the largest Christian presence in the Arabic world is found in Egypt, though still considered a minority when compared to the whole population of that country. It is mainly represented by the historic yet active Coptic Church, a North African form of the Eastern Orthodox, and by other Christian mainline denominations.

Not all Arabs are Muslims, and most Muslims are not Arab, either. Indonesia (the largest Muslim country in the world), Iran, Pakistan, and Turkey are Muslim but non-Arab countries, and large populations in Africa, the Far East (like India), and the former Soviet Union (in Central Asia) are Muslim but culturally and ethnically non-Arab. In addition, the number of

Muslims in the West (Europe and North America) is rapidly growing as a result of migration, conversion, and natural growth.

2. All Middle Easterners are Arabs. This is not true; Iran is a Middle Eastern country, but it is Persian; Cyprus is a Middle Eastern island, but half of its population is Greek and the other half is Turkish; and Turkey is another non-Arab nation. The Arab world, however, spreads out beyond the Middle East designation to include all of North Africa. The common denominator among Arab countries is the use of the classical Arabic language and, in most cases, the mainstream Islamic faiths and traditions. Arabic is the official and universal language. However, each country or region has its own colloquial version of that classical language that is a lower form of Arabic for daily use. Neighboring countries and communities understand each other well, but as one travels farther afield, communication and comprehension decrease as the differences in the spoken language and accent become more obvious and pronounced.

3. All Arabs are primitive people. Unfortunately, most foreigners have misleading pictures about the Arabs and the Middle Easterners. "The first images that come to the Westerner's mind when he [or she] thinks of the Arabs are sand, desert, camels, oil wells, irrational mobs . . . and the like" (Hamady, 1960, p. 229). This is a stereotype. "The Western world must realize that ignorance about Arabian culture and history is not 'bliss,' but a detriment to international relations" (Hamada, 1990, p. 128). That is also true for Westerners and expatriates who are interested in investing money and making business deals in the area. Many organizations started projects in the Middle East without adequate preparation or consultation. The results have been mainly negative and unpleasant for everyone involved.

In addition, not all the Middle East countries are deserts or rich. Although some are wealthy and well-established, others are struggling and still developing. Lebanon, for example, led the region in terms of education, culture, and income per capita, and it has no oil, deserts, or major shrines. For decades it was called the Switzerland of the Middle East, but internal and regional wars waged on its territories have made that label a thing of the past. Unfortunately, small nations often pay the price of regional conflicts and become victims of world politics. Lebanon now has significantly deteriorated and disintegrated, and the Lebanese people deeply grieve the loss of their uniqueness, accomplishments, and identity. There are fears that the superpowers want to resolve the regional crisis at Lebanon's expense (cf. Abi-Hashem, 1999), for example, by giving South Lebanon to a new Palestinian state and naturalizing the hundreds of thousands of Palestinian guests and refugees that have fled to Lebanon since late 1940s. In light of the unpredictable politics in the region, Lebanon may become another Cyprus or perhaps a second Palestine. Lebanon is losing its role as a leading and progressive nation in the whole Middle East.

As with other nations spread over a large geographic area, the Arab peoples have a wide variety of societies, subcultures, economical levels, and traditions. Because the region is deeply rooted in the land, many traditions and characteristics have been transferred through the generations and woven like threads of gold into the social fabric of people. Moreover, the long heritage and rich mixture of cultures in the Middle East are a direct result of its strategic location at the crossroads of major civilizations that met and interacted there. That is still true as the West and the East converge at the gates of all major ports and cities. That is even more true now with the increased trends of internationalization and globalization.

4. All Arabs are fanatics and terrorists. Unfortunately, to many Westerners the term *Arab* is synonymous with *radical*, *uncivilized*, *fanatic*, or even *terrorist*. This misconception could be the result of ignorance or a biased media. Some Arabs, living or traveling in the West, identify themselves as Middle Easterners to avoid the stereotypes associated with the term *Arab*, especially after the events of September 11, 2001.

Arab culture and Islamic traditions have lately come under media scrutiny, in part to satisfy curiosity about or outright confusion around them. In reality, there are different types of Muslim communities: (a) the *traditional*—simple folks, mostly rural, who enjoy a peaceful community and a rich cultural heritage; (b) the *secular*—mostly educated and business oriented people who live in fairly open, progressive, or complex communities; (c) the *fundamental*—highly dedicated radicals, committed and fervently zealous to their sociopolitical and religious causes; (d) the *moderate*—people with balanced views and practices, whether individually or in groups; and (e) the *national*—people who strive to establish a regime that applies Islamic law and regulations to all aspects of personal life and communal affairs (cf. Voll, 1982).

GEOPOLITICAL REALITIES AND DYNAMICS

The psychosocial and ethnopolitical elements are in a state of flux in the Middle East. There are internal tensions within individual countries and external turmoil among neighboring countries. Frequent political, cultural, and ideological clashes lie at the heart of all Middle East crises. That is true of Israel as it is of the surrounding Arab countries. The rise of many renewal movements and the emergence of radical, extreme, and fanatical groups have reshaped the whole climate of the Middle East and North Africa.

The hard issues highlighted in this chapter reveal the multifaceted nature and the magnitude of conflicts in the Middle East, especially pertaining to Israel and Palestine. The complexity and tension appear to be increasing on many levels: (a) the geopolitical, (b) the religio-ideological, and (c) the sociocultural (Abi-Hashem, 1992, 2000; Awwad, 2001; Barakat, 1993; Dwairy,

1998; Esposito, 1997; Freedland, 2002; Hamady, 1960; Mortimer, 1982; Moussalli, 1998; Peristiany, 1965; Shahak & Mezvinski, 1999; Storey & Utter, 2002).

Barakat (1993, p. 270) poignantly observed several characteristic features of the Arab and Islamic world during the recent decades: the centrality of religion, the attempt to integrate capitalism into Arab systems, the absence of future-oriented rationalism, social and political fragmentation, repressive socialization and neopatriarchy, dominance of traditionalism over creativity, duality of Westernization and *salafiyya* (ancestralism), disequilibrium in the Arab ego, and the prevalence of traditional mentality.

Although resolution and relative peace have been established on a few fronts in the Middle East, the long-term prognosis does not look good. It has been evident in recent months that events are taking a turn for the worse. This raises a fundamental question: Is the peace process in the Middle East clinically dead? Are we past hope and resolution?

What has been labeled a "peace process" is presently a paralyzed and crippled process. The word *process* should imply an unfolding of events toward a resolution of the conflict. However, this particular process in the Middle East has become stalled and immobilized. Can such a "process" be revived? In the opinion of many observers, a full and permanent peace at the present time is not possible. What complicates the situation is the presence of different perspectives, local needs, styles of negotiation, sets of expectations, political ambitions, styles of communication, and cultural mindsets. These factors were clearly obvious during the Gulf War, revealing a deep gap and sharp contrast between the Eastern mentality versus Western mentality in dealing with the other country, whether in pursuing a passive peace or in conducting a massive war (cf. Abi-Hashem, 1992).

The major parties in Israel and Palestine have failed badly in preparing their public for a new mental perspective or for the cognitive leap toward ultimate compromise (Freedland, 2002). In general, some Arab and Muslim leaders have been reluctant to change their tone or policy toward Israel. "Grudging behavior by one side fueled grudging behavior by the other, leading to a vicious cycle of skirted obligations, clear-cut violations, and mutual recriminations" (Agha & Malley, 2002, pp. 10–11). The radicals within each camp are undermining the position of the moderates in their respective societies. All these dynamics are making the prospect for resolution more difficult. "The mounting death tolls on both sides seem to confirm the notion that conflict management rather than conflict resolution should be the order of the day, and that now is the time for taking incremental steps in order to rebuild the torn fabric of trust" (Agha & Malley, 2002, p. 10).

"'The peace process may not be clinically dead, but it's about to die,' said Nabil Khatib, director of a Palestinian media center at Bir Zeit University. 'It's a depressing situation especially because it's not just due to the tough issues, but to psychology'" (Morris & Demick, 2000, p. A23). Similarly, Agha and Malley (2002) have argued that slow or small negotiations are not fruitful anymore:

> Rather than bring the two sides closer, negotiations serve to play up remaining disagreements and to play down the broad scope of actual convergence. The time for negotiations has therefore ended. Instead, the parties must be presented with a full-fledged, non-negotiable final agreement. . . . Mistrust, enmity, and suspicion are the consequences of the conflict, not its cause. A deal should not be made dependent on preexisting mutual trust; the deal itself will create it. (p. 12)

The authors made the case for such a comprehensive deal because they believed that designing a full resolution package is possible provided that each party's core issues and interests are protected. Finally, as a matter of principle, any political effort must await the end of violence so as not to reward it. However, like the situation with Iraq, violence appears to be a byproduct of the political confusion and turmoil. The relationship between Israelis and Palestinians "is unfortunately destined to remain a conflictual one. . . . It would be historical anomaly for a conflict between two fundamentally unequal antagonists to be resolved without violence" (Agha & Malley, 2002, pp. 12–13).

It may be possible to resolve the crisis provided that there is an external nonbiased party offering help and guidance and a semblance of goodwill among the parties. What is needed fundamentally is mutual understanding, genuine acceptance, training in cross-cultural empathy, and an ability to contain the chronic accumulated resentment. Clear thinking, positive planning, and decisive external intervention from neutral, able, and caring parties are desperately needed to defuse the current deadly violence and to make some healthy progress.

In recent decades, Islamic religious movements have been trying to develop political activism, social reformism, and liberation theology against very difficult conditions. "The natural question that has faced a number of scholars writing on Islamic resurgence is whether resurgence and modernity are, indeed, compatible" (Abu-Rabbi', 1996, p. 248). According to Sivan (1985), radical Muslim groups are trying to combine medieval theology with modern politics. They have rejected Western values, broken off with pan-Arabism, and begun an activist movement on their own.

Arabs also experience a tension between traditionalism and secularism as contemporary Islam keeps evolving. In many quarters of the Middle East, the efforts to integrate social justice, progressive lifestyle, and pure Islamic faith have been either extremely careful and cautious or quite liberal and rapid. This fact has created a whole new set of sociocultural dynamics. Perhaps a new overall Arab-Muslim renaissance and enlightenment are needed to reconcile the demands of the new emerging cultures with the old and familiar world of tradition.

HISTORICAL AND RELIGIOUS BACKGROUND

The Middle East is a place where ancient civilizations meet modern societies and lifestyles. It has a strategic location and serves as the gateway to three major continents. In the majority of places life is meaningful, easy, productive, and tranquil. Its people are open, friendly, and hospitable. They are fairly universal in their faith or ecumenical in their worldview. They are still rooted in the land, as they deeply cherish their traditions, faith, and values. Most urban people operate well within the modern and complex lifestyles without losing their social customs, religious identity, or cultural heritage (cf. Hourani, 1991).

Dwairy (1998) identified four major periods in Arab history, each representing a distinct layer in the Arab cultural heritage (pp. 6–15): (a) the illiterate period (*Aljahiliyya*), the period preceding Islam, during which collectivism and hierarchy of authority were the main social characteristics; (b) the Islamic empire, when Arab-Islamic armies conquered the surrounding countries and expanded from Iran in the East to Spain in the West, passing through North Africa; (c) the stagnation period, a time of deterioration of cultural status and political power mainly between the 14th and 18th centuries; and (d) the renewal, the emergence of traditionalism, spiritualism, and fundamentalism as ways of effecting a new cultural synthesis that can hold its own in competition with Western modernity and liberalism.

The rise and expansion of Islam in the second period as a strong religious, cultural, and political movement has resulted in the birth of a major world civilization that enjoyed significant prosperity and advances in architecture, science, and literature while most of Europe was still living in the dark ages. That was definitely the golden age of Islam. Many Muslim groups today are trying to restore that former glory. That many Muslim nations have great financial resources, mainly from oil (aka *black gold*), makes them feel especially blessed by God (Allah) and therefore deeply obligated to preserve and spread His only true way (Youssef, 1991).

According to Choueiri (1990), although Islam traditionally was an expansionist movement, the fundamentalist hybrid is basically conservative and reactionary, constantly trying to exclude Western influences from the Muslim cultures. Choueiri also called for deeper investigation of Islamic subjects such as reformism, revivalism, and radicalism.

Islam is not merely theological; it is also sociopolitical. Some sociologists have even argued that Islam is an ideology (Malik, 2000; Moussalli, 1998). It can be stated that there are two basic types of Muslims: the social-cultural and the political-ideological. Obviously, Islam has elements that can be applied to a social order and a political system. Therefore, there is no great differentiation between what is religio-spiritual and what is civil-secular. This very fact reflects the strength and richness of Islam on the one hand and the apprehension and limitation most secular and non-Muslim people feel about it on the other (cf. Esposito, 1996; Hoveyda, 1998; Malik, 2000).

There are five or six basic beliefs and tenets of Islam:

1. *Al-shahaada*—the profession, testimony, or confession of faith, that is, that there is a single God and that Mohammad is His messenger.
2. *Al-salaat*—prescribed prayers recited five times daily, in public or private, facing Mecca.
3. *Al-zakaat*—giving alms to the poor and needy, especially around holidays.
4. *Al-sa'owm*—fasting, mostly limited to the holy month of Ramadan.
5. *Al-hajj*—pilgrimage to Mecca at least once in a lifetime.

Some scholars add to this list *jihad*, which translates as striving for a holy cause or serving Allah with fervent zeal and supreme effort. Jihad thus has a personal as well as a communal dimension. It can mean "fighting a holy war," which is believed to be the duty of every Muslim, just as it can mean a struggle against vice, such as corruption, threat, or injustice (Johnson, 2002). It is also called for when there is a need to defend, empower, or reform the Islamic *ummah* (community).

Thus, *jihad* can be applied on a personal, communal, or national level (low vs. high jihad). Firestone (1999) tried to trace the origins of jihad and found that it has played a crucial role in the recent geopolitics of the Middle East. After reviewing the Qur'an and early Islamic literature, Firestone concluded that the idea of jihad originated in the first generation of Islam. Throughout history, perhaps, "Islam owes much of its popularity as a major world religion to this tenet" (Hamada, 1990, p. 164). Given these facts and tendencies within the various Islamic sects and groups, it would be wiser (and safer) for foreign powers and world policymakers not to provoke the committed and already agitated Muslim masses into wrath but to be very careful in dealing with them and their systems of thought (cf. Hamada, 1990).

Al-Shari'a, the set of Islamic laws and regulations, embodies the core values and blueprints for living, both on the interpersonal and national level. The Shari'a consists of many rules, laws, and interpretations. Many devout Muslims believe that as long as they observe the Shari'a, then all will be well and the Islamic order will flourish (cf. Ahmad, 1999; Voll, 1982).

WHY SO MANY GROUPS ARE ANGRY WITH THE WEST

Many people, groups, and regimes are angry with the West in general and hostile toward the United States in particular for fundamental cultural, socioeconomic, and political reasons.

Cultural and Moral Invasion

According to Dwairy (1998), the major developments of the 20th century in communication, education, technology, and mass media resulted in Western invasion of almost every sector of the Arab Islamic world. That intense and substantial exposure introduced the ideas of individualism and liberalism and therefore have challenged the fundamentals of authoritarianism and collectivism there.

> In the last two centuries, the cultural debate has focused on the questions of traditionalism versus modernity, and authenticity (*asala*) and specificity (*khususiyya*) versus Westernization. . . . Some extremists call for Westernization, and others call for Islamic fundamentalism. The majority of Arabs fall somewhere in the middle. . . . There is a division of opinion about the basis of authority. (Dwairy, 1998, p. 11)

These Arab-Muslim communities have been reacting negatively to what they consider corruption in the West, and especially the United States, which constantly exports products, including lifestyles, music, magazines, movies, and so on to countries with traditional values. Other Western values like extreme individualism, self-sufficiency, personal autonomy, self-fulfillment, privacy, and seeking what feels good have been gradually invading the East and changing its sociological nature and family structure (cf. Abi-Hashem, 1997). Medved (2001) stressed that the American entertainment industries are presenting an ugly version of the United States to the rest of the world. Hollywood's obsessive fascination with the wild and dark side of human nature and its emphasis on excitement and deviance have produced deep reactions in other countries. Part of any honest answer to the question of why other people hate the United States, Medved asserted, should include the mass media, the movies, the television shows, and the popular music America is exporting around the globe.

Choueiri (1990) described Islamic fundamentalism as a contemporary product of the clash between the traditional values and ideologies and the influences of capitalism and socialism of the Western world. Strict Islamic fundamentalists reject secularization and view it as a harmful influence of the Western Christian tradition. Some Islamists even perceive secularism as a source of corruption, dictatorship, and serious violation of human rights, freedom, and liberation (Tamimi & Esposito, 2000).

Economic and Financial Exploitation

The use of cheap labor in foreign countries to produce American goods, the bold advertisement of unhealthy products (e.g., cigarettes); the quick establishment of greedy business deals; and the aggressive marketing of American products without careful consideration for local peoples' values, welfare, and traditions have created further negative feelings and attitudes in many parts of the world, including the Muslim world.

In addition, those who have little or nothing envy the level of affluence, comfort, and consumption of those who have a lot and want more. The huge variety of items, the attractive and colorful packaging, and the high level of waste in the West add to the imbalance of the world's resources. The fact that the United States protects corporate giants at home and abroad at the expense of impoverishing many developing countries also has created deep resentment in people who lack the bare necessities of life (J. N. Morgan, 2002).

Many communities feel that much good is coming out of the United States. Americans have been pioneers in humanitarian aid, educational endeavors, technological help, missionary service, and social development. Yet, out of America also come scores of products, items, and trends—Coca-Cola, McDonalds, Marlboro, and Hollywood films—that are intrusive and harmful to many vulnerable societies. News networks such as CNN, ABC, CBS, and FOX can be seen in every village around the world. These invasions are definitely eroding local cultures and traditions and eventually imposing a global mindset, lifestyle, and worldview. Muslims no less than others are wary of this economic cum cultural penetration.

Political and Imperialistic Manipulation

The United States often is perceived as trying to rule the world; it pursues its foreign policy with little or no consultation, consideration, or coordination with respective national leaders and local constituencies. The role of the United States in the Middle East has been mainly biased and inconsistent. U.S. foreign policy continues to aggravate and provoke many groups either because of its denial of the clear facts on the ground or because of its arrogance and indifference to the will of the inhabitants of the region. It appears to quickly shift its alliances of convenience and to renege on its promises and long-term commitments. U.S. support of certain leaders, parties, or groups changes from season to season; sometimes the support turns to hostility, apparently after they have served some underlying purposes. Occasionally, the United States gets heavily involved in one spot, and then suddenly abandons it, leaving behind total chaos. Its foreign policies have been rather confusing and unclear, frequently characterized by poor judgment and lack of global common sense. It has been said that the wind of politics has no clear morality or ethics—it has only hidden interests and temporary benefits.

Arabs and Muslims are specifically angry at the U.S. government for its unconditional and excessive support of Israel. That the United States gives Israel "carte blanche" to do as it pleases regardless of Israel's misbehavior and policies have offended many leaders and sociopolitical groups in the Arab and the Islamic world ("Undercurrent of Hostility," 2002). In addition, U.S.

policy toward Iraq has been a major source of anger in the Arab world. The severe sanctions and restrictions against Iraq, imposed following the Gulf War in 1990, have caused huge devastation and taken an unbelievable human toll. The more recent threats of a U.S. invasion have compounded the situation and created tremendous sympathy for and solidarity with Iraq.

Military and Unilateral Expansion

The constant U.S. flexing of muscles, intimidating use of force, and unilateral policing of the world are major reasons for anger and resentment. Such behavior is perceived as arrogant and self-serving. People in developing countries have a love–hate relationship with the West. They understand that the United States is seeking to guard its own interests by supporting oppressive regimes and using superior technological weapons against those without them (J. N. Morgan, 2002). The new doctrine of preemption, however, is considered the most chilling and dangerous concept in foreign policy so far. The United States claims "the right to strike, pre-emptively, at any nation which it decides is developing weapons of mass destruction or supporting terrorism. It is carte blanche for war on the world" (Steele, 2002b, p. 12).

The cold war mentality still prevails in many parts of the Middle East (Abi-Hashem, 1992), and it has not totally disappeared from Europe, either. The West in general and the United States in particular are still perceived as agents of imperialism. Some Islamist groups believe that Muslim soil is sacred and should not be polluted by a non-Muslim presence, and especially the presence of foreign troops, which are associated in their collective memory with the early European Crusaders.

> In the aftermath of the cold war, the United States was in search of an enemy. Now, it's found one: terrorism. Terrorism is dangerous, but it's not the only threat . . . [As other threats have grown] the United States has failed to assume leadership role in addressing them . . . [the U.S.'s] arrogant unilateralism is worrying the world. Defining the terrorist attacks as an act of war made it easier to carry out military operations. The U.S. is confusing Terrorism with the precepts of classic war. ("The Last Word," 2002, p. 56)

The United States is perhaps the world's largest and best magnet for terrorism. This may be due to the U.S. sale of weapons to various dictators and groups, training assistance, and technology sharing (cf. Moen, 1993). These facts have indirectly promoted a market for aggression and created a global industry for terrorism. The United States sorely needs a cultural enlightenment, especially in the area of global awareness and sensitivity. Being powerful, wealthy, and "number one" in many domains does not automatically translate into being seasoned, considerate, or even culturally relevant. On the contrary, it may be the source of resentment and anger.

UNDERSTANDING FUNDAMENTALISM
AND RELIGIOUS MILITANCY

Fundamentalism generally is associated with religion. Because religion is inseparable from culture and political life, fundamentalism has largely become part of the societal and political agenda.

In its various forms, fundamentalism depends for its existence on significant social, political, technological, and intellectual transition (Armstrong, 2000). The media have flooded us with coverage of topics related to Islamic militancy, but, in fact, religious militancy is also found among many other faiths and spiritual traditions (Medved, 2002). It has been historically part of most conflicts and wars. According to Moussalli (1998), Islamic fundamentalism tends to transfer sociopolitical concepts into religio-ideological concepts and vice versa; certain theological ideas can be transferred into political mandates and a case for militant action.

Although the concept of *jihad* parallels the concept of *holy war* in other faiths (Armstrong, 2000), many believe that jihad is much more serious, distinct, and pronounced (cf. Esposito, 1996; Hoveyda, 1998; Malik, 2000). Jihad can be launched on many levels and can take several shapes and modalities (B. Barber, 1996; Firestone, 1999; Johnson, 2002). It can be applied to an individual's quest toward purity and piety, to a community's striving toward reformation and renewal, or to a nation's fight against deviation and corruption. Radical groups rely on their (mis)interpretation of jihad to justify their passions, intentions, and actions. Conversely, extreme forms of jihad appeal to those with impulsive tendencies, rigid mentalities, and innate needs to be acknowledged as worthy (cf. Woodberry, 2002).

Some extremists are ready to go abroad and die in suicide missions in order to undo evil, correct blasphemy, or retaliate for mistreatment and oppression of other Muslim communities in the world. They regard their activities as fulfillment of a divine duty. Actually, they believe that if they die in the process they are martyrs, worthy of great honor in this world and great reward in the next.

Woodberry (2002) explained Islamic fundamentalism and militancy as follows:

> most fail to grasp the diversity within Islam and its roots. The Qur'an is comprised of recitations by Muhammad, believed to come from God, to meet the needs that arose on specific occasions. Some were peaceful; others were militant. Therefore, either position can be argued for by selecting specific verses or illustrations from history. (p. 4)

According to Hitchcock (2001), "The two common explanations of terrorism are a sense of injustice and religious fanaticism, and both are real enough. . . . Religion is indeed a volatile substance, precisely because it is the realm where good and evil meet" (p. 3).

However, Mozaffari (1996, as quoted in Storey & Utter, 2002) defined *Islamic fundamentalism* or *Islamism* as a militant and antimodernist movement growing out of a belief that Islam is simultaneously a religion (*deen*), a way of life (*dunya*), and a form of governing state (*dawla*). Therefore, "the Islamic fundamentalists . . . believe in the absolute indivisibility of the three famous D's. This characteristic marks the main difference between them and the liberal Muslims . . . " (p. 129).

In Arabic, the word *fundamentalist* could be translated as *muta'assib* (super conservative) or *usoolee* (someone who holds onto the roots of his faith and its fundamentals). It can take many forms and be manifested in passive and peaceful ways or in aggressive and militant ways (cf. Woodberry, 2002). Osama bin Laden is believed to have developed an extreme branch of *usooliyyia* (fundamentalism) after he left Saudi Arabia.

Super conservatives, fundamentalists, and Islamic extremists are trying to promote radical activism, purism, confrontation with the West, and even militancy. According to Woodberry (2002), "Islamist movements normally arise from the interaction of feeling of trauma, local conditions, and a millennial ideology" (p. 5). Moreover, to the radical Islamist, other people who cause harm, oppression, and injustice are enemy of the faith. So, true Muslims should strive even with their lives until justice and purity prevail.

Islam has many defenders. Akbar (1999); J. Cooper, Nettler, and Mahmoud (2000); Courbage and Fargues (1998); Dalacoura (1998); Eltahawy (2002); Halliday (1996); Hefner (2000); Hunter (1998); Kurzman (1998); and Lawrence (1998) have defended Islam against accusations that it is violent, is intolerant of other religions, violates human rights, opposes modernity, subjugates women, is incompatible with democracy, is aggressive, and hates the West. Such thinkers view Islam as a universal religion (and Muslims as a multiethnic community, a mosaic) that is more influenced by the current sociocultural and political systems than it is influencing them. Many prominent writers claim that "liberal Islam" is alive and well and is actually compatible with the world's contemporary culture.

THE QUESTION OF ISRAEL, THE PROBLEM OF PALESTINE

According to some, the roots of the Israeli–Palestinian conflict go back to biblical times when the tension regarding the promised land between the seed of Abraham (Isaac vs. Ishmael) began. In modern times each party has shown a clear psychological ambivalence and vacillation about committing itself to a long-term binding treaty. We have looked at Islamic militancy; Jewish fundamentalism and militancy deserve equal attention and analysis. Shahak and Mezvinski (1999) found that Jewish religious groups in Israel and in the West have three characteristics in common: They are radicals, they oppose the Palestinians in all shapes and forms, and they largely disagree among themselves. Rigid party leaders, on both sides, often show signs of arrogance and paranoia, which affect their political judgment and military behavior. Consequently, they become more addicted to force and bloodshed and increasingly fearful of trusting their fragile destiny to the other side (Seale, 2002). These dynamics have usually alienated the moderate and open-minded elements in both societies. Breaking this deadlock may have to await the replacement of the old guard with new and young leadership on both sides that has good intentions, practical approaches, and realistic mindsets. If empowered, they can find closure to the devastating crisis and reverse the cycle of deterioration and destruction.

In the minds of most Palestinians, fighting is culturally and religiously necessary in order to defend and restore their roots, honor, and dignity, which are directly related to the land. Their relationship with their land is psychologically very intimate. For the average Israeli immigrant, safety and affordability are paramount. The immigrants look for affordable housing anywhere (including settlements), and they want to be secure, comfortable, and prosperous. These are obvious and pronounced differences between the two populations regarding their emotional attachment to the land and their set of future goals and priorities.

According to Karon (2002), Israel now faces a fundamental political choice in its relations with the Palestinians. Israelis are sharply divided over whether the way out is to complete the separation into two states. Those who are looking for a military victory got bad news from Martin van Creveld, a world-renowned military historian, who warned that Israel cannot defeat the Palestinians (quoted in Karon, 2002, ¶ 2). Though Israel may have one of the strongest conventional armies, fighting against an enemy armed only with stones and assault rifles, the asymmetry is reversed when it comes to political will. "The readiness of the Palestinian militants to die in order to inflict pain is mirrored in growing doubts among Israelis" (¶ 2). Whereas Israeli soldiers weep over their dead comrades, the relatives of Palestinian suicide bomber proudly display their martyr's pictures. Similarly, funerals of dead Palestinian fighters motivate hundreds more to continue the struggle at any cost (also see Zoroya, 2002). All this "creates a fundamental weakness on the Israeli side, one familiar to the Soviets who fought in Afghanistan and the Americans in Vietnam" (¶ 2).

Historically, the United States and Britain both helped establish the state of Israel about 55 years ago. They still find themselves obliged to act on its behalf. Moreover, the Israeli government and the "aggressive lobbying in Washington" on its behalf ("Key Points," 1991, p. 15) apply tremendous pressure on U.S. foreign policy to act favorably toward Israel. Israel has been symbolically described as the 51st state and the stubborn daughter of America. Most probably, Israel was a major force behind first Gulf War and the current U.S. efforts to drum up support for a second Gulf War. Observers of the Middle East believe that Israel dragged the United States to fight Iraq, destroy its strength, and eliminate its regime, even as it publicly remained outside the physical action. In fact, it was praised for its self-restraint and good conduct during the first Gulf War (Abi-Hashem, 1992).

On the other hand, the Arab nations have been frustrated with their inability to find a unified and comprehensive way to deal with the challenge of Israel. "The fact that a few million Israelis can conquer all of Palestine, occupy neighboring Arab lands and check the collective power of 200 million Arabs has been a source of deep humiliation, even shame, throughout the Arab world" (Khouri, 1991, p. 7).

It is now clear that Israel's goal seems to be to weaken or even to eliminate the possibility of any Palestinian entity or presence. Israel freely expands into Palestinian territory; controls Palestinian resources; opens or closes roads, factories, and schools; and puts severe and daily pressure on Palestinians. Israel knows that these measures may drive some Palestinians to leave the country and others to act in desperation and hysteria, which in turn gives Israel a green light to exercise more punishment, restriction, and subtle oppression. Israel justifies its own aggression as legitimate self-defense and retaliation, or in post-September 11 language, as its own war against terrorism. Some suspect that Israel actually does not want opposition to its policies within Palestine and the Arab-Muslim world to fade. Israel has used those hard-line positions as reasons to expand territorially and to build a huge offensive arsenal.

Palestinians and Israelis have similar tragic histories. Both peoples have been mistreated and by now have identical mental and emotional dynamics. Both are acting and reacting out of their basic fears, aspirations, victimization, needs, hurts, and anger. They keep persecuting and massively projecting on each other. They have so much in common yet they are so different in their developmental stages. They share the same ground and face the same destiny, yet they want to eliminate each other. Whereas the radical Palestinians are fueled by an ideological–sociopolitical jihad and holy war, right-wing Jewish groups are probably fueled by their wish to undo anti-Semitism and unconsciously avenge their accumulated mistreatment and hurts. The Israelis are finally enjoying a powerful status and exercising superior military force over those around them, something they actually lacked for centuries. They ought to remember, however, that psychologically it is easy for the one who has been abused to become an abuser.

According to Herlinger (2002), not only politicians but also many community and church leaders in the West are reluctant to openly criticize Israel's behavior and policies. They are afraid of being accused of anti-Semitism or labeled as the "friends of radical Palestinians" (p. 7). Many analysts believe that the United States cannot be an effective mediator in the conflict; although its foreign policy has intermittently shown many surges of reasonable calls to ameliorate this intensely polarized situation, it inevitably swings back to heavily favor Israel and its demands. Many Arab, Muslim, and other international leaders have been frustrated with U.S. policy and have lost hope and trust that its initiatives in the Middle East will bear fruit.

According to Dwairy (1998), a Christian Palestinian psychologist who lives and works in Israel,

> If Arabs are the people most misunderstood by the West, Palestinians Arabs are the most misunderstood Arab people. Political conflicts and historical events have dehumanized them and overshadowed their national tragedy, culture, and other human aspects of their lives . . . Publications about Arabs in English . . . that make the connection between Arab mental health and sociopolitical issues are very rare. (p. xvii)

Today in the Arab-Muslim world, analysts and critics are engaged in self-searching and honest reflection on the condition of their countries. These critics see the long-term stagnation, unhealthy practices, and fragmentation of the Arab world as shameful and destructive. According to Abu Fadel (2002), some Arab writers and poets are creating small local discussion groups and Internet Web sites (even in places like Damascus, Syria), calling for nonviolent opposition to Israel. They are advocating Gandhi's approach to political struggle as the only way to a resolution and a victory over Israel. As for now, Steele conceded, this is "pure fantasy, of course. There is no Palestinian Gandhi, no Israeli Martin Luther King, in sight or over the horizon waiting to emerge" (2002, p. 14). Nonetheless, moderate Arabs believe that most Israelis still have a human heart and glimpse hope in the midst of a long dark history that, ultimately, the people of Israel will appreciate a peaceful struggle in the name of good will and humanity.

It is unfortunate that the potentials of both sides of the divide right now seem to be wasted and their cultural heritage totally buried in endless conflict and hate. Each community has much goodness, assistance, and social grace to offer the other.

CONCLUSION

Peace is a profound and beautiful concept. It is *shalom* in Hebrew, *salaam* in Arabic, and *paix* in French. These terms convey more than merely the absence of trouble, conflict, and war; rather, they carry rich meaning and bestow generous blessing upon the hearers. *Shalom* is a wish for well-being and wholeness. *Salaam* is a greeting for goodness. In the Middle East, the term *peace* has been confused, misused, and rather abused. Its connotations have been mixed with hidden agendas and private intentions, and the real notion of peace has lost its cultural depth, philosophical meaning, and spiritual blessing. Depending on who is delivering the rhetoric and who is listening (or being lectured to), the word *peace* has been recently so easy to utter, but so difficult to define, and its content so hard to constitute and construct.

The language of peace is shaped by different cultural perspectives. Each side or party in the Middle East has its own mindset, needs, agendas, expectations, and worldview. Each group presents a convincing case for its vision, yet has overwhelming fears and apprehensions. On one side, the Palestinians are grieving the loss of their identity, land, power, heritage, and future. On the other side, the Israelis are establishing their new homeland, identity, power, heritage, and future. For one, it is a paradise lost. For the other, it is a paradise found.

Large communities in many parts of the Middle East are very distressed, even hopeless, being caught in the middle of tension and deep agony. Their inevitable reactions of anxiety, loss, fear, and resentment are resulting in severe depressions, marked helplessness, and traumatic symptoms. Families are being divided, properties damaged, and relatives and close friends scattered. Life in general is being constantly disrupted, and the living conditions are becoming increasingly impoverished and unbearable. For the young and energetic population, this situation is creating in them extreme attitudes and dangerous behaviors. Oppression and destruction will naturally give birth to a new generation of political radicals, freedom fighters, altruism seekers, and perhaps more martyrdom admirers (Zoroya, 2002).

For the mental health workers, serving in such turbulent places may be a great challenge, but it is greatly needed, and it can be quite rewarding. Local caregivers of all kinds are disheartened and exhausted like the rest of the communities around them. In many cases, social workers, educators, clergy, counselors, and healthcare professionals are isolated by artificially erected barriers and green lines. Some choose to work alone in order to keep a low profile for obvious security reasons. Regardless of the price, they live their lives and serve with courage and grace.

Here I would like to extend a broad call to psychologists, mental health professionals, political activists, and culturally sensitive caregivers of all types to engage creatively in international service and to try to restore sound and compassionate ethics into the world of politics. There are many opportunities to volunteer one's time and talents in troubled places and to provide some desperately needed care. We can help free the political process from its disruptive biases, manipulations, and psychosocial stereotypes and reduce the arrogance and sense of superiority that are plaguing our world. We can listen to the needy, empathize with the oppressed, and bridge the gap between those who have and those who have not so that the potential for wars, terrorism, and suffering is diminished.

4

THE SOCIAL CONSTRUCTION
OF TERRORISM

ROM HARRÉ

If the then government of Afghanistan had declared war on the United States at 8 am EST on September 11, 2001, the attacks on New York and Washington would have been air raids.

—Anonymous EU Representative

I propose to discuss some of the social psychological aspects of the complex phenomenon of contemporary global international terrorism using the recently developed principles of discursive psychology. According to that point of view, the key to the psychological genesis of many social phenomena lies in the language and other symbolic systems with which they are described, thought about, and commented on and the projects that are created for dealing with them. In general, from the point of view of discursive psychology, any social phenomenon has two aspects. There is the pattern of actions performed by those involved, that is, their intended doings and sayings. Then there is the pattern of acts that are the socially significant meanings of the patterns of action, for the actor and for those to whom the acts are directed. Personal and collective interpretations are, not infrequently, different in some particular cases. Whose interpretations have hegemony is the topic of that branch of discursive psychology called *positioning theory*. How actions are interpreted as acts, it is argued, determines the subsequent events that follow from them.

Acts of terrorism must be subjected to the same style of analysis and explanation as such simple social acts as the way people greet each other by shaking hands. In both cases there are actions the social effectiveness of which depends on the way these actions are given meaning as acts. In nearly all cases of interest there is a dominant collective consensus as to what this or that action means in this or that context among these or those people; this and similar processes have been called *social constructions*.

Just as actions are socially constructed as acts by attributions of meaning, so too are actors typified as those who perform acts of these kinds. Someone who pays for someone else's meal at a restaurant may be typified as a gracious host or as a social climber depending on how the act of setting forth the Platinum American Express Card is interpreted. Those who perform actions that are said to be "acts of terror" attract the label *terrorists*.

The first task then is to ask what seems like a lexicographical question: What are the necessary and sufficient conditions for using the words *act of terror* and *terrorist*? Only when we have explored this question can we go on to discuss the sources and consequences of the social constructive acts by which these attributions were made.

THE CONCEPTS *ACTS OF TERROR* AND *TERRORIST*

What does it mean to call someone a *terrorist* and his or her acts *acts of terror*? If the category attributions are not simple descriptions but psychologically potent labels, what is their import?

Does a particular act by an actor make that person a terrorist? Or is it rather how that person's action is categorized and described that makes that person a terrorist? Could two people perform essentially the same act, but one be perceived by others to be carrying out acts of terror and the other perceived to be simply doing a job? Someone who uses explosives to bring down a building may be committing a war crime, if he knows that civilians are inside, or he may simply be clearing a construction site.

Is the intention of the actor enough to ground the attribution of *terrorist*? Are the perpetrators of road rage attacks terrorists? One can argue that they aim to get their way by inducing alarm and fear in their victims, but clearly such people are not properly called *terrorists*. So it is not simply our interpretations of people's motives that determine how we label them. The road rage perpetrator has no political agenda.

Are the relevant and potent categorizing acts and actors wholly the work of other people, or do the discourses of the activists who kill people and destroy property in pursuit of a political agenda have an important role in categorizing them as terrorists? In recent years those who perpetrate acts others label *terror* frequently make claims to being motivated by noble ideals and driven to their attacks by the indifference of those who should have listened to their catalog of grievances and woes. How are the competing story lines to be balanced in making the attribution?

There seem to be at least three questions to be answered:

1. Are the words *terror* and *terrorist* applied solely on the basis of the actions some people perform? The answer drawn from the above examples is surely no. It is the objective behind the actions that counts.
2. Is the intention to cause terror and to kill and maim a sufficient condition for using these labels? Again the examples above suggest that it is not. The actions must be interpreted as directed toward a political end, acknowledged but not accepted as legitimate by the targets of attack. It may be that the ends are accepted as legitimate but the use of death and destruction as the means is rejected.
3. Is a certain kind of justificatory rhetoric the ground for the damning attribution? In some cases the attackers might excite pity rather than fear in their actual or putative victims.

None of these proposals seem to reach the heart of the matter. I now turn to reflect on some of the terror organizations of our time.

WHO AND WHAT ARE THESE PEOPLE?

The Stern gang, Euskadi Ta Askatasuna (ETA), the Irish Republican Army (IRA), the Bader-Meinhoff gang, the al-Qaeda network, Carlos the Jackal, and all the others are only too ready to offer the rest of society justificatory manifestos and declarations concerning their aims and why they have been driven to resort to the means they have. In contrast to the perpetrator of a road rage attack who has no further aim beyond his or her rage, those whom we call terrorists are openly and explicitly political in their claims. Yet, it is clear that these organizations do not rely on rational persuasion to attain their ends. The means is violence, whatever the end may be.

In World War II, the leaders of the three major allies, Britain, the Soviet Union, and the United States, met several times to hammer out and publicly declare their war aims. Was the U.S. and British invasion of France, which resulted in mass death and destruction, an act of terror? One might argue that the acts of an army are not acts of terror, but what sort of army? Is the IRA really an *army* at war with the army of another power? No existing state recognizes this organization as a legitimate part of its state apparatus, so one might argue that it is not an army at all.

So here we seem to have a criterion for using the label *terrorist*. By definition, members of the established armed forces of a duly constituted nation cannot commit the acts of violence we call *terrorism*. Organized groups, which are not organs of some state and that kill people and destroy property, are prima facie "terrorists."

Do you have to kill people to be labeled a terrorist? What about hunger strikers and the suffragettes who chained themselves to railings in London—how are we to label them? They did violence to their own bodies to further their causes. Such people may touch our emotions, but it is pity rather than terror that is evoked. Here then is a second criterion. A person properly called a terrorist is one whose actions are meant to create alarm and terror in certain people, sometimes in the citizens of a whole nation (as with the acts of al-Qaeda), and sometimes within the members of a narrow social class (as with anarchists of the 19th century, whose target was the authoritarian rulers of nation states). The means must be the infliction of death or the making of threats of death so that the level of actual fear and apprehension in a certain group of people should reach the level necessary to react.

These are just some of the many tricky issues that must be tackled in following the work of the social construction of persons as terrorists and their performances as acts of terror. No doubt other contributors to this volume will discuss the psychological theories held by activists themselves as to the effect on other people of their violent attacks. My interest is in the discursive methods by which activists are labeled as terrorists and the consequences of so doing. It is the new social psychological concept of positioning that I turn to in an effort to understand the constructionist processes that have been going on and have always gone on in the face of the violence of a certain class of political activists.

A basic distinction that I will take for granted between acts of war between nations and acts of terrorism is itself carved out of a gray area. What do we make of "state-sponsored terrorism" as a concept? What is the difference between the way we classify the Japanese attack on Pearl Harbor and the way we classify the IRA Birmingham pub bombing? The Japanese government planned and executed that attack, whereas the Irish government had nothing to do with the slaughter in Birmingham. Why has the attack on the Twin Towers been called an act of terrorism and the response labeled with the oxymoron "the war on terror"? The Taliban who evidently supported the al-Qaeda network were the government of Afghanistan. The conceptual issue seems to me to hinge on the degree of independence that it is presumed al-Qaeda had from the Taliban regime. Otherwise one is obliged to conclude that the Afghan government attacked the Twin Towers and that this was an act of war. The "war on terrorism" would then properly be called "the war between Afghanistan and the United States and its allies." By making a tripartite distinction between al-Qaeda, the Taliban regime, and Afghanistan proper, the distinction between a national war and the new political entity, a war on terrorism, is made conceptually possible.

This raises some very delicate issues about the support some Americans gave the IRA, support that has never been forbidden by the U.S. government. Al-Qaeda managed to kill about 3,000 people, whereas the troubles in Northern Ireland have cost about 4,000 lives.

MANDELSTAM'S DISTINCTION

In a widely reported recent interview on the radio, the British politician Peter Mandelstam argued for a distinction between two groups of unofficial "warriors" who used acts of violence intended not only to kill but to induce terror.

> I think the distinction we have to make is not between good and bad terrorists. It is between those terrorists who have political objectives and are prepared to negotiate these objectives at the end of the day and engage in some sort of dialogue and ultimately some sort of political or peace process. I don't call them terrorists when they reach that stage. They are resisters. They are freedom fighters or whatever. They are like territorial, as opposed to international, terrorists. And its at what stage of development they are at, what attitude they have to politics, whether they are prepared to engage [in discussions, that makes the difference]. (Mandelstam, 2001)

Mandelstam's distinction was based on reflections on what the point of an attack might be. Is it intended as an act of revenge for a real or fancied wrong, complete in itself, or is it just one aspect of the pursuit of a policy the ultimate point of which is political? Mandelstam's two categories could be more precisely defined somewhat as follows:

1. Terrorist: a person who uses violence but whose convictions or aims leave no place for a possible shift from violent acts to political negotiation. The suicide bomber is an extreme example of this category. Because the act of violence is also the moment of death for the actor, there can be no place at a future negotiating table for him (or more rarely, her). If there were to be some moment at which al-Qaeda would be prepared to discuss the future of Palestine, it would, at best, be in the remote future. The current phase of its activities is surely confined to acts of revenge on and punishment of the nations that they believe have humiliated them and their co-religionists.
2. Freedom fighter: a person whose ultimate aim is a political settlement of some passionately held problem. The person so classified is one for whom terrorist acts are taken to be instruments of a political process.

Mandelstam seems to believe that it is possible to transition from the one state to the other. This reflects an important point in the social constructionist position. A socially constructed category is not a description of a person's permanent attributes or even of a person's transitory attributes at all. It is the category to which a person has been assigned. For that reason such a person can be reassigned to another category if the circumstances permit it or if it seems advisable. There is a limitation to this reassignment in that in certain circumstances people tend to try to make concrete the attributes of the category to which they have been assigned. Each act of assignment is also an act of positioning, ascribing or denying rights and duties to the person so positioned. As a terrorist, an armed person has no right to attempt to kill or wound someone of the target side. As a soldier of a power with which we are at war, however, we admit that right. Soldiers are not tried for murder after the war has ended. War crimes do not include hostile but legitimated acts.

Although Mandelstam's distinction is useful, there are certainly some difficulties with this rather simplistic dichotomy as a social psychological category pair. One is the existence of political declarations and manifestos issued by the activists. Mandelstam's distinction suggests that we should refer to people as terrorists only if they refuse to abandon their weapons and come to the negotiating table. This does not seem to capture very well the rules for the use of the concept of *terrorist*. EOKA, the terrorist organization that aimed at uniting Cyprus with Greece, did indeed eventually negotiate. Moreover, although they did not achieve their political aims, the setting up of part of Cyprus as an independent Greek state brought an end to the terror campaign. Before turning to negotiation they did many of the things that would justify the use of the word *terrorist* to describe them.

From the point of view of the social psychologist, the distinction between the two labels *terrorist* and *freedom fighter* is of great importance, because it has implications for subsequent acts of positioning, by both activist and victim.

Assuming that a distinction could be defended, would it exhaust the attributes that might be used in the social construction of the category of *terrorist* and the labeling of certain activists with it? Here is another possibility. Let us consider a hypothetical case. A civil war is in progress in some South American country. Some armed groups support the legitimate government, others oppose it. The government of a foreign power covertly supports the group that opposes the legitimate government. Is this an example of cross-border terrorism? This seems to me to be an intermediate case between the dichotomous categories proposed by Mandelstam. His categories are not strict because a given group of activists can drift across the line of demarcation between terrorists and freedom fighters.

POSITIONING THEORY

I now sketch some of the recent developments in social psychology that are relevant to the questions that I have raised in the first part of this chapter. These questions center on the grounds for using a certain fateful vocabulary to describe certain people and their actions and the possible consequences of so describing them.

Elementary Positioning Theory

A *position*, according to positioning theory (van Langenhove & Harré, 1999), is a cluster of rights and duties to perform certain social acts that an individual may occupy in the course of a strip of life. Unlike roles, positions generally are ephemeral and dynamic. A person may position himself or herself or may be positioned by others. In both cases the positioning can be explicit or implicit, exhibited only in what people say and do and what the others around allow them to say and do. Positions are relational, too. Even in reflexive positioning, when one positions oneself as having a certain moral character or a certain set of rights and duties that has not yet been acknowledged by the others, the concepts have relational connotations. If one positions oneself as generous, this implies there is both a donor and a recipient of gifts and favors.

In many cases the basic position defined in terms of rights and duties may rely on another prior act of positioning. The prior act may consist of attributions of psychological and characterological attributes to some individual, which open up or close down access to certain rights and duties. People positioned as *stupid* are not given the right to make complex decisions for a group. People who are positioned as reliable may find themselves saddled with the duty to turn off the lights and lock the doors at the end of the office day.

For convenience, I refer to the former kind of positioning as an act of moral positioning and the latter an act of characterological positioning. In discussing the positioning that has gone on in the case of Osama bin Laden, the leader of the al-Qaeda network, one sees both levels of positioning being performed by Western leaders and newspaper commentators. What may seem like amateur psychologizing of little diagnostic value turns out to be profoundly important when seen as characterological positioning.

When a pattern of moral positions has been established, the rest of the conceptual structure tied in with positions cuts in. What individuals say or do is interpreted in light of how they are positioned. Furthermore, these actions are in almost all cases capable of being seen as the enactment of this or that story line. Usually these story lines follow well-established narrative conventions of the cultural system in which they occur.

For instance, the story line could be that of "martyr for a cause." Or it could be "heroic leader of a crusade." Both bin Laden and President Bush have adopted the latter story line in their mutual acts of positioning. Bush uses the story line to position bin Laden as a terrorist and himself as a knight to the rescue. Bin Laden uses the same story line to position himself as the defender of the weak and the United States as an oppressor and, among other things, the supporter of the unjust regime of Israel.

Narrative Conventions

If an act of positioning is to be effective, the story line must not dominate the discourse. To the extent possible, it must draw on one of the plots that the members of the culture have taken in as part of a standard repertoire. Many of these are culled from fairy tales or folk tradition. We do not need to elaborate the story of the wolf and the three little pigs to appreciate the plot. Brave knights set out to right the wrongs perpetrated on the poor and unfortunate and rescue fair ladies from their captors. That is what brave knights do! No explanation required. No one needed a gloss on *Monty Python and the Holy Grail*.

Labeling: Ascribing Socially Efficacious Meanings

It is now apparent that *labeling theory* was one of the earliest manifestations of what we would now recognize as a social constructionist analysis. One of the earliest examples was Aaron Cicourel's deservedly praised study of the social psychological processes that were set in motion by the administration of formal juvenile justice. Cicourel (1976) found that many youngsters committed crimes but that only some found their way into the courts. In the course of the administration of justice the ones who were caught were labeled *delinquent*, *criminal*, and so on. Subsequently this group went on to more persistent and elaborate criminal activity, although before the labeling process the two groups of youngsters were not distinguishable in any psychologically or criminologically relevant way. In summary, the delinquents knowingly or unknowingly lived up to their labels.

Research on the effect of nicknaming on personality displays and social behavior showed the same sort of phenomenon (J. Morgan, O'Neil, & Harré, 1977). Children, particularly, tended to live up their nicknames. Observable differences between the personalities and behavior of children prior to and after being nicknamed were readily tied to the wider connotations of the nickname.

An Example of Positioning Discourses

In the two examples that follow I look at acts of positioning, the exploitation of narrative conventions and the use of labels.

Here is an excerpt from a speech by Osama bin Laden:

> Our Islamic nation has been tasting [horror] for more [than] eighty years, of humiliation and disgrace, its sons killed and their blood spilled, its sanctities desecrated.
>
> God has blessed a group of vanguard Muslims, the forefront of Islam, to destroy America. These [Muslims] have stood in defense of their weak

children, their brothers and sisters in Palestine and other Muslim nations. . . . I tell them that these events have divided the world into two camps, the camp of the faithful and the camp of infidels. Every Muslim must rise to defend his religion. The wind of faith is blowing and the wind of change is blowing to remove the evil from the Peninsula of Muhammad, peace be upon him. ("A Nation Challenged," 2001, p. B7)

To a social psychologist there is nothing startling about this speech. The story lines are familiar. A history of degradation and oppression is told. Heroic defense of the weak is called for. This is run together with another story line, that of jihad, the call to arms to defend the faith and the faithful. It is equally the story line of the Crusades, of Hitler's invasion of Sudetenland, and so on.

The labeling and positioning is implicit but quite clear. "America" is implicitly labeled as *infidel* and *evil*. Given that there are beings of this sort threatening the faithful, al-Qaeda, as the leader in the "camp of the faithful," is positioned as having the *duty* to destroy "them." It is interesting that the other moral component of a "position," namely "right," is not as clearly set out here as it is in President Bush's positioning discourse. It seems to lie in the phrase "God has blessed a group of vanguard Muslims . . ." My reading of this is the implication that this group has not only the duty to destroy the infidel, but as legitimated by God, they also have the right to do so.

Here is a speech delivered by George W. Bush, president of the United States, reported in the same issue of the *New York Times*.

This military action is a part of our campaign against terrorism. In this conflict there is no neutral ground. If any government sponsors the outlaws and killer of innocents, they have become outlaws and murderers themselves. We're a peaceful nation. Yet as we have learned so suddenly and so tragically, there can be no peace in a world of sudden terror. In the face of today's new threat the only way to pursue peace is to pursue those who threaten it. We defend not only our precious freedoms but also the freedom of people everywhere to live and raise their children free from fear. ("A Nation Challenged," 2001, p. B6)

This is the rhetoric of the founding fathers. The terms would be entirely familiar to the orators and architects of the American Revolution. The jump from the local to the universal has always been a theme of American rhetoric; "Give us your poor and your oppressed" was addressed to the authoritarian regimes of Europe.

Let us now look at this speech with the eye of the positioning analyst. "We," the United States and its allies, are labeled as the champions of freedom and so positioned as having the right to defend everyone's freedom. This positioning is overt. The labeling of "someone" as a government-sponsored gang of killers implicitly positions al-Qaeda as the enemies of freedom, which the United States has not only the right but the duty to destroy.

Look at the symmetry between these speeches when analyzed within positioning theory. Each protagonist sets out a story line of wrongs to be righted. Each performs both implicit and explicit acts of positioning arrogating to the group each represents both the duty and the right to attack the other.

Social psychology is not political analysis; rather, it aims at understanding how political and moral stances are generated. It is quite another question to discuss their moral qualities. That is not the task of the social psychologist, but of the person who makes these analyses as a citizen, a politician, and so on. The evident symmetry of the discursive constructions of Osama bin Laden and George Bush certainly does not entail a corresponding symmetry in the moral stances each takes.

CULTURAL PSYCHOLOGY AS AN ANALYTICAL SCHEME

Is my terrorist your freedom fighter? Are Chechnyans bandits or patriots? Is my patriot your turncoat? Is Paul Revere a hero or a traitor? Is the American preference for serial monogamy morally better or worse than the European preference for lovers and the sanctity of marriage? By whose standards should these matters be judged?

The possibility of *moral relativism*, the belief that different cultures have different but equally compelling systems of moral and political conceptions, is of ancient origin. Aristotle was well aware that different political arrangements that were equally workable were based on different fundamental moral principles. He made a catalogue of the constitutions of the Greek city-states, displaying the many differences. Nevertheless Aristotle was a moral relativist only in the way an anthropologist of our day might be. He recorded different ways of life. Yet, he himself argued for a fundamental and universal form of the good life, the pursuit of excellence in all the ways of which a human being is capable. The condition of *eudaimonia*, of the well-lived life, was one to which everyone not only could but also should aspire (Aristotle, 1947, Book III, chap. 12).

The recent development of cultural psychology (Cole, 1998) is closely linked to the philosophical thesis of relativism. For the purposes of this discussion I focus on those aspects of cultural psychology which, when translated into philosophical terms, appear as moral relativism. If we believe that there is good evidence that the forms of thought, feeling, and action characteristic of different cultures have distinct characteristics, then we have taken the first step toward the stance of cultural psychology. Furthermore, if different cultures have distinct ways of making judgments about human conduct, it might well be that those assessments of people's actions, which we call *moral*, might also be culturally variable. This touches on a point that came up in the discussion of the social construction of categories. If categories are socially constructed and there are rival constructions of certain acts, then there is bound to be some debate about which construction has hegemony. From an objective viewpoint, we might be inclined to say that neither had. That is moral relativism.

The beginnings of cultural psychology in the sense I have just described are ancient. For our purposes the origin of this department of psychology in modern times can be ascribed to the anthropologists Boas (1928) and Benedict (1934). Each culture can be thought of as applying an implicit principle of selectivity to arrive at what is locally regarded as an absolute. Here is how Benedict (1934) introduces the principle: "Every human society everywhere has made . . . [a] selection in its cultural institutions. Each from the point of view of another ignores fundamentals and exploits irrelevancies" (p. 24). The implication is that there is no overall rationale for the selections made by a culture. The selections are the result of the vagaries of history.

The Boasians offered two main supports for the principle of tolerance. The principle is supported if we can find two societies in which the same actions are given different moral assessments (i.e., interpreted as different acts). Thus in Western Europe not fleeing in the face of the enemy displays courage, a moral virtue, whereas among the Chewong of South East Asia not fleeing displays folly and lack of consideration for others, a moral failing. Cultural psychologists can find plenty of examples of this sort of duality. Eating pigs is praiseworthy in Eastern Europe but an abomination to Jews and Muslims.

The second line of support for the principle of tolerance comes from a somewhat tendentious concept, "being right for a culture." For example, polygyny might be right for a culture in which the number of women exceeds that of men or domestic labor is in short supply. Radcliffe-Brown (1952) further tightened the notion of right for a culture with the concept of "necessary for social/biological survival" (p. 152). Cultural practices exist, so he claimed, because "they are part of the mechanism by which an orderly society maintains itself in existence" (p. 152). This applies as much to methods of agriculture as it does to the more cognitive aspects of culture, such as the standards of correct reasoning, emotional styles, and intuitions of acceptable or unacceptable conduct.

From the point of view of social psychology, the conventions of correct conduct and the criteria for assessing people and actions are what count. The ultimate philosophical question as to whether some conventions and criteria are implicit in all cultural practices in all eras is of small importance. The social psychological research program must look both at the overt moral system preached in a culture and actual practice. There are likely to be two story lines in use, one expressing a cultural ideal and the other shaping actual conduct. Most people in the United States think the law should be obeyed, yet nearly all drivers routinely exceed the official speed limit and drink more than the permitted maximum before driving. Social psychology is based on an implicit principle of tolerance.

It follows that for the social psychologist it is not a question of who is good and who is evil, but how activists and defenders make sense of actions as morally or legally assessable acts. In summary, the social psychologist is or should be concerned to catalogue the ways good and evil are understood in various cultures and how rhetorics of moral outrage, moral approval, and so on are constituted and used.

CONCLUSION

The social constructionist approach to the study of any psychological phenomenon bids the analyst pay close attention to the discursive conventions by which sense is made of a situation. In most cases this involves the construal of actions as acts of various kinds, within the framework of active positioning of activist and defender as terrorist and patriot. The principle of tolerance is one way of expressing the need for the psychologist to stand back from joining the moral community to which he or she belongs. The stance of the informed outsider must be maintained whether the research project is into the phenomenon of terrorism or into the rhetoric used, say, in fundraising for a hospice.

A normative construction stands between the activist and the defender. Generally there are two constructions, that of the defender by the activist and that of activist by the defender. Each construction has an associated story line that serves as the resource to shape the response of both parties to an act of terror, the perpetrator and the victim. To stand back and analyze the social psychological aspects of the activities of the IRA or the Stern Gang or al-Qaeda as well as those who defend existing social orders against them is not to condone terrorism. Each of us is a member of one or more existing social orders and as a citizen has a moral duty to take a stand. To understand the psychological sources of these assaults and the psychological devices by which the responses of the defenders are orchestrated, we must suspend our revulsion at acts of mass murder. There are many studies of the former problem. This chapter is an attempt to open up ways of addressing the latter.

5

CULTURAL PRECONDITIONS FOR POTENTIAL TERRORIST GROUPS: TERRORISM AND SOCIETAL CHANGE

FATHALI M. MOGHADDAM

Someone asked Mulla why fish cannot talk in the water.
"Neither could you, if you were under water," he remarked.
—Mehdi Nakosteen, *Mulla's Donkey and Other Friends*

Stories about Mulla Nasreddin, such as the one above, are part of an Eastern Sufi tradition of exploring and imparting wisdom. An idea I take from this story is that environments can place certain powerful restrictions on all beings, irrespective of who and what they are—neither people nor fish can talk under water. In line with this emphasis on the overwhelming influence of context, my primary concern in this discussion is on the cultural conditions that are more likely to give rise to and strengthen potential terrorist groups. At the outset I want to clarify three ways in which this discussion is limited. First, I refer to *potential* terrorist groups, because the preconditions I identify do not make it inevitable that a group will commit acts of terror. Rather, the identified preconditions increase the probability of this outcome. Second, the preconditions I focus on are cultural, but they are no doubt influenced by material conditions. However, in this discussion I am not concerned to examine the relationship between material and cultural

I want to thank Rom Harré and Don Taylor for their helpful reviews of an earlier draft of this chapter.

conditions. Third, I am not concerned with the personality of terrorists and the kinds of minds they might have when considered as isolated individuals (e.g., see Pearlstein, 1991), although there may also be some limited merit in such reductionist approaches. In the domain of criminal behavior there is much value in psychological profiling, with a focus on dispositional characteristics at the individual level, but I view this approach as less useful and less effective in the domain of terrorism. One key difference between them is that, unlike most criminals, terrorists strongly believe that justice and fairness are on their side, and this belief arises out of a collaboratively constructed and maintained worldview (White, 2002). Thus, although from one perspective terrorists are morally disengaged (Bandura, 1990), from their own perspective they are morally engaged.

I present four major propositions. The first proposition asserts that the most effective approach to understanding terrorism is through cultural and collective rather than dispositional and individualistic analysis (following Geertz, 1973; Moghaddam, 2002). Second, I propose that a cultural examination enables us to develop a cultural profile of the conditions in which potential terrorist groups are most likely to evolve and even thrive. The third proposition is that the most salient and central feature of the cultural profile of potential terrorist groups is certain styles of perceiving societal change and stability. Such perceptions, I argue, evolve and are sustained in large part through the (often self-imposed) isolation of potential terrorist groups. The fourth proposition is that the most important preconditions for the emergence of terrorist groups are the same, irrespective of whether such groups are antistate or state-supported. Thus, although my main concern in this discussion is not with state terrorism (for broader discussions of the issues, see Chomsky, 2001; George, 1991), the preconditions I identify extend to at least some types of state terrorism.

The main focus in this discussion is on universal features of the cultural conditions giving rise to potential terrorist groups. At the same time, I acknowledge that there are fundamental differences in the behavior of different terrorist groups around the world: Islamic and Jewish terrorist groups operating in the Middle East, Catholic and Protestant terrorists groups operating in Northern Ireland, to name just a few, are all different from one another in important ways. Although such differences are important, all terrorist groups arise out of certain cultural conditions that have universal features, and it is these features that are the focus of this chapter. My analysis builds on previous discussions of the beliefs systems, values, and other cultural characteristics of terrorist groups (e.g., Blazak, 2001; D. E. Kaplan & A. Marshall, 1996; Rapoport, 2001; White, 2002), fine-grained case studies of the behavior of terrorists (e.g., Crawshaw, 1988), as well as more general discussions and studies reflecting on the conditions giving rise to terrorism (e.g., Atran, 2003; F. Barber, 2001; Hoffman, 1998; Kennedy, 1998; Laqueur, 1999).

Under the circumstances that surround the Ik, the larger a family grows, the less security it can offer. The ideal family, economically speaking and within restricted temporal limits, is a man and his wife and no children. Children are useless appendages, like old parents. Anyone who cannot take care of himself is a burden and a hazard to the survival of others... . The other quality of life that we hold to be necessary for survival, love, the Ik also dismiss as idiotic and highly dangerous. There is also a joking relationship called "friendship." But all this makes sense in the strictest economic terms, in terms of survival, and individual survival at that. If they achieve social survival it is purely accidental; there is no intent so to do. (Turnbull, 1972, p. 134)

Colin Turnbull's detailed case study of the Ik presents a horrifying portrait of how a group can come to adopt patterns of behavior that most people in most societies would consider to be inhuman. The Ik were formerly a hunting and gathering group, but after World War II they were confined to a small area on the Kenya–Uganda border. They could no longer roam their traditional routes, hunting game and gathering food wherever it was to be found. With physical confinement came extremely harsh living conditions and excessive competition for individual survival. Children would steal food from parents, old people would be abandoned to die, young girls would exchange sexual favors for daily food. The behavior of the Ik was utterly transformed.

Turnbull's case study of the Ik is part of a wider research literature that highlights the elastic, changeable nature of human behavior and the idea that there are multiple human natures rather than one human nature (Ehrlich, 2000). Even what we consider to be essential and pervasive features of human societies, such as love and friendship, can be fundamentally transformed beyond recognition under certain conditions. Turnbull's analysis strongly suggests that it was the characteristics of the conditions and the emergent Ik collective meaning system that evolved, rather than some unique feature of Ik individuals, that gave rise to the documented destructive behavioral patterns. In other words, the Ik individual was not able to resist the influence of the collective culture; to rephrase S. Engel (2000), the Ik context became everything.

About the same time that Turnbull, an anthropologist, published his now classic book *The Mountain People* (1972), Stanley Milgram, a social psychologist, conducted research that was reported in his ground-breaking work *Obedience to Authority* (1974). Milgram's research also demonstrated the powerful impact that context can exert on individual behavior: Adults with psychologically normal personality profiles obeyed an authority figure to inflict deadly harm on others. Milgram's research falls in a long experimental tradition, going back at least to the studies of Sherif in the 1930s, demonstrating how arbitrary group norms and other features of the cultural context can fundamentally shape some aspects of individual behavior (see Moghaddam, 1998, chap. 7; Sherif, 1936).

In illuminating the particular aspects of behavior that can be highly influenced by cultural context, Moghaddam (2002) distinguished between *performance capacity*, behaviors constrained by stable biological characteristics of humans, and *performance style*, behaviors that take place in networks of, and are influenced by, meaning systems. For example, performance capacity determines the ability of a person to see the colors on the U.S national flag from 200 yards away; performance style influences how this individual interprets the U.S. flag (e.g., "That flag stands for freedom and democracy" vs. "That flag represents the Great Satan"). In this discussion, then, we are concerned with performance style rather than performance capacity, with interpretations of the world and collaboratively constructed meaning systems, and not "abilities" as determined by biological characteristics of isolated individuals. In particular, our focus is on those aspects of meaning systems that are associated with the cultural preconditions giving rise to potential terrorist groups.

CULTURAL PRECONDITIONS GIVING RISE TO TERRORIST GROUPS

Certain cultural conditions are more likely to give rise to potential terrorist groups, irrespective of the characteristics of the individuals in such conditions. The following is a set of such preconditions, a kind of checklist that could be used to identify the probability of potential terrorist groups evolving in a culture. First, considered in isolation, each item on the checklist is not of much significance as an indicator. The preconditions must be considered as a whole. Second, this is a case in which the whole is more than the sum of its parts, so we must attend to the Gestalt that can emerge when all the preconditions are present. Third, even when all of the preconditions are present, there may evolve groups with the potential for carrying out terrorist acts, but this potential may never be realized. Fourth, although all of the preconditions play an essential role, two in particular play the role of "catalysts" and should be given special attention. They are , first, isolation of the group from mainstream society and, second, a particular style of viewing societal change. These are discussed more extensively below.

The cultural preconditions that give rise to potential terrorist groups can be viewed as lying on a continuum, with preconditions associated with societal and structural features at one end and preconditions associated with the individual and self-perceptions at the other end. However, it is important to see these "individual" characteristics as arising out of socialization, as being culture-based and changeable, and not as part of some set of fixed, inherently stable characteristics within individuals. Toward the center of the continuum are preconditions associated both with societal conditions and conditions within groups that actually or potentially carry out acts of terror. Keeping in mind this continuum, the conditions are as follows: (a) isolated groups, often through deliberate withdrawal; (b) a categorical "good vs. evil" view; (c) a perception of the present society as illegitimate and unjust; (d) a perceived need for radical societal change; (e) a belief that an ideal society is an end that justifies any means; (f) a view that acts of terror are effective means to destabilize existing society; (g) a perception that one has a vital duty to bring about societal change; (h) a belief in self-improvement through one or more acts of terror; (i) the experience of the self in inflated, fragile, and protected terms; and (j) a perception that it is easier to stay in rather than to exit the terrorist group.

Existence in Isolation

Despite the great difficulty of defining *terrorism* (H. H. A. Cooper, 1978, 2001), there is general consensus that secrecy and isolation are two important characteristics of potential terrorist groups. In almost all cases potential terrorist groups take part in activities, including the gathering, assessment, and storage of information and the development of plans, and they also hold some key views and goals that they attempt to keep secret, particularly from government authorities. In most cases the ideas of potential terrorist groups about the nature, role, and necessity of communications with others are different from those in the larger society. Necessity dictates that potential terrorist groups divulge as little information as possible about themselves to outsiders and that the information communicated be misleading. This means that secrets are kept from even close friends and family members.

In terms of lifestyle and group organization, potential terrorist groups tend to be fundamentally different from the larger society (Rapoport, 2001). This is in large part because of the need for secrecy. To maintain a high level of secrecy, potential terrorist groups typically practice a high level of isolation or develop "shadow lives." That is, in addition to their public and ordinary lives, they develop a parallel, secret, and isolated group life. For example, a baker is a loving son and brother and a friendly neighbor, but he may also has a secret life unknown to all but a few.

Isolation from the rest of society serves a number of important catalytic functions, in addition to maintaining secrecy. In fact, it is a more important precondition than almost all the other preconditions. First, isolation serves to maintain and strengthen ethnocentrism (LeVine & Campbell, 1972), supporting the "we are right, they are wrong" attitude among group members. The extreme views of the group members do not come under critical scrutiny and are never really tested against other views, because they are not allowed to see the light of day. Second, isolation serves to heighten group conformity and cohesion, so that there is less chance of rebellion. Studies of groups, including cults and minority religious groups (e.g., Hostetler, 1980; Jackson & Perkins, 1997), demonstrate that isolation is an important means through which group conformity and cohesion are maintained. Third, isolation serves to solidify the influence of the leadership (see discussions of realistic conflict theory in Taylor & Moghaddam, 1994). This is partly because the external threat is highlighted and exaggerated through isolation, and under conditions of external threat the position of the leadership is strengthened. Through further discussions of the other main preconditions, the central catalytic role of isolation will be clarified.

Isolation is also a hallmark of, and one of the two most important preconditions for, groups used to perpetrate state terrorism. Such groups are typically trained in isolation and are required to maintain tight secrecy over their identities. However, in some cases the state finds it useful to propagate and even exaggerate the power and extent of state terrorist groups, without labeling them as terrorist groups, as a means of putting fear into opposition groups.

A Categorical "Good vs. Evil" View of the World

The psychological and often physical isolation of the potential terrorist group is associated with a categorical view that divides the world into "good vs. evil" and "us vs. them". Some aspects of the categorization process are not unique to such isolated groups. Categorization is a pervasive cognitive process that enables humans to more effectively deal with the potentially infinite amount of information in the environment, and categorization of social phenomena is a central part of the human social life (see McGarty, 1999). However, the social and sometimes physical isolation of potential terrorist groups, as well as their particular in-group norms, serves to exaggerate the consequences of categorization. An extensive literature mainly using the minimal group experimental paradigm suggests that under certain conditions categorization even on what seems to be a trivial basis can lead to intergroup bias (see Taylor & Moghaddam, 1994, chap. 4). Categorization can also be the basis of stereotype development (Oakes, Haslam, & Turner, 1994), and the physical and psychological isolation of terrorist groups enhances the stereotypes of the in-group and out-group. Associated with this is *within-group minimization*, a perception that the in-group is more homogeneous than it is, and *between-group exaggeration*, a perception that the differences between groups are greater than they are.

Potential terrorist groups, and these include state-supported terrorist groups, are more likely to thrive in cultural conditions that nurture categorical thinking and that depict the world as consisting of groups with fundamental differences. In such contexts, people are not treated as individuals who share characteristics with all humanity, but rather as group members whose salient characteristics are exclusively determined by group membership. Consequently, the only thing that matters is whether a person is a Catholic or Protestant, Black or White, Arab or Israeli, and so on. Cultural conditions conducive to such thinking can, albeit unwittingly, be strengthened by mainstream politicians who divide the social world into "good and evil."

Perception of Present Society as Illegitimate and Unjust

An important component of the belief system giving rise to potential terrorist groups is that society as it exists presently is illegitimate and unjust. (Social identity theory is one of several major theories that give importance to these factors in inter-group relations; see Tajfel & Turner, 1986.) Illegitimacy is typically associated with perceptions of a violation of a "higher order," for example, as seen to arise from divine or other holy sources (and influences religious terrorism), or as assumed to arise from "nature" and the natural environment (and influences environmental terrorism).

The lack of legitimacy may be seen to arise from an absence of a religious foundation. An example is the perceived violation of religious "laws," as in the case of an Islamic society (e.g., Saudi Arabia, stationing of U.S. troops in the "holiest land" of Islam) that is seen to be moving "too far" away from Islamic values, or a non-Islamic society (e.g., United States) that is seen to cause historically Islamic societies to move toward Westernization and secularization. Such perceptions can be used to justify terrorism against those viewed as responsible for illegitimacy, including terrorism against minority groups, such as against women who attempt to come out from under the veil in Islamic societies.

Closely associated with the perception of illegitimacy is the perception of society as unjust. (*Society* here could also refer to the larger world society.) The perceived injustice often arises out of a belief that those in power are not upholding the "correct" values strongly enough, or that they are subjugating individuals and groups who try to uphold the "correct" values. Thus, for example, the Orange Order and the Irish Republican Army (IRA) in Northern Ireland and the Shining Path in Peru (to name but a few) have propagated a view of their respective societies as unjust, just as the Islamic jihad has propagated a view of the larger society of the international order, dominated by the United States, as being unjust.

Claims of societal illegitimacy and injustice are typically assessed through criteria that are subjective and even arbitrary, rather than objective. Majority groups put forward various criteria that typically favor their position, and minority groups put forward other alternative criteria and claims. Consider, for example, the alternative claims and positions of the more radical feminist groups, Black Power groups, gays, and other minority groups, since the 1960s versus the position of the White, male majority group and the U.S. Federal Government. In conditions allowing for public scrutiny and debate, even radical groups that engage in dialogue tend to become incorporated within the larger societal discourse, and to eventually help shape the discourse, as well as to become influenced by it themselves. However, groups that are isolated are more likely to rigidly maintain their own arbitrary criteria and claims, because there is less possibility that their views on the illegitimacy and injustice of society is directly challenged. Rather than moving closer to other segments of society, they are even more likely to move further apart. In this way, potential terrorist groups are influenced by their isolation to move further away from the rest of society.

In the case of state-supported terrorist groups, isolation affords greater opportunities for the development of a perception that those attempting to bring about societal change are unjust and lack legitimacy. Thus, state-supported terrorist groups typically view society as legitimate and just, and political reformers as traitors (to "the leader," "the nation," "the true religion," and so on).

Perception of the Need for Radical Societal Change

Among the cultural preconditions that nurture potential terrorist groups, none is more important than those related to societal change: first, a perceived need for radical societal change; second, the perception that the existing system does not allow for normative avenues to achieve societal change toward the ideal society; and third, the conviction that the ideal society is an end that justifies any and all means. Just as group isolation and secrecy is a "structural" catalyst for other preconditions, the perception of a necessity for societal change serves as a psychological catalyst for the other preconditions. Potential terrorist groups are associated with cultural conditions that nurture a need for what Watzlawick, Weakland, and Fisch (1974) have described as a "change of change," that is, a complete change from one system to another, rather than reform or change within an existing system. Given the radical nature of this goal, it is not surprising that a "change of change" is often sought through revolution, and terrorism is seen as one means to move society closer to revolution.

A wide range of theories, from macro theories such as Marxist theory and elite theory (Moghaddam, 2002, chap. 2) to micro psychological theories such as relative deprivation theory (Gurr, 1970), give importance to the role of a perceived need for radical societal change in group mobilization. Both Marxist theory and elite theory propose that a vanguard or "counter-elite" is needed to raise consciousness and make the proletariat or the "Anonelite" aware of the necessity of societal change. Dissatisfaction with the present social system, and awareness of cognitive alternatives, is also given central place in social identity theory (Tajfel & Turner, 1986).

The direction of the desired change varies across cultures. In some cases, a need is seen for a change back to some assumed "golden age" when justice was supposed to have prevailed. For example, attempts to return to an era when "Christian values" or "Islamic values" or "Jewish values" ruled and there was (ostensibly) no injustice. In other cases, the emphasis is on radical societal change toward some perceived ideal goal, such as the classless society.

There is also some commonality in the perception of the inevitability of radical societal change. For example, from the perspective of some who seek to establish a classless society, the historical march toward such a society is inevitable in the long term. Just as feudalism was followed by capitalism, capitalism will be followed by socialism, the dictatorship of the proletariat, and the classless society. However, "vanguards of the proletariat" can play an important role in this historical process. For those motivated by religious convictions and desiring a religious form of an ideal society, also, the ultimate goal is often seen to be inevitable, but individuals and groups must play a role in guiding society back on the "correct" path. State-supported terrorist groups also focus on a "correct" path, but one that is determined by the state rather than by political reformers.

Perception of a Lack of Legal Means of Achieving Change

An important distinction can be made between normative and non-normative means of attempting to change society (Taylor & Moghaddam, 1994). Normative means are within the bounds of acceptable behavior, as defined by both informal "commonsense law" as well as formal "black letter law" (see Finkel, 1995). For example, in democratic societies the ideal is that individuals and groups attempting to bring about change compete for political office in open elections. Being elected to political office is seen as a normative and effective means of influencing societal change. In dictatorships, also, there are normative avenues for attempting to bring about change, although they are far more limited. For example, in Iran and Saudi Arabia, normative channels for change exist within the strict confines of religious orthodoxy: Change can be brought about as long as it does not violate the interpretation of Islam endorsed by the rulers at the time.

An important feature of cultures that provide fertile ground for the growth of potential terrorist groups, including state-supported ones, is a widespread perception, justified or not, that there are no legal means to change society to some ideal form. The idea that this perception of a "closed system" will lead to rebellion and perhaps the collapse of the existing social order is found in both early and more recent writings. For example, this idea is clearly set out in Plato's *Republic*, where he warns the rulers that if they do not allow circulation of talent, so that talented individuals can rise from lower ranks to join the rank of rulers, and individuals born into the top rank but without the requisite talent can fall to lower ranks, then "the State will be ruined" (*The Republic*, 1987, Book Three, § 415c). The same idea is central to Pareto's elite theory (1935), developed some 2,500 years after Plato's *Republic*. More recent intergroup theories and experimental studies suggest that this perception is associated with attempts to instigate action through non-normative means (Taylor & Moghaddam, 1994). Moreover, an important shift takes place from individual to collective action: the attempt to mobilize collectivities against the current system.

Belief That the Ideal Society Justifies Any Means

Associated with a perception that normative means are not available for changing society toward the ideal society is a perception among terrorist groups, including those supported by the state, that the ideal society is an end that justifies any and all means of action. Because society as it exists is perceived to be illegitimate and unjust and to have unfair laws, and because all normative paths for moving toward, or back to, the ideal society are closed, then non-normative means are seen as necessary and justified. As stated in the title of a book about the Japanese terrorists responsible for the 1995 nerve gas attack on a Tokyo subway, this may even reach the extreme of "destroying the world to save it" (Lifton, 2000). This explains the close association often noted between terrorism and crime.

One of the major challenges confronting terrorist groups is that of gathering adequate resources to support themselves and their activities. The perception that the "ends justify the means" opens up many non-normative avenues for accumulating resources, including bank-robbery, drug smuggling, kidnapping, and other types of criminal activity. The link between drug trafficking and terrorism has a long history (Lupsha, 1987) and has perhaps become even more prominent in the 21st century, as evident by events in Colombia, Afghanistan, and elsewhere. A more recent but fast-rising threat is the use of biological terrorism (Kuhr & Hauer, 2001).

The most troublesome consequence of the worldview that justifies means through ends is the willingness to sacrifice human life toward the greater goal. Normative values upholding the sanctity of human life are cast aside, and the terrifying outcome is a willingness to die in order to kill almost as a routine part of existence. The solemnity of death is lost in this culture; killing becomes a victory and a cause for celebration. This radically different approach to death and killing arises, and is sustained, through the isolation of the terrorist group.

It is in this context that we can better understand the actions of Middle Eastern suicide bombers and the utter failure of terror management theory (Greenberg, Arndt, Simon, Pyszczynski, & Solomon, 2000) and other similar Western attempts to explain certain types of terrorism. Terror management theory and other similar explanations rest on the assumption that individuals consciously or unconsciously fear death and are first and foremost concerned to stay alive. This assumption makes sense from the perspective of Western liberal values, but it is misleading in the context of a culture that gives value to martyrdom and the sacrifice of one's life for the great cause. As clearly demonstrated by the terrorists of September 11, as well as by the actions of thousands of "martyrs" in the Middle East over the last few decades, as well as thousands of "heroes" in Western and non-Western societies who in particular historical periods have sacrificed their lives to try to destroy "the enemy," in some cultural contexts it is an honor and a privilege for individuals to sacrifice their lives. Rather than fearing death, these individuals rush to their fate as a way of playing their part in a larger struggle.

Belief in Acts of Terror to Destabilize Society

An important difference between state-supported and anti-state terrorist groups concerns the issue of stability: State-supported terrorist groups view terrorism as an effective means of maintaining the stability of society, whereas anti-state terrorist groups view terrorism as an effective means of destabilizing society. Thus, for anti-state terrorist groups the ethic that "ends justify means" is closely tied to what is assumed to be a practical strategy: bringing about change through acts of terror. This function is assumed to be served particularly through a supposed "consciousness raising" function of terrorist acts. The general population is assumed to be unable to perceive the real, illegitimate, and unjust nature of the existing society and therefore needs to be "awakened."

Acts of terror are assumed to serve a number of functions toward "awakening" the general population. First, they serve to demonstrate the vulnerability of the rulers and the fragility of socio-political order. The rulers can be attacked and the existing order can be weakened, damaged, and made unstable. This is assumed to embolden the general population, which is thought to ultimately want to move toward the ideal society envisaged or endorsed by the potential terrorist group. In this sense, the act of terror is sometimes assumed by terrorists, such as the Oklahoma City bombers (see Linenthal, 2001), as a "spark" that will ignite the explosion of the masses and result in a revolution. Second, acts of terror are assumed to strengthen the terrorist group, by improving confidence and sometimes (when robbery and other such crimes are involved) by increasing in-group resources.

It may appear from the above discussion that the general public should be viewed as suffering something akin to "positive illusions," incorrect and exaggerated rosy picture of society and how just and fair it is. The members of potential terrorist groups, on the other hand, may be seen as suffering from "depressive realism," seeing the world "as bad as it really is." However, it would be wrong to assume that the members of potential terrorist groups are depressed individuals. Far from it, as becomes clear in the following sections— these individuals tend to be optimistic about the changes they can bring about and the "inevitability" of their ultimate victory in the struggle toward the ideal society.

Perception That the Group Can Bring About Societal Change

Potential terrorist groups, including state-supported ones, are more likely to flourish in cultural contexts where groups have the opportunity to be isolated and thus to cultivate the perception that the members have a vital role to play to bring about societal change. Through the role envisaged for the group, each individual comes to see herself or himself as having a vital role in societal change. In this regard, the role of narratives, concerning group traditions, past history, and self-presentation in the larger society, become particularly important.

Narratives have roles in relation to the past, the present, and the future (see Bruner, 1991). Given the need for secrecy, terrorist groups are reluctant to leave written records; they rely especially on verbal narratives. First, narratives help construct group traditions and convey a strong sense of historical destiny. In this way, group members come to perceive themselves as belonging to a much larger movement with long histories, rather than isolated and alone (even though, for all practical purposes they may in fact be isolated and alone). Second, narratives operate to place the group in a "vital" role in the present and help to direct actions toward the ideal future.

Close attention to narratives can also help outsiders better understand the forward looking, optimistic view of those who carry out terrorist acts. From the perspective of mainstream Western society, it is difficult to comprehend that acts of terror, including suicide bombings by "martyrs," are generally carried out by groups who view themselves as helping to improve the world. This remains one of several blind spots in analyses of terrorism conducted from a Western viewpoint, as reflected by terror management theory and the like. It is not a fear of death and escape from dark unknowns that propel suicide bombers, but joy and optimism in a life that is assumed to eventually follow, a life that promises to be much better than the harsh realities of the present existence, which holds so few possibilities for collective in-group improvement in living conditions, employment, education, and so on.

Belief That Societal Change Improves the Group Situation

Terrorist acts are more likely to arise in cultural contexts that encourage potential terrorist groups, including those supported by the state, to believe there is more to gain through terror than other avenues of action. The "gain" might be a believed paradise in the afterlife, or it may simply be tangible material and nonmaterial benefits for members of one's family.

Interpretations of holy books, such as the Qur'an, that justify and glorify "martyrdom" play an important cultural role in the nurturance of suicide bombings and other acts of terror. Such interpretations have proved to be politically powerful in a number of settings, including the struggle against colonialism, as in the case of the Algerian struggle against French rule; the fight against traditional monarchies, as in the case of the struggle to topple the Shah in Iran; and the struggle against foreign invaders, such as the fight to expel the Soviet army from Afghanistan. In all these cases, the belief that "martyrdom" is a necessary and laudable means toward the desired end took hold in the wider society and swelled the ranks of particular groups.

However, the supreme sacrifice of giving one's life for a cause is not alien to Western societies; indeed, it is often depicted as a highly valuable act. For example, one of the most influential of Dickens's novels, A Tale of Two Cities, ends with one man giving his life to save another, and the last words of the novel are said by the "martyr": "It is a far, far better thing that I do, than I have ever done; it is a far, far better rest that I go to, than I have ever known" (Dickens, 1859/1963, p. 320). This same sentiment is in the minds of suicide bombers, who also believe their situation is about to improve.

A Protected, Unstable, and Inflated View of the Self

Since the return of the "self" to psychology in the last few decades of the 20th century, self-esteem has gained central place as a part of explanations for various types of "bad" behavior. In particular, the "problem of low self esteem" has been assumed to underlie an enormous array of problems, including poor school performance, prejudice, and acts of aggression. Received wisdom from this tradition implies that terrorists must suffer low self-esteem.

However, even if we accept assumptions underlying the traditional measures of self-esteem (see Sabat, Fath, Moghaddam, & Harré, 1999), the low self-esteem hypothesis is clearly discredited by extensive findings showing that the groups assumed to have low-self esteem actually do not have this "problem" (see Moghaddam, 1998, chap. 10). Indeed, rather than low self-esteem, if there is a problem it may be related to protected, unstable, and inflated views of the self (following Baumeister, Boden, & Smart, 1996). A "protected" view of the self and the in-group evolves in large part through the isolation of the potential terrorist groups. The lack of opportunities for feedback from those outside the in-group also serves to protect unstable and inflated views of the self, views not based on reality. For example, a view of the self as "revolutionary," "supported by the people," "engaged in a sacred cause," "leading others toward a better life," and the like could more likely be successfully challenged by others if sufficient opportunities arise for communications with outsiders.

Perception of Difficulty of Leaving the Terrorist Group

Terrorist groups are examples of what Coser (1974) calls *greedy groups*, meaning they make absolute claims on the loyalty and resources of their members, with no exceptions or exits permitted. Members of such groups experience two sets of pressures: pressures from the larger society, which serve to further isolate them, and pressures from within the groups to maintain group loyalty and prevent exit of any kind. The first set of pressures can lead to a perception among members that there is no way out because the authorities, or at least an important influential elite within society, are not willing to consider any possible avenues for communication and change. Also, the perception often exists that there is no possibility of a fair trial for individuals who attempt to exit from potential terrorist groups. This perception can be strengthened by the establishment of military courts specifically for the trials of suspected terrorists, reenforcing the impression that they will be denied any chance of a fair trial

The second set of pressures, those exerted within the groups, is exaggerated by the isolation of such groups. Members gradually come to live at least a part of their lives (what I have called *shadow lives*) in a high state of secrecy. The closer a group moves toward carrying out acts of terror, the greater the pressure to maintain secrecy. Early in their involvement with such groups, members feel they can still exit safely. However, a "tipping point" is reached, beyond which the cost of exit of a group member is seen as too great for the group to bear. Sometimes members become explicitly aware of both the closed nature of the group and the terrible consequences of attempted exit from the group.

However, it would be too simplistic to interpret a suicide bombing, or other similar types of terrorist action, as arising from pressure within the terrorist group. Rather, such actions evolve out of a much larger cultural context, sometimes involving major movements that influence the interpretation of religious laws, written and unwritten.

CONCLUSION

The thrust of my argument is that terrorist groups, including state-supported ones, are more likely to evolve when certain cultural characteristics are present, and these I have termed the *preconditions* for the rise of such groups. In this final section, I further clarify what I do and do not mean by putting forward these preconditions, and then I examine the particularly important perceived link between terrorism and societal change.

What I Do and Do Not Mean

Given the prevalence of hierarchical models in psychology, put forward by Freud, Erikson, Maslow, Piaget, and Kohlberg, among others (see Moghaddam, 2002, chap. 11), it might be assumed that the preconditions I have postulated follow this tradition and are also part of a hierarchical model.

Such a model might predict a unidirectional, stepwise progression, so that, for example, step one might be "isolation" and the last step might be "the perception that is easier to remain rather than exit from terrorist group." However, I am not proposing a hierarchical model, nor do I see the preconditions as forming any kind of stepwise progression. Rather, the cultural preconditions I have outlined could be met in any order: they might be met all at once, or in a stepwise manner, depending on cultural conditions.

However, two preconditions are more important than the others: Isolation serves as a "structural" catalyst, and the perception of a need to radically change society is a psychological catalyst. Although these two have central importance, all the preconditions reinforce one another and work as a Gestalt.

A stipulation I propose is that all the preconditions have to be met before a group implements an act of terror. At the same time, it is also possible that all the preconditions are met, but a potential terrorist group stops short of actually undertaking terrorism. The preconditions identified increase the probability of terror being carried out, they do not make it a certainty.

Terrorism and Societal Change

Finally, as psychologists we should pay particular attention to the preconditions associated with terrorism and societal change and more specifically with the perception that society has to change and that acts of terror (which acts may be claimed to be acts of liberation) are necessary for bringing about change toward the ideal society. It is essential to understand these perceptions as arising out of a larger culture and being imbedded in narratives adopted by a wider population, rather than being unique to small isolated groups of potential terrorists.

For Western researchers to better appreciate the important role of the cultural preconditions leading to suicide bombers and other such actions, it is useful to reflect on instances in the history of the West where self sacrifice, martyrdom, heroism, and the like were widely supported and encouraged. For example, before the Vietnam War, there was widespread support among U.S. citizens for the idea of fighting and dying for one's country. The popular narratives of the time reflected the widespread support that heroism and self-sacrifice had among the general U.S. population. To understand why individual soldiers were willing to sacrifice their own lives during World War II, for example, it is necessary to consider the wider culture and the collaborative construction of "the good soldier," "the good Christian," and so on. In a similar manner, one can only understand the lone suicide bomber by considering the larger context from which he or she emerges and is often lauded as a martyr.

II

PSYCHOSOCIAL CONTEXT

6

THE ROLE OF SELECTIVE MORAL DISENGAGEMENT IN TERRORISM AND COUNTERTERRORISM

ALBERT BANDURA

Self-sanctions play a central role in the regulation of inhumane conduct. In the course of socialization, people adopt moral standards that serve as guides and deterrents for conduct. After personal control has developed, people regulate their actions by the sanctions they apply to themselves. They do things that give them self-satisfaction and a sense of self-worth. They refrain from behaving in ways that violate their moral standards because such behavior brings self-condemnation. Self-sanctions thus keep conduct in line with internal standards.

However, moral standards do not function as fixed internal regulators of conduct. Self-regulatory mechanisms do not operate unless they are acti-

Some sections of this chapter include revised, updated, and expanded material from the following two sources:

Bandura, A. (1986). *Social foundations of thought and action: A social cognitive theory.* Englewood Cliffs, NJ: Prentice Hall. Copyright 1986 by Prentice Hall. Adapted with permission.

Bandura, A. (1990). Mechanisms of moral disengagement. In W. Reich (Ed.), *Origins of terrorism: Psychologies, ideologies, theologies, states of mind* (pp. 161–191). Cambridge, England: Cambridge University Press. Copyright 1990 by Cambridge University Press. Adapted with permission.

121

vated, and there are many psychological processes by which control reactions can be disengaged from inhumane conduct (Bandura, 1986). Selective activation and disengagement of moral self-sanctions permit different types of conduct despite the same moral standards. Figure 6.1 shows the locus in the process of moral control at which moral self-censure can be disengaged from reprehensible conduct. The disengagement may center on redefining harmful conduct as honorable by moral justification, exonerating social comparison, and sanitizing language. It may focus on agency of action so that perpetrators can minimize their role in causing harm by diffusion and displacement of responsibility. It may involve minimizing or distorting the harm that flows from detrimental actions. The disengagement may include dehumanizing the victims and blaming them for bringing the suffering on themselves.

The way in which these moral disengagement practices operate in the perpetration of inhumanities is analyzed in detail in later sections of this chapter.

These psychosocial mechanisms of moral disengagement have been examined most extensively in the area of political and military violence. This limited focus tends to convey the impression that selective disengagement of moral self-sanctions occurs only under extraordinary circumstances. Quite the contrary. Such mechanisms operate in everyday situations in which decent people routinely perform activities that further their interests but have injurious effects on others. Self-exonerations are needed to eliminate self-prohibitions and self-censure. This chapter analyzes how the mechanisms of moral disengagement function in terrorist operations.

Terrorism is a strategy of violence designed to promote desired outcomes by instilling fear in the public at large (Bassiouni, 1981). Public intimidation is a key element that distinguishes terrorist violence from other forms of violence. Unlike the customary violence in which victims are personally targeted, in terrorism the victims are incidental to the terrorists' intended aims, and the violence is used mainly as a way to provoke social conditions designed to further broader aims.

Several features of terrorist acts give power to a few incidents to induce widespread public fear that vastly exceeds the objective threat. The first terrorizing feature is the unpredictability of who will be targeted and when or where a terrorist act will occur. The second feature is the gravity of terrorist acts that maim and kill. With the magnified lethality of the weapons technology, terrorists can now wreak destruction on a massive scale. A third feature of terrorist acts that render them so terrorizing is the sense of uncontrollability that they instill. The fourth feature that contributes to a sense of personal and societal vulnerability is the high centralization and interdependence of essential service systems in modern life. A single destructive act that knocks out communications, transportation, and power systems and damages safe water and food supplies can instantly frighten and harm

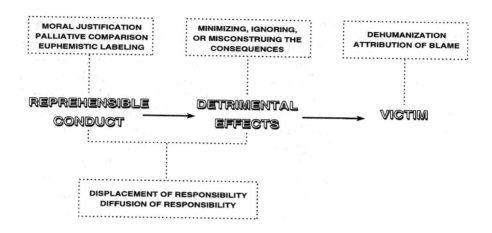

Figure 6.1. Mechanism through which moral self-sanctions are selectively activated and disengaged from detrimental behavior at different points in the self-regulatory process. From *Social Foundations of Thought and Action: A Social Cognitive Theory* (p. 376), by A. Bandura, 1986, Englewood Cliffs, NJ: Prentice Hall. Copyright 1986 by Prentice Hall. Reprinted with permission.

vast numbers of people. The combination of unpredictability, gravity, vulnerable interdependence, and perceived self-inefficacy is especially intimidating and socially constraining (Bandura, 1990).

In coping with problems of terrorism, societies are faced with a dual task. The first is how to reduce terrorist acts; the second is how to combat the fear they arouse. Because the number of terrorist acts is small, the widespread public fear and the intrusive and costly security countermeasures pose the more serious problems. Utilitarian justifications can readily win the support of a frightened public for curtailment of civil liberties and violent counterterrorist measures. A frightened and angered citizenry does not spend much time agonizing over the morality of lethal modes of self-defense.

The term *terrorism* is often applied to violent acts that dissident groups direct surreptitiously at officials of regimes to force social or political changes. So defined, terrorism becomes indistinguishable from straightforward political violence. Particularized threats are certainly intimidating to the martial and political figures who are personally targeted for assassination and create some apprehension over destabilizing societal effects. However, such threats do not necessarily terrify the general public as long as ordinary civilians are not targeted. As I show later, terrorist tactics relying on public intimidation can serve other purposes as well as serve as a political weapon.

From a psychological standpoint, third-party violence directed at innocent people is a much more horrific undertaking than political violence in which political figures are personally targeted. It is easier to get individuals who harbor strong grievances to kill hated political officials or to abduct advisors and consular staffs of foreign nations that are alleged to support oppressive regimes. However, to cold-bloodedly slaughter innocent women and children in buses, department stores, and airports requires more powerful psychological machinations of moral disengagement. Intensive psychological training in moral disengagement is needed to create the capacity to kill innocent human beings as a way of toppling rulers or regimes or of accomplishing other political goals.

MORAL JUSTIFICATION

One set of disengagement practices operates on the construal of the behavior itself. People do not ordinarily engage in reprehensible conduct until they have justified to themselves the morality of their actions. In this process, destructive conduct is made personally and socially acceptable by portraying it as serving socially worthy and moral purposes. People then act on a moral imperative. Moral justification sanctifies violent means.

Radical shifts in destructive behavior through moral justification are most strikingly revealed in military conduct. People who have been socialized to deplore killing as morally condemnable can be rapidly transformed into skilled combatants, who may feel little compunction at and even a sense of pride in taking human life. Moral reconstrual of killing is dramatically illustrated in the case of Sergeant York, one of the phenomenal fighters in the history of modern warfare (Skeyhill, 1928). Because of his deep religious convictions, he registered as a conscientious objector, but his numerous appeals were denied. At camp, his battalion commander quoted chapter and verse from the Bible to persuade him that under appropriate conditions it was Christian to fight and kill. A marathon mountainside prayer finally convinced him that he could serve both God and country by becoming a dedicated fighter.

The conversion of socialized people into dedicated fighters is achieved not by altering their personality structures, aggressive drives, or moral standards. Rather, it is accomplished by cognitively redefining the morality of killing, so that it can be done free from self-censuring restraints. Through moral sanction of violent means, people see themselves as fighting ruthless oppressors who have an unquenchable appetite for conquest or as protecting their cherished values and way of life, preserving world peace, saving humanity from subjugation to an evil ideology, and honoring their country's international commitments.

Over the centuries, much destructive conduct has been perpetrated by ordinary, decent people in the name of righteous ideologies, religious principles, and nationalistic imperatives (Kramer, 1990; Rapoport & Alexander, 1982; Reich, 1990/1998). Throughout history countless people have suffered at the hands of self-righteous crusaders bent on stamping out what they considered evil. Voltaire put it well when he said, "Those who can make you believe absurdities, can make you commit atrocities." Adversaries sanctify their militant actions but condemn those of their antagonists as barbarity masquerading under a mask of outrageous moral reasoning. Each side feels morally superior to the other. Acting on moral or ideological imperatives reflects a conscious offense mechanism, not an unconscious defense mechanism.

The politicization of religion has a long and bloody history. In holy terror, perpetrators twist theology and see themselves as doing God's will. In 1095, Pope Urban II launched the Crusades with the following impassioned moral proclamation: "I address those present, I proclaim it, to those absent, Christ commands it. For all those going thither, there will be remission of sins if they come to the end of this fettered life." He then dehumanized and beastialized the Muslim enemies: "What a disgrace if a race so despicable, degenerate, and enslaved by demons, should overcome a people endowed with faith in Almighty God and resplendent in the name of Christ! Let those who once fought against brothers and relatives now rightfully fight against the barbarians under the guidance of the Lord."

Islamic extremists mount their jihad, construed as self-defense against tyrannical, decadent infidels who seek to enslave the Muslim world. Bin Laden ennobled his global terrorism as serving a holy imperative (Borger, 2001; Ludlow, 2001): "We will continue this course because it is part of our religion and because Allah, praise and glory be to him, ordered us to carry out jihad so that the word of Allah may remain exalted to the heights." In the jihad they are carrying out Allah's will as a "religious duty." The prime agency for the holy terror is thus displaced to Allah. By attribution of blame, terrorist strikes are construed as morally justifiable defensive reactions to humiliation and atrocities perpetrated by atheistic forces. "We are only defending ourselves. This is defensive jihad." By advantageous comparison with the nuclear bombing of Japan, and the toll of the Iraqi sanctions on children, the jihad takes on an altruistic appearance: "When people at the ends of the earth, Japan, were killed by their hundreds of thousands, young and old, it was not considered a war crime, it is something that has justification. Millions of children in Iraq are something that has justification." Bin Laden beastialized the American enemy as "lowly people" perpetrating acts that "the most ravenous of animals would not descend to." Terrorism is sanitized as "the winds of faith [that] have come" to eradicate the "debauched" oppressors. His followers see themselves as holy warriors who gain a blessed eternal life through their martyrdom.

Israeli prime minister Yitzhak Rabin's assassin was similarly acting on a divine mandate, using the rabbinical pursuer's decree as moral justification. In his view, those who give over their people and land to the enemy must be killed. As he explained, the killing was meant to prevent transfer of land to Palestinian control: "Maybe physically, I acted alone but what pulled the trigger was not only my finger but the finger of this whole nation which, for 2,000 years, yearned for this land and dreamed of it."[1]

Paul Hill, the Presbyterian minister, also justified the killing of a doctor and his elderly assistant outside the abortion clinic as carrying out God's will: "God's law positively requires us to defend helpless people. God has used people, who are willing to die for their cause to save human life. I'm willing to do that" (see Footnote 1).

Although moral cognitive restructuring can be easily used to support self-serving and destructive purposes, it can also serve militant action aimed at changing inhumane social conditions. By appealing to morality, social reformers are able to use coercive, and even violent, tactics to force social change. Vigorous disputes arise over the morality of aggressive action directed against institutional practices. Powerholders often resist, by forcible means if necessary, pressures to make needed social changes that jeopardize their own self-interests. Such tactics provoke social activism. Challengers consider their militant actions to be morally justifiable because they serve to eradicate harmful social practices. Powerholders condemn violent means as unjustified and unnecessary because nonviolent means exist to effect social change. They tend to view resorting to violence as an effort to coerce changes that lack popular support. Finally, they may argue that terrorist acts are condemnable because they violate civilized standards of conduct. Anarchy would flourish in a climate in which individuals considered violent tactics acceptable whenever they disliked particular social practices or policies.

Challengers refute such moral arguments by appealing to what they regard as a higher level of morality derived from communal concerns. They see their constituencies as comprising all people, both at home and abroad, who are victimized either directly or indirectly by injurious institutional practices. Challengers argue that, when many people benefit from a system that is deleterious to disfavored segments of the society, harmful social practices secure widespread public support. From the challengers' perspective, they are acting under a moral imperative to stop the maltreatment of people who have no way of modifying injurious social policies because they are either outside the system that victimizes them, or they lack the social power to effect changes from within by peaceable means. Their defendants regard militant action as the only recourse available to them.

Clearly, adversaries can easily marshal moral reasons for the use of aggressive actions for social control or for social change. When viewed from divergent perspectives, violent acts are different things to different people. In conflicts of power, one person's violence is another person's selfless benevolence. It is often proclaimed that one group's criminal terrorist activity

---

[1]A copy of the newspaper article this material was extracted from is available from Albert Bandura, Department of Psychology, Stanford University, Stanford, CA 94305.

is another group's liberation movement fought by heroic freedom fighters. This is why moral appeals against violence usually fall on deaf ears.

MORAL JUSTIFICATIONS AND THE MASS MEDIA

The mass media, especially television, provide the best access to the public because of its strong drawing power. For this reason, television is increasingly used as the principal vehicle of social and moral justifications of goals and violent means. Struggles to legitimize and gain support for one's causes, and to discredit those of one's foes, are now waged more and more through the electronic media (Ball-Rokeach, 1972).

Terrorists try to exercise influence over targeted officials and nations through intimidation of the public and arousal of sympathy for the social and political causes they espouse. Without widespread publicity, terrorist acts can achieve neither of these effects. Terrorists, therefore, coerce access to the media to publicize their grievances to the international community. They use television as the main instrument for gaining sympathy and support for their plight by presenting themselves as risking their lives for the welfare of a victimized constituency whose legitimate grievances are ignored. The media, in turn, come under heavy fire from targeted officials who regard granting terrorists a worldwide forum as aiding terrorist causes. Security forces do not like media personnel tracking their conduct, broadcasting tactical information that terrorists can put to good use, and interposing themselves as intermediaries in risky negotiation situations. Social pressures mount to curtail media coverage of terrorist events, especially while they are in progress (Bassiouni, 1981).

ADVANTAGEOUS COMPARISON

How behavior is viewed is colored by what it is compared to. By exploiting the contrast principle, reprehensible acts can be made righteous. The more flagrant the contrasting inhumanities, the more likely it is that one's own destructive conduct would appear trifling or even benevolent. Thus, terrorists minimize their killings as the only defensive weapon they have to curb the widespread cruelties inflicted on their people under tyrannical regimes. In the eyes of their supporters, risky attacks directed at the apparatus of oppression are acts of selflessness and martyrdom. Those who are the objects of terrorist attacks, in turn, characterize their own retaliatory violence as trifling, or even laudable, by comparing it with the carnage and terror perpetrated by terrorists. In social conflicts, injurious behavior usually escalates, with each side lauding its own behavior but condemning that of its adversaries as heinous.

Advantageous comparisons also draw heavily on history to justify violence. Terrorists are quick to note that the French and Americans got their democracies through violent overthrow of oppressive rule, and the Jewish people got their homeland by paramilitary violence. Terrorists claim entitlement to the same tactics to rout those they regard as their oppressors. A former director of the CIA effectively deflected, by expedient comparison, embarrassing questions about the morality and legality of CIA-directed covert operations designed to overthrow an authoritarian regime. He explained that French covert operations and military supplies greatly aided the overthrow of oppressive British rule during the War of Independence, thereby creating the modern model of democracy for other subjugated people to emulate.

Social comparison is similarly used to show that the social labeling of acts as terrorism depends more on the ideological allegiances of the labelers than on the acts themselves. Airline hijackings were applauded as heroic deeds when East Europeans and Cubans initiated this practice, but condemned as terrorist acts when the airliners of Western nations and friendly countries were commandeered. The degree of psychopathology ascribed to hijackers varied depending on the direction of the rerouted flights. Moral condemnations of politically motivated terrorism are easily blunted by social comparison because, in international contests of power, it is hard to find nations that categorically condemn terrorism. Instead, they often back the perpetrators they like but condemn those they repudiate.

Violent countermeasures to deter terrorists from future assaults inevitably sacrifice innocent lives. Democratic societies face the fundamental moral dilemma of how to justify countermeasures that are taken to stop terrorists' atrocities without violating the values of their society in defense of those values (Carmichael, 1982). Because of many uncertain factors, the toll that counterterrorist assaults may take on innocent life is neither easily controllable nor accurately calculable in advance.

Moral justification of violent countermeasures by expedient comparison relies heavily on utilitarian principles. The task of making retaliatory violence morally acceptable from a utilitarian perspective is facilitated by two sets of judgments. First, nonviolent options are judged to be ineffective to achieve desired changes. This removes them from consideration. Second, utilitarian analyses affirm that one's injurious actions may prevent more human suffering than they cause. Curbing terrorism benefits humanity and the social order. Thus, on the assumption that fighting terror with terror will achieve a deterrent effect, it is argued that retaliatory assaults will reduce the total amount of human suffering.

As Carmichael (1982) noted, utilitarian justifications place few constraints on violent countermeasures because, in the utilitarian calculus, sacrificing the lives of some innocent persons can be greatly outweighed by halting terrorist massacres and the perpetual terrorizing of entire populations. However, the utilitarian calculus is quite slippery in specific applications.

Lethal countermeasures are readily justified in response to grave threats that inflict extensive human pain or that endanger the very survival of the society. However, the criterion of "grave threat," although fine in principle, is shifty in specific circumstances. Like most human judgments, gauging the gravity of threats involves some subjectivity. Moreover, violence is often used as a weapon against threats of lesser magnitude on the grounds that, if left unchecked, the threats may escalate to the point of extracting a heavy toll on human liberties and suffering. Gauging potential gravity involves even greater subjectivity and hence fallibility of judgment than does assessment of present danger. The future contains many uncertainties, and human judgment is subject to a lot of biases (Nisbett & Ross, 1980). Assessment of gravity prescribes the choice of options, but choice of violent options often shapes evaluation of gravity itself. Thus, projected grave dangers to the society are commonly invoked in the moral justification of violent means to squelch present objections. The perturbing appearance of national impotence in the face of terrorist acts creates additional social pressures on targeted nations to strike back powerfully.

EUPHEMISTIC LANGUAGE

Language shapes the thought patterns on which people base many of their actions. Activities, therefore, can take on a markedly different character depending on what they are called. Euphemistic language is used widely to make harmful conduct respectable and to reduce personal responsibility for it (Lutz, 1987). Euphemizing can be an injurious weapon. People behave much more cruelly when assault actions are given a sanitized label than when they are called *aggression* (Diener, Dineen, Endresen, Beaman, & Fraser, 1975).

In an insightful analysis of the language of nonresponsibility, Gambino (1973) identified the different varieties of euphemisms. One form relies on sanitizing language. Through the power of sanitized language, even killing a human being loses much of its repugnancy. Soldiers "waste" people rather than kill them. What most people call bombs, the military calls "vertically deployed anti-personal devices." Bombing missions are described as "servicing the target," in the likeness of a public utility. The attacks become "clean, surgical strikes," arousing imagery of curative activities. The civilians the bombs kill are linguistically converted to "collateral damage." Many are victims of bombs that were "outside current accuracy requirements." Soldiers killed by misdirected missiles fired by their own forces are the tragic recipients of "friendly fire."

The agentless passive form serves as a linguistic device for creating the appearance that harmful acts are the work of nameless forces, rather than people (Bollinger, 1982). It is as though people are moved mechanically but are not really the agents of their own acts. Gambino further documented how the specialized jargon of a legitimate enterprise can be misused to lend an aura of respectability to an illegitimate one. Deadly activities are framed as "game plans," and the perpetrators become "team players," a status calling for the qualities and behavior befitting the best sportsmen. The disinhibitory power of language can be boosted further by colorful metaphors that change the nature of destructive activities.

Cognitive restructuring of harmful conduct by moral justifications, sanitizing language, and expedient comparisons is the most effective set of psychological mechanisms for disengaging moral control. Investing harmful conduct with high moral purpose not only eliminates self-censure so destructive acts can be performed without personal distress and moral qualms. Sanctification engages self-approval in the service of destructive exploits. What was once morally condemnable becomes a source of self-valuation. Functionaries work hard to become proficient at them and take pride in their destructive accomplishments.

DISPLACEMENT OF RESPONSIBILITY

Moral control operates most strongly when people acknowledge that they are contributors to harmful outcomes. The second set of disengagement practices operates by obscuring or minimizing the agentive role in the harm one causes. People will behave in ways they normally repudiate if a legitimate authority accepts responsibility for the effects of their conduct (Diener, 1977; Milgram, 1974). Under displaced responsibility, they view their actions as stemming from the dictates of authorities rather than from their own personal responsibility. Because they feel they are not the actual agent of their actions, they are spared self-condemning reactions.

In terrorism sponsored by states or governments in exile, functionaries view themselves as patriots fulfilling nationalistic duties rather than as freelancing criminals. Displacement of responsibility not only weakens moral restraints over one's own detrimental actions but diminishes social concern over the well-being of those mistreated by others (Tilker, 1970).

Self-exemption from gross inhumanities by displacement of responsibility is most gruesomely revealed in socially sanctioned mass executions. Nazi prison commandants and their staffs divested themselves of personal responsibility for their unprecedentedly inhumane acts (Andrus, 1969). They claimed they were simply carrying out orders. Self-exonerating obedience to horrific orders is similarly evident in military atrocities, such as the My Lai massacre (Kelman, 1973).

In an effort to deter institutionally sanctioned atrocities, the Nuremberg Accords declared that obedience to inhumane orders, even from the highest authorities, does not relieve subordinates of the responsibility for their actions. However, because victors are disinclined to try themselves as criminals, such decrees have limited deterrent effect without an international judiciary system empowered to impose penalties on victors and losers alike.

In psychological studies of disengagement of moral control by displacement of responsibility, authorities explicitly authorize injurious actions and hold themselves responsible for the harm caused by their followers (Milgram, 1974). However, the sanctioning of pernicious conduct in everyday life differs in two important ways from Milgram's authorizing system. Responsibility is rarely assumed that openly. Only obtuse authorities would leave themselves accusable of authorizing destructive acts. They usually invite and support harmful conduct in insidious ways by surreptitious sanctioning systems for personal and social reasons. Sanctioning by indirection shields them from social condemnation should things go awry. It also enables them to protect against loss of self-respect for authorizing human cruelty that leaves blood on their hands. Implicit agreements and insulating social arrangements are created that leave the higher echelons blameless.

Kramer (1990) described the great lengths to which Shiite clerics go to produce moral justifications for violent acts that breach Islamic law, such as suicidal bombings and hostage-taking. These efforts are designed not only to persuade themselves of the morality of their actions but also to preserve their integrity in the eyes of rival clerics and other nations. The Islamic religious code permits neither suicide nor the terrorizing of innocent people. On the one hand, the clerics justify such acts by invoking situational imperatives and utilitarian reasons, namely that tyrannical circumstances drive oppressed people to resort to unconventional means to route aggressors who wield massive destructive power. On the other hand, they reconstrue terrorist acts as conventional means in which dying in a suicidal bombing for a moral cause is no different than dying at the hands of an enemy soldier. Hostages typically get relabeled as spies. When the linguistic solution defies credibility, personal moral responsibility is disengaged by construing terrorist acts as dictated by their foe's tyranny. Because of the shaky moral logic and disputable reconstruals involved, clerics sanction terrorism by indirection, they vindicate successful ventures retrospectively, and they disclaim endorsements of terrorist operations beforehand.

Nation states sponsor terrorist operations through disguised, roundabout routes that make it difficult to pin the blame on them. Moreover, the intended purpose of sanctioned destructiveness is usually linguistically disguised so that neither issuers nor perpetrators regard the activity as censurable. When condemnable practices gain public attention, they are officially dismissed as only isolated incidents arising through misunderstanding of what, in fact, had been authorized. Efforts are made to limit the blame to subordinates, who are portrayed as misguided or overzealous.

A number of social factors affect the ease with which responsibility for one's actions can be passed to others. High justification and social consensus about the morality of an enterprise aid in the relinquishment of personal control. The legitimacy of the authorizers is another important determinant. The higher the authorities, the more legitimacy, respect, and coercive power they command, the more willing are people to defer to them. Modeled disobedience, which challenges the legitimacy of the activities, if not the authorizers themselves, reduces the willingness of observers to carry out the actions called for by the orders of a superior (Meeus & Raaijmakers, 1986; Milgram, 1974; Powers & Geen, 1972). It is difficult to continue to disown personal agency in the face of evident harm that results directly from one's actions. People are, therefore, less willing to obey authoritarian orders to carry out injurious behavior when they see firsthand how they are hurting others (Milgram, 1974; Tilker, 1970).

Perpetration of inhumanities requires obedient functionaries. They do not cast off all responsibility for their behavior as if they were mindless extensions of others. If they disowned all responsibility, they would be quite unreliable, performing their duties only when commanded to do so. In situations involving obedience to authority, people carry out orders partly to honor the obligations they have undertaken (Mantell & Panzarella, 1976). In fact, they tend to be conscientious and self-directed in the performance of their duties. It requires a strong sense of responsibility to be a good functionary. One must, therefore, distinguish between two levels of responsibility: A strong sense of duty to one's superiors and accountability for the effects of one's actions. The best functionaries are those who honor their obligations to authorities but feel no personal responsibility for the harm they cause.

Displacement of responsibility also operates in situations in which hostages are taken. Terrorists warn officials of targeted nations that if they take retaliatory action they will be held accountable for the lives of the hostages. At different steps in negotiations for the hostages' release, terrorists continue to displace responsibility for the safety of hostages on the national officials they are fighting. If the captivity drags on, terrorists blame the suffering and injuries they inflict on their hostages on the officials for failing to make what they regard as warranted concessions to remedy social wrongs.

DIFFUSION OF RESPONSIBILITY

The deterrent power of self-sanctions is weakened when the link between detrimental conduct and its effects is obscured by diffusing responsibility. This is achieved in several ways. Responsibility can be diffused by division of labor. Most enterprises require the services of many people, each performing fragmentary jobs that, taken individually, seems harmless. The partial contribution is easily isolated from the eventual function, especially when participants exercise little personal judgment in carrying out a subfunction that is related by remote, complex links to the end result. After activities become routinized into programmed subfunctions, people shift their attention from the meaning of what they are doing to the details of their job (Kelman, 1973).

Group decision making is another common bureaucratic practice that enables otherwise considerate people to behave inhumanely, because no single individual feels responsible for policies arrived at collectively. Where everyone is responsible, no one really feels responsible. Social organizations go to great lengths to devise sophisticated mechanisms for obscuring responsibility for decisions that may affect others adversely. Collective action, which provides anonymity, is still another diffusion expedient for weakening self-restraints. Any harm done by a group can always be attributed in large part to the behavior of other members. People act more cruelly under group responsibility than when they hold themselves personally accountable for their actions (Bandura, Underwood, & Fromson, 1975; Diener, 1977; Zimbardo, 1969).

DISREGARD OR DISTORTION OF HARMFUL CONSEQUENCES

To be able to perpetrate inhumanities requires more than absolving oneself of personal responsibility. Other ways of weakening moral self-sanctions operate by minimizing, disregarding, or distorting the effects of one's action. When people pursue activities that harm others, they avoid facing the harm they cause or minimize it. If minimization does not work, the evidence of harm can be discredited. As long as the harmful results of one's conduct are ignored, minimized, distorted, or disbelieved, there is little reason for self-censure.

It is easier to harm others when their suffering is not visible and when destructive actions are physically and temporally remote from their injurious effects. Our death technologies have become highly lethal and depersonalized. We are now in the era of faceless electronic warfare, in which mass destruction is delivered remotely with deadly accuracy by computer and laser controlled systems.

When people can see and hear the suffering they cause, vicariously aroused distress and self-censure serve as self-restrainers (Bandura, 1992). In studies of obedient aggression, people are less compliant to the injurious commands of authorities as the victims' pain becomes more evident and personalized (Milgram, 1974). Even a high sense of personal responsibility for the effects of one's actions is a weak restrainer of injurious conduct when aggressors do not see the harm they inflict on their victims (Tilker, 1970).

Most organizations involve hierarchical chains of command, in which superiors formulate plans and intermediaries transmit them to functionaries who then carry them out. The farther removed individuals are from the destructive end results, the weaker is the restraining power of injurious effects. Disengagement of moral control is easiest for the intermediaries in a hierarchical system—they neither bear responsibility for the decisions, nor do they carry them out or face the harm being inflicted (Kilham & Mann, 1974). In performing the transmitter role, they model dutiful behavior and further legitimize their superiors and their social policies and practices.

A Pulitzer Prize was awarded for a powerful photograph that captured the anguished cries of a little girl whose clothes were burned off by the napalm bombing of her village in Vietnam (Chong, 2000). This single humanization of inflicted destruction probably did more to turn the American public against the war than the countless reports filed by journalists. The military now bans cameras and journalists from battlefield areas to block disturbing images of death and destruction that can erode public support for resolving international dispute by military means. With the advent of satellite transmission, battles are now fought on the airwaves over "collateral damage" to shape public perceptions of military campaigns and debates about them. For example, in the escalating cycle of terrorism and military retaliation in the Middle East, the Arab news network, Al-Jazeera, airs graphic real-time images of death and destruction round-the-clock (El-Nawawy & Iskandar, 2002). In the Iraq war, reporters were again allowed to accompany combat forces to present a different perspective from the one broadcast by Al Jazeera. Satellite television has thus become a strategic tool in the social management of moral disengagement at the locus of the human consequences of lethal means.

The aim of terrorists is to inflict widespread destruction. The moral dilemma for targeted nations is how to conduct counterterrorist operations that abide by just war standards. The magnitude of civilian casualties accompanying military campaigns is typically minimized by focusing mainly on "collateral damage" resulting directly from military strikes. When the counterstrikes destroy power, water, sanitation, and food distribution systems, they leave in their wake ill and malnourished populations who face a daily struggle to survive. High-tech bombardment may reduce the number of civilians killed, but it vastly increases the human toll when it destroys a nation's infrastructure.

ATTRIBUTION OF BLAME

Blaming one's adversaries or compelling circumstances for harmful acts is still another expedient that can serve self-exonerative purposes. In this process, people view themselves as faultless victims driven to extreme means by forcible provocation rather than acting on a deliberative decision. Conflictful transactions typically involve reciprocally escalative acts. One can select from the chain of events a defensive act by the adversary and portray it as the initiating provocation. Victims then get blamed for bringing suffering on themselves. Those who are victimized are not entirely faultless because, by their behavior, they contribute partly to their own plight. Victims can, therefore, be blamed for bringing suffering on themselves. By fixing the blame on others or on circumstances, not only are one's own injurious actions made excusable, but one can even feel self-righteous in the process.

Victim blaming by ascription of responsibility figures prominently in attribution theory (Weiner, 1986). However, the mechanism by which blaming spawns inhumane conduct has received less attention. In social cognitive theory (Bandura, 1986), victim blaming functions as a means of disengaging moral self-sanctions that operate in concert with other means serving the same purpose.

Terrorist acts that take a heavy toll on civilian lives create special personal pressures to lay blame elsewhere. Irish Republican Army guerrillas planted a large bomb that killed and maimed many family members attending a war memorial ceremony in a town square in Enniskillen, Northern Ireland ("IRA 'Regrets' Bombing," 1987). The guerrillas promptly ascribed the blame for the civilian massacre to the British army for having detonated the bomb prematurely with an electronic scanning device. The government denounced the "pathetic attempt to transfer blame" because no scanning equipment was in use at the time.

Observers of victimization can be disinhibited in much the same way as perpetrators are by the tendency to infer culpability from misfortune. Seeing victims suffer maltreatment for which they are held partially responsible leads observers to derogate them (M. J. Lerner & Miller, 1978). The devaluation and indignation aroused by ascribed culpability, in turn, provides moral justification for even greater maltreatment. That attribution of blame can give rise to devaluation and moral justification illustrates how the various disengagement mechanisms are often interrelated and work together in weakening moral control.

Self-vindication is easily achievable by terrorists when legitimate grievances of maltreatment are willfully disregarded by powerholders so that terrorist activities are construed as acts of self-protection or desperation. Oppressive and inhumane social conditions and thwarted political efforts breed terrorists who often see foreign government complicity in their plight through support of the regime that they see as victimizing them. Those who become radicalized carry out terrorist acts against the regime as well as the implicated foreign nations. Violent countermeasures are readily resorted to in efforts to control terrorist activities when the social conditions breeding discontent and violent protest are firmly entrenched in political systems that obstruct legitimate efforts at change. It is much easier to attack violent protests than to change the sociopolitical conditions that fuel them. In such skirmishes, one person's victim is another person's victimizer.

DEHUMANIZATION

The final set of disengagement practices operates on the targets of violent acts. The strength of moral self-sanctions partly depends on how perpetrators view the people toward whom the violence is directed. To perceive another as human enhances empathetic reactions through a sense of common humanity (Bandura, 1992). The joys and suffering of similar persons are more vicariously arousing than are those of strangers or of those divested of human qualities. Personalizing the injurious effects experienced by others also makes their suffering much more salient. As a result, it is difficult to mistreat humanized persons without risking self-condemnation.

Self-censure for cruel conduct can be disengaged or blunted by stripping people of human qualities. Once dehumanized, they are no longer viewed as persons with feelings, hopes, and concerns but as subhuman forms. They are portrayed as mindless "savages," "gooks," "satanic fiends," and the like. Subhumans are regarded as insensitive to maltreatment and influenceable only by harsh methods. If dispossessing one's foes of humanness does not weaken self-censure, then the latter can be eliminated by attributing demonic or bestial qualities to them. They become "Satanic fiends," "degenerates," "vermin," or other bestial creatures. It is easier to brutalize victims, for example, when they are referred to as "worms" (Haritos-Fatouros, 2002).

"Evil" has become very much in vogue as the current form of demonization. It conjures up the image of an unfathomable pernicious force that ruthlessly drives evildoers. As previously noted, inhumanities are typically perpetrated by people who can be quite considerate and compassionate in other areas of their lives. They can even be ruthless and humane simultaneously toward different individuals. This selectivity of moral engagement is strikingly illustrated by Goeth, a Nazi labor commandant. While dictating a letter replete with empathy and compassion for his ailing father, he sees a captive on the grounds who he thinks is not working hard enough. He whips out his revolver and callously shoots the captive. The commandant is both overcome with compassion and is savagely cruel at the same time. By using a description in the guise of an explanation, ready attribution of violence to evil stifles analysis of the determinants governing inhumane conduct.

Studies of interpersonal aggression give vivid testimony to the disinhibitory power of dehumanization (Bandura et al., 1975). Dehumanized individuals are treated much more punitively than those who have been invested with human qualities. When punitiveness does not achieve results, this is taken as further evidence of the unworthiness of dehumanized persons, thus justifying even greater maltreatment. Dehumanization fosters different self-exonerative patterns of thought. People seldom condemn punitive conduct, and they create justifications for it when they are directing their aggression at persons who have been deprived of their humanness. By contrast, people strongly disapprove of punitive actions and rarely excuse them when they are directed at persons depicted in humanized terms.

Under certain conditions, the exercise of power changes the users in ways that are conducive to further dehumanization. This happens most often when persons in positions of authority have unconstrained coercive power over others. Powerholders come to devalue those over whom they wield control (Kipnis, 1974). In a simulated prison experiment (Haney, Banks, & Zimbardo, 1973), even college students, who had been randomly chosen to serve as either inmates or guards and who had been given relatively unrestrained power, began to treat their charges in degrading, tyrannical ways. Thus, role assignment that authorized use of coercive power overrode personal characteristics in promoting punitive conduct. Systematic tests of relative influences similarly show that aggressive modeling and normative pressures exert considerably greater power over aggressive conduct than do people's personal characteristics (Larsen, Coleman, Forbes, & Johnson, 1972).

The overall findings from research on the different mechanisms of moral disengagement corroborate the historical chronicle of human atrocities: Conducive social conditions rather than monstrous people are required to produce heinous deeds. Given appropriate social conditions, decent, ordinary people can be led to do extraordinarily cruel things.

As alluded to in previous analyses, moral disengagement involves social machinations, not just personal intrapsychic ones. In moral justification, for example, people may be misled by those they trust into believing that violent means prevent more harm than they cause. The benefits that are socially declared may be exaggerated or just pious rhetoric masking less honorable purposes. Cultural prejudices shape which human beings get grouped and dehumanized and the types of depraved attributes ascribed to them. Social systems are structured in ways that make it easy for functionaries to absolve themselves of responsibility for the effects of their actions. Communication systems can be institutionally managed in ways that keep people uninformed or misinformed about the harm caused by the collective action. In summary, moral disengagement is a product of the interplay of both personal and social maneuvers.

PROMOTION OF EMPATHIC HUMANENESS
THROUGH MORAL ENGAGEMENT

Psychological research emphasizes how easy it is to bring out the worst in people through dehumanization and other means of self-exoneration. The sensational negative findings receive the greatest attention. Thus, for example, the aspect of Milgram's research on obedient aggression that is most widely cited is the evidence that good people can be talked into performing cruel deeds. However, to get people to carry out punitive acts, the overseer had to be physically present repeatedly ordered them to act cruelly as they voiced their concerns and objections and accepted responsibility for any harm caused. Orders to escalate punitiveness to more intense levels are largely ignored or subverted when remotely issued by verbal command. As Helm and Morelli (1979) noted, this is hardly an example of blind obedience triggered by an authoritative mandate. Moreover, what is rarely noted is the equally striking evidence that most people steadfastly refuse to behave cruelly, even in response to strong authoritarian commands, if the situation is personalized by having them see the victim or requiring them to inflict pain directly rather than remotely.

The emphasis on obedient aggression is understandable considering the prevalence and severity of people's inhumanities toward one another. However, there is considerable theoretical and social significance in the power of humanization to counteract cruel conduct. Studies examining this process reveal that, even under conditions that weaken self-deterrents, it is difficult for individuals to behave cruelly toward others when they are humanized or even personalized a bit (Bandura et al., 1975).

Experimental research underscores the centrality of a sense of common humanity in the development of interpersonal empathy (Bandura, 1982). Seeing one's welfare as tied to the well-being of others arouses empathic reactions to their joys and sufferings. Conversely, competitive and discordant experiences, in which another's gain brings suffering to oneself, create counter-empathy. Similarly, people respond empathically to the emotional experiences of others simply depicted as in-group members, and counter-empathetically to those portrayed as out-group members, in the absence of having shared any experiences with them. If a sense of mutuality has been created, so that the joys and distresses of an out-group member foretell similar experiences for the observers, correlative outcomes transform disempathy to empathy. In the international strife sparked by the September 11th terrorist attack, both sides in the conflict trade heavily on polarizing rhetoric of "us" versus "them" with ascriptions of evil to each other (Mandel, 2002).

The exercise of moral agency has dual aspects, inhibitive and proactive (Bandura, 1999). The inhibitive form is manifested in the power to refrain from behaving inhumanely. The proactive form of morality is expressed in the power to behave humanely. In the latter form of morality, people do good things as well as refrain from doing bad things. The investment of common humanity at each locus of moral self-regulation tends to foster humaneness. In the exercise of proactive morality, people act in the name of humane principles even when social circumstances dictate expedient, transgressive, and detrimental conduct. They disavow the use of "worthy" social ends to justify destructive means. They are willing to sacrifice their well-being rather than accede to unjust social practices. They take personal responsibility for the consequences of their actions. They remain sensitive to the suffering of others. Finally, they see human commonalities rather than distance themselves from others or divest them of human qualities.

TRANSFORMATIVE POWER OF HUMANIZATION

The transformative power of humanization is graphically illustrated in the midst of the military massacre in My Lai (Zganjar, 1998). An American platoon, led by Lt. Calley, had massacred 500 Vietnamese women, children, and elderly men. Detailed analyses of the massacre in this village have documented how moral self-sanctions were disengaged from the brutal collective conduct (Kelman & Hamilton, 1989). A ceremony, 30 years in coming, was held at the Vietnam Veteran's Memorial honoring extraordinary heroism of prosocial morality in the midst of this carnage. Thompson, a young helicopter pilot, swooped down over the village of My Lai on a search and destroy mission as the massacre was occurring. He spotted an injured girl, marked the spot with a smoke signal, and radioed for help. Much to his horror, he saw a soldier flip her over and spray her with a round of bullets. Upon seeing the human carnage in an irrigation ditch and soldiers firing into the bodies, he realized that he was in the midst of a massacre.

He was moved to moral action by the sight of a terrified woman with a baby in her arms and a frightened child clinging to her leg. He explained his sense of common humanity, "These people were looking at me for help and there is no way I could turn my back on them." He told a platoon officer to help him remove the remaining villagers. The officer replied, "The only help they'll get is a hand grenade." Thompson moved his helicopter in the line of fire and commanded his gunner to fire on his approaching countrymen if they tried to harm the family. He radioed the accompanying gunships for help, and together they airlifted the remaining dozen villagers to safety. He flew back to the irrigation ditch where they found and rescued a 2-year-old boy still clinging to his dead mother. Thompson described his empathetic human linkage: "I had a son at home about the same age."

The affirmation of common humanity can bring out the best in people. The transformative power of humanization is further illustrated in a daughter's mission of vengeance (Blumenfeld, 2002). Her father, a New York rabbi, was shot and wounded in Jerusalem by Omar, a Palestinian militant. Twelve years later she set out to gain revenge by forcing him to confront his victim's humanity. In the course of exchanging letters under a concealed identity with the jailed gunman, the parental victim, militant gunman, and filial avenger were humanized in the process. In a dramatic courtroom parole hearing, the daughter identified herself to Omar as she pleaded for his release from prison, vowing he would never hurt anyone again. He wrote to her father likening his daughter to "the mirror that made me see your face as a human person," which "deserved to be admired and respected." This is a case of hatred that breeds escalative cycles of violence turned into mutual compassion. At the national level, Nelson Mandela singularly displaced hatred of apartheid with reconciliation by affirming common humanity.

GRADUALISTIC MORAL DISENGAGEMENT

Disengagement practices do not instantly transform considerate persons into cruel ones who purposely set out to kill other human beings. Rather, the change is achieved by gradual disengagement of self-censure. Terrorist behavior evolves through extensive training in moral disengagement rather than emerging full-blown at the outset. The path to terrorism can be shaped by fortuitous factors as well as by the conjoint influence of personal predilections and sociopolitical inducements (Bandura, 1982). Development of the capability to kill is usually achieved through an evolvement process, in which recruits may not recognize the transformation they are undergoing (Bandura, 1986; Franks & Powers, 1970; Haritos-Fatouros, 2002). The disinhibitory training is usually conducted within a communal milieu of intense interpersonal influences insulated from mainstream social life. The recruits become deeply immersed in the ideology and functional roles of the group. Initially, they are prompted to perform unpleasant acts that they can tolerate without much self-censure. Gradually, their discomfort and self-reproof are weakened to ever higher levels of ruthlessness through extensive performance and through extensive exposure to aggressive modeling by more experienced associates. The various disengagement practices form an integral part of the training for terrorism. Eventually, acts originally regarded as abhorrent can be performed callously. Inhumane practices become thoughtlessly routinized.

Escalative self-disinhibition is accelerated if violent courses of action are presented as serving a moral imperative, and the targeted people are divested of human qualities (Bandura et al., 1975). The training not only instills the moral rightness and importance of the cause for militant action; it also creates a sense of eliteness and provides the social rewards of solidarity and group esteem for excelling in terrorist exploits.

Sprinzak (1986, 1990) has shown that terrorists, whether on the political left or right, evolve gradually rather than setting out to become radicals. The process of radicalization involves a gradual disengagement of moral self-sanctions from violent conduct. It begins with prosocial efforts to change particular social policies and opposition to officials, who are intent on keeping things as they are. Embittering failures to accomplish social change and hostile confrontations with authorities and police lead to growing disillusionment and alienation from the whole system. Escalative battles culminate in terrorists' efforts to destroy the system and its dehumanized rulers.

MORAL DISENGAGEMENT IN THE MERCHANDISING OF DEATHLY WARES

The preceding analyses have been concerned mainly with how disengagement mechanisms are enlisted in the service of terrorist violence and in combating terrorism by violent means. These same mechanisms are also heavily enlisted by terrorist entrepreneurs, who supply militant states with the lethal tools to terrorize their own people or to equip the terrorist groups they sponsor. Frank Terpil, who became a terrorist entrepreneur after he fell from grace at the CIA, provides vivid testimony to these psychological mechanisms (Thomas, 1982).

This deathly operation is especially informative because it reveals in stark detail that those who trade in human destruction do not do it alone. They depend heavily on the collective moral disengagement of a vast network of reputable citizens managing respectable enterprises. Terpil masked his death operations in the euphemisms of a legitimate business fulfilling "consumer needs" under the sanitized name Intercontinental Technology. To spare himself any self-censure for contributing to human atrocities, he actively avoided knowledge of the purposes to which his weapons would be put. "I don't ever want to know that," he said. When asked whether he was ever haunted by any thoughts of human suffering his deathly wares might cause, he explained that a weapons dealer cannot afford to think about human consequences. Banishing thoughts of injurious consequences frees one's actions from the restraints of conscience. "If I really thought about the consequences all the time, I certainly wouldn't have been in this business. You have to blank it off."

Probes for any signs of self-reproach only brought self-exonerative comparisons. When asked if he felt any qualms about supplying torture equipment to Idi Amin, Terpil replied with justification by advantageous comparison with employees' production of napalm at Dow Chemical. As he put it, "I'm sure that the people from Dow Chemical didn't think of the consequences of selling napalm. If they did, they wouldn't be working at the factory. I doubt very much if they'd feel any more responsible for the ultimate use than I did for my equipment." When pressed about the atrocities committed at Amin's torture chambers under the sanitized designation State Research Bureau, Terpil repeated his depersonalized view, "I do not get wrapped up emotionally with the country. I regard myself basically as neutral, and commercial." To give legitimacy to his "private practice," he claimed that he aided British and American covert operations abroad as well.

What began as a psychological analysis of the operator of a death industry ended unexpectedly in an international network of supporting legitimate enterprises run by upstanding conscientious people. The merchandising of terrorism is not accomplished by a few unsavory individuals. It requires a worldwide network of people, including reputable, high-level members of society, who contribute to the deathly enterprise by insulating fractionation of the operations and displacement and diffusion of responsibility. Some people manufacture the tools of destruction. Others amass the arsenals for legitimate sale. Others operate storage centers for them. Others procure export and import licenses to move the deathly wares among different countries. Others obtain spurious end-user certificates that get the weaponry to embargoed nations through circuitous routes. Still others ship the lethal wares. The cogs in this worldwide network include weapons manufacturers; former government officials with political ties; ex-diplomatic, military, and intelligence officers who provide valuable diplomatic skills and contacts; weapons merchants and shippers operating legitimate businesses; money raisers to finance terrorist activities; and bankers laundering and moving money through legitimate financial systems. By fragmenting and dispersing subfunctions of the enterprise, the various contributors see themselves as decent, legitimate practitioners of their trade rather than as parties to deathly operations.

Even producers of the television program *60 Minutes* contributed to Terpil's coffers ("CBS Reportedly Paid 2 Fugitives," 1983). Terpil skipped bail to a foreign sanctuary after he was caught selling assassination equipment to an undercover FBI agent. He was tried in absentia. The District Attorney confronted the lead reporter of the program about a payment of $12,000 to an intermediary for an interview with the fugitive, Terpil. The reporter pleaded innocence through various disengagement maneuvers.

MORAL JUSTIFICATION IN THE USE OF COUNTERTERRORIST MEASURES

A comprehensive analysis of terrorism must also address how targeted nations grapple with terrorist violence. Hostage taking is a common terrorist strategy for wielding control over governments. If nations make the release of hostages a dominant national concern, they place themselves in a highly manipulable position. Tightly concealed captivity thwarts rescue action. Heightened national attention along with an inability to free hostages independently conveys a sense of weakness and invests terrorists with considerable importance and coercive power to extract concessions. Overreactions in which nations render themselves hostage to a small band of terrorists inspires and invites further terrorist acts. Hostage taking is stripped of functional value if it is treated as a criminal act that gains terrorists neither coercive concessionary power nor significant media attention.

Extreme retaliatory attacks that cause widespread death and destruction may advance the political cause of terrorists by arousing a backlash of sympathy for innocent victims and moral condemnation of the brutal nature of the attacks. To fight terror with terror often creates a ready supply of recruits prepared to die for their cause, even by suicidal martyrdom. Brute means also provide new justification for violence that escalates terrorism rather than diminishes it. Indeed, some terrorist activities are designed precisely to gain worldwide support for their cause and to provoke curtailment of personal liberties and other domestic repressive measures that might breed public disaffection with the system. Extreme countermeasures can, thus, play into the hands of terrorists.

Efforts to reduce societal vulnerabilities with better counterterrorist technologies beget better terrorist tactics and devices. A security officer characterized such escalating adaptations well when he remarked that, "For every 10-foot wall you erect, terrorists will build an 11-foot ladder." Technological advances are producing more sophisticated terrorizing devices that increase societal vulnerability.

Some nations pursue the policy that terrorist acts will be promptly answered with massive deathly retaliation, whatever the cost, on the grounds that this is the price one must pay to check terrorism. Opponents of such policies argue that retaliatory overkill only fuels greater terrorism by creating more terrorists and increasing public sympathy for the causes that drive them to terroristic violence. Vigorous debates are fought over whether massive retaliation curbs terrorism or breeds an escalative cycle of terror.

At the geopolitical level, nations increase their vulnerability to terrorism by foreign marriages of convenience that prop up oppressive regimes. These life conditions, which spawn enmity, wrath, and political instability, become the breeding ground for terrorism. In the short-term solutions, terrorists must be routed and made to bear the consequences for their destructive acts. Here the issue of concern is whether military force is used in accordance with just war principles or in vengeful ways that violate the society's moral standards. The long-term solutions require promoting social reforms that better the life conditions of people. A focus on fighting violence with violence while neglecting needed long-term remedies is likely to produce an escalative cycle of terror and retaliation.

The preceding discussion has centered mainly on how terrorists invoke moral standards to justify human atrocities and selectively disengage these standards in conducting terrorist activities. Terrorism and fighting it with military force involve two-sided moral disengagement. Moral justification is brought into play just as surely as selecting and executing counterterrorist campaigns. This poses more troublesome problems for democratic societies than for totalitarian ones. Totalitarian regimes have fewer constraints against using institutional power to control media coverage of terrorist events, to restrict human rights, to sacrifice individuals for the benefit of the state rather than make concessions to terrorists, and to combat terrorist threats with lethal means. Terrorists can wield greater power over nations that place high value on human life and personal liberties. This constrains the ways they can act.

The terrorist attacks by the al-Qaeda network on U.S. consulates and military installations abroad and the devastating strike on the U.S. homeland presented a grave national threat with reverberating domestic and international consequences. It shattered the sense of national invulnerability, crippled major sectors of the society with worldwide economic repercussions, heightened cultural clashes between secular modernists and religious fundamentalists within Islamic nations and against Western nations, reordered geopolitical debates and international alliances, and launched widespread retaliatory military campaigns abroad to root out terrorist sanctuaries. It was a different order of terrorism conducted by a well-financed elusive enemy operating through a worldwide network aimed at fomenting a holy war between the Western world and the Islamic world. The terrorist strikes called for national protective countermeasures to deter further terrorist attacks.

Fighting terrorism with military force presents moral dilemmas on the execution of military means. Midway through a nationwide study on selective disengagement of moral agency in support of military force, the nation witnessed the demolition of the World Trade Center and part of the Pentagon by the al-Qaeda network (McAlister, Bandura, Morrison, & Grussendorf, 2003). The terrorist strike raised the level of moral disengagement. The higher the moral disengagement, the stronger the public support for immediate retaliatory strikes against suspected terrorist sanctuaries abroad and for aerial bombardment of Iraq. Further research is needed to determine how the level of moral disengagement affects the form, scope, and intensity of countermeasures the public supports.

The just war principles of necessity, proportionality, discriminativeness, and humanity (Walzer, 1992) provide some guidelines for defensive military campaigns. They specify the just grounds for resort to military force and the form, scope, and intensity of military means that are morally defensible. Viewed from this framework, military counterstrikes are justified as the last resort after nonviolent means have been exhausted; the military campaign is limited to the level of force needed to eradicate the threat; and the counterstrikes are conducted in ways that minimize civilian casualties.

Just cause is a further principle of justifiability. A military intervention may fulfill the previously mentioned standards but be used for economic and strategic self-interest. The force must be used for a just cause rather than for vengeance, control of resources, or geopolitical advantage. Just causes can be undermined by brute means. Unilateral military intervention can also taint humanitarian intentions with geopolitical designs. The oft-ready transmutation of allies of convenience into foes and foes into allies of convenience creates skepticism about avowed just causes. By advantageous comparison, authoritarian regimes legitimize their own brutal practices against militant dissidents within their society by likening their brutality to the war on terrorism.

Morally calibrated countermeasures that involve restrained and discriminate use of military force help to gain and maintain domestic and international support. Cooperation with nation states is essential because uprooting terrorist threats must be pursued internationally. The aid of allies is even more critical for the tough and lengthy occupation and reconstruction programs required in the aftermath of war. Because of the geographic dispersion of the terrorist enemy, success requires a unified effort by countries to rid themselves of not only the terrorists in their midst but also of the ills within their societies that breed embittered and alienated populations. States must ameliorate these conditions largely by pushing for change from within. Foreign unilateral interventions can readily convert, in the eyes of the Islamic world, an antiterrorism campaign into a holy intercultural war. Indeed, morally undisciplined force is likely to beget more embittered terrorists willing to die in defense of their values and way of life.

The mounting of a counterterrorist military campaign creates a moral suasion war through airwaves on the construal and justification of the interventions. M. B. Smith (2002) provides a thoughtful analysis of the metaphoric labeling of retaliatory countermeasures as "War on Terrorism." Actual wars involve battles between states that end with the emergence of a victor. In contrast, the al-Qaeda enemy is a decentralized, loosely interconnected network operating surreptitiously worldwide without clear boundaries and extending its reach by coordinating the activities of dispersed affiliates. It is a new type of global enemy that is mobile, has no fixed geographic boundaries, and cannot be eradicated by ousting a leader. Suicide terrorism as an act of martyrdom serves as one of its weapons that defies control. This creates a situation where an incomplete military end is likely because dismantling a terrorist operation in a particular locale does not eliminate the threat elsewhere. For example, with porous borders and proxy ground forces of suspect allegiance, the massive Afghanistan military campaign relocated rather than eradicated the core al-Qaeda leadership, that continues to operate as a resurgent terrorist force spreading terrorism worldwide against an expanded range of coalition foes. In addition to selecting targets of high symbolic and economic value, the broadened aim breeds fear internationally by hitting easily accessible targets that are neither predictable nor protectable. Given globally dispersed semi-autonomous terrorist cells with ample replacement recruits for captured or slain operatives, this is not a readily winnable war. Recurrent terrorist attacks heighten sociopolitical pressures to deploy electronic tracking systems for large-scale domestic and international surveillance.

War metaphors create a mindset for war that helps to mobilize patriotic public support for military initiatives. Gilovich (1981) documented the power of comparative framing of military operations in enlisting support for military means. For instance, in judging how the United States should respond to a totalitarian threat toward a small nation by another country, people advocated a more interventionist course of action when the international crisis was likened to Munich, representing political appeasement of Nazi Germany, than when it was likened to another Vietnam, representing a disastrous military entanglement. The U.S. National Security Advisor likened allied opposition to a United Nations authorization of the use of force against Iraq to the appeasement of Hitler in the 1930s (Bernstein & Weisman, 2003). The Prime Minister of Great Britain similarly equated the opponent in the UN Security Council with the Nazi appeasers of yesteryear. Confinement by no-flight zones, continuous aerial surveillance, and bombardment of defensive and communications facilities, and disallowance of oil revenues is hardly appeasing treatment. Likening the terrorist threat to the so-called "axis of evil" to the axis powers of World War II provided further moral justification for military action. To bring the threat by comparative framing even closer to home, preemptive disarmament of Iraq was likened to the Cuban missile crisis.

The war metaphor also supported wartime restrictions on privacy rights and civil liberties. Justification by advantageous historical comparison vindicated the restrictions. The public was reminded that Lincoln did it during the Civil War, and Roosevelt did it during World War II. Under a high sense of personal vulnerability, concern for personal safety outweighs protection of privacy and civil liberties. Indeed, antiterrorism laws, granting the government broad domestic surveillance powers to access, scan, and profile information on personal activities without public oversight and accountability, received widespread public support.

One must distinguish between justification of self-defense by military force and justification of the military means used in the pursuit of the just cause. Routing al-Qaeda from their sanctuaries in Afghanistan was justifiable in terms of just war standards. It was achieved with remarkable swiftness by combining unrelenting aerial bombardment with Afghan warlords serving as the proxy army. Many of the international reactions, especially in Muslim societies, centered on the proportionality of force, the civilian toll, and the rightness of intention in the expansion of the war on terrorism to Iraq.

Drawing on historical contrast, the U.S. Defense Secretary acknowledged the inevitability of civilian causalities, but added, "We can take comfort in the knowledge that this war has seen fewer tragic losses of civilian life than perhaps any war in modern history" (Shanker, 2002). The military architect of the campaign downplayed reports of civilian casualties on the grounds that they are impossible to estimate reliably: "And so all of us have opted not to do that" (Coille, 2002). In the public view, precision-guided weapons spare innocents.

Televised scenes of Afghans celebrating the rout of the brutally tyrannical Taliban regime documented the humanitarian aspect of the military campaign. Civilian liberation from state terrorism with virtually no Allied casualties and seemingly minimal "collateral damage" persuaded even vocal critics of the use of lethal force that military means could serve as a humanitarian intervention. Some prominent liberalists became humanitarian hawks promoting the use of military power. Aerial bombardment together with proxy ground forces, which worked surprisingly well in Kosovo and speedily in Afghanistan, represent a model of warfare that the general public could support with few moral qualms. Ill-fitting metaphors can spawn military initiatives that beget continuing terrorism rather than restore public safety. Kosovo has become the operative metaphor for the times (Packer, 2002). Routing the autocratic regime from Kosovo in a finite military operation did not incite a worldwide Serbian network to terrorize the United States and its Allies. By contrast, routing al-Qaeda from Afghanistan relocated much of the terrorist menace in an open-ended battle with Islamic extremists operating worldwide in the name of a holy war.

The sorrowful experience in Vietnam created low tolerance for a protracted war that piles up casualties and erodes public support. As a consequence, military doctrine now favors "overwhelming force" that gets the job done fast with minimal combat casualties. In Iraq, this doctrine took the form of a massive missile barrage to paralyze the enemy with "shock and awe." A devastating assault is hard to square with the discriminateness, proportionality, and casualty standards of morally justifiable war. Vigorous debates will be fought over the justness of the lethal means in the geopolitical war.

Satellite broadcast technology heightened the war of words and imagery regarding "collateral damage." Whereas the Western media were highlighting the humanitarian benefits of military force, Al-Jazeera satellite television was showing vividly the heavy civilian toll of the military campaign in Afghanistan along with constant images of carnage from the Israeli–Palestinian conflict. Discriminate aerial bombardment requires reliable ground intelligence to spot the enemy. To spare Allied lives, the feuding Afghan warlords did the ground fighting and provided some of the ground intelligence. Reports of questionable reliability wreaked havoc on families bombed in villages and wiped out political rivals where tribal factions sought advantage in local power struggles.

Collateral damage extends beyond the direct impact of military strikes on civilians. Al-Jazeera expanded the meaning of *collateral damage* to the disastrous aftermath of the military campaign—a war-ravaged infrastructure and huge displaced populations in squalid refugee camps left to fend for themselves without the basic necessities of life. With Allied reluctance to commit security ground forces that would put their soldiers in harm's way, feuding warlords took control over their fiefdoms, some resumed the lucrative international heroin trade, and others even restored the medieval tyranny, especially toward women, that was so brutally practiced by the Taliban. Generous payments to the warlords, the allies of convenience, to fight the war and to hunt the al-Qaeda and the Taliban nourished a state of national anarchy.

The hunt for the elusive al-Qaeda got downgraded, and bin Laden was declared irrelevant in favor of a preemptive military campaign against Iraq. The metaphoric war on terrorism evolved into an actual one. The initial labeling of the war on terrorism as a "crusade" fought under the code name "Infinite Justice" suggesting, in Arabic translation, the trumping of God as the ultimate authority, inflamed Islamic fundamentalists. Leaders of the Christian Right poured fuel on the fire by characterizing the Prophet Muhammad as a terrorist and Palestinians as interlopers who must be stripped of control of the holy land, thus rekindling the religious crusade of yore.

Opponents of going to war with Iraq questioned the rightness of intention. Many critics worldwide voiced distrust and cynicism that the war on terrorism provided a pretext for promoting less pious agendas (Clymer, 2002). The rush to preventative war roused the undercurrent of indignation among alienated allies over how the United States uses its matchless power and sought to counterbalance it with threats to veto a war resolution. Critics warned that unilateral resort to awesome military power, embellished with grandiose visions, would make the world more liable to terrorism than safer from it. Bin Laden, who had been presumed dead, resurfaced on Al-Jazeera praising recent terrorist strikes, trumpeting the evil intentions of the poised infidel invaders, and calling Islamists worldwide to action to disable the enemy.

Saddam's regime was militarily boxed in by no-flight zones with continuous aerial surveillance by Allied warplanes and bombardment of defense and communication facilities. Some nations questioned the justification of the priority accorded to the threat and timing of a preemptive strike against Iraq that did not seem to pose much of a threat under the stringent containment. They viewed the planned invasion as a war of choice, not necessity. Critics of a military invasion and occupation argued that UN inspectors destroyed more weapons of mass destruction than did the Gulf war. The Military containment and deterrence had worked for over a decade. They prescribed a coercive, but nonviolent alternative, including an expanded and intensified inspection program backed up by an arms embargo, unfettered aerial surveillance, extensions of the no-flight zone nationwide, and multinational soldiers to guard inspected military installations and prevent rearmament (Walzer, 2003). They lobbied for forceful inspecting and dismantling weapons of mass destruction and their production facilities under the international charter and auspices rather than through armed invasion with its prolonged aftermath of uncertain scope and magnitude.

The utilitarian standard provided justification for armed intervention as a necessity even if it had to be done unilaterally. A preemptive strike would prevent a projected massive future threat to humanity. The public was reminded that Hussein was a monstrous despot who terrorized and gassed his own people and invaded a neighbor state. Containment was dubbed a failure and dismissed as an option, and the magnitude of the threat was amplified. Although militarily contained and apparently not tied to al-Qaeda, in defiance of UN resolutions, Hussein was a deceptive obstructionist to arms inspection and was producing chemical and biological weapons that he might pass on to organized or freelancing terrorists. Moreover, his efforts to create atomic weapons posed an even graver international threat. The utilitarian justification presented a stark contrast: Inflict small harm now preemptively or suffer massive human destruction by a nuclearly armed despot. The projected human threat was personalized and made to be immense and pervasive because a "dirty" nuclear bomb could be smuggled into any city and detonated. No one was safe any longer from a nuclear strike. The clear choice in this humanitarian crisis: responsible preventive military offensive or international timidity. The President maintained that the military overthrow of Saddam's regime was morally obligatory to defend the American people against this grave threat. In the stark contrast of the dichotomous options and the rightness of the cause, moral considerations and potential international repercussions held low priority for a frightened populace.

The utilitarian benefits of a military campaign against Iraq were vigorously contested (Kaysen, Miller, Malin, Nordhaus, & Steinbruner, 2002). The U.S. administration depicted the outcomes in predominately positive terms—removal of a horrific regional threat of mass destruction, democratization of a despotic regime, and liberation of its terrorized people. Critics argued that the planned intervention was mischaracterized as a "preemptive" war that forestalled an imminent attack by an enemy, when, in fact, it was a "preventive" war to disarm and supplant a regime reined in and constrained militarily and by severe economic sanctions.

They voiced concern about a new doctrine of anticipatory military self-defense against a presumptive threat in future years. The critics (Kaysen et al., 2002) enumerated a host of potentially disastrous consequences of military intervention. It would inflame the Muslim world and only escalate international terrorism; derail the global efforts to eradicate the terrorism spawned by the al-Qaeda network and other Islamic terrorist groups; expand the ranks of ultraconservative Islamists and undermine the efforts of modernists and reformers working toward an Islamic pluralism; unleash ethnic warfare in the Mideast region; damage relationships and partnerships with allies; subvert international laws that protect the rights of nations and ensure the equitable application of the laws; undermine the nation's moral position as a force for good by violating its own values; and burden the nation with staggering long-term costs of warfare, occupation, peacekeeping, and national reconstruction.

The U.S. administration and their advisors countered the forecast of these sobering risky outcomes with a more optimistic consequential scenario. Saddam ruled by fear not loyalty, so an invasion would bring a quick end to his terrifying reign. Rejoicing of the liberated Iraqis would affirm the moral rightness of the military remedy. Rapid military success would turn detractors and private approvers into appreciative public supporters for the democratization not only of Iraq but of the entire region.

The Iraqi regime, depicted as an imminent and grave biochemical threat conspiring with terrorists and poised to unleash their weapons of mass destruction if attacked, was speedily routed as an enemy more in the likeness of rogue armed combatants than a mighty military machine. Geopolitical disputes arose over who should preside over the reconstruction of the nation and who should look for the chemical and biological weapons and nuclear facilities that were the main justification for the military invasion. Within this deeply fissured multireligious nation, the power vacuum was quickly filled by exiles with political ambitions, ethnic separatists, and clerics jockeying for power to create an Islamic nation in opposition to a pluralistic secular one. The sociopolitical war presents more daunting challenges than did the military war.

Given the potential escalative chain of events, societies face the challenge of eliminating weapons of mass destruction in a morally defensible way. If terrorism is to be defeated, societies must address the life conditions that drive people to deadly terrorist missions. This is a daunting challenge not amenable to quick fixes. Islamic terrorists come mainly from populations living in an environment of poverty, political oppression, gross inequities, illiteracy, and a paucity of opportunities to improve their lives. More advantaged members who have been alienated and radicalized by embittering experiences in their efforts to promote the social changes they desire usually spearhead militant activism (Bandura, 1973; Sprinzak, 1990). In cultural milieus where suicide bombing is hailed as gaining blessed martyrdom, this mode of terrorism is institutionally embraced and socially applauded as divine retribution for the humiliation and suffering inflicted by the enemy (Lelyveld, 2001). Educational development provides the best means of escape from poverty and the promotion of national development. However, this institutional resource is squandered when educational systems are used more for indoctrination in reactionary theology than for cultivation of the talents needed to thrive in modern global society.

All too often, American foreign policy forges marriages of convenience with autocratic rulers who preside over their people with oppressive force to ensure self-preservation. These life conditions arouse the wrath of disaffected populations toward the United States and its allies for propping up the authoritarian regimes financially and militarily. The population is further inflamed by Islamic fundamentalists through the politicization of religion to rally support for terrorist operations against secularism and the supporters of the enemies of their medievalist strain of Islam. The scourge of terrorism presents a great humanitarian challenge on how to make it in people's self-interests to live together agreeably in a pluralistic society embedded in modernity and global interdependence. If the war on terrorism is to be won, it requires extensive enabling support of the moderate voices within these societies who have a progressive vision of how to integrate the benefits of modernization with humanist principles that uphold human rights, equality, and dignity.

7

UNDERSTANDING AND RESPONDING TO GROUP VIOLENCE: GENOCIDE, MASS KILLING, AND TERRORISM

ERVIN STAUB

To prevent mass violence, we must understand its origin, whether we are considering the Holocaust, the genocide of the Armenians, the genocide in Rwanda, the "autogenocide" in Cambodia, the mass killings in Bosnia, the disappearances in Argentina, or terrorism around the world. These include social conditions, cultural characteristics, the relationships between groups, and the psychological processes of groups and individuals. In this chapter I describe influences that contribute to mass violence. I briefly discuss prevention, including response to terrorism, and I consider what is required to eliminate the social and cultural conditions and psychological processes that give rise to group violence.

The conception of origins that follows is based primarily on my previous research (Staub, 1989) and its elaboration in later publications. These publications also develop conceptions of and practices required for prevention, in part derived from understanding the roots of violence (Staub, 1989, 1998, 1999, 2002, in press; Staub & Pearlman, 2001; see also Charny, 1999). The chapter also draws on the work of others. The conceptions of origins and prevention have been developed with a focus on genocide, mass killing, and what is currently called *ethnopolitical violence*. Here I extend these conceptions to some degree, taking into consideration issues related to and information coming from the study of terrorism.

Terrorism is usually defined as violent acts, frequently by small groups of people, against noncombatants. However, increasingly in wars civilian populations have been targeted, normalizing, to some extent, violence against noncombatants. The firebombing of German and Japanese cities by allied forces during World War II is an example. Moreover, terrorist groups, whether they try to change repressive systems or respond to or claim to respond to injustices, often see themselves as fighting a war (McCauley, in press).

INSTIGATORS OF COLLECTIVE VIOLENCE

One starting point for mass violence is difficult conditions in a society, such as severe economic problems, great political conflicts, rapid social changes, and combinations of these factors. These have intense psychological impact. They frustrate basic needs in whole groups of people—universal psychological needs for security, for a positive identity, for feelings of effectiveness and control, for positive connections to people, and for a comprehension of reality (Staub, 1989, in press; see also Burton, 1990; Kelman, 1990).

Another starting point is conflict between groups, especially about "vital" interests. An important issue is how such conflicts become intractable, that is, violent and extremely resistant to resolution (Staub & Bar-Tal, in press). This might be the case due to material, objective elements (e.g., the difficulty of dividing territory that two groups need for living space, as in the Palestinian–Israeli conflict). But even more it may have to do with psychological elements. The territory is part of the groups' identity. There has been a history of mutual devaluation, distrust, and fear. The basic needs are frustrated by the relationship between the groups, for example, by calling into question a group's identity. Such psychological issues make the conflict especially difficult to resolve.

Frequently, violence is a response to demands by a subordinate group for greater rights, or it may arise as political movements advocate social change. The violence may be started by either side, the dominant group that resists change or the subordinate group as it tries to bring about change. An evolution of increasing violence can lead to mass killing or genocide, to extreme terrorist acts, or both. In Argentine in the 1970s, groups working for social change began to engage in terrorism, with mass killing (the "disappearances") being the response by the military government (Staub, 1989).

Conflicts between groups, especially intense and violent conflicts, frustrate basic human needs. Dominant groups, when faced with demands from a subordinate group, protect not only their rights and privileges, but also their security, identity, and their version or particular comprehension of reality.

In the worldview they have developed, their social position represents the "right" social arrangements. Often it is a combination of difficult life conditions and group conflict that jointly frustrate basic needs and give rise to the psychological and social processes that lead to violence.

Great differences between groups in a society, in power and privilege, can persist for a long time without violence. However, when groups begin to experience relative deprivation and come to view their situation as unjust, the conflict may become a live one. In the modern age, with many modes of communication that enable people to compare themselves not only to real others but also to images of wealth and the good life, feelings of frustration at their relative deprivation and powerlessness may emerge and can become intense. People's need for a positive identity (who I am if I have so little whereas others have so much) and for effectiveness and control (why can't I and people in my group improve our lives) are frustrated. The desire for justice, an important motive, may in part be constituted out of such basic needs.

One of the important "difficult life conditions" in the modern age is great and rapid cultural change. Even great positive changes, such as social movements like the civil rights movement and feminism in the United States, require significant psychological adaptation (Staub, 1996). Societies that are both traditional and repressive, that do not allow freedom of expression or the exchange of ideas, face special difficulties in handling the tremendous changes in the modern world in technology, knowledge, entertainment, and mores that seep into societies even when barriers have been set up.

Self-interest is another instigator. The combination of intense devaluation of a subgroup in society and its challenge to the dominant group, can lead to actions by the dominant group that lead to the destruction of the subgroup. Mass killing or genocide of indigenous peoples have often been in part due to the desire to gain land or develop resources where these groups have lived (Hitchcock & Twedt, 1997; Totten, Parsons, & Charny, 1997). Self-interest also creates or maintains violence in groups that may have started out with positive ideals, working for social change and justice and improving the conditions of life for some group, but have come to use violent means (McCauley & Segal, 1989). Over time their life may come to be organized around violence, which becomes both an end in itself and a way of making a living and maintaining status. The guerillas in Colombia may be an example of this.

PSYCHOLOGICAL AND SOCIAL PROCESSES IN TURNING AGAINST THE OTHER

Ideally, groups would respond to instigating conditions by cooperative efforts to improve conditions or by dealing with them through negotiation and mutual concessions. Instead, psychological and social processes may arise that turn one group against another and lead to violence.

One way for individuals to handle difficult life conditions or group conflicts that frustrate their basic needs is to turn to some group for security, identity, connection to other people, effectiveness, or comprehension of reality in a changing or changed world. This may be their ethnic group, their nation, the dominant social group they are part of, some political or ideological movement, or a religious group. In addition to gaining support and connection, they can elevate themselves by elevating this group, its ideals, and actions (Tajfel, 1978). They can also elevate themselves by devaluing and then harming others.

Instigating factors like difficult life conditions or group conflicts may give rise to basic needs in many people, thereby creating the conditions for political and social movements. However, some people, perhaps because of their individual life histories or specific circumstances or both, may be more affected and more inclined than others to join groups and ideological movements in response to social conditions

In a *New York Times* column, Thomas L. Friedman (2002) described the terrorists of September 11, 2001, as educated young men from middle class families in the Arab world who went to Europe for more education. The narrowness of the experience and worldview they grew up with clashed with the complex, modern world they encountered in Europe. In addition, as Muslims, they experienced a lack of respect and marginality in Europe. They joined local prayer groups or mosques, where they became radicalized. They went off to Afghanistan, where they received training in Osama bin Laden's training camps.

The ideology of a strict religion at home and later as preached in the mosques, the difficulty of integrating their past understanding of the world with their new experiences in a much different world, the lack of satisfaction of basic needs when they lived in Europe such as positive identity (respect) and connection to the world around them, the influence of the religious groups they entered, the sharp lines between us and them that these influences have created probably all entered into the formation of these terrorists. However, their earlier life experiences, whether in their families of origin or elsewhere, must have also been important, because not all young men from the same Arab countries who went to Europe became terrorists.

Part of the elevation and affirmation of the self and the group happens through scapegoating another group, which is blamed for life problems or for the existence of conflict. This leaves oneself and one's group blameless, provides an explanation of the difficulties of life (they caused it), and creates a community among those who scapegoat. The scapegoated group may be to some degree responsible, but not to the extent or in the way it is blamed. Or it may be blameless, like Jews who were accused of being responsible for Germany's defeat in World War I, but a history of devaluation or other factors make the group an easy target for scapegoating.

The United States is seen by people in Arab countries as in some ways blameworthy for their problems because of a variety of policies and practices. These include support of repressive governments in the Arab world (and elsewhere), U.S. policies toward Iraq, and U.S. support for Israel. Before Iraq's invasion of Kuwait, the United States supported Saddam Hussein, a violent dictator, and then after driving Iraq out of Kuwait, it insisted on the continuation of a worldwide embargo that has not accomplished its aims but has harmed many people in that country. However, Arabs are not the only ones who see terrorism against the United States as a response to U.S. foreign policy. A telephone poll of 275 opinion leaders in 24 countries conducted for the *International Herald Tribune* and the Pew Research Center between November 12 and December 13, 2001, has shown that 76% of those polled in Islamic countries believe this; so do 36% in Western Europe; and still more in Asian, Latin American, and Eastern European countries (each over 50%; McCauley, in press).

In addition to U.S. foreign policy, negative reactions to the United States may arise for other reasons. The United States is probably scapegoated to some degree because it is one of the important originators of cultural changes, which are difficult for traditional societies to handle, especially those that are also repressive. Thus, the United States may be viewed as a source of the confusion that is inherent in our times.

Ideologies are another important response to instigating conditions. People have visions of ideal social arrangements that describe a better life either for a particular group or for all humanity, such as nationalism (the vision of a more powerful, wealthier, and often ethnically pure nation), communism, or Nazism. Even "Hutu power" in Rwanda, a vision elevating Hutus in relation to Tutsis and offering the image of a society not only dominated by Hutus but "purified" of Tutsis, can be seen as an ideology (see des Forges, 1999; Staub, 1999). Ideological visions can be positive, but those that arise in response to difficult life conditions or group conflicts are often destructive. They identify enemies who must be "dealt with," which in the end usually means destroyed, in order to fulfill the ideology.

Ideologies are seemingly always involved in genocide and mass killing. They usually have a central role in terrorism. In the case of genocide and mass killing, the ideologies are often secular. The Nazis wanted to achieve racial purity and a Germany with more living space (Hilberg, 1961). The Khmer Rouge in Cambodia wanted to create total social equality (Barron & Paul, 1977; Staub, 1989). However, religion itself can also be regarded as an ideology, a vision of creating a better world by creating social arrangements and living life according to the precepts of the religion.

Religion has often been used as a means of identifying others as enemies, even when the ideology itself is secular. The Nazis saw Jews as the enemy; the Serbs in Yugoslavia and Bosnia with a nationalistic ideology identified Muslims as the enemy. Obviously, Osama bin Ladin and his followers have created an ideology in which religion is central. However, as in the case of secular ideologies, the social conditions and the needs and motives that arise from them are important in making religion a vehicle for destruction.

Islam is not unique in being used as a vehicle for violence. Christianity has given rise to tremendous violence, through the inquisition and the Crusades in the Middle Ages, the persecution of "heretics" (that is, people who even to a small degree tried to change the existing religious dogma), the persecution by Catholics of Protestants, and the persecution of Jews. Although central to most religions is the belief in and advocacy of the love of the other, most religions at least implicitly define its adherents as true believers and those outside the faith as misguided or even the enemies of the true faith. This makes them potential scapegoats and ideological enemies in the face of difficult life conditions, conflicts, or internal processes, crises, and evolution within the religion itself.

THE EVOLUTION OF DESTRUCTIVENESS

As scapegoating and ideology turn one group against another, members of one begin to take hostile actions against members of the other. This sets in motion a process of evolution. Individuals and whole groups "learn by doing" and change as a result of their own actions.

As they harm others, the perpetrators of violence as well as the whole society they are part of begin to change. *Just world thinking* (Lerner, 1980), the belief that the world is a just place and those who suffer must have somehow deserved their suffering, leads to greater devaluation of the victims. As they further harm the other, perpetrators and even bystanders come to exclude the victimized group and its members from the moral realm, the realm in which moral values and standards apply. They often replace moral values that protect other people's welfare with values such as obedience to authority, loyalty, or adherence to the higher values of the ideology. In the end, there may be a reversal of morality; killing the identified enemy may come to be seen as right and moral (Staub, 1989).

As the evolution progresses, individuals change, the norms of group behavior change, and new institutions are created to serve violence. These may range from paramilitary groups to regular government institutions, such as those in Germany that dealt with arrangements having to do with the extermination of Jews. This evolution also takes places in the case of intractable conflict, and among those who engage in violence as a response to actions directed at them. For example, as the violence in the Israeli–Palestinian conflict intensified in 2000–2002, both societies came to be organized around the conflict, each group intensely devaluing the other group and regarding its own cause as the only just cause (Staub & Bar-Tal, in press).

Such an evolution also takes place in terrorist groups. In the course of the evolution, enmity intensifies. For example, ideological movements that become genocidal over time, and those that come to use terror (and the two can coincide), may start as political movements. The Baader-Meinhof gang in Germany is one example. One of its leaders, Ulrica Meinhof, started out with student demonstrations against the U.S. nuclear weapons in Europe (Demaris, 1977). When the group was formed, it initially engaged in political action (McCauley & Segal, 1989). However, because bringing about political and social changes is difficult, some groups become increasingly radical over time. (For other instances of the radicalization of individuals who later become terrorists, see Billig, 1984, 1985; Crenshaw, 1986; McCauley & Segal, 1989).

One may assume that an ideological movement or a terrorist group exists at least in part to serve the basic needs of its members. For instance, as members learn to view social reality through the prism of the group ideology, they gain a new comprehension of reality as well as a positive identity by working for a better future and gaining recognition for it from others in the group. They gain effectiveness and control through group actions. Membership also provides deep connections to people. However, the ideals of the ideology can also express genuinely held values, initially held by some and progressively adopted by most members. In the end, members are motivated to act for both "cause and comrades."

The fulfillment of both the ideological vision and of basic needs requires progress in a group's efforts. However, progress in effecting social change is often slow, even in an open society. In trying to have an effect, members of the group may feel they must engage in more extreme actions. The internal dynamics of terrorist groups facilitate radicalization: To gain status, members of the group are likely to advocate more extreme actions and beliefs (McCauley & Segal, 1989). Getting attention for the group, which often entails violent action, is also justified by the goals of gaining public support for the cause and thereby also attracting new members.

Thus, both "learning by doing" or change that results from the group's own actions, and the internal dynamics of groups contribute to an evolution toward increasingly radical ideologies and violent means to fulfill them. Commitment is maintained by mutually reinforcing support within the group, the continued propagation of ideals, the idealization of leaders, an increasing separation from the rest of the world (and thus lack of corrective input), and even by the sacrifices that members of the group make for the fulfillment of goals.

As the group engages in more and more violence, the destruction of the enemy can become its highest goal. Members of the group may develop fanatic commitment to the goal of fulfilling the ideology by destroying its opponent. Fanaticism means that a particular goal becomes of paramount importance, with total commitment to it, all other goals being subordinated to it.

The suicide bombers are an extreme example of how life itself can become subordinated to what are the loftiest goals in the perpetrators' minds. The process of sacrificing one's life for the goal is facilitated when a whole society comes to cherish and idealize extreme sacrifice for the cause; religious beliefs may enter the picture, making it appear that the person who commits suicide in the course of harming the enemy will be rewarded in the afterlife. Mystical beliefs may even develop that this person will not be truly dead. Beliefs and ideology merge to shape the dynamics of the larger group as well as of the smaller group that carries out such acts.

Young Palestinian suicide bombers seem attracted by the vision of freeing their group and helping it achieve a better life; by support in their larger community and even their immediate families; by promises of fame, better financial condition for their families, and a happy afterlife; and perhaps even by the mystical belief I noted. After they have made the decision to become suicide bombers, they are also continually surrounded by other members of the terrorist group, who provide support and bar access to outside influences that may induce them to change their minds (Post, 2001).

CULTURAL FACILITATORS OF GROUP VIOLENCE

Certain cultural characteristics are conducive to the emergence of psychological and social processes that initiate violence in response to instigating factors. These characteristics have usually been present in societies that had in the past perpetrated genocide or mass killing or given rise to terrorism.

Cultural Devaluation

One characteristic that can contribute to violence is a history of devaluation of another group or subgroup of society. The devalued group is usually selected as a scapegoat or ideological enemy. Devaluation can vary in form and degree. It might consist of beliefs that the other is lazy, or of limited intelligence, or manipulative, or morally bad, or a dangerous enemy that intends to destroy society or one's own group. A devalued group that does relatively well—its members are reasonably well off—is an especially likely victim. This was the case of the Jews in Germany, the Armenians in Turkey, and the Tutsis in Rwanda (Staub, 1989, 1999). It may also be the case that the enmity of some groups hostile to the United States is intensified by a combination of a negative view of the United States and negative reactions to its strength and power.

Sometimes two groups develop intense, mutual hostility, which I have referred to as an *ideology of antagonism* (Staub, 1989, pp. 250–251). Seeing the other as the enemy, and themselves as an enemy of the other, becomes part of the group's identity. This makes group violence more likely.

The dividing lines between groups that can give rise to devaluation and hostility are many and varied. Divisions may be based on religion, wealth, and status, place of residence (i.e., in cities as opposed to rural areas; this was the case in Cambodia, where such distinctions corresponded to divisions in wealth and power), political beliefs and programs, and ethnic membership (especially when groups strive for rights or power or try to establish their independence).

Hostility to the out-group also depends on threat to and attack on the in-group. McCauley (in press) suggested that when threat lessens, stereotypes of out-groups become more positive. He noted that after the Oslo Accords, support for terrorism among Palestinians declined; it later rose when Sharon, less friendly to Palestinians, came to power. The conditions that influence and may mitigate level of hostility in an intractable conflict require further exploration.

Inequality, Relative Deprivation, and Injustice

People who are poor or have limited power and rights sometimes join forces in groups and movements with the declared aim of correcting their circumstances and the wrongs they entail. In difficult times, characterized by economic problems or great social change, usually such people are especially affected. Their experience of relative deprivation (Pilisuk & Wong, 2002) and injustice may intensify.

Members of ideological groups are often heterogeneous. The supporters of Nazism in Germany came from varied social and economic groups, moved by the combination of culture and difficult social conditions (Staub, 1989). Often people who have not directly experienced poverty or suffered from substantial inequality join those who have and may assume leadership positions (because they tend to be better educated and are better equipped than the majority of group members). They may join because their own basic needs have been frustrated in other ways (one of these may be harsh treatment or neglect as children), and they may be looking for a sense of identity and community that a movement can provide. Or they may join because they are compassionate and have moral principles that lead them to identify with those who are affected by difficult conditions or are unjustly treated. Other reasons for joining may include the desire for power that the leadership of a movement might provide.

Conditions in a society may limit opportunities and create a sense of hopelessness even in people whose background is not underprivileged. This may be true of some young men in Saudi Arabia. According to media reports Mohammed Atta, the leader of the September 11 attacks, could not find a job in Egypt upon his return from Europe (Friedman, 2002). In Rwanda, economic and other problems diminished the opportunities for many young men, who joined paramilitary groups (the *interahamwe*) that became the primary perpetrators of the genocide (des Forges, 1999).

Strong Respect for Authority

Strong respect for authority makes it especially difficult to deal with instigating conditions. When people are accustomed to being led, in difficult times they are more likely to seek new leaders, who often lead ideological movements. They are also unlikely to oppose the evolution of violence and more likely to follow direct orders to engage in violence. Germany, for example, has been a society with very strong respect for people in authority (Staub, 1989). In Rwanda, a very hierarchical society, many Hutus responded to direct orders to join in the killing of Tutsis (des Forges, 1999). The inclination to follow authority also tends to increase—even when it is less a part of a culture—in response to threat, danger, or attack. This seems to have happened in the United States after the attacks on September 11, 2001.

In terrorist groups there is often strong hierarchy, sometimes with leaders who are described as charismatic. However, charismatic leadership is a relational process, a function of both the characteristics of the leader and followers (Post, 2001). Many of those who join may want to relinquish burdensome selves and to submit themselves to powerful leaders, but are actively looking for such leaders. In addition, life in terrorist groups is dangerous, a condition that tends to intensify hierarchy and obedience to authority. This picture is complicated somewhat by conflict and competition among the leaders in some terrorist groups, like the Baader-Meinhof gang in Germany (McCauley & Siegel, 1989).

Still, many terrorist groups are extremely hierarchical and are often headed by a single figure who assumes paramount importance for group members. Post (in press) noted that when such a leader is captured or killed, as in the case of Abimael Guzman, the leader of the Peruvian Shining Path group, or Abdullah Ocalan, the leader of the Kurdish separatist group in Turkey, the movement is fatally weakened or stopped. For this reason, he noted, Osama bin Laden organized the leadership of al-Qaeda on the basis of semi-autonomous groups.

Monolithic and Autocratic Versus Pluralistic and Democratic Societies

The more varied the values in a society, and the greater the extent that all groups can participate in societal processes, the less likely is the evolution toward mass violence. People are more likely to oppose harmful, violent policies and practices that may lead to genocide. In totalitarian and autocratic systems that are unwilling to allow opposition, with strong state and police controls, both genocide (Fein, 1993) and the mass killing of citizens that has sometimes been described as state terror (Pilisuk & Wong, 2002; Rummel,

1994) are more likely than in systems that allow opposition. Democracies (Rummel, 1994), especially mature ones (Staub, 1999) that are pluralistic and have a well-developed civic culture, are unlikely to engage in genocide.

As I have noted, terrorism may be more likely, in contemporary times, by citizens of traditional and repressive societies, which seems to describe many Arab countries at the beginning of the 21st century. Revolutions in communication and travel have set in motion great changes in the world, even in traditional societies with repressive systems that try to keep out change. Because these societies do not allow engagement with much of what is modern and new, they make it especially hard for people to integrate the new and the old. When a repressive society has an ideology that is successful in shaping the thinking of citizens, dissatisfaction may lead to displacing anger from leaders and to scapegoating subgroups of the society or outsiders.

Although mature democracies tend not to engage in genocide or mass killing at home (the mass killing of native Americans in earlier times may be an exception), they have supported other governments that engage in mass killing in their own countries. The United States supported Iraq before its invasion of Kuwait even as it engaged in killing its own Kurdish citizens using chemical weapons. The United States and Britain supported Indonesia when over a million of its citizens were killed, identified as communists but often because of their ethnic Chinese background or for other reasons (Charny, 1999).

In contrast to genocide and mass killing, terrorism is not uncommon within democracies. Germany, Italy, Japan, Spain after Franco, and the United States are among the many countries that have experienced the killing of civilians by other civilians who wanted to promote some cause. Social arrangements may frustrate the basic needs and important goals of some subgroups in societies that find no easy or reasonable recourse. Personal life circumstances may frustrate the needs and goals of many individuals. In societies that stress material success and are highly competitive, some people will fail. Such current frustration may combine with earlier experiences of suffering. Ezekiel (1995) found that many of the young followers of right wing, racist movements in the United States have had childhood experiences of intense deprivation and abuse. As one "solution," some people may turn to ideologies that are created out of already existing cultural elements, such as White supremacy. They may engage in terrorist actions that represent at least symbolically a movement toward the creation of a racially pure country.

Unhealed Wounds of Past Victimization or Suffering

Groups that have been victimized in the past, whether through genocide or in other ways, may feel deeply wounded psychologically. Without healing, members of the group may feel diminished and vulnerable, and they may see the world as a very dangerous place. At times of difficulty or in the face of conflict, they may engage in what they deem necessary self-defense. However, this could be the perpetration of violence on others (Staub, 1998; Staub & Pearlman, 2001).

In the case of the Palestinian–Israeli conflict, the horrendous experience of the Holocaust, combined with the early attacks on Israel by Arab states and continued lack of acceptance of Israel by them, are likely to have greatly enhanced Israel's sense of vulnerability. This may have contributed, for example, to what appeared to be greater than necessary use of force in response to the stone throwing that started the "second Intifada." The history of the Palestinians suggests that they are also a deeply wounded people.

What is true of groups is also true of individuals. Many people are wounded from events in their lives. As children they may receive persistent harsh treatment at the hands of parents or peers. They may be abandoned by important people in their lives. Such experiences shape people's ongoing perceptions of events and affect their response to them. Past victimization as a member of a group combined with painful personal experiences may make people especially vulnerable to destructive ideological movements.

Summary: Influences Leading to Group Violence

The combination of social conditions and culture set the stage, making group violence, including terrorism, more or less likely. The immediate circumstances of individuals—their own personal life circumstances, associations with people with a particular political or ideological orientation, and so on—may lead them to join an ideological movement or a terrorist group. Other relevant factors include one's past history and personality, which may intensify the need for identity and community, the willingness to submit the self to a leader, or the development of empathy and caring for others that may lead to the adoption of ideologies that offer a better life for people. Research on terrorist groups shows that the dynamics of the group are important. This is also likely to be true of ideological movements that lead to mass killing or genocide. However, such large-scale violence, when it involves a movement usually occurs only after the movement becomes a system and government.

THE ROLE OF BYSTANDERS

The passivity of bystanders greatly encourages perpetrators. It helps them believe that what they are doing is right. Unfortunately, bystanders are often passive and sometimes even support and help perpetrators (Barnett, 1999; Charny, 1999; Staub, 1989, 1999).

Internal bystanders (members of the population out of which the group arises that perpetrates the violence) often go along with or participate in discrimination and ignore the violence against victims. As a result, just like perpetrators, they change. Like perpetrators, bystanders, as members of the same society, have also learned to devalue the victims. They have also been affected by instigating conditions. It is difficult for them to oppose their group, especially in difficult times and in an authority-oriented society. To reduce their guilt, and their empathy, which make them suffer, bystanders often distance themselves from victims. Over time, some become perpetrators.

In the case of terrorist groups or extreme ideological movements of other kinds, over time many potential bystanders lose influence, because the group cuts itself off from the rest of the world. However, they retain potential influence over the "base community" of the terrorist or ideological movement, which in turn retains some influence over the movement. When this base community uses its influence (e.g., the community in Northern Ireland condemning some especially violent act of the Irish Republican Army), it does affect subsequent behavior of the terrorist group (Post, 2002a).

External bystanders, outside groups, and other nations usually remain passive, continue with business as usual, or even support extremist or violent groups as they move toward or even engage in mass killing or genocide (des Forges, 1999; Powers, 2002; Staub, 1999). Nations do not see themselves as moral agents. They are guided by national interest, which is usually defined as wealth, power, and influence. When they have ties to another country, they tend to support its leaders and system. This may be due to personal connections, like France supporting the regime of Habyarimana in Rwanda between 1990 and 1994 in part because of the good personal relationship between Francois Mitterand, the French president, and Habyarimana (des Forges, 1999). They may also give support to repressive, unjust, or violent systems in the belief that stability or some other factor is in their interest. They do not usually advocate positive social changes or act to protect a persecuted group.

There has been increased interest in "human rights" at the end of the 20th century. This has found expression in UN and other international conventions. Interventions, like those in Bosnia and Kosovo (especially the latter), although highly imperfect in nature (Staub, 1999, in press), express this trend in action. The policies and practices of the United States after the attacks of September 11 have for now put a halt to this trend. In exchange for support in the war against terrorism, the United States accepts without complaint the persecution of opposition and minority groups around the world, whether they be Chechens in Russia or religious "cults" or dissidents in China, Malaysia, or elsewhere who are now referred to by governments as *terrorists*. The voice of the rest of the international community is also silent.

THE ROLE OF LEADERS

The inclinations of a population that result from the interplay of culture and instigating conditions create the possibility of mass murder. To some degree, the people select leaders who respond to their inclinations and fulfill their needs. Still, leaders and the elite have an important role in shaping and influencing events. They may scapegoat and offer destructive ideologies and use propaganda to intensify negative images and hostility. They may create institutions, such as media and paramilitary groups, that promote or serve violence (Staub, 1999). Political scientists and other scholars often see such leaders as acting to gain support or enhance their power (Allport, 1954).

However, leaders are also members of their society; they are affected by life conditions and group conflict and at least in part act out of the motives and inclinations described above. They may have learned to devalue groups that the society has devalued. They may carry the wounds that their group has suffered. They may have had direct family losses as a result of the victimization of their group, as in the case of some Serb leaders in Bosnia (Staub, 1999). Destructive leadership is also often the result of an evolution within the group toward violence, as well as of group dynamics as the group interacts with other groups and the rest of the world.

OTHER INFLUENCES

An additional influence contributing to genocide that has been suggested may arise from a sudden shift in government combined with "state failure," which means the failure of the new government to deal effectively with problems that face the society. An ongoing war (and not only a civil war) also adds to the probability of mass killing or genocide. The genocides of the Jews and Armenians were perpetrated during wars that did not involve the victims. Economic interconnections between a country and other countries make genocide and mass killing less likely (Harff, 1996; Melson, 1992).

HALTING PERSECUTION AND VIOLENCE

When violence against a group has become intense, halting it requires action by nations and the community of nations. Early warning is important, but it is not enough. Usually, as in the case of the genocide in Rwanda in 1994 (des Forges, 1999), when information about impending violence is available, the international community does not respond. For this to change requires changes in values and actions by citizens that influence their governments. It also requires institutions to formulate and effect responses by the community of nations. Interconnected institutions within the UN, regional organizations, and national governments are needed (Staub, 1999).

Appropriate actions include diplomatic efforts to warn perpetrators as well as offers to mediate and incentives to stop violence. Such efforts must be accompanied or followed, as needed, by withholding aid, imposing sanctions and boycotts, and related actions. Ideally sanctions would be designed to affect primarily leaders and elites, like confiscating their foreign bank accounts. At times, force may be necessary. However, early actions, especially preventive actions, are likely to reduce the need for force (Carnegie Commission on the Prevention of Deadly Conflict, 1997; Staub, 1999). Unfortunately, as I have noted, the movement toward engaging in such actions may become a casualty of the war against terrorism.

PREVENTING MASS VIOLENCE

Preventive actions by bystanders or "third parties" are important to thwart the likelihood of mass violence. Promoting healing among previously victimized groups as well as potential perpetrators, who if not wounded before their violent actions are likely to be psychologically wounded by them, reduces the likelihood of new or renewed violence. Healing furthers the possibility of reconciliation (Staub, 1998; Staub & Pearlman, 2001). Creating positive connections between groups, for example, through shared efforts in behalf of joint goals, helps people overcome past devaluation and hostility. Coming to understand the other's history and culture is also important.

The perception of justice by both parties following conflict and violence is also essential to stopping violence. This is difficult to come to, because groups usually have very different perceptions of past events and therefore different views of reestablishing justice. Establishing what has happened, for example, through truth commissions and international tribunals, can contribute. The punishment of especially responsible perpetrators (but not revenge on a whole group) is important (Staub, 1999). Assumptions of responsibility and expressions of regret by perpetrators (or by both parties, when violence was mutual), can further the process of healing, forgiveness, and reconciliation.

Understanding how violence originates, along the lines described in this chapter, can be helpful. In work in Rwanda, developing such an understanding as part of a more elaborate intervention seemed extremely beneficial (Staub, Pearlman, Hagengimana, & Gubin, 2002; Staub & Pearlman, 2001). The intervention consisted of brief lectures on the origins of genocide, the impact of trauma and victimization on groups and on avenues to healing, and extensive discussions in which participants applied the information they received to their own experience. Participants discussed in small groups their own painful experiences during the genocide, receiving empathic support from one another. Both Tutsis and Hutus seemed very positively affected by this and seemed more able to accept the horrible events they had experienced.

The participants in this training worked for local organizations that worked with groups in the community. Some of the participants used this approach, integrated with whatever approach they have traditionally used, with community groups. We compared the effects of this approach with the effects of a traditional approach (groups led by individuals we had not trained) and control groups. Community members who received the "integrated" training showed 2 months after the end of the training a reduction in trauma symptoms and a more positive orientation toward members of the "other group" both over time and in comparison with those who received either traditional training or no training (Staub et al., 2002).

Perhaps an understanding of how violence originates can also be used to help develop shared collective memories, a shared understanding of past history by groups that have harmed each other. This is now recognized as extremely important for a peaceful future following intractable conflict and violence (Staub & Bar-Tal, in press). In a workshop, a group of Rwandese national leaders thought this was very important for their country and discussed it extensively, but many thought it impossible to achieve at this time (Staub & Pearlman, 2002). However, considering how the harmful acts of the other group, as well as of one's own group, have come about using a framework about the origins of violence described here and used as part of the intervention in Rwanda, may help provide a perspective in which the role of both the self and the other can be recognized and responsibility shared.

Other important influences in preventing violence are economic development and democratization. Economic development has been a focus of ideas about prevention (Carnegie Commission, 1997). However, significant economic development may not even be possible without addressing structural, social, and psychological elements. Without social changes, in many places economic development would primarily benefit the elite and may even increase relative deprivation. It would more likely be beneficial if there were democratization, special attention to improving the conditions of everyone's life in society, and attention to the psychological needs of people and psychological relations between groups. Democratization is of great value in its own right. It creates pluralism, moderates respect for authority, and can provide the conditions for lessening differences in power and privilege.

SPECIAL ISSUES RELATED TO TERRORISM

Terrorism may be even more difficult to address than mass killing or genocide. In poor and nondemocratic societies people may have little realistic opportunity to improve their lives by political means. In reasonably wealthy, democratic societies there may still be unfairness and suffering that have either social or personal origins or both. Individuals or whole subgroups may turn for the satisfaction of basic needs and grievances to small groups that provide them with a sense of community and a vision but may become violent over time.

To combat terrorism it is important to address, as much as possible, the roots of despair and to enhance need satisfaction. This requires promoting pluralism, democracy, economic development, and decent material conditions for people and addressing the psychosocial needs of individuals and communities. In the terminology of this chapter, such policies and practices would help fulfill basic human needs.

Within the United States, the terrorist attacks of September 11 have created great empathy for the relatives of those who were killed. The resulting suffering could also be a source of empathy for people in other countries who suffer from persecution and violence or simply from economic deprivation and poverty. It could lead to a commitment to offer more help for people around the world, not only financially but also expertise to create their own capacity for manufacturing and agricultural production and in other realms. I have noted, however, that the experience of September 11 has not led the United States and other nations to become more constructive bystanders. A positive sign, at the time I am writing this, is a small increase by President Bush of foreign aid. Can the existing although as yet limited knowledge by psychologists about the reduction of violence be used to advocate constructive policies and practices?

Another important issue is the socialization of children. The rank and file of extreme racist groups, at least in the United States (Ezekiel, 1995), tend to be young people who have experienced much pain and suffering, including harsh treatment and abuse, in their early years. Warmth and affection and positive guidance satisfy basic needs and make it less likely that children join ideologically extreme, socially destructive, and potentially violent movements. In addition, they contribute to the development of caring for other people. The development of inclusive caring, caring that extends beyond the group, is especially important for preventing terrorism and creating a nonviolent world (Staub, 2002). Humanizing "others" is a necessary condition for caring about their welfare, which in turn is essential to reduce violence between groups.

CONCLUSION

We need to explore further the specific or unique determinants of different forms of violence, such as government persecution, conquest, revolution, civil war, terrorism, as well as conditions and influences that lead to these forms of violence to evolve into mass killing or genocide. Testing our capacity to predict group violence is important (Harff, 1996; Staub, 1999). So is the development of techniques to help groups to heal and reconcile (Agger & Jensen, 1996; Staub & Bar-Tal, in press; Staub et al., 2002; Staub & Pearlman, 2001). Creating positive bystandership by nations and nongovernmental organizations, as well as learning about effective modes of bystander behavior, are essential for prevention. Citizen involvement is required for moving nations to act in behalf of persecuted people. To create a less violent world, the development of knowledge in this realm and its application have to go hand in hand.

8

TERRORISM AND THE
QUEST FOR IDENTITY

DONALD M. TAYLOR AND WINNIFRED LOUIS

Who are these terrorists who attacked the United States on September 11, 2001? It is disturbing enough that they were willing to kill civilians, but what about suicide terrorists who take their own life in the process? The more we learn, the more we are forced to reject the naïve view that they are psychologically deranged or evil. Rather, we see terrorists as individuals who are tactically motivated in their use of violence (see also U.S. Department of State, 2000). Terrorism is used because it is effective in garnering attention for low-power groups and their unpopular causes. In total, 405 people were killed by terrorists in 2000, and only 19 of these were U.S. citizens. Yet this modest number was sufficient to create widespread fear and anxiety.

In this chapter we explore the role that psychological identity might play in fostering conditions that are conducive to the recruitment of terrorists. Specifically, we apply a theory of the self that emphasizes collective identity to define the circumstances that favor recruitment. Our theory is not designed as a replacement for analyses that have applied other psychological and social psychological processes to understanding terrorism (e.g., Unger, 2002). What we offer is an additional process that may provide insights into the conditions necessary for terrorism to take hold.

We begin with a definition of terrorism and a brief review of some of the more traditional applications of social psychological theory. We then outline a broadly based theory of the self and explore the implications of the theory for the recruitment of terrorists. In the final section we examine some of the important social norms that facilitate and regulate the behavior of terrorists.

SOCIAL PSYCHOLOGY OF TERRORISM

Title 22 of the United States Code, §2b56f(d) defines *terrorism* as "politically motivated violence perpetrated against noncombatant targets by subnational groups or clandestine agents, usually intended to influence an audience." The rational basis for terrorist actions rests on the argument that groups cannot achieve their political ends by military confrontations because they are too weak to defeat their enemies; they cannot engage their enemies by political means because they are too marginal ideologically. Targeting noncombatants with a view to instigating widespread fear, anger, and societal polarization in the enemy population may be the only method available to groups that are no match for their enemy in terms of military or political power.

Terrorist groups emerge, then, where a group has little power and where severe economic conditions, political conflict, threats to vital national interests, and rapid social change are paramount (see Staub, chap. 7, this volume). All these are exacerbated by feelings of relative deprivation that arise in an age of global communication in which television and other media facilitate social comparison with the real and imagined wealthy, glamorous lifestyles of high-power nations and groups. Given such desperate conditions, the social psychology of social influence offers insights into the processes by which terrorists might be recruited and their behavior channeled (see Louis & Taylor, 2002; D. M. Taylor & Bougie, 2002). The legacy of the traditional social influence literature is that the power of conformity affects us all. From Asch's famous (1956) experiments on group conformity to Milgram's (1965) classic obedience experiments, one conclusion is inescapable: Ordinary people turn to their peers and legitimate authorities for basic information about appropriate attitudes, values, beliefs, and behavior. After he or she is recruited, the terrorist, like anyone else, is influenced greatly by the social group if it has a clearly defined chain of authority and if the appropriate norms are articulated clearly and unanimously.

In North America it is clear that conformity to the norms of marginal subgroups can explain behaviors that society at large views as unacceptable or extreme. From street gangs to religious cults, including those that involve mass suicide, concrete examples can be found in which individuals' violent or self-destructive behavior is directed by powerful group norms. The examples are common enough, and their circumstances documented sufficiently, to conclude that even members of groups that seem radically bizarre to the wider society are behaviorally driven by understandable and well-known social influence processes. The People's Temple, a religious cult led by the Reverend Jim Jones, came under investigation by a Congressional committee in 1978 that visited the temple's settlement in Jonestown, Guyana. Jones orchestrated the suicide deaths of more than 900 of his followers who died either of their own volition or at their parents' hands. The Heaven's Gate cult had its headquarters in Rancho Santa Fe, California. On March 26, 1887, 39 members took their own lives believing they were bound for a better life. In an insightful analysis, Aronson (2000) concluded that "it is hard to accept the fact that more than nine hundred people in the single location of Jonestown could all be extraordinarily weak, docile, or crazy—or that each and every one of the thirty-nine members of the Heaven's Gate (without a single dissenter) could be unbalanced in the same way" (p. 27).

Our purpose in underscoring the importance of the role played by normal social influence processes for societally marginal groups is to support our view that basic psychological processes may equally operate in recruiting terrorists. Who are the people who are likely to be attracted to the People's Temple and Heaven's Gate cults? For our purposes the question becomes the following: Who are likely candidates for terrorist activities generally, and the elite suicide terrorists in particular? To answer these questions, we turn our attention to a theory of the self.

SEARCH FOR COLLECTIVE IDENTITY

We focus our attention on the concept of the self because we believe it to be central for understanding human behavior. The capacity to self-reflect is uniquely human, and as such it allows individuals to form a concept of the self. The self-concept, then, is a pivotal cognitive process that organizes experience, guides behavior, and provides the individual with meaning. We offer in this section a theory of the self (see D. M. Taylor, 1997, 2002) that we argue has universal application, but one that might be usefully applied to understanding the recruitment of terrorists.

The self-concept is multidimensional, but two fundamental distinctions are central to the present analysis. The first important distinction contrasts *identity* and *esteem*. The identity component (or alternatively, the descriptive, cognitive, or knowledge component) is the one that describes who I am. In contrast, the esteem (or alternatively, the evaluative or emotional component) focuses on my evaluation of myself. Thus, identity answers the question, *who* am I? whereas esteem answers the question, am I *worthy*?

A second fundamental distinction must be made between an individual's *personal* self and his or her *collective* self. The personal self refers to those characteristics or attributes that individuals believe are unique to them. When a woman describes herself as intelligent, shy, and loyal, she is defining the constellation of attributes that make her unique. However, the same person might also describe herself as a young, Black woman. These are aspects of the individual's collective identity in that they refer to attributes that the individual shares with other members of the categories *young*, *Black*, and *woman*.

By crossing these key dimensions of the self, identity versus esteem, and personal versus collective, we arrive at four distinct components to the self-concept: Personal Identity, Personal (Self-)Esteem, Collective Identity, and Collective Esteem. These four components of the self-concept are not theoretically novel. The literature on the self has long distinguished between identity, knowledge, and cognition on the one hand and evaluation, emotion, and esteem on the other (see Baumeister, 1997). Social identity theorists deserve credit for introducing the role of collective identity in understanding the self (Tajfel & Turner, 1979, 1986). Traditionally, theorists of the self have focused exclusively on personal attributes of the self, and it was social identity theorists who argued that membership in social categories also contributes to an individual's self concept.

Where our theory of the self departs from tradition is in terms of the role played by each of the four components. D. M. Taylor (1997, 2002) argued that whereas each of the four components plays a pivotal role for a healthy sense of self, certain components have psychological precedence. Specifically, Taylor argued that collective identity has psychological priority over the other three components, and in turn, personal identity has precedence over personal (self-) esteem. The hierarchical arrangement of the four components is adapted from Taylor (2002) and is presented in Figure 8.1.

The precedence of collective identity arises because the attributes that comprise an individual's personal identity are relative. When an individual perceives herself as intelligent, she is really saying, "I perceive myself to be more intelligent than others who make up my reference group." The college student does not perceive herself as "intelligent" compared with grade school students or to Einstein. Thus, in order for individuals to define what attributes are unique to them, they must have a norm or standard to serve as a comparative template (see also referent informational influence theory, Terry & Hogg, 1996). This is precisely the role of collective identity. Collective identity is a description of the group to which individuals belong, which serves as the normative backdrop against which they can articulate their unique attributes. In summary, without a clearly defined collective identity, an individual cannot engage in the normal comparative processes that would allow for the development of a personal identity. In this sense, collective identity is primary. The collective identity of a terrorist organization describes the group's beliefs, values, attitudes, and goals. Moreover, it specifies the routes an individual might take to internalize the values and achieve the goals. The indi-

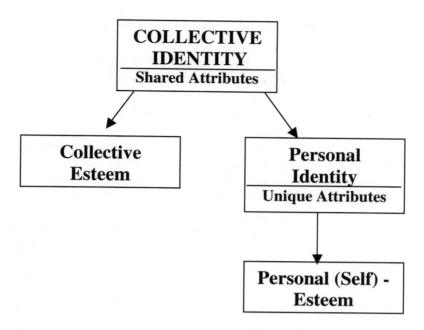

Figure 8.1. Hierarchical configuration of the four components of the self-concept. Note: This figure is based on Taylor (2002).

vidual terrorist now has a template against which to formulate his or her own personal identity.

By extension, it would be impossible for an individual to develop personal (self-)esteem without the benefit of a clearly defined personal identity. Personal (self-)esteem is a form of self-evaluation that requires a concrete basis for engaging the evaluative process. An individual must know who he or she is—must know his or her unique attributes—in order to arrive at an evaluation of the self. In this sense, personal identity is a necessary prerequisite for personal (self-)esteem.

What we are proposing here runs counter to most thinking about the "self." The usual analysis focuses attention on the individual and her or his personal identity and esteem (e.g., Baumeister, 1999). We argue that this emphasis is misguided, because personal identity and esteem are essentially derivative. Whereas we view personal identity as the pivotal aspect of the self for individual functioning, logically it is impossible to form a personal identity without a collective identity to serve as a basis of reference. Collective identity then has psychological primacy, and this primacy has profound implications. Free will, the belief that individuals make choices and are responsible for those choices, is as central a belief as there is. An individual's choices in life are extensions of her or his personal identity. However, personal identity can only be articulated against the backdrop of a clearly defined collective identity.

COLLECTIVE IDENTITY, CULTURE, AND RELIGION

Each of us has as many collective identities as the number of groups to which we belong and with which we share characteristics. These collective identities range from ethnic and gender groups to work and leisure groups. In our view, one of them has special precedence, and that is our cultural, and in some instances religious, collective identity.

Cultural identity, and in some cases religious identity, has a special status because it is the identity that purports to cover every aspect of a person's life. We link culture and religion because both have the potential to be all-inclusive. Devout Jews, Muslims, Buddhists, and Christians do view their religion as a template for every detail in their life. Thus, culture and religion *can* be synonymous in terms of how pervasive they are as collective identities. We underscore *can*, however, because for many people their religion is not an identity that is central to every aspect of their life. People may be nominally Christian and to a certain extent follow Christian tenants, but their Canadian/Western culture, for example, is pervasive. More broadly, where a society makes a sharp distinction between religion and secular culture, or between church and state, religion and culture may not be synonymous.

Why is cultural collective identity so important? Surely I take my professional identity seriously, and, like it or not, my gender identity is very much a part of who I am. However, my professional collective identity provides me only with a blueprint for job-related activities, and my gender identity is not always applicable. Indeed, in a variety of circumstances my gender identity would be an inappropriate basis for guiding my behavior: Who I hire and promote should not be based on gender. By contrast, my cultural collective identity equips me with a template for every facet of life, including family structure, child rearing, appropriate behavior with members of the opposite sex and elders, how to cope with death, occupational structure and status, and explanations for the unknown, just to name a few. A cultural identity provides its members with a shared history and a set of broadly based and valued goals, along with detailed informal normative information about how to pursue the valued goals defined by the collective identity. Thus, cultural–religious collective identity is socially defined and represents the individual's most pervasive and all-inclusive collective identity.

The pervasiveness of cultural collective identity is precisely why it is so resilient. It apparently cannot be destroyed at the point of a gun, as assimilation was attempted and failed in the former Soviet Union. Witness the ethnic or cultural revival of the myriad newly formed states whose cultural identity was suppressed under the old Soviet Union. Nor, apparently, can culture be eradicated and peoples assimilated by positive inducements that attempt to replace their own culture or religion with one that has more material resources to offer. Newcomers were attracted to North America where the streets were purported to be paved with gold. All that was asked was that newcomers agree to have their heritage cultures "melted" away so that they would become culturally American. Yet cultural distinctiveness continued to thrive to the point that America now views itself as multicultural. Indeed, whereas traditional theory focused on the inevitability of assimilation, cultural relativity and multiculturalism have become the new theoretical model (see D. M. Taylor, 1991).

The present theory of the self makes very clear predictions in terms of psychological health and subjective well-being. Individuals with a clearly defined cultural collective identity are poised to develop a healthy, functioning self. That is, a clearly defined collective identity is a necessary prerequisite for engaging in the process of defining a personal identity and, by extension, personal (self-)esteem.

In every culture there are always some individuals who, for a variety of reasons, have not internalized a clear schema of their cultural or religious collective identity. However, there are also entire groups who struggle in a cultural collective identity vacuum. Specifically, severely disadvantaged groups whose culture and religion have been destroyed by the exploitation of more powerful cultural groups have no clearly defined collective identity to offer their members. Such an analysis has been applied to the plight of aboriginal people whose culture was destroyed by European incursion and African Americans whose culture was destroyed by slavery (see D. M. Taylor, 1997, 2002).

We now turn our attention to the application of our theory of self to understanding how members of certain groups may be attracted to terrorism in general and suicide terrorism in particular.

TERRORISM AND COLLECTIVE IDENTITY

There are, in the international arena, a number of disadvantaged groups about whom North Americans know very little. Other groups are often in the news, but there is little in-depth understanding of group members' actual daily living conditions. North Americans may have some difficulty understanding their own role in the conditions we describe that may be conducive to the rise of terrorism.

Our analysis of the role of collective identity in attracting terrorists begins with the examples that have dominated North American news since the September 11 terrorist attack on New York and Washington. Two groups are particularly salient. The first is the al-Qaeda network of terrorists, and the second is the Palestinian terrorists whose acts have been so frequently depicted in North American media as part of the protracted conflict with Israel. Both groups have a religious underpinning, but our analysis would also apply equally to others such as the Japanese Red Army, the Euskadi Ta

Askatasuna (ETA) in Spain, and the Shining Path in Peru. These are terrorist groups whose collective identity is not so linked to religious identity. The groups we focus on here, al-Qaeda and Palestinian groups such as Hamas, not only engage in terrorism but also frequently use suicide terrorists that serve to exacerbate fear and reinforce the perception that they must be psychologically deranged or inherently evil. Much has been written about the "hopeless" conditions of the groups from which terrorists are recruited (Staub, chap. 9, this volume). The emphasis in these discussions is the feelings of anger and frustration that would accompany desperate economic conditions and widespread relative deprivation arising out of global communication depicting wealthy Western nations.

Most important for our analysis, however, is not the extent to which objective living standards are tragically poor, but rather the extent to which longstanding collective identities have been disrupted. That is, a clearly defined collective identity provides individual group members with a sense of the structure of society, its rationale, how to navigate life successfully, and what to value and strive for. Even where there is widespread poverty, and living conditions are desperate for the vast majority, people can at least engage in a number of psychological coping mechanisms against the backdrop of a clearly defined collective template.

It might be argued that the creation of societies built around a fundamentalist Islamic ideology was designed specifically to provide a group with an absolutely clear collective framework within which to articulate a healthy personal identity and sense of well-being. The revolution in Iran with its return to fundamentalist Islam and the rise of the Taliban in Afghanistan might be two among many prototypical examples. Surely, regardless of how one evaluates the restrictive norms of such states, it can be argued that each individual group member was provided with the clearest possible collective identity within which to function psychologically.

On the surface this may be true. At a more profound level, however, the sudden implementation of a fundamentalist religious collective identity as a reaction to a more secular collective identity would produce a chaotic collective identity for most. All of a sudden, established norms, values, and goals are replaced with new ones that are often totally at odds with the previous collective identity. The values, specification of goals, and the specific normative routes to their achievement are in disarray. Moghaddam (2002) addressed this issue from a social more than identity perspective by observing that revolution involves a paradox. "On the one hand, a government is overthrown, and rapid and dramatic changes are made in the laws of the land and the economy. On the other hand, an invisible hand seems to pull things back to the way they were, so that soon people feel that nothing has changed" (p. 33).

For those who have previously lived with a fundamentalist religious ideology as their collective identity template, the sudden new regime is not threatening and indeed may offer new opportunities, rewards, and status. For example, religious leaders whose role was relatively impotent in the context of a secular collective identity may suddenly discover newfound power and status. For the vast majority, however, the sudden change is psychologically threatening, because they no longer have a clear collective identity to serve as a guide to their individual behavior. So threatening is this loss of collective identity that despite the threat of severe punishment, many will continue to function in a clandestine manner using their original collective identity as the functional template. Moghaddam (2002), for example, has described how despite what appear to be well-defined restrictive laws, many people in newly fundamentalist Islamic nations (e.g., Afghanistan after the Taliban; Iran after the revolution) engage in a wide spectrum of individual actions that indicate clearly that they are attempting to operate with their original secular collective identity.

This clinging to old collective identities in the face of dramatic change is not a novel observation. The fall of apartheid in South Africa produced dramatic changes for Black and White South Africans alike. Yet despite a clear racial change in political leadership and the emergence of a new Black elite, for many ordinary Blacks and Whites, pre-apartheid role relationships have continued.

In the face of social upheaval, who are particularly vulnerable in terms of a confused collective identity? It has to be young people who are future oriented, who are anxious to get ahead but have no clear collective identity to provide them with the mechanisms and infrastructure for defining themselves, promoting a positive identity, and achieving their goals. Those young people who are born into disadvantage would experience profound hopelessness but might not be expected to instigate political action. In the absence of leadership and without the opportunity to contemplate how to generate a new collective identity (or in the language of social identity theory, contemplate "cognitive alternatives"; Tajfel & Turner, 1986), disadvantaged young people would experience profound demotivation and apathy. What of those young people who have more education and commerce with the world, even where that commerce is, as Moghaddam (2002) described, listening to the BBC or Voice of America via underground radio? It is not the least advantaged, but those who are relatively privileged members of disadvantaged groups, who emerge as leaders (see D. M. Taylor & McKirnan, 1984). We contend that these ambitious young people are the prime candidates not only to engage in, but also to organize and lead, terrorist activities.

Take the case of Osama bin Laden. He was highly educated in Saudi Arabia but like many of his generation found himself with no outlet for his intellectual talent, there being no streamlined link between training and job opportunity. He, along with so many educated others of his generation, had no collective blueprint for actualizing his ambitions. Moreover, his commerce with global communication made it clear to him that there is a clearly defined and powerful enemy—the West in general and the United States in particular—and that the nations and peoples who have been victimized are Muslim.

An educated and cosmopolitan individual, devoid of a collective identity from which to derive a personal identity, he turns his attention to crafting a clear collective identity. The elements of the collective identity include all of the richness that Islam as a collective identity can provide. However, an essential feature of a functioning collective identity, we have argued, is that it specifies not only what is important and valued in society, but how societally valued goals and status can be achieved: contingencies between behavior and societal success. Where, as in many Muslim nations, deprivation is so widespread that getting ahead seems impossible, people may seek to construct and incorporate a new understanding of social contingencies, a new collective identity. Once the most powerful culture in the world (viz., Western culture in general and the United States in particular) is judged to be the sole cause of Muslim deprivation, the conclusion is inevitable. Individual advancement can be accomplished only by raising the entire Muslim world out of disadvantage. That can be accomplished only by confronting the most powerful culture in the world. You can't confront such a powerful enemy through the usual military and diplomatic channels, and thus organized terrorism becomes the default solution. Now bin Laden has a clearly defined collective identity that is forward-looking and motivating.

OFFERING RECRUITS A COLLECTIVE IDENTITY

Leaders of terrorist organizations such as bin Laden must now engage in the recruitment process, and naturally their attention is going to turn to young men and women. These young people find themselves at a time in their life when they are looking to the future with the hope of engaging in meaningful behavior that will be satisfying and get them ahead. Their objective circumstances including opportunities for advancement are virtually nonexistent; they find some direction from their religious collective identity but the desperately disadvantaged state of their community leaves them feeling marginalized and lost without a clearly defined collective identity.

Let us take, by way of illustration, the plight of those in refugee camps (see Palmer & Taylor, 2000). As many as six million displaced peoples live in refugee camps around the world, some for as long as three generations. They have no official legal status and little or no opportunity for education, work, sanitation, and social services. To make matters worse, whereas every refugee might hope to be granted asylum in some country of opportunity, each knows that his or her chances are virtually zero. Why? Because refugees with greater resources make their way to a desirable country directly by plane or boat and request asylum. For every refugee who makes it to a developed nation through his or her own resources, there is one less who can be taken from a refugee camp. The young people who languish in refugee camps live out their life with not merely a confused collective identity, but an empty collective identity. Regardless of the cultural historical content that might be transmitted to them, a critical aspect of that collective identity, namely the specification of paths by which valued societal goals can be achieved, is absent.

Many inhabitants of refugee camps may not be in a position to generate a collective identity on their own, and so they may find attractive a terrorist organization's offer of a very well defined collective identity that offers a clearly defined route for improving conditions for the individual and the group as a whole. The collective identity of the terrorist is extremely compelling. It has the familiarity of a religious basis that needs no affirmation. It has a clearly defined explanation and rationalization for the current malaise that young people in particular and most of society are experiencing. It offers a clearly defined route for addressing the malaise along with a clearly delineated plan for how the individual can advance to the point of receiving ever-increasing status and respect. The collective identity offered by a terrorist organization is not only clear but simplistically clear, it is espoused without even minor variation by every member of the organization, and it is forward-looking with the promise of better conditions for the group and the individual.

However, not all members of such disadvantaged groups are attracted to collective action in the form of terrorism. By exploring the collective identity of those who might not be attracted to terrorism, we might better grasp the attraction of terrorism for young recruits. First, no matter how disadvantaged a group is, there is always a segment of society that is privileged. It may be the religious elite, the political elite, or the economic elite, but in either case these are group members whose privilege depends upon the status quo, and as such they are not attracted to any new collective identity. Second, the majority of group members cling to the collective identity they know, even when that collective identity is not serving them well. Beyond the Muslim nations that are the focus here, and the example of South Africa described earlier, in North America we have witnessed the impact of families coping with a lost collective identity when mines close down, fishing stocks run out, timber becomes scarce, and the family farm is gobbled up to make way for urban expansion. Similarly, in disadvantaged nations and communities, where life has been made chaotic by the foreign policies of powerful nations, embargoes, and local conflicts, ordinary people struggle to use the collective identity they were socialized into, even though the expected contingencies are not met. Younger people, who have not the same commitment to a collective identity that is outmoded, are caught with no clear replacement template within which to work. These are prime candidates for a new collective identity. What could be more attractive than an organization that offers a clearly defined identity that validates a confused young person and offers a clear set of guidelines for how to better the life for the individual and indeed for the entire group?

NORMATIVE STRUCTURE OF
TERRORIST COLLECTIVE IDENTITY

What a clear collective identity provides is a framework for individual behavior, that is, a clearly defined set of group norms. There are certain structural features to these norms that can be underscored when considering the collective identity of terrorist groups in particular. Whereas a clear collective identity allows an individual to engage in the important psychological processes of forming a personal identity and personal (self-)esteem, there are times when the individual simply follows the behavioral norms specified by the collective identity. Specifically, in an intergroup situation, where an individual's group identity is made salient, the individual's own group, or in-group, specifies the appropriate attitudinal and behavioral norms to follow, especially with respect to the out-group. Theoretically, then, social identity theorists posit that in-group norms serve as the exclusive guide to behavior when an individual's collective identity is made salient in an intergroup context (Terry & Hogg, 1996; Terry, Hogg, & White, 2000; J. C. Turner, Hogg, Oakes, Reicher, & Wetherell, 1987).

Individuals are guided by their personal identity for the most part and only shift to following in-group norms when the intergroup situation makes group, or collective, identity salient. For terrorists, however, as for other soldiers, their personal identity, indeed their very existence may be built around the norms of their collective or in-group identity, because the relationship of the terrorist group to the powerful out-group identity is constantly salient. Moreover, terrorist groups are very much in the minority within their own society. Thus, in addition to having, by definition, a chronic orientation to the intergroup conflict, terrorist groups may, merely because of their minority status, experience collective identity salience (e.g., Feather, 1995). The unique position of a terrorist group, therefore, points to the potent role that in-group norms play in shaping terrorists' behavior.

The social psychology of minority influence underscores how a terrorist group can provide its members with a clearly defined collective identity. Research indicates consistently that for a minority to influence a majority, minority group members must speak loudly, repeatedly, and with one voice (Moscovici, 1985, 1994). Terrorist groups are very much a minority in their own society, and usually their views are considered extreme. As such, terrorist collective identity norms must be highly salient for individual members, the norms must be extremely simple with no latitude for interpretation, and the norms must be espoused constantly. Thus, if nothing else, terrorist group members have an ultra-clearly defined and nonnegotiable collective identity. Such clarity satisfies an important psychological need for individual members of terrorist groups and offers insights into why a terrorist organization may be so attractive for certain members of disadvantaged groups.

This consistency and extremism may be necessary to engage out-group attention. However, it is precisely the social psychological processes that give rise to the structure of terrorist group's identity that makes them appear so fanatical. This extremism and fanaticism make it extremely difficult to engage terrorist groups in political negotiations that might involve some compromise and accommodation. Indeed, so simple, extreme, and unyielding are the collective identity norms of terrorists groups that they may become dysfunctional in resolving intergroup conflict not only by the threatened advantaged out-group but by the broad disadvantaged group on whose behalf the terrorists are acting. For example, extremists who spearheaded the women's movement, the warriors who rocked mainstream society to protect aboriginal lands in North America, militant civil rights protagonists in the United States, and terrorist cells that advocated the political separation of Québec from Canada or the Basque region from Spain, all lost power and influence once the powerful out-group appeared to be motivated to resolve intergroup issues. At the point of negotiation more moderate members of the disadvantaged groups, not terrorists, became the leaders. Indeed, where a terrorist leader does inherit the mantle of leadership in the negotiation process, the leader may be forced to distance himself or herself from the inflexible and extreme collective identity norms of the terrorist group, as may be argued to have been the case with Sinn Fein in Ireland. We argue then that a dynamic understanding of these conflicts over time suggests that the terrorist arms of a political movement may be instrumental in motivating a previously obstructionist powerful advantaged group to come to the bargaining table.

However, it appears often to be the case that the terrorists themselves are then discredited and rejected by their successors. The actual rejection of violence and willingness to engage with the powerful advantaged group are conditions that may allow moderate leaders to negotiate effectively with the advantaged group, rather than engendering or misperceiving bad faith and hostility. In addition, however, the moderates' ostentatious, strategic rejection of violent tactics and willingness to engage in negotiations can be exchanged for advantaged group recognition and concessions in the context of more militant disadvantaged group factions ready to resume or escalate violence if negotiations fail (see also Gurr, 1970; Louis & Taylor, 2002; Osgood, 1962).

ROLE OF THE OUTGROUP IN DEFINING TERRORIST IDENTITY

We began our analysis of the structure of the collective identity norms for terrorist groups by focusing on the primacy of in-group norms. Indeed, social identity theorists have argued that in-group norms are the exclusive guide to behavior when collective identity is made salient. In the context of theorizing about collective action, we have challenged this view (see Louis & Taylor, 2002) and have proposed that the out-group may play a vital role in shaping group behavior. Focusing on the role of outgroup norms for the collective identity of terrorist groups allows us to gain further insight into the structure of the collective identity norms for terrorist groups.

Louis and Taylor (2002) have argued that often an in-group focuses on an out-group not only for strategic reasons, but out of a psychological need to form a clear collective identity with respect to in-group norms. A number of implications for the structure of terrorist group's collective identity arises from the role that out-group norms may play in the identity process.

First, we have stressed that terrorists themselves are motivated to understand the stressful conditions of disadvantage that their group confronts: An answer is needed to the question of why their group is suffering. Belief in the existence of injustice, the identification of a malevolent enemy propagating the injustice, and the attribution of in-group suffering to that enemy may greatly simplify the stressful challenge of understanding social inequality. Just as advantaged-group members are motivated to blame the disadvantaged for their own suffering with just world thinking (M. J. Lerner, 1971), disadvantaged group members may adopt as a global heuristic for understanding their suffering the belief in an unjust world (see also Crocker & Major, 1989; Staub, 2001). This heuristic may be psychologically valuable because it can be an accurate representation of how the intergroup inequality developed and is being maintained, thereby providing a useful guide to disadvantaged group action. However, even if the representation is inaccurate, a coherent understanding of the social inequality as caused by an evil and oppressive out-group may also be psychologically valuable. It reduces uncertainty and allows for the externalization of blame for extreme disadvantage, and, in so doing, protects self-esteem.

A second insight concerning identity processes in terrorism, we argue, arises when we understand terrorism as fundamentally interactive. A teenager in a refugee camp who turns toward a life as a teacher or spiritual leader is working for his or her group but within the group: The behavior is oriented toward his or her own community. Usually in the context of a refugee camp such within-group alternatives are not available, and so teenagers in a refugee camp are likely to turn toward working for their group outside their group in the form of terrorist activities: The behavior is oriented toward the powerful enemy. Thus, we argue that if terrorists face uncertainty and confusion in developing a model for their own cultural or religious group's collective identity, they may direct their emotional energy into rejecting the out-group-dominated present. In fact, the more uncertain and ambiguous it is to affirm the relevance and meaning of their own collective identity, the more likely it may be that terrorists would be drawn to the comparatively uncomplicated identity paradigm of defining themselves as "not the out-group." Similarly, if terrorists disagree among themselves regarding the values that they would try to instantiate if their own group gained power, they may orient their time and attention to derogating the values of the out-group (enemy) culture. In fact, the more incoherent and conflictual the social representation of their own cultural values, the more likely it might be that terrorists would rely on the comparatively uncomplicated communication option of rejecting the out-group values, which are easy to identify consensually.

In the social influence literature, rejecting out-group norms because of their influence source rather than their content has variously been labelled *reactance* (Brehm, 1966; Heilman, 1976) or *anticonformity* (Nail, MacDonald, & Levy, 2000). The link we are making is between influence processes, on the one hand, and political strategy, on the other. For disadvantaged groups oriented toward rejection of the status quo, the power of the advantaged group power may be a politically important focus (e.g., a social movement that proclaims itself "Resistance!" and advertises with slogans "Fight injustice!" and "Resist racism!"). Even when there is no agreed-on blueprint for the future—and perhaps most often when there is no agreed-on blueprint for the future—clarity may be achieved, and motivation for political action may be sustained, by rejecting the out-group political model and values expressed by the existing system, which was defined by the powerful out-group. A similar argument has been made in the form of "disaffection" models of political protest (e.g., Bynner & Ashford, 1994; Gurr, 1970). Individuals who are disadvantaged socioeconomically are thought to vent their feelings of dissatisfaction with protests aimed not at achieving a positive goal for one's self or one's group, but rather at expressing rejection of the powerful out-group "societal" norm. Thus, deliberately and ostentatiously rejecting the enemy influence may provide terrorist organizations with a psychological anchor for a new collective self and a new action orientation, in the absence of any positive dimensions on which to define a collective identity (Louis & Taylor, 2002).

Research on stigmatized minorities within particular societies suggests that the defensive rejection of the out-group should be considered as a motivational force in addition to, or even instead of, positive attachment to the in-group (e.g., Britt & Heise, 2000; H. P. Kaplan & Liu, 2000). By ostentatious anticonformity, disaffected individuals express a collective identity derived from the rejection of another group's norms. Thus, al-Qaeda terrorists may be argued to have abandoned the focus on positive outcomes (social or economic power for the Muslim in-group) because the low likelihood of achieving the positive outcome was emotionally distressing. The conjunction of low power to achieve positive outcomes for a broad Muslim in-group and the perception that the American out-group is responsible for thwarting in-group goal achievement produced a focus, in the terrorist minority, on achieving negative outcomes for the out-group.

To the extent that this pattern of influence predominates, it is ironically the established, powerful group's norms that determine the form that terrorist actions take. Simply put, terrorists are actively focused on violating powerful out-group norms. The social power of the terrorists' behavior is derived from the behavior's offensive quality; the powerful out-group's norms signal to the terrorist group the behaviors that are most shocking. Greater degrees of orientation toward the powerful out-group produce greater intensities of reactance by terrorists, rather than compliance. First, rejecting the powerful group's norms and values may become an end in and of itself; second, hurting the powerful group may come to be seen as benefiting the in-group; third, the powerful out-group's attention may become the reinforcement that terrorist behavior attempts to elicit, so that outrage may be seen as preferable to being ignored by the powerful out-group.

POTENTIAL FLASH POINTS

We have argued that in addition to disadvantaged economic and political conditions, issues of psychological identity may offer insights into the recruitment of individuals for terrorist activities generally and suicide terrorist actions in particular. We have introduced a theory of the self that argues for the primacy of cultural collective identity in the development of a healthy, functioning "self." The implications of the theory are that individuals who lack a clearly defined cultural or religious collective identity are psychologically desperate. In this context, terrorist organizations fill a necessary psychological void. What makes terrorist groups particularly attractive is their simplistic worldview that offers recruits a clear collective identity. Specifically, the clear collective identity is one that has a rich and familiar religious base, with a clearly defined enemy, along with a set of clearly defined norms for appropriate behavior—a set of behaviors that allow both the individual and the group to dramatically improve their depressed conditions.

For illustrative purposes, we conclude by considering two groups that we would argue presently suffer from having no clearly defined collective identity. The two groups we have in mind are not experiencing conditions that would lead to the rise of terrorism. However, we should not imagine that there might not be a sudden rise in terrorism if the societal vulnerability continues and new threat factors are introduced.

Russian citizens live in circumstances that leave them devoid of any clearly defined collective identity. The fall of communism, where a clearly defined collective identity was in place, has not been replaced with any clearly defined collective template. Individual Russian citizens have no template for how to get ahead, how to gain prestige, or what the payoffs are for long-term investment of time in developing particular skills and training. That is, those of us raised and socialized into capitalism know intimately what goals to pursue, how to pursue them, and their consequences. The template must be extremely well-defined if we are willing to sacrifice immediate salary for years of education with the promise of an even bigger salary at some unspecified time in the future. For the average Russian citizen, capitalism is a mere label with some vague connection to life in the West. It certainly is not a clearly defined template with a well-defined road map for getting ahead and articulating, let alone achieving, important goals in life. The result is that no clear personal identity can be formed, and individuals are left with the option of pursuing immediate gratification. Alcohol and drug misuse has spiraled out of control and HIV has become endemic. Indeed, the only understandable collective schema is one built on organized crime, and those involved are indeed motivated and goal directed. The Russian example demonstrates the consequences of a collective identity vacuum. As yet there is no link to terrorism primarily because there is no identified outside powerful enemy.

One of the themes of recent news out of Afghanistan is the extent to which the world may be lured into a false sense of security now that a new government has been installed to replace the Taliban. There was a surprising degree of accommodation among potential rival leaders such that the world breathed a comfortable sigh of relief. Forgotten in the process is any appreciation of just how chaotic life is for most Afghans. There is such a paucity of infrastructure that education, health care, justice, and fiscal and military stability are in disarray. The Taliban may have been oppressive, but no one can argue that there weren't a clearly defined set of goals and structure to society. The point is that the vacuum left by the departure of the Taliban is as much a psychological vacuum as one related to fiscal stability and infrastructure. For the average person there is no clear collective identity that spells out the nation's goals and the precise mechanisms for getting ahead. Ordinary individuals cannot engage their own personal identity with respect to the context of their life because there is no clear collective identity to call upon. Again, we regard this identity vacuum as a dangerous potential flash point.

9

MALEVOLENT MINDS:
THE TELEOLOGY OF TERRORISM

A terrorist act is a particular form of complex humanitarian emergency that is usually designed to influence people far beyond the primary victims and responders. This factor exerts a profound influence on the characteristics of the violence used. The development of appropriate prevention, mitigation, response, and recovery programs must begin with an assessment of terrorists' goals, motivation, and rationalization of their actions. I consider several watershed terrorist events to illustrate typical terrorist goals, explore the three general types of terrorist motivation developed by Hoffman, and cite some of the sociocultural and contextual factors that impel terrorists to embark on a campaign of violence.

In general philosophical terms, *teleology* is the study of the manifestations of design or purpose in nature under the assumption that natural processes are ultimately determined by their utility in an overall natural design. At least metaphorically, acts of terrorism are manifestations of the worldview or ultimate purpose of the actors. The development of appropriate responses

The views expressed in this work are my own and do not reflect the official policy or position of the Department of the Army, Department of Defense, or the U.S. Government.

187

to terrorism should properly begin with an analysis of this worldview. Our understanding of the motivation of terrorist actors can affect our capacity to respond and hence the extent of our vulnerability. The orderly and systematic analysis of terrorist motivation can provide valuable clues about strategies for responding to terrorism in terms of both protection and mitigation activities (antiterrorism) and for direct action involving preemption, interdiction, or retribution (counterterrorism). Our understanding of terrorist motivation also affects the development of planning and training activities focused on the management of the consequences, particularly the psychological impact of major terrorist events. The development of strategies for both defensive deterrence (the protective measures of antiterrorism) and offensive deterrence (the retaliatory measures of counterterrorism) should be guided by an understanding of the terrorist's presumed goals, motivation, and justification. In this process one may seek answers to questions about the terrorist's objectives, interest in negotiation, likely choice of weapons, and other key issues that can shape our response.

Whether the terrorists are foreign or domestic, one may make several generalizations about the relationship between their respective goals, tactics, and techniques of operation: (a) terrorists generally represent subnational groups, (b) their tactics generally reflect a form of asymmetrical warfare that is very similar to traditional forms of guerrilla warfare, (c) their motivations are largely political or cultural even if individual attacks conform to conventional forms of criminality, and (d) assaults are typically conducted against noncombatants.

TERRORISM AS COMPLEX EMERGENCIES

Historically, disaster management and humanitarian assistance planners have divided disasters or emergencies into three general categories: natural, technologic, and complex. Natural disasters include common geologic and meteorologic events such as floods, tornadoes, earthquakes, or volcanic eruptions. They can certainly be catastrophic for those directly affected, but they are relatively common and do not typically carry with them any meaningful security or political implications especially in developed and politically stable environments. Technologic emergencies, such as transportation accidents and catastrophic infrastructure failure, are generally the result of human error and do not typically represent acts of intention or malice. For these natural and technologic events, emergency and disaster response assets in the United States are generally well organized. Operators are capable of mounting a response at the local and national levels with a reasonably high degree of efficacy. Complex humanitarian emergencies (CHEs), however, are fundamentally different from such events in their causes, psychological impact, and response requirements.

The precise definition of complex emergencies is the subject of some debate, but the central themes of such disasters are illustrated in the definition offered by the London School of Health and Tropical Medicine (cited in Burkle, 1999), which describes them in part as "situations in which the capacity to sustain livelihood and life is threatened primarily by political factors, and in particular, by high levels of violence" (p. 3). Frequently, CHEs emerge from the synergistic distress of failing political infrastructure confronted with a catastrophic economic or natural disaster. The disintegration of the former Yugoslavia and the Rwandan genocide of 1994 are illustrative of CHEs at the state level. On a somewhat smaller scale, terrorist acts may also be viewed as a form of CHE because of the presence of political motivation and violence. Across a wide range of individual terrorist acts, political motivation surfaces as a central organizing principle. Such acts are usually directed at a specific target but are clearly intended to have a political and psychological impact on a much larger scale.

In responding to disasters, planners and emergency responders typically organize training and allocate resources along four dimensions: prevention, mitigation, response, and recovery. In the case of complex emergencies, and in acts of terrorism in particular, the political aspects of the event exert a dramatic effect on both the psychic impact of the events themselves and the strategies used to defend against and respond to them. In the development of the Department of Homeland Security, the government has underscored that a successful response to terrorism requires an integrated and coordinated multisectoral effort including contributions from military, law enforcement, diplomatic, economic, political, public health, and social sectors. In developing such complex responses it is useful to examine elements of the presumptive motivation and justification of terrorist events by the actors.

FACTORS INFLUENCING THE PSYCHOLOGICAL IMPACT OF TERRORIST EVENTS

Terrorist acts are defined to a large degree by their impact, and especially their psychological effects. It is important to understand what factors are involved in producing these effects, as one might reasonably assume that terrorists are aware of them and plan accordingly.

Certain situational factors make terrorist acts more psychologically damaging than natural or technological emergencies. In natural calamities or unintentionally caused technological disasters, the resulting psychological fallout is not as devastating because these events are understood to be the unintended result of circumstances beyond human responsibility and therefore unpreventable. These acts of God or nature or human error are also seen as unusual occurrences not attributable to malevolence. In terrorist events, however, the infliction of physical and psychological pain is the specific purpose of the behavior; the elements of malevolence and intent frame the experience in a different and more psychically damaging context (Burkle, 1999).

In an address to the First Harvard Symposium on the Medical Consequences of Terrorism, Flynn (1996) cited three clusters of factors that interact in complex ways to determine the impact of terrorist events: (a) the characteristics of the event itself, (b) the psychological fallout from the event, and (c) the behavioral health services available to those affected. Clearly, the third factor, the availability of accessible and culturally acceptable behavioral health services, is a critical issue, but these services address essential elements of consequence management that are beyond the scope of this chapter. However, Flynn's first two factor clusters concerning event characteristics and psychological fallout are useful to explore because they may provide insight into the terrorist's goals and objectives. Flynn reported that terrorist events typically have characteristics that tend to increase the probability of adverse psychological consequences. Whereas many natural and technologic disasters have some of these characteristics, terrorist events frequently have most of them.

I examine these characteristics and comment on their possible role in illuminating the connection between terrorist goals and methods.

Little or No Warning

The absence of warning reduces one's perceived sense of control over the environment and increases the sense of vulnerability. In an ideal world, one would like to be able to both predict and control one's environment. At a minimum, one might tolerate the inability either to predict or to control but not both. When one is unable to either predict or control one's environment (i.e., to prevent, avoid, or mitigate threats), the resulting sense of helplessness can generate profound distress.

This characteristic is well explicated in Seligman's cognitive model for depression (1975). Using ethologic studies, Seligman determined that when an animal learns it has no control over adverse events, it may develop what he labeled *learned helplessness*. Transferred to human behavior, this learned helplessness has three components. The first is a deficit in motivation: When one learns that one's efforts have no effect on the environment, one stops responding. In effect, one says, "Why bother?" The second deficit concerns cognition: If one learns one has no control, the learning tends to become overgeneralized to a wide range of issues, and this interferes with the ability to learn later that one can have control. The third is an emotional deficit: The perception of loss of control creates pervasive passivity.

Although it is doubtful that terrorists review the psychological research as part of their planning process, it is reasonable to assume that what scientists can demonstrate empirically, terrorists do understand intuitively. Terrorists do not plan their acts in ignorance or in a vacuum; acts precipitated without warning are clearly designed to maximize the victims' perception of loss of control over the environment.

Perception of the Potential for Reoccurrence

This is closely related to the notion of loss of control. The message is that if it happens once, it can happen again, and people are not safe anywhere. This illustrates one of the main themes of terrorism: to compromise the sense of security that traditionally exists between a government and its citizenry. By demonstrating the inability of the government to protect the populace, the terrorists recapitulate their goals of inducing a sense of loss of control among victims. Over time this disruption in the state's ability to maintain security can easily impair the government's ability to retain its credibility or even its tenure.

Multiple attacks over time have an emotional effect that is more synergistic than cumulative. In the instance of a natural or technologic disaster there is a definitive end. People can process the psychological fallout from the event through normal mechanisms of psychological unburdening, grieving, and seeking of appropriate support. That terrorist events reflect the conscious intent of human will precludes the ability of the victims to determine when the threat is truly over.

Serious Threat to Personal Safety

Studies of combat veterans and victims of violent crime confirm that unintended exposure to extreme risk is associated with future psychological symptoms. Members of the military, police, fire, and rescue services and other emergency responders routinely face highly stressful or life-threatening circumstances, but their activities often carry with them some degree of volition, often accompanied by highly evolved training and support structures. Purposeful and voluntary participation in high-risk events can certainly cause psychic distress, but the issues of choice and the protective elements of training, equipment, and a shared sense of coherence of response tend to ameliorate much potential psychological fallout. It is the quality of unanticipated risk imposed on those who are unprepared that makes terrorist events so psychologically disruptive.

Exposure to Gruesome or Grotesque Situations

Exposure to gruesome or grotesque situations concerns event responders, primary victims, and the general public in slightly different ways. Those involved in rescue efforts directly concerned with body recovery and body identification are at enhanced risk. This is an especially important risk factor if the responder does not customarily deal with deceased persons or has not been properly briefed on the situation prior to arrival at the site. Even morgue workers or others who routinely work with deceased persons may be affected if the victims have sustained massive loss of corporeal integrity. In the case of large explosive events this is not unusual. The effect may be enhanced if the responder has had or develops a spontaneous emotional link to the victim, even if the link is oblique. For example, Mitchell (1990) reported a case in which a veteran paramedic responded to a traffic accident in which one of the fatalities, a young girl, suffered substantial disfigurement. The paramedic reported that he experienced overwhelming emotional distress only when he discovered that the victim was clutching a small doll of a type he had recently given his own daughter, who was about the age of the victim. Clearly, even among trained professionals, the forging of a meaningful emotional link, however unbidden, can erode the personal–professional boundaries that would normally provide an element of protective emotional distance.

Diminished Health Status

In addition to the immediate trauma caused by the event, primary victims of a terrorist attack may suffer protracted or permanent disabilities that impair their ability to adjust to the distress of the event. Causes may include injuries requiring multiple surgeries, need for long-term medical care or rehabilitation, disfigurement, chronic pain, or other conditions that are commonly associated with crush, blast, or burn injuries. In an investigation of the physical injuries associated with the Murrah Federal Building blast, the Oklahoma State Department of Health (Injury Protection Service, 1996) reported that 842 people were injured as a direct result of the blast or during escape after the blast, 83 of whom required hospitalization for their injuries. The report concluded; "At least two-thirds of the injuries among hospitalized persons will likely or certainly result in disability" The physical, emotional, and social impact of these conditions can disrupt the ability of the victim to gain emotional closure on the event and can lead to increased psychological risk.

By using bombs or other devices that create disability as well as death, terrorists can impose long-term suffering on the perceived enemy and institutionalize ongoing evidence of their ruthlessness, commitment, and ability to overcome the security measures of the target group. The disabilities of individual victims also serve as reminders of the terrorist's ability to inflict damage on the resources of the target community, to include its medical, legal, social, and economic resources and institutions.

Potential for Unknown Health Effects

If a terrorist event were to involve a chemical, biological, nuclear, or radiologic assault, victims would be confronted not only with the immediate destruction and disability imposed by the initial event but also with the fear of future effects on their own health, the health of loved ones, or that of future generations. Whereas chemical agents tend to work quickly, some biological agents have delayed effects, and radiologic agents may cause damage that takes years to manifest. The persistent fear of a "time bomb" medical malady carries with it the tyranny of the unknown, particularly if the presumed disorder may affect fertility or genetic integrity. This serves to institutionalize the acts of the perpetrators through the creation of what could be called a multigenerational threat.

One finds a model for this in the atmospheric radiation leak that took place at the Three Mile Island Nuclear Station in Pennsylvania on March 28, 1979. Although the leak was small, the emotional impact of possible radiation poisoning was very dramatic for the population near the power plant. Media reports of the event were highly sensational, a situation that was circumstantially exacerbated by the release of the movie *The China Syndrome* the same month.

Following the leak, President Carter ordered a commission to investigate the accident. The commission was an ad hoc group headed by John G. Kemeny, president of Dartmouth College. Other members represented the Nuclear Regulatory Commission, the U.S. Environmental Protection Agency, and the U.S. Department of Health, Education, and Welfare. In October 1979 the commission published its report; it found no significant increases in cancer rates, developmental abnormalities, or any other index of radiation poisoning. The report did note the following, however: "The major health effect of the accident appears to have been on the mental health of the people living in the region of Three Mile Island and the workers at TMI" (n.p.). Multiple investigations by academic institutions and government agencies soon after the accident and in the years following have found similar results (Uranium Information Centre, 2001). Although the Three Mile Island accident was a technological disaster, the unintended effect resembles a terrorist event, not as a function of the intent of the responsible parties, but of the psychic effects. The idea of a silent, invisible, noiseless, odorless, tasteless agent whose lethality might take years to materialize was an emotional threat of Mephistophelean proportions.

SYMBOLISM OF TARGET SELECTION

Because acts of terrorism are designed to provide a credible threat to the power or image of the state or other target group, targets may be selected primarily for their symbolic value. This is one of the central organizing principles of terrorism and is reflected across a range of attacks and targets. Aside from making statements of discontent to the leadership of the target group, it also sends a message to the populace that targets include cultural institutions as well as physical ones. In selecting culturally significant targets, terrorists threaten not only physical security, but also the very social systems and cultural institutions that define the culture itself. Obviously, the attacks of September 11, 2001, are particularly distressing examples, but less cataclysmic acts are also illustrative. The bombing of American embassies in Dar Es Salaam, Tanzania, and Nairobi, Kenya are vivid examples.

The symbolic aspect of targeting frequently extends to governmental institutions or business facilities in an effort to generate a destabilizing political or economic action against state institutions or their representatives. In Colombia, for example, rebels bombed an international oil pipeline 152 times in the year 2000 alone (U.S. Department of State, 2000). In addition, Colombian terrorists espousing political views from both left and right have kidnapped or killed journalists, members of the judiciary, and union leaders not only to demonstrate their capacity for interpersonal violence, but to assault the cultural institutions of a free press, the rule of law, and individual economic opportunity. Similarly, suicide bombers operating in Israel typically attack retail shopping areas, public transportation, fast food outlets, and other institutions emblematic of a stable and comfortable social existence. In a less grisly act condemned around the world, the Taliban of Afghanistan destroyed two large Buddhist statues they considered a threat to the spiritual purity they sought to impose on the population. The destruction of the statues did not result in the loss of life, but the impact of the event on the worldwide Buddhist population would satisfy many peoples' definition of terrorism.

Whether the particular targets are individuals, economic venues, religious icons, legal institutions, or social agencies, the symbolism of the target is a key element in understanding the ultimate purposes or function of a terrorist act.

IMPRESSION MANAGEMENT

As we have noted, for many terrorists, the mechanics of the assault are often less important than the symbolic message of the action. It follows that one of the most important collateral objectives for terrorists is to maximize the role of the media in a bid to spread their message and images. As a practical matter, the sheer drama of a terrorist event is ideally suited to exploit both the immediacy of electronic media and the staying power of print media. Terrorists are aware that mass media coverage of their acts can produce a level of public exposure that would be difficult to duplicate, even through the most sophisticated and expensive of commercial advertising campaigns. Even for terrorists who do not publicly acknowledge their activities, their ability to make their message known through the media is highly confirmatory of their potency and is a powerful incentive to act.

The task of selecting and studying potential targets is greatly facilitated by the location of many of their targets in free and open societies. Since the fall of the Berlin Wall, we have seen the proliferation of pluralistic states with representational governments, free presses and stable legal systems. These states tend to have a relatively high degree of personal freedom and provide easy access to a large amount of publicly available information. These freedoms have made it easier for terrorists to operate and virtually assured of maximum media exposure and (in the event of their apprehension) of a degree of legal protection far beyond what they might expect in their native environments. Ironically, these are often the very freedoms the terrorists seek to destroy in their attempt to destabilize the political machinery of the target government.

In addition to the symbolic value, terrorists typically consider a range of other political and logistical issues in target selection; factors include accessibility, vulnerability, publicity value, financial commitment, probability of success, possible retribution, and any idiosyncratic values of particular interest to the operators.

It is a truism that terrorism has been with us since the dawn of human conflict, but in the three decades preceding the assaults of September 11, 2001, there were at least five events in which target selection issues shaped America's perception of terrorism and illustrated the value that terrorists attach to the link between target image and emotional impact (Grosscup, 2002). The first was the attack on Israeli athletes at the Munich Olympics in September 1972; the second was the bombing of the U.S. Embassy in Beirut in April 1983; the third was the attack on the World Trade Center in New York in February 1993. These were followed by the sarin attack in the Tokyo subway system and the bombing of the Murrah Federal Building in Oklahoma, in March and April 1995, respectively. Although terrorist attacks are invariably highly emotionally charged events, these five events were psychologically significant in slightly different ways; each illustrated different but important aspects of the terrorist's motivation and goals, symbolism of the targets, use of the media, and tactical strategy.

The attack on Israeli athletes at the 1972 Munich Olympics was the first terrorist event that had real-time televised coverage; it transfixed a worldwide audience of half a billion people and illustrated several important philosophical principles common to many terrorist agendas. In classical Greece, wars were suspended during the Olympics and armies were prohibited from conducting maneuvers in order to permit attendees and competitors to travel in safety. In the modern age, the Olympic Games have been suspended only during the two world wars. By targeting the Olympics, the terrorists conveyed the unmistakable message that they viewed no political or social institution, no matter how universal, apolitical, historic, or revered, as sacrosanct. In addition to the production of shock and horror, the perpetrators of the Munich assault induced a worldwide sense of vulnerability by demonstrating that accepted rules of order and conduct were no longer operative. It also provided a dramatic example of the complex relationship between terrorism and the media and begged the question of the proper role of the media in reporting terrorist events (Becker, 1996).

The second event was the suicide bombing of the U.S. Embassy in West Beirut in April 1983. A lone bomber drove a pickup truck loaded with explosives into the building. The explosion cost the lives of 63 people, 17 of them Americans. Aside from the obvious symbolism of an attack on a U.S. governmental outpost, this assault was significant because it was the first modern use of a suicide bomber in a terrorist event. It was particularly difficult for Americans to understand what sort of worldview would permit an assailant to purposefully kill himself in a political act. It turned out to be an event that would provide a template for many terrorist acts to follow, to include the suicide bombings of the Marine Corps Barracks and the French Paratroopers quarters (also located in Beirut) in October of that year.

The third event is now called the first World Trade Center bombing. The terrorists' plan called for the destruction of the foundation of one tower such that it would collapse into the other tower, destroying both. Had the plan worked, the projected number of dead and injured would probably have been in the range of tens of thousands. Whatever the eventual loss of life might have been, the ultimate goal of the assault was to send a message to Americans that their homeland was not immune from a form of assault that had previously been limited primarily to targets overseas. Although our nation achieved much of its position of world leadership through participation in wars, they were geopolitical conflicts fought by our military forces deployed to foreign shores under the authority of national leadership. The World Trade Center bombing of 1993 made the United States a battleground for the first time since the Civil War, and it was a form of war for which we were not prepared, initiated by nonstate actors against a civilian target. This first assault on the World Trade Center is an exemplar of many of the operating principles of the terrorist ethos: The idea of subnational aggressors perpetrating unannounced assaults against innocents virtually defines the term *terrorism*.

The Aum Shinrikyo's sarin attack in the Tokyo subway system on March 20, 1995, riveted the world's attention, not so much for the number of deaths (12), or even for the number of injured (3,794; Council on Foreign Relations, 2003), but because of the contextual issues involved. Although chemical weapons had been used in the Iran–Iraq War in the early 1980s and by Iraq against the Iraqi Kurdish population in 1987, the context involved state actors. In the Tokyo attack, it was the first time that a subnational terrorist group used a chemical agent as a weapon of mass destruction in a civilian environment. The facility with which the act was carried out also imbued the populace with a profound sense of vulnerability. The selection of a crowded subway system as the target made it clear that the death toll was limited only by the lack of sophistication of the agent dispersal system on the part of the perpetrators.

In addition to generating generalized feelings of vulnerability, the Aum Shinrikyo attack also had a dramatic impact on Japan's collective sense of national order. Japan is a largely homogeneous nation whose cultural institutions and system of social interaction have been steeped for centuries in the traditions of security, civility, harmony, and social order. This fact takes on additional psychological significance because the chief architect of the assault was Japanese.

The date April 19, 1995 is remembered by many in much the same way as December 7, 1941. The difference is that the bombing of the Murrah Federal Building in Oklahoma City was done not by a foreign power as an act of war, but by a native son as an act of revenge. It made Americans painfully aware that the terrorist threat does not emanate from foreign shores alone. The statistics associated with the effects of the blast were stunning: 168 killed, 19 of them children; 853 injured; 7,000 people deprived of a workplace. The psychological reverberations of the event were also dramatic; at least 190,000 people attended funerals for the victims, and more than 387,000 people personally knew at least one person who was killed or injured in the blast. This was not just a tragedy or a crime; it was and continues to be a major public health event, especially concerning mental health services.

Shortly after the explosion in Oklahoma City, a spokesman for the Militia of Montana, an antigovernment extremist group, announced to the press: "Expect more bombs" (Southern Poverty Law Center, 1997b, p. 3). This vividly confirmed that it was not necessary to look overseas to find anti-American sentiment as a source of potential violence. According to the Militia Task Force of the Southern Poverty Law Center (1997b), there were, at the time of the Oklahoma City bombing approximately 850 formally constituted domestic "Patriot" organizations whose shared value was the repudiation of the U.S. Government. Today that number has declined, but there are also more than 600 racist, neo-Nazi, and other hate groups whose capacity for terrorist violence is of great concern (Southern Poverty Law Center, 1997a).

In slightly different ways these watershed events all illustrate commonly interactive themes of terrorist operations involving the perpetrators' goals, motivation, and justification.

GOALS, MOTIVATION, AND JUSTIFICATION

It has been a general observation of many terrorism researchers that whereas terrorist acts typically involve acts of destruction, the general goal of terrorism is not the destruction itself—it is the production of fear. Often, the intent is to induce not only concern about personal vulnerability among individuals, but to produce a long-term climate of general anxiety by affecting broad areas of the cultural fabric of the target group. By disrupting the sense of trust in public security, economic institutions, and stability of the social environment, the terrorist seeks to destroy the implicit and explicit social contract between the government and the governed—to destroy the collective confidence individuals invest in social institutions and the national leadership.

Terrorists may also have more specific objectives related to their particular political or social agenda, which may include recognition of their cause, intimidation of leaders, coercion, provocation of overreaction, support of an existing insurgency, or simple retribution (Interagency OPSEC Support Staff, U.S. Government, 1996). They may also seek to inspire and incite members of other marginalized, disaffected, or disenfranchised groups. This is particularly appealing to terrorist groups that attempt to polarize the target community or to militarize a situation that would otherwise be resolved through social or political mechanism. For terrorists, the ability to militarize an otherwise political situation serves to provide a more level playing field for them by pursuing a strategy that enhances the relative power of physical violence over legal or institutionally mediated alternatives. In effect, the message becomes, " I may not have the political power to beat you in court, but I have the physical ability to beat you in the alley behind the courthouse!"

The United States as Target: Terrorist Motivation

Whether the target is a government building, a business, an individual, or the entire body politic, there seems to be no shortage of enmity for U.S. institutions and citizens. It is important for Americans to understand how contextual issues, including perceptions of the U.S., relate to the motivation of terrorists both foreign and domestic. For many, the greatest barrier to achieving this often lies in the inability to leave their own mindset behind.

It is important to remember that the United States supports regimes and has long-standing relationships with governments that may themselves experience significant internal dissent. This may be especially important in countries where the dissent comes from well-organized factions or dissident groups who view the United States as an enemy by proxy. In these circumstances, terrorists may view acts against Americans or American institutions as a way of simultaneously striking a blow at the United States while making their own government less appealing in the eyes of American leadership. One finds an example of this in the relationship the United States has developed with Pakistan in the aftermath of the September 11 attacks. Although the national leadership of Pakistan has been very supportive of U.S. efforts against terrorists operating in the region, Pakistan also suffers from significant levels of internal dissent among a passionately vocal and active minority of its citizens. Examples may be found in the number of Pakistanis who support the values of the Taliban regime and in the murder of American journalist Daniel Pearl.

In a related vein, the United States also has relationships with nations confronted by secessionists who seek their own political autonomy. Many such separatist groups are motivated by a zeal for nationalism and autonomy that is often shaped along ethnic or religious lines; they want to carry on what they see as the mission of their forbearers by establishing or re-establishing their historic homeland. This trend has been especially visible since the great colonial powers began to grant independence to their former possessions. Particularly since the disaggregation of the former Soviet empire, the number of groups seeking autonomy has increased dramatically. It is interesting to note that there were 50 original signatories to the United Nations Charter of 1945; today there are 190 member states.

In addition to U.S. relationships with internally troubled governments, the worldwide presence of American corporations, their products, and ubiquitous trademarks carry with them American social values and enhance our visibility. The notion of American cultural hegemony is a theme that is reflected in explorations of the cultural aspects of terrorist motivation, including economic and religious issues. Particularly among theocratically governed populations, the very notion of having a secular government may be in itself, viscerally offensive, to say nothing of consumerism, an open press, empowerment of women, and multiculturalism.

It is also true that Americans as a group have historically demonstrated poor security practices or even negative attitudes about security issues. These factors also tend to prioritize U.S. targets in the minds of some terrorists. This may have a particularly important impact on U.S. military personnel in foreign locations. Consider the comments of a leader of the Turkish Workers and Peasants Liberation Party:

> The American military man is a perfect target. He is a symbol of American interests overseas. His death weakens the ties between America and our country's military rulers. American military people are paid to risk their life for their country. Do not hesitate to kill them, kill their wives, their children. Make American order them back home or risk open rebellion in Washington. American military members are highly visible targets. They seem to intentionally behave in such a way as to be culturally obnoxious and alienate themselves for no apparent reason. (U.S. Air Force Special Operations School, 1996, n.p.)

Unfortunately, these feelings often extend to civilian representatives of the U.S. government as well. The United States currently has civilian and or military personnel in virtually every nation around the world, thus maximizing the appearance of cultural invasion and concomitantly expanding the potential number of available targets in areas easily accessible to terrorists.

Justification

What is it that permits an otherwise normal person to make a conscious decision to commit violent acts of such magnitude against unknown and defenseless others? For many it appears the philosophy is no more complicated that the idea that the ends justify the means. Terrorist operators may think they have no meaningful alternatives for changing the circumstances that trouble them. Statements made by various terrorist groups and individuals often reflect the view that they can not accept the world as it is and feel they must take dramatic action now, however violent, to achieve a greater good in the long term. It is this notion of the promise of things to come that is the hallmark of many culturally or religiously motivated terrorists, a theme to which I return later.

Individual terrorists are impelled to action by a broad range of motives, but for purposes of general classification it may be useful to examine the taxonomy promulgated by the U.S. Army's Command and General Staff College (*U.S. Army Field Manual*, as cited in Terrorism Research Center, 1997). It is a robust general framework for examining the role of historic, personal, cultural, and contextual issues in the development of terrorist motivation. Aside from its descriptive aspects, the schema also gives some insights into factors affecting the decision to use terror tactics and types of weapons most likely to be used. This model incorporates some of the research done at RAND (Hoffman, 1993) and cites three general motivational categories (see Figure 9.1).

The Rationally Motivated Terrorist

In the sense it is used here, the term *rational* does not carry with it the connotation of a positively adapted, socially appropriate response. In the context of terrorism, *rational* is defined narrowly by Hoffman (1993) to simply denote perpetrators who think through the goals and possible consequences of their acts. Their motivation derives from the potential utility of a particular act as envisioned by the planners. Decisions about the use of terrorism tend to be made through analysis of the presumed cost–benefit ratio of the intended actions.

Were it not for sinister motives, one might expect terrorists of this type to sound a lot like legitimate military authorities planning an operation or even business executives developing an advertising campaign. Often, the rationally motivated terrorist represents a constituency with well-defined and at least theoretically achievable goals that may involve political, social, economic, or other specific objectives. The potential commission of a terrorist act is weighed against the risk of reprisal from opposing elements and the possible loss of support from the group's constituency.

Terrorism analysts have often pointed out that among rationally motivated terrorists, the terrorists' relationship with their constituency exerts a strong

Motivation	Context	Negotiate?
Rational	Political	High
Psychological	Personal	No
Cultural	Group	No

Figure 9.1. Probability of willingness to negotiate or use weapons of mass destruction by Hoffman typology.

influence on both target selection and types of violence. One finds an example of this in some of the bombings initiated by the Provisional Irish Republican Army. In some instances a target would be selected and the bomb placed, after which a group member would make a phone call to warn of the presence of the device and the scheduled time of its detonation. Rationally motivated terrorists may also concentrate their attacks on nonpopulated targets such as infrastructure. Property damage, however great, carries with it a much lower risk of reprisal and social condemnation than the loss of life. In this way the group demonstrates its capacity for violence but does not risk the loss of support from a constituency that may reject the killing or injury of innocents.

The terrorist group's relationship with its constituency may also extend to the notion of group membership itself. As a general rule, every handful of core terrorist operators who actually commit acts of violence are supported by a structure that evolves outward in an onion-layer fashion to include tens of thousands to hundreds of thousands of persons who provide varying degrees of support. Near the center are several dozens to several scores of people who manage finances, transportation, logistics, housing, training, and related activities. The process continues outward to those who would never provide direct tactical support but find they can endorse the general goals of the terrorist group and may provide financial, political, philosophical, or moral support. These supporters often construe the terrorists' motives in more benign or praiseworthy terms that might characterize them as liberators, freedom fighters, or defenders of the culture.

The question for the rationally motivated terrorist might be, "Will this terrorist act work for my desired purpose, given the present sociopolitical conditions?" The cost–benefit orientation of the rationally motivated terrorist is important to recognize; it may give clues about the degree to which the prospective actors may be willing to negotiate for remedies that are available to the government. Often, "carrot and stick" approaches by authorities may be effective in decreasing the motivation for violence, especially if the concessions can be framed in ways that permit the terrorists to maintain credibility with their constituency in the absence of violence.

The Psychologically Motivated Terrorist

One might reasonably argue that all terrorists are to some degree "psychological," if only because their activities represent conscious thought and behavior. In the context of Hoffman's (1993) taxonomy, however, the term *psychological* is applied to terrorist motivation in a very general sense to characterize the essential role of psychic distress as a motivational issue for the perpetrators. The point is well illustrated by the adage "Passionate anger can sometimes fill an empty life." In the case of the psychologically motivated terrorist, the impetus to commit acts of violence is often related to a profound sense of failure or inadequacy for which the perpetrator may seek redress through revenge. The question of these terrorists might be expressed as follows: "How can I use terrorism to develop and maintain a sense of identity, mastery and self esteem?"

For these terrorists, the attraction to terrorism is typically based on the psychic benefits of group affiliation. Often, the ability to achieve and maintain membership in the group actually holds a much stronger attraction than the stated political objectives of the organization. It is the process of being a terrorist and the consensual validation it brings that is important, not necessarily the achievement of stated goals. Hoffman noted that if these groups achieve any meaningful progress toward their espoused goals, they often adopt increasingly radicalized positions characterized by increasingly nonachievable goals. The development of these goals may become necessary for the organization, because the attainment of true success would threaten their continuing need to exist. Viewed in this light, one may see how the terrorists' diffuse, contradictory, illogical, or unrealistic objectives, which seem self-defeating to outside viewers, actually represent an adaptive response of sorts. For those terrorists who cling to the group for their identity, there is no meaningful goal; there is only the process of being a terrorist.

Leaders of these groups may be very charismatic. To understand the role of leaders in groups of psychologically motivated terrorists it is useful to consider the two necessary conditions for the emergence of charismatic leadership. First, the leader must be perceived to be profoundly significant. This significance is a necessary but not sufficient requirement. To be truly charismatic, the profound significance of the leader must also be accompanied by the perception on the part of the observers that their affiliation with the leader permits them to attain some degree of the leader's significance for themselves. It is this emotional profit motive of sorts that actually binds the adherent to the leader—a situation that is highly confluent with the emotional needs of the psychologically motivated terrorist. Groups that are so strongly enmeshed typically tend to resemble culturally or religiously motivated groups in that they do not tolerate ambiguity. In contrast to the rationally motivated terrorists, there is no interest in debate or dissent; negotiation both within the group and with outside authorities is anathema. Among these groups it is not unusual for group members or leaders who show a willingness to negotiate to be killed by members of their own organization. In the event the group consensus evolves to a more moderate position, the more radical members often depart to form splinter groups.

One finds a variation of the psychologically motivated terrorist in the lone wolf operator, for whom the validation of the self is not derived through group affiliation, but through the sense of power, mastery, and autonomy that attends to the ability to make unilateral decisions. Lone wolf terrorists may have a small support system, but they do not typically share power in any meaningful way. It is not unusual for lone wolf terrorists to have deep-seated feelings of alienation and anger, and to view themselves as victims.

One is reminded of the background of Oklahoma City bomber Timothy McVeigh. According to members of his legal defense team, McVeigh was possessed of a background in racist and antigovernment extremist ideology that was accompanied by a profound sense of disappointment in his life. After a successful enlistment in the Army, during Desert Storm he failed in his attempt to join the Army's Special Forces; he left the service in late 1991. The standoff at the Branch Davidian compound at Waco, Texas, and the FBI's confrontation with the Weaver family at Ruby Ridge, Idaho, confirmed McVeigh's distorted perceptions about the federal government and impelled him to take action. For all of its horror, the bombing of the Murrah Federal Building represented little more than an act of protest and revenge by one who viewed his government as despotic.

Because McVeigh's alienation contained strong elements of in-group/out-group dynamics and cultural polarization, he also represents some of the elements of a culturally motivated terrorist.

The Culturally Motivated Terrorist

According to Hoffman (1993), the motivation for these groups to commit violent acts typically derives from an almost primordial fear of cultural extermination or the loss of cultural identity. The essential question for them is this: "How can I use terrorist tactics to stop the threat to my culture / faith / ethnic group / clan / tribe?" Not surprisingly, the most important and volatile aspect of cultural identity is often religion, especially in national or cultural groups who are largely governed or socially defined by a particular system of faith. In these groups, religious values represent the idealized state of the group; provide a system of social norms; and answer essential existential questions about cosmology, proper conduct, purpose in life, and afterlife. In Afghanistan under the Taliban, for example, Islam provided not only a system of religious faith as understood in the West, but the entire system of civil and criminal law, political organization, and social behavior (Goodwin, 1998). In such a theocratic environment it is easy to see how a perceived threat to the faith would be construed as a threat to the group's existence in its entirety, not only in this life, but in the next. It this case, it is not the system of faith itself that creates the problem, but the perception of the threat to the faith.

Although the brand of Islamic fundamentalism espoused by al-Qaeda and related organizations is a clear example, it is important to note that the principles of religious fundamentalism or ethnic purity exist in many groups. One has only to look at history's dismaying record of religious or ethnically based genocidal conflicts to fully apprehend the potential destructive power of such belief systems. From the medieval Crusades to the Ku Klux Klan, the Holocaust of the Nazis and the fratricidal lunacy of the former Yugoslavia, religion and cultural separatism can easily fuel the engines of political violence.

The relative degree of volatility that attends religious or culturally motivated violence is strongly influenced by the adherents' perception of nonbelievers (Terrorism Research Center, 1997). The impetus to act is particularly strong among groups that focus on the presumed ability of outsiders to corrupt their moral values, or dilute their cultural identity. These two threats, cultural erosion and moral degradation, are especially explosive in combination. Among fundamentalists, those who believe in the literal interpretation of their respective religious or philosophical texts, the risk of nonaction is compelling (Scott, 2001).

Sullivan (2001) has described the central elements of such a perceptual framework as principles that help explain the motivation of religious terrorists:

> In a world of absolute truth, in matters graver than life or death, there is no room for dissent and no room for theological doubt. Hence the reliance on literal interpretation of texts—because interpretation can lead to error and error can lead to damnation . . . without infallibility there can be no guarantee of truth. Without such a guarantee, confusion can lead to hell. (p. 46)

In this worldview, the failure to respond to the utmost of one's ability would be tantamount to an acceptance of damnation. It is a small leap, then, to imagine the level of commitment that would derive from the need to protect one's eternal soul. Certainly the group or political mechanism perceived as the greatest source of the threat (e.g., a hegemonic foreign power, pluralism, consumerism, moral relativism, secular humanism, globalism) would be considered the most viable cultural contaminant of the faith.

The range of sources for such contamination is daunting. For example, Ignatieff (1997) has commented on the role of globalization as a potential threat to cultural identity. Whereas many in the developed world happily view globalization as an opportunity for the increased exchange of ideas, culture, and commerce, others see only the potential eradication of their cultural identity. For some, the Internet has come to symbolize the outward manifestation of the threat of globalization at the individual level. For some, the Internet represents the way in which technology can turn the world into a threatening supermarket of instantaneous information, options, and questions that can dissolve social boundaries and dilute the efficacy of traditional cultural values. It is not simply the magnitude of the threat, but the rate at which the threat can evolve and transform itself. To the fundamentalist, the threat may be cataclysmic (Afemann, 1997).

Hoffman's (1993) terrorist taxonomy makes an important contribution to our understanding of terrorist motivation by describing three critical ideas that clarify motivational aspects of religious terrorism in particular. For terrorists who believe their acts are conducted in service to a Supreme Being, their efforts do not represent simply political statements or acts born of frustration, but sacramental acts, conducted with a profound sense of the absolute moral certainty and rectitude of their behavior, carried out with divine sanction. In this context, one can see the enormity of the challenge confronting planners seeking to develop policies and strategies to address terrorist motivation at its source.

CONSIDERING THE FUTURE

One of the realities of the post September 11, 2001, environment is the dramatic shift in the sources and severity of security threats for Americans. Galdi (1995) observed that in the future, ethnicity, theology, and special interests may replace the historic role of geography, nationalism, and political ideology as sources of conflict in the world. There is much evidence to support his contention.

Terrorist acts destroy property, equipment, and lives. The destruction of buildings and equipment is less important than the taking of human life, but even the loss of life is less damaging than terrorism's broader psychic impact. Terrorist acts, whatever their source or intent, seek to destroy the psychological security that defines the victim's way of life. In the United States in particular, our national spirit is defined less by the presence of a homogeneous people than by the sense of our shared history as Americans. If it is true that terrorism is a cruel form of theater, then it is also true that the plot involves the attempted assassination of the cultural institutions and social systems that define our way of life.

Regrettably, the terrorist threat to the United States is expanding in terms of the number of actors and the destructive potential of their weapons. All the traditional forms of state-sponsored terrorism continue to be performed on the world stage, particularly among separatists, ethnic purists, and religious fundamentalists. Perhaps more disturbing is the proliferation of individual terrorists or small groups who have become actors if only to vent their private frustrations over real or imagined injustices.

It is important, therefore, for strategic planners, policy makers, emergency responders, and the public at large to remain aware not only of the physical risks to our people, but of the motivation and psychic intent of the perpetrators. The constituent elements of the terrorist's motivation carry with them important heuristic guidance that can help us shape our prevention and response to terrorist acts as individuals, as organizations, and as a nation.

10

TERRORISM FROM A PEACE PSYCHOLOGY PERSPECTIVE

RICHARD V. WAGNER AND KATHERINE R. LONG

Several years ago, while preparing the Table of Contents of the edited volume *Peace, Conflict, and Violence: Peace Psychology for the 21st Century* (Christie, Wagner, & Winter, 2001), the editors sought an author for a chapter on terrorism. No experts in the psychology of terrorism were readily apparent. Of the several prominent nonpsychologists who were contacted, none were available. Reluctantly, the editors proceeded with publication without a chapter on terrorism.

In the aftermath of September 11, peace psychology finds itself again in need of a statement on its role, its relevance in helping us understand and respond appropriately to terrorist acts. Granted, in the past century there have been violent acts carried out against civilians, such as the bombings of Dresden and Hiroshima and the massacre at Babi Yar, that have been more destructive than those perpetrated on New York City and Washington, DC. However, the latter events attained special salience for a variety of reasons, including the prominence of the victims, the perceived invulnerability of

We are grateful to Michael Wessells, Daniel Christie, Susan Opotow, and members of Richard V. Wagner's Fall 2002 course, Psychology of Social Conflict, for their helpful comments on an earlier version of this chapter.

the United States, and the visual drama of the attack, coupled with the U.S. capacity to respond extensively and with extremely destructive power. Furthermore, there is an ever-increasing worldwide destructive capacity of weapons heretofore available only to "rational" world powers. Now, thanks to the ubiquitous licit and illicit arms trade networks, these weapons are available to almost anyone with sufficient funds and wherewithal (expertise, materials, protected sites). Terrorism is no longer confined geographically, either in terms of targets or sponsoring organizations. It is not restricted to single or small groups of actors engaging in hit-and-run activities resulting in relatively small numbers of casualties. Nor is it confined to people who have a stake in the future of the cause that the terrorist acts intend to further. It is much more difficult now to generalize and predict specifically who will become terrorists; who supports them; and when, where, and how they will strike.

PSYCHOLOGY AND TERRORISM

Terrorism is behavior. Psychology is the study of behavior. Ergo, psychologists should be studying terrorism. With a few exceptions (e.g., Bandura, 1990; McCauley, 1991; see also psychiatrists such as Lifton, 1999, and Post, 1990), academic and scientific psychologists have not been prominent in the study of terrorist behavior, either historically or contemporaneously. True, September 11 has altered this lack of focus on terrorism. The preliminary responses of psychologists have been, understandably, almost entirely in the realm of "practice," that is, in the treatment of those affected by the events. Psychologists made themselves available throughout the regions directly affected, as well as elsewhere in the United States wherever people expressed personal concern about coping with the aftermath of September 11. The "next available" copy of the American Psychological Association's (APA's) *Monitor on Psychology* (November, 2001) featured articles on helping school children (pp. 38–40), military families (pp. 44–45), and practitioners themselves (pp. 36–37) to cope with the aftermath of September 11. Yet there were also reflections on how psychology can help understand terrorism. For example, former APA President Philip Zimbardo argued that we can never "stop future terrorism . . . unless we know what are the root causes of the hatred against America" (2001, p. 49) and how to blunt that hatred.

Peace psychology as an arm of APA (Division 48: Society for the Study of Peace, Conflict, and Violence) is well-positioned to contribute to our understanding of terrorism. Peace psychology "seeks to develop theories and practices aimed at the prevention and mitigation of direct and structural violence . . . (and) promotes the nonviolent management of conflict and the pursuit of social justice" (Christie et al., 2001, p. 7). This definition of the scope and interests of peace psychology makes plain how relevant the field is to the analysis of the behavior of terrorism. Many psychologists, whether they consider themselves "peace psychologists" or not, are well-qualified to explore the key questions concerning the "prevention and mitigation" of terrorist behavior. This includes directly violent behavior or the more insidious, structural violence that can lead people to see terrorism as their only effective means of responding to perceived injustices. The importance of psychology is made clear in APA's charge to its Subcommittee on Psychology's Response to Terrorism, namely to "contribute scientific knowledge and expertise to the goal of ending and addressing terrorism" (Ronald F. Levant, quoted in Martin, 2002, p. 28).

In this chapter we present a peace psychological perspective on terrorism. We focus on the basic causes of terrorism, as well as what we consider the most effective responses to terrorist acts. In the process, we recognize that psychology is just one discipline, one area of expertise among many that are essential to understanding the causes of terrorism and the most effective ways of preventing its further occurrence and mitigating the destructive effects it can have on future nonviolent responses to conflict. We leave the issue of helping people to cope with the effects of terrorist acts in the capable hands of psychology's numerous practitioners (including the related International Peace Practitioners Network).

What constitutes a "peace psychological perspective"? A common model espoused by many in the field recognizes (a) two types of violence—direct and structural—and (b) three categories of responding to violence in an effort to prevent its recurrence or further development —peacekeeping, peacemaking, and peacebuilding. *Direct violence* refers to physical or psychological harm inflicted directly by one or more persons (or communities or nations) upon another person or persons (or communities or nations). It is one person hitting another; it is gangs rumbling; it is "ethnic cleansing"; it is war. It is a gas attack in a Tokyo subway, a suicide bombing in Jerusalem, a 767 flown into the World Trade Center. Structural violence, on the other hand, is indirect violence perpetrated upon people by impersonal social structural elements of a society. It is poverty in many areas of the world (Third and First), exploitation of child labor, suppression of free speech, destruction of vital natural resources, and denial of ethnic and cultural identity and sovereignty.

Peacekeeping refers to efforts to stop ongoing violence, but without resorting to violence in the process. Separating combatants is one example, as the United Nations has done in order to prevent a recurrence of bloodshed between Greek and Turkish Cypriots. Another example was the use of U.S. federal troops to integrate schools in Arkansas and Alabama in the 1950s.

Peacemaking refers to attempts to reduce, manage, or resolve destructive conflicts. It is negotiations to resolve a labor contract; it is elders in an Amazonian indigenous community deciding between two families' competing land claims (Wagner & Wray, 1995); it is Algerian diplomats mediating an agreement between the United States and Iran to secure the release of U.S. hostages (Slim, 1992).

Peacebuilding takes peacemaking a step further by promoting the conditions of social justice and positive approaches to peace (Galtung, 1996). This philosophy presumes that building the conditions that remove the structural bases of destructive conflict must be the ultimate goal of a psychology of peace. It is, for example, an economic system that institutes management and worker control over the means of production and compensation for labor; it is respect and recognition of the legitimacy of others' perspectives that may differ from one's own; it is a social system that guarantees equal justice for all and the exclusive use of nonviolent means to resolve conflict.

Peace psychologists recognize the critical differences among peacekeeping, peacemaking, and peacebuilding, as the foregoing examples illustrate. They sit along a continuum of reactive to proactive processes and temporary to permanent solutions to violent conflict. Peacekeeping merely keeps the lid on a turbulent situation, perhaps allowing for future constructive steps to be taken; peacemaking removes the current causes of conflict; peacebuilding, however, is proactive and involves longer term, more abstract and utopian goals than peacemaking. Furthermore, once implemented, conditions established through peacebuilding are likely to be more long-lasting and to require much less "maintenance" than those deriving from peacekeeping or peacemaking (Wagner, 1988).

DEFINING TERRORISM

Before we explore a peace psychological approach to the causes of and responses to terrorist acts, it is essential that we understand what we mean by *terrorism*. We recognize the difficulties inherent in any attempt to reach consensus on such a definition. There is the inevitable problem of perspective, as the voluminous attribution theory research points out. One person's terrorist may very well be another's freedom fighter, depending on whether the focus is on the actor or the recipient. Taking into account cultural biases is also necessary when trying to develop a universally acceptable definition. Finally, we must recognize that terrorism can be both direct, overt acts of one or more persons against one or more others, and indirect as in the detrimental practices or policies of an institution or organization against one or more persons. However, in the context of this volume, we limit our definition to direct, overt terrorism, leaving structural terrorism for another day.

For our purposes, we focus on the means used when defining *terrorism* ("Understanding Terrorism," 2002). From this perspective, *terrorism* refers to violent acts directed deliberately at innocent people designed to achieve a certain political, ideological, or emotive goal. The terrorist act is symbolic, meant "to intimidate a watching popular audience" (Crenshaw, 2000, p. 406). The goal may be specific and instrumental, such as promoting a particular political, military, or ideological cause, or it may be emotive, such as vengeance or punishment for real or imagined wrongs. Establishing that terrorism is simply a strategy adopted by a group to achieve some sort of end allows us to examine the specific groups that use such a strategy and explore the possible motives behind their actions (Harmon, 2000).[1]

ROOTS OF TERRORISM

In a terrorist group each individual may have his or her personal reasons for joining the group, and certainly it is essential to understand those reasons. However, a peace psychological analysis focuses on the group bases for the creation of terrorist collectivities. This restriction means, further, that we do not consider criminal or pathological terrorism (Post, 2002a). A peace psychological perspective focuses rather on the social and political structural bases of terrorist behavior. It is important to note that because perception is an integral part of the perspective, how much the bases of terrorist behavior reflect reality may be a matter of degree.

Conflict is the initial source of all forms of terrorism. Conflict arises when two or more people or groups have mutually exclusive goals: Two teams cannot both win a basketball game; a group that wants clean, safe streets may be impeded by another that wants lower taxes; Israel and Palestine cannot both have sole possession of the city of Jerusalem. Our question here is this: What are the conditions that would lead a group of people to choose the extremely destructive tactic of terrorism as their response to conflict?

We see four different categories of motives or needs as basic to structural causes of the kind of unrest that singly or, more often, in combination can lead to terrorism (Burton, 1987). The first is what Staub (2001) referred to as difficult life conditions, that is, hunger, sickness, and shelter for oneself or one's family. Staub argued that the "tremendous life problems" (p. 77) in Germany in the 1920s and early 1930s were, at least in part, a cause of the terrorist activity the Brown Shirts engaged in prior to Hitler's ascension to power. Major gaps between the resources of haves and have-nots in many Latin American countries may well have led to the development and support for various terrorist guerrilla groups, such as the Sendero Luminoso (Shining Path) in Peru and FARC in Colombia. Kristof (2002) warned that neglect of the plight of the poor in Latin America looms as a potential crisis for the United States in its relations with the Southern hemisphere. People with few material resources, having little to lose, are prime candidates for joining extremist organizations that promise better living conditions as soon as the haves are removed from power. Muslims living in poverty may be attracted

---

[1]By this definition, the U.S. atomic bombing of Hiroshima and Nagasaki and the Allied bombing of Dresden during World War II could be considered terrorism. Civilians were the intended victims; the goal was to demoralize Japan and Germany and thereby hasten the end of the war.

to Osama bin Laden and al-Qaeda by the perception that they are fighting the prosperous United States, and Palestinian suicide bombers are alleged to be enticed by the monetary rewards promised their families.

The second basic need is for security (Christie, 1997), the lack of which often leads to fear. Ralph White (1984) made the distinction between realistic fear and exaggerated fear, the latter being based in a perception of danger that is a distortion of reality (to the extent that reality can be determined). Although the perception of danger may be as real to a party as true danger, the distinction gains importance when we consider the implications. For White, realistic fear is "healthy." It is realistic to fear another terrorist attempt to produce a catastrophic attack in the United States; this kind of fear should lead to realistic measures to prevent such an attack. An exaggerated fear, on the other hand, is by definition partly unrealistic and therefore is likely to lead to ineffective measures to avoid the feared event. Ineffective measures can have negative consequences. They can lead to heightened emotional responses to presumed creators of the threat, which in turn can lead to scapegoating. The U.S. government has made major efforts (at least rhetorical) to prevent just such scapegoating of Arab-Americans in the wake of the World Trade Center and Pentagon attacks. Exaggerated fear can also lead to escalation in the violence of the response to the threat. Finally, it can lead to erroneous analyses of what realistically should be feared and thus to inappropriate responses to the real threat. The current U.S. focus on homeland security, for example, may lead to a false sense that we are taking all the necessary steps to prevent further catastrophic acts of terror, and in the process, we may be missing the importance of contending with the original and ongoing causes of the terrorist threat.

The third basic need is for self-determination, that is, the ability to make one's own decisions about "life, liberty, and the pursuit of happiness." Numerous rebel groups that seek either political power or autonomy illustrate this root of terrorism. The Tamil Tigers, who currently seek autonomous status in Sri Lanka, are one such example. So are the guerrilla groups in Chechnya, the rebels in Kashmir, and the various competing factions terrorizing rural communities in Angola and other parts of southern Africa (Wessells & Monteiro, 2001).

The need for self-determination is, at base, an issue of power. A fear of losing power may, in fact, be one possible reason for state terrorism, that is, terrorist tactics used by those in power against their populace in order to maintain the subjugation of the latter. The Argentine and Chilean military terrorized segments of their respective populations during the 1970s as a means of securing political control they had recently acquired (Lira, 2001; Lykes, 2001). Joseph Stalin systematically terrorized his people through large-scale execution and incarceration during the 1930s to solidify his position as Premier in the USSR (White, 1984), and the Slobodan Milosevic regime promoted ethnic cleansing in an attempt to maintain Serbian control of Bosnia and Kosovo (Oberschall, 2001). State terrorism can also take place indirectly. Such is the case when one nation supports a rebel group's terrorist activities in a rival nation it wants to weaken, such as current Pakistani support of Kashmiri rebels and clandestine U.S. support of Nicaraguan "freedom fighters" (Contras) in the 1980s.

The fourth basic need is for social respect, that is, others' acknowledgement of the value of one's social identity, of the ethnic, religious, or cultural membership group. Some conflicts based in the social need for respect have long histories. The "Troubles" in Northern Ireland derive from an intractable conflict between Protestants and Catholics that had its roots in the 1688 Battle of the Boyne, in which Catholics supporting deposed English King James II were defeated by the Protestants led by William III of Orange (Pick, 2001). There is, therefore, a 300-year history of Catholic attempts to reverse (or at least remove) the Protestant domination of the political and economic structure of Northern Ireland.

However, the recognition that such respect is a critical human need seems to have emerged in Western consciousness only in the last decades of the 20th century, *realpolitik* having been the prevailing political philosophy theretofore. The increasing salience of respect for social identity probably derives both from the colonial legacy of national boundaries that do not coincide with ethnic geographical boundaries as well as from the decline in superpower rivalry following the demise of the USSR in the mid-1980s. We have seen the increasing importance of ethnic, religious, and cultural identity in the Middle East, where national boundaries (e.g., Israel, Iraq, Jordan, and Lebanon) were imposed upon previously nomadic people. One result has been political power falling into the hands of one ethnic group antagonistic to various others arbitrarily placed within its borders, an obvious case in point being Saddam Hussein's Ba'athist group's dominion over Shiite majority and Kurdish minority groups living in Iraq. Tragic events in Africa, too, have unfolded as a result of colonial insensitivity to ethnic boundaries in the political divisions imposed in the 19th century, and recent ethnic violence in the former Yugoslavia can be traced the post-World War II imposition of statehood on a conglomeration of antagonistic ethnic groups, especially the Serbs, Bosnians, Kosovars, and Croats.

The demise of the U.S.–USSR rivalry has left exposed many ethnic divisions and antagonisms that had been cloaked by the over-arching conflict between Communism and Capitalism. With the removal of the military and political pressures that supported dictatorial regimes wedded either to the U.S.-led or Soviet-led blocs, the underlying social identities gained increasing salience. Former U.S. clients, such as Shah Reza Pahlevi in Iran, were no longer unequivocally supported, leaving them vulnerable to overthrow by groups whose identity was submerged in the cause of fighting communism. The same can be said about members of the Soviet bloc. With varying degrees of difficulty, the former Yugoslavia broke into several ethnic nations (Croatia, Serbia, Montenegro, Bosnia, Kosovo); Czechoslovakia became the Czech Republic and Slovenia; and the USSR itself experienced the departure of several of the Soviet Socialist Republics and its own reconstitution as Russia. Such a redistribution of political power, and the emergence of a seeming multitude of social identities, would not have been tolerated during the East–West confrontation, but the 1990s found no basis for the maintenance of the artificial submersion of ethnic identity.

The relevance of respect for one's social identity is not restricted to social identity based in ethnicity. It can have roots in political identity, as may have been the case of the Maoist Shining Path in Peru, or in religious identity, as in the case of the Aum Shinrikyo sect with its terrorist gas attack in the subway of Tokyo in 1995 (Post, 2002a), and most recently the radical Muslim al-Qaeda.

What are the conditions that account for the attractiveness and influence of Osama bin Laden and al-Qaeda? In terms of our analysis, they are capitalizing on the convergence of several roots of terrorism. Reports indicate that many of their supporters come from areas of the Middle East with widespread poverty, where the rich are clearly allied with and sustained by Western nations. The perceived reasons for the Western support—ready access to oil reserves—promote the expansion of the gap between rich and poor, rather than the benefits of the sale of oil being passed along to those most in need.

Furthermore, self-determination is nonexistent in most cases. The West is seen as dictating the policies of the ruling elite, or the elite choose policies that maintain their place in power. The majority of Egyptians, Saudi Arabians, and Jordanians, for example, reportedly feel powerless in determining their own destinies.

Respect for social, ethnic, and religious identities appears minimal at best. We continually hear the complaint that Western influences are destroying traditional Muslim familial and community values. For example, young adults' preferences for Western garb, Western music, and freedom to come and go as they please convey an implicit devaluation of centuries of Muslim heritage.

Put these four factors together—difficult conditions, insecurity, lack of self-determination, and devaluation of traditional values—and you have an ambience conducive to an effective extremist ideology and action. Al-Qaeda has capitalized quite effectively on the disgruntlement arising from the frustrations felt by segments of the Middle Eastern population. Bin Laden is reported to be very charismatic, hence the power of the heroic image and mythology that surrounds him and attracts many adherents to his cause. Al-Qaeda has allied itself politically with various militant groups, especially with those harboring specific grievances in their own countries, thereby increasing their attractiveness and perceived legitimacy as the champion of the powerless. The indoctrination processes they have developed insulate adherents from outside influences, strengthening their hold on people who have joined their extremist cause.

In al-Qaeda's scheme, religious belief dictates that the greater Muslim society be cleansed of corrupting Western influences that have invaded many Muslim countries. It is not only Westerners, but the current leadership in many moderate or West-leaning Middle Eastern countries that are the targets of Muslim terrorism. Presumably they believe that by intimidating Western governments and the regimes they support in Moslem nations, Muslims can regain their social identities as the True Believers and legitimate disciples of the Prophet Mohammed.

RESPONDING TO TERRORISM

Certainly many peace psychologists recognize that a person or group engaging in violent behavior must be stopped by the most effective means available: constraint or, as a last resort, destruction. Realistic precautions, including realistic homeland security programs, should be instituted to protect against further terrorist attack. Whenever possible, however, peace psychologists promote nonviolent responses to violence—not necessarily as a personal philosophy (though for some it is very much a matter of personal or religious belief) but because the overwhelming majority of the evidence indicates that responding to violence with violence only provokes further violence (M. Deutsch, 1983).

As stated earlier, the peace psychology paradigm recognizes three different types of constructive responses: peacekeeping, peacemaking, and peacebuilding. The appropriateness and effectiveness of each depends on the particular conditions surrounding the conflict. Peacekeeping, such as placing neutral troops between two warring groups, is most appropriate when antagonists can find grounds only for negotiating a truce, not an agreement that resolves their current conflict. The roots of conflict remain such that when the buffer is removed, hostilities often resume. If terrorism has been a part of the conflict, as is true in the Israeli–Palestinian case, then resumed conflict is likely to include resumed terrorism. Certainly it is possible that a period of nonconflictual contact or communication between separated parties may lead to the establishment of tolerance and mutual acceptance, but basically, peace "kept" must be maintained indefinitely, unless constructive measures are taken to promote positive relations. It would seem, then, that peacekeeping is not in the long run an effective response to terrorism.

Peacemaking is a more promising measure. Negotiating to right certain injustices, to provide food and security to a beleaguered ethnic group, for example, may remove the reasons for or the support for terrorism. The very act of negotiating provides a measure of respect or recognition of another group's social identity, one of the major causes of unrest. However, negotiating with those perceived as terrorists or supporters of terrorism is anathema to those against whom the terrorism is perpetrated: Israeli politicians are hardpressed to negotiate with the Palestine Liberation Organization; the British were extremely reluctant to meet with members of the Irish Republican Army; and the United States refuses to negotiate with supporters or representatives of al-Qaeda ("you're either for us or you are against us"). Getting perceived supporters of terrorism and victims to the negotiating table is often only possible through the offices of third parties (e.g., the United States in the case of Israelis and Palestinians).

Such peacemaking efforts, when successful, usually deal either with very specific aspects of the conflict (e.g., territory to be occupied and controlled by Palestinians on the West Bank; nature and representation of various parties in a Northern Ireland government) and do not address the ultimate bases of the conflict (e.g., the occupation of land formerly belonging to Palestinians; the second-class citizenship endured by the Catholics for centuries in Northern Ireland). The Israeli–Palestinian Oslo Accords ultimately failed because they did not address these basic issues sufficiently. Furthermore, in the case of the major terrorist activity we face today—with its roots in real or perceived social structural injustice and frustration of basic human needs—peacemaking solutions are likely to provide only temporary relief from terrorism. The Israeli–Palestinian conflict has seen numerous negotiated and mediated agreements—cease fires, troop removals, land exchange, the Oslo Accords—yet somehow truly constructive relations have never evolved and terrorist activity resumes, each time more extensively than before. Interim agreements may have been made with respect to the current factors in dispute, but peaceful relations have not been built to withstand future contentions on fundamental issues. Perhaps given sufficient time for goodwill and trust to develop, peacemaking can have long-lasting effects.

Clearly, peacemaking alone is not sufficient to prevent the recurrence of terrorism. There are, however, specific peacebuilding procedures that can enhance the possibility of establishing the sort of relations between contending groups that decrease or eliminate the likelihood that future conflict will lead to a resumption of support for terrorist activity. Goodwill and trust are essential to the peacebuilding effort, so the question becomes how to build trust between parties that have been so contentious that one has resorted to terrorism either out of frustration or vengeance, or as a tactic to soften an otherwise unbeatable opponent. Or, in the case of current Middle Eastern terrorism, perhaps the most realistic scenario is building trust with and between those who are presently not in contention, as an important step in preventing the spread of terrorism beyond its current boundaries.

One psychological process that is crucial in peacebuilding is what R. K. White (1986) referred to as realistic *empathy*. Antagonists each must be able to understand the perspective of the other party—not agree or sympathize with the other but merely understand why they think and react the way they do. This is a process central to the dual-concern model of conflict style (Blake & Mouton, 1964; Rubin, Pruitt, & Kim, 1994). This model proposes that conflict be viewed in the context of each party's concern for its own welfare as well as for the welfare of the other. Degrees of concern for oneself and for the other obviously can vary greatly. To build peaceful relations, it is necessary for people to respond in ways appropriate to meeting each other's needs, that is, to have high concern both for their own and for the other's aspirations. Realistic empathy might allow Palestinians to understand the Israelis' realistic obsession with security, and Israelis to understand the Palestinian concerns with self-determination and a recognition that their lands have been wrested from them over the past 50 years. It might also allow them to appreciate the resultant sense of humiliation Palestinians may feel (Lindner, 2002). Such understanding is essential if Israelis and Palestinians are to develop trust and begin to build peaceful relations with one another.

How do we promote mutual empathy between antagonists? One such method is to provide opportunities for members of contending parties to communicate their basic needs and perspectives on how the other is impeding their ability to satisfy those needs. An excellent example is the communications workshop format developed three decades ago by Herbert Kelman (cf. Kelman, 1986) to help Arabs and Israelis begin to understand the nature and intensity of their respective beliefs about the other. This model has been adopted by others (e.g., Rothman, 1992) and implemented in various settings involving ethnic groups in conflict (e.g., Korostelina, 2002, in the Crimea, and Ohanyan & Lewis, 2002, in Georgia and Abkhazia). Hearing your adversary voice his or her perspective can be a major step in developing the empathy that helps parties build mutual trust and understanding.

Reconciliation is another measure that can build (or rebuild) trust between antagonists. "Truth and Reconciliation" commissions have been established in South Africa (de la Rey, 2001) as well as in Chile (Lira, 2001). These commissions allow aggrieved parties to voice their anger, to describe the injustices experienced, and sometimes to face those who have "aggrieved" them. Often, an element of reconciliation is some kind of an apology. The effect essentially is to institute a sense that justice prevails, to recognize the evil of the acts perpetrated, and to restore respect for the social identity of those formerly demeaned. Additionally, such procedures can have the important psychological effect of a sense of validation and recognition of the suffering undergone. Acceptance of such a process by former antagonists or their representatives can be a major factor in reconciling and establishing trust between parties formerly in intense conflict, and thereby to remove the reasons for either party to engage in extreme behavior—such as terrorism—to "right" wrongs that have occurred in previous years. The nature of postconflict reconstruction can be an essential feature in building peace in a region devastated by terrorism and other forms of violent conflict (Wessells & Monteiro, 2001).

Often it is difficult for adults who have been engaged in protracted conflict to overcome the obstacles to building peace relations with a former adversary. As a result, many peace psychologists see educating youth as a key to long-term peace (e.g., Abu-Nimer, 2000; Cairns, 1996). Programs promoting the use of cooperative methods of handling conflict in schools (e.g., D. W. Johnson & R. T. Johnson, 1989) may, in the process, begin to establish an ethic of resolving conflict in peace and with justice, a necessary step for overcoming protracted conflict the schoolchildren's parents have failed to resolve. Perhaps the ultimate goal is to "promote the culture of peace in children" (Schwebel, 2001, p. 1). Such a dramatic change in the worldwide tendency to choose violence as a means of handling conflict may be necessary if we are to rid the world of terrorism.

LIMITATIONS IN ANY PSYCHOLOGICAL ANALYSIS OF INTERNATIONAL BEHAVIOR

Before concluding our peace psychological analysis of terrorism, we should mention several limitations. First, there is the inevitable question of generalizing across various levels of analysis—from individual behavior to groups, to communities, to nations. If we study the development of antipathy between co-workers, can we apply our findings to friction between gangs or ethnic communities or neighboring countries? Is personal humiliation of a single U.S. citizen, for example, the same as the humiliation the United States felt following its defeat in Vietnam; or is the humiliation one feels when losing a legal dispute with a neighbor of the same order as the humiliation one feels when one's country faces international economic sanctions or loses a war? Levinger and Rubin's (1994) list of similarities and differences in conflict at different levels of analysis serves fair warning that the principles developed in two-person conflicts may not be applicable in larger groupings.

Tetlock (1998) similarly urged caution, noting that the application of social psychological principles to world politics is tenuous because "the tape of history runs only once" (p. 870). The world clearly does not operate like a laboratory with its control groups and random assignment of participants. Hence, post facto analysis becomes the rule rather than the exception, and this is replete with the problems inherent in delayed recall and biased perspective on value-laden events. Attempts to avoid these difficulties by the use of hypothetical scenarios present a whole new set of methodological problems, especially the huge gap between imagining violence and experiencing it in real life.

Not only is there a gap between hypothesis and reality, there is a theory-application gap. Blight (1987) has pointed out that policymakers generally perceive psychological theory to be irrelevant to the realities of making the tough decisions. They probably share the general societal view of psychology as a treatment-oriented profession and therefore perceive psychologists as naïve when it comes to the reality of policymaking. This was particularly evident during the latter stages of the Cold War: Psychologists (e.g., M. Deutsch, 1983) emphatically declaimed the dangerous, irrational, "malignant spiral" of the nuclear arms race, yet the race went on and on. The *realpolitik* philosophy that fuels arms races and eye-for-an-eye conduct predominates in much of the world. Psychologists and policymakers have difficulty appreciating one another's perspectives, to the detriment of constructive policy as well as ecologically valid empirical work on issues of group, community, and international violence.

Finally, we must remember that theory and research on issues of international importance are prone to be affected by different cultural perspectives. The overused statement that one person's terrorist is another's freedom fighter contains a cultural element at the very least (Montiel & Anuar, 2002). Salem (1993) argued that "the centrality of the idea that peace is necessarily 'good' and war is 'bad' is, to some degree, peculiar to the Christian worldview" (p. 362), thereby challenging the peace psychologist's focus on promoting nonviolent means of resolving conflict. Arguing about the truth of any of these statements of belief is not the point: Recognizing that most psychological theory and research about violence are based on Western models of psychology is the point. We are well advised to recognize that the psychological "truths" we propound are subject to the criticism of cultural bias.

CONCLUSION

The question posed in this chapter is, from a peace psychological perspective, how should we respond to terrorism. Answers to this question depend upon several things. First, what is the goal of the response: to strike back in vengeance—in which case peace psychology is irrelevant—or to prevent terrorism from recurring? Second, what is our perception of the terrorists' reasons for terrorizing. If we see terrorists as pathological, then again peace psychology is irrelevant—our choice would be to directly and violently contain or eliminate the terrorists. If, on the other hand, we see terrorists as *rationally* choosing to perpetrate violence, then our analysis must consider the causes of terrorism. These causes often include real or imagined injustice in meeting basic human needs for coping with difficult life conditions, insecurity, lack of self-determination, and disrespect for one's social identity.

For the peace psychologist, the most logical and ultimately successful means of responding to terrorism is one or more of the three nonviolent responses we have described: peacekeeping, peacemaking, and peacebuilding.

Often there is a progression from peacekeeping to peacemaking to peacebuilding (Lederach, 1997). Peace psychologists recognize that we cannot just settle for preventing current violence or resolving one more conflict but must ultimately choose methods that establish relations based on mutual trust, cooperation, and justice.

III

CONSEQUENCES OF TERRORISM

11

THE PSYCHOSOCIAL AFTERMATH OF TERRORISM

YAEL DANIELI, BRIAN ENGDAHL, AND WILLIAM E. SCHLENGER

This chapter summarizes briefly the empirical literature on the psychological impact of terrorism, viewed through the lens of a comprehensive conceptualization of trauma and its consequences. We begin with some first-hand observations of the aftermath of September 11 in New York City by Yael Danieli and then outline the conceptual framework that organizes our thinking. We then review epidemiologic studies of terrorism conducted in the United States and in other nations, and we describe what is known about preventive and treatment interventions. We close with some initial conclusions and recommendations for the future next steps.

THE AFTERMATH: SOME REFLECTIONS

The terrorist attack on September 11, 2001, is a watershed event, a defining moment in the way of being in New York, the United States, and the world. As with other massive human-made catastrophes, it became for many a demarcating rupture that maps and orients all other events and experiences as before or after it. Shortly after the event, many felt that "nothing will ever be the same" and that there was no going "back to normal." Thus, the individual and collective challenge is to create a new normality; follow new rules of behavior; search for new ways of being safe and secure; relate in new ways to oneself, others, and the world; and reassess and find meaning and values on personal, interpersonal, societal, national, and international levels.

The central question for the "new normality"—for which there is neither a single nor a simple answer—is: How do we live with growing levels of threat, anxiety, fear, uncertainty, and loss? The post-September 11 demoralization has been compounded not only by the economic decline and stock market drop, but also by the crises of civil liberties and of trust in the efficacy of the protective role of the government and other institutions—all fundamentals of American life—by the lingering threats of other forms of terrorism and by ongoing and imminent wars. Who can we trust? On whose judgment can we rely? Do we have a meaningful direction?

September 11th changed much of our public and private discourse and pervaded virtually every dimension of life in New York City. Everyone appears to be accommodating the new schedule of loss and sorrow: What kind of commemorations? When? What forms and rituals and customs of bereavement? How do we build, how high; and where do we build, work, and live from now on? Architects consider lowering the orphaned skyline, symbolic of the sobering of the exuberant, sometimes brash, New York spirit. Yet geography, including urban geography, is destiny (Erikson, 1963). Much of the carefree attitude has been lost. New York seems to be shadowed by an imperceptible yet omnipresent sense of sadness. The vanishing of the "tribute of lights"—the lights beamed upward in the shape of the twin towers—was experienced by many as reliving the loss of the towers themselves.

People felt attacked as a community and they responded as a community. Thousands volunteered in any way they could. New York's cosmopolitan and socially/culturally/racially/ethnically/religiously diverse texture was reflected in the lives lost as well as in the diverse needs and the necessarily varied responses. Doing something, anything, seemed to help lessen the shock and the sense of helplessness. Contrast that with the experience of professionals in Rwanda, for example, who—without any medical or technological aid—felt that anything they did helped. Hospital personnel in New York City—in full readiness and with every medical and technological advances available—were overwhelmed with helplessness exacerbated by the tragic fact that few, if any, survivors arrived.

Many survivors of previous trauma living in the United States were particularly affected by September 11 because, until then, they had viewed America as their "last place of safety." For some, specific aspects of the terrorist attacks (e.g., incineration for Holocaust survivors; "this is exactly like El Salvador;" "It's like time disappears") served as triggers or symbols of past trauma, reactivating stress symptoms of past traumata (see, for e.g., J. D. Kinzie,

Boehnlein, Riley, & Sparr, 2002). Their "homeostasis" may be destroyed (Zahava Solomon, personal communication, May 7, 2002). American former prisoners of war (POWs), having lived through the attack on Pearl Harbor, combat, and imprisonment, were also affected by September 11. Rodman and Engdahl (2002) found a small but significant increase in posttraumatic stress disorder (PTSD)-related distress among 117 World War II and Korean War POWs surveyed in July, 2002.

On September 11, many Americans came to realize for the first time that there are people who hate them. Typically, they rushed to ensure that they and their children did not respond by hating all Arabs. Many lost the sense of invulnerability and the American naive, unselfconscious assumption of being universally loved and esteemed (see Slouka, 2002).

New Yorkers, heartened by the outpouring of national and international solidarity and support, felt comforted by this embrace, as if it helped balance the foreign assaulting evil. Americans discovered in themselves heroism, renewed patriotism, camaraderie, and caring. The patriotic attitudes were evident as ongoing threats, such as the anthrax attack, emerged. There was great support for a war on terrorism, both domestically and internationally. Over time, international support seems to have become qualified, and in some cases we may have slid back into complacency (Peterson, 2002) or moved into a phase of numbness. In time, as expected, thus honeymoon was followed by disappointment, anger, finger-pointing, and accusations of neglect. Worse, inequities and even corruption have been alleged regarding the funds made available for the families of victims.

September 11 has also created an unprecedented surge of interest in trauma (and self-proclaimed expertise therein). Many existing groups have committed themselves to volunteer their service to those in need following the terrorist attacks. Other groups, particularly around New York City, were created specifically for this purpose. Many professions, including psychology, responded overwhelmingly on all levels. Various societies, institutions, and organizations generated feature publications from their unique perspectives. Providers dealing with the psychosocial needs of victims of trauma worldwide applied approaches based on their experience and training (Danieli, Rodley, & Weisaeth, 1996; Green et al., 2002; Weine et al., 2002).

TRAUMA AND THE CONTINUITY OF SELF: A MULTIDIMENSIONAL, MULTIDISCIPLINARY INTEGRATIVE (TCMI) FRAMEWORK

Massive trauma causes such diverse and complex destruction that only a multidimensional, multidisciplinary integrative framework (Danieli, 1998) is adequate to describe it. An individual's identity involves a complex interplay of multiple systems, including the biological and intrapsychic; the interpersonal—familial, social, communal; the ethnic, cultural, ethical, religious, spiritual, natural; the educational/occupational; the material/economic, legal, environmental, political, national, and international. These systems coexist along the time dimension, creating a continuous sense of life from past through present to the future. Ideally, one should have free psychological access to and movement within all these identity systems. Each system is the focus of one or more disciplines that may overlap and interact, such as biology, psychology, sociology, economics, law, anthropology, religious studies, and philosophy. Each discipline has its own views of human nature, and it is these views that inform what the professional thinks and does.

TRAUMA EXPOSURE AND "FIXITY"

Trauma exposure can cause a rupture, a possible regression, and a state of being "stuck" in this free flow, which Danieli (1998) has called *fixity*. The intent, time, duration, extent, and meaning of the trauma for the individual and the survival strategies used to adapt to it determine the degree of rupture and the severity of the fixity. Fixity can be intensified in particular by the conspiracy of silence (Danieli, 1982, 1998); the survivors' reaction to the societal—including healthcare and other professionals—indifference, avoidance, repression, and denial of the survivors' trauma experiences (see also, the second wound; Symonds, 1980); and homecoming stress (D. R. Johnson et al., 1997). This conspiracy of silence is detrimental to the survivors' familial and sociocultural (re)integration by intensifying their already profound sense of isolation and mistrust of society. It further impedes the possibility of their intrapsychic integration and healing, and it makes the task of mourning their losses impossible. Fixity may increase vulnerability to further trauma. It also may render immediate reactions to trauma (e.g., acute stress disorder) chronic, and, in the extreme, become life-long (Danieli, 1997) *posttrauma/ victimization adaptational styles* (Danieli, 1985), when survival strategies generalize to a way of life and become an integral part of one's personality, repertoire of defense, or character armor.

These effects may also become intergenerational in that they affect families and succeeding generations (Danieli, 1998). In addition, they may affect groups, communities, societies, and nations. Studies by Rich (1982), Klein (1987), and Sigal and Weinfeld (1989) have validated Danieli's descriptions (Danieli, 1985) of at least four differing post-Holocaust adaptational styles of survivors' families.

Klein-Parker (1988); Kahana, Harel, and Kahana (1989); and Helmreich (1992) confirm this heterogeneity of adaptation and quality of adjustment. The heterogeneity of responses of families of survivors to their Holocaust and post-Holocaust life experiences emphasizes the need to guard against expecting all victims/survivors to behave in a uniform fashion and to match appropriate therapeutic interventions to particular forms of reaction.

The recognition of the possible long-term impact of trauma on one's personality and adaptation and the intergenerational transmission of victimization-related pathology still await explicit inclusion in future editions of the diagnostic nomenclature. Until they are included, the behavior of some survivors, and some children of survivors, may be misdiagnosed, its etiology misunderstood, and its treatment, at best, incomplete. This framework allows evaluation of each system's degree of rupture or resilience and thus informs the choice and development of optimal multilevel intervention. Repairing the rupture and thereby freeing the flow rarely means "going back to normal." Clinging to the possibility of "returning to normal" may indicate denial of the survivors' experiences and thereby fixity.

Immediately following September 11, Danieli (2001) suggested that more than ever, issues related to the time dimension emerged as paramount. First was the imperative to resist the culturally prevalent (American) impulse to do, to find quick fixes, to focus on outcome rather than process, to all too swiftly look for closure, and to flee "back to normal." Second, knowing that there will be long-term effects of the disaster and of the immediate interventions, it is imperative to recognize the necessity for and importance of long-term commitment to providing optimal care, and to examine systematically every short-term decision from a long-term perspective. She also noted the necessity of considering at-risk times (e.g., family holidays, anniversaries) as well as the at-risk groups.

Integration of the trauma must take place in all of life's relevant systems, and it cannot be accomplished by the individual alone. Systems can change and recover independently of other systems. Rupture repair may be needed in all systems of the survivors, in their community and nation, and in their place in the international community. To fulfill the reparative and preventive goals of trauma recovery, perspective and integration through awareness and containment must be established so that one's sense of continuity and belongingness can be restored. To be healing and even self-actualizing, the integration of traumatic experiences must be examined from the perspective of the totality of the trauma survivor's family and community members.

A major factor in the rejection of the initial World Trade Center reconstruction designs was the city's requirement that they include as much commercial space as had been lost, an exercise in "going back to economic normal," while not attending fully to all other relevant systems in need of repair. "We can reconstruct buildings and infrastructure, but how do you reconstruct dreams and feelings?" Not considering the totality of the needs of the communities involved is like "building from the roof down" (Pasagic, 2000), a guarantee of failure, if not immediately, then certainly in the future.

REACTIONS AND RESPONSES TO TERRORISM

The definition of terrorism is complex and subject to considerable debate and argument. Chapters 1 (Marsella) and 2 (Hallett) in this volume contain detailed discussions of the definitional problems. Generally, terrorism entails systematic, yet unexpected, violent attacks or threats of violence, to intimidate or coerce—especially against defenseless civilians. It is used in a calculated manner and is driven by an element of hatred and/or political purpose.

Regardless of the weapons used, terror is psychological warfare. It may be massive or small scale; it may be sustained (long term) or a one-time event. In terms of its effects, it is more malignant than natural and technological disasters. Its impact extends far beyond those actually killed or injured.

Mass panic, marked by nonsocial and irrational flight, as depicted in disaster movies, is, in fact, a rare response to disaster. Mass anxiety and the outbreak of multiple unexplained symptoms (i.e., nausea, vomiting, headache) are common (Pastel, 2001). They may be the main threat in the face of a bio-weapons attacks (Moscrop, 2001). Experiences in the Tokyo sarin gas attack suggest that the psychological casualties may outnumber the physical casualties by approximately four to one (Kawana, Ishimatsu, & Kanda, 2001).

The long-term social and psychological effects of an episode of chemical or biological attack, real or suspected, are likely to be as damaging as the acute effects, if not more so (Wessely, Hyams, & Bartholomew, 2001). Medically unexplained physical symptoms, such as those now associated with Gulf War syndrome, challenge patients, clinicians, scientists, and policymakers.

Terrorism's effects are defined narrowly in both of the world's primary nosologies, the 10th edition of *International Classification of Diseases* (ICD-10; World Health Organization, 1992) and the 4th edition of *Diagnostic and Statistical Manual of Mental Disorders* (DSM–IV; American Psychiatric Association, 1994). The most frequent effects include acute stress disorder (ASD) in the short term, and PTSD in the longer term. Additional disorders that frequently occur after exposure to trauma include depression, other anxiety disorders, and substance abuse. Conversion and somatization disorders may also occur, and they are more often observed in non-Western cultures (Engdahl, Jaranson, Kastrup, & Danieli, 1999). Complicated bereavement (Horowitz, 1976) and traumatic grief (Prigerson & Jacobs, 2001) have been noted as additional potential effects.

Shear and colleagues (2001) defined *traumatic grief* as a constellation of symptoms, including preoccupation with the deceased, longing, yearning, disbelief and inability to accept the death, bitterness or anger about the death, and avoidance of reminders of the loss. Research shows that traumatic events that are man-made and intentional, unexpected, sudden, and violent have a greater adverse impact than natural disasters (Norris, 2002).

PTSD has been found to be associated with stable neurobiological alterations in both the central and autonomic nervous systems. Neuropharmacologic and neuroendocrine abnormalities have been detected in the noradrenergic, hypothalamic-pituitary-adrenocortical, and endogenous opioid systems. These data are reviewed extensively elsewhere (Friedman, Charney, & Deutch, 1995). The proposed diagnoses of "complex PTSD" (Herman, 1992) and "disorder of extreme stress not otherwise specified" (DESNOS; Roth et al., 1997) that were considered for but not included in *DSM-IV* (American Psychiatric Association, 1994) represent attempts to go beyond the basic 17 symptoms of PTSD and associated features. Although several of the DESNOS descriptions, such as survivor's guilt, are included as associated features of PTSD, many believe that it is a construct in its own right. Similarly, to Danieli (see the TCMI Framework above), the descriptions of complex PTSD and DESNOS emphasize profound personality changes following repeated exposure to man-made traumata; these are allowed in *DSM–IV* only as associated features but not as a distinct diagnosis, and these descriptions recognize alterations in the survivor's world assumptions and values.

In each of these instances, however, the entity represents a hybrid that mixes aspects typically conceptualized as belonging to Axis I (clinical syndromes defined by the presence of specific symptom constellations) and Axis II (personality disorders—"enduring pattern of inner experience and behavior that . . . is pervasive and inflexible . . . is stable over time, and leads to distress or impairment"; American Psychiatric Association, 1994, p. 629). The *ICD-10* (World Health Organization, 1992) category of "enduring personality change after catastrophic experience" (p. 209) is more consistent with Danieli's notion of posttrauma/victimization adaptational styles, but the *ICD-10* description focuses on adjustment rather than adaptation and is far narrower than Danieli's. Additional systematic research is needed to document in detail the long-term course of the aftermath of repeated exposure to man-made trauma, including terrorism.

Exposure to trauma may also prompt review and reevaluation of one's self-perception, beliefs about the world, and values. Although changes in self-perception, beliefs, and values can be negative, varying percentages of trauma-exposed people report positive changes as a result of coping with the aftermath of trauma ("posttraumatic growth," Tedeschi & Calhoun, 1996). Survivors have described an increased appreciation for life, a reorganization of their priorities, and a realization that they are stronger than they thought. This is related to Danieli's (1994b) recognition of competence versus helplessness in coping with the aftermath of trauma. Competence (through one's own strength and/or the support of others), coupled with an awareness of options, can provide the basis of hope in recovery from traumatization.

Within the same context, Peterson (2002) assessed the values, strengths, and virtues before and after September 11 in convenience samples of Americans, using a cross-sectional, Internet-based survey approach. Although not generalizable to Americans as a whole, the results are still of interest. Among the 24 strengths assessed, 6 were higher after September 11 than before: love, gratitude, hope, kindness, spirituality, and teamwork. This finding is consistent with the predictions of the so-called terror management theory, which holds that people "manage" the terror of confronting their mortality by increasing their identification with culturally salient values. Six months after September 11, however, gratitude, hope, and love scores were lower, although only gratitude had returned to its pre-September 11 level. Kindness, spirituality, and teamwork, however, were higher 6 months after September 11.

Children exposed to large-scale traumatic events may experience significant worries and fears, concerns about personal safety and security, nightmares (either resembling or seemingly unrelated to the traumatic events), separation anxiety, and somatic complaints. In addition, children may experience changes in sleep and appetite, and school performance may be adversely affected by difficulties with concentration, attention, and increased activity levels. Other reactions common in children include an increased sensitivity to sounds such as sirens, increased startle response, and a decreased interest in once pleasurable activities. As they attempt to cope with and process traumatic events, younger children may engage in posttraumatic play and ask questions or talk about the event repeatedly. Among older children, concerns about safety and security may extend to a sense of a foreshortened future. In addition, adolescents may exhibit withdrawal, substance abuse, and risk-taking behaviors, as well as a fascination with death and suicide. Finally, extensive viewing of media coverage appears to negatively affect children of all ages. Interventions with children must consider the distinct differences between adult and child responses (Gurwitch, Sullivan, & Long, 1998).

INTERNATIONAL RESEARCH FINDINGS

With the exception of the Oklahoma City bombing, prior to September 11, the United States has largely been spared terrorist attacks on its land in comparison with the rest of the world. Seeking guidance from the experience of the rest of the world, we summarize below some of the existing empirical studies on the aftermath of terror. The examples in this section represent primarily studies on the effects of continued terrorism. We then summarize studies conducted in the United States.

Abenhaim, Dab, and Salmi (1992) contacted all known survivors of terrorist attacks occurring in public places in France between 1982 and 1987; 254 participated in the survey. PTSD was present in 9% of uninjured and moderately injured survivors but in 31% of severely injured ones. Major depression was found in 13% of all survivors and was unrelated to severity of injury. Three days after a 1996 terrorist bombing of a bus in India, 11 of 31 survivors studied had diagnosable psychiatric disorders (i.e., acute stress reaction, depression, and dissociative amnesia). The most common symptoms were depersonalization (interpersonal detachment); feeling things were not real; sleep disturbances; loss of appetite; nightmares; situational anxiety; depression; irritability; dulled feelings; self-blame; guilt; loss of interest; suicidal ideas; and worry about money, spouse, work, and children (Gautam et al., 1998).

Eleven people were killed and 60 injured in the Enniskillen bombing of November 1987 in Northern Ireland. Survivors were psychologically appraised 6 months and 1 year later. At 6 months 50% had developed PTSD. This group comprised more females than males; however, all victims were highly distressed. No correlation was found between psychological distress and physical injury, calling into question previous assertions to the contrary (Curran et al., 1990). Acknowledging the role of ideology in reinforcing the continued participation of both Catholic and Protestant youth in the "Troubles" in Northern Ireland, Cairns and Toner (1993) created an innovative program to transform the ideological rift into a force for reconciliation. Their program included discussion regarding ideological differences that usually arise in the context of developing peer relationships.

W. Austin (1989) examined how Filipinos have reacted to the continuing presence of terrorist violence (i.e., ambush, murder, kidnapping, and property destruction). Among the effects of terrorism were both social and individual changes, an increase in political corruption, and some economic decline. Individual adaptations to terrorism included increased fear and anger, decreased mobility, a focus on immediate safety, and habituation toward terrorist acts. Among survivors of the massacre of a South African church congregation, religious beliefs and practices were frequently used to construct a meaningful retrospective narrative of the massacre (Ogden, Kaminer, Van Kradenburg, Seedat, & Stein, 2000). Kawana, Ishimatsu, and Kanda (2001) found that, even 5 years later, psychological aftereffects remained among survivors of the Tokyo sarin gas attack.

Kilpatrick, Best, Smith, and Falsetti (2002) evaluated services provided to family members affected by the Pan Am 103 terrorist bombing. These services included an international toll-free telephone number and informational hotline, a secure Internet Web page to provide updates about the trial, funding for mental health services, travel funds to attend the trial, assistance with travel arrangements, and a Lockerbie trial handbook. The most frequently used resources included the trial handbook and Web page. These innovative services allowed accurate information to be disseminated to large numbers of people. Although the death of family members was identified as a cause of major disruption in people's lives, and approximately half of the individuals contacted reported that they had emotional or behavioral problems serious enough to consider seeking therapy, only about one-third used mental health services. Reasons for low mental health care utilization included beliefs that they could handle their difficulties on their own with the support of friends, family, and clergy; stigma associated with obtaining services; and lack of funds. However, 90% of victims who did use services evaluated them positively.

Coping with chronic recurrent attacks and threats of attacks has, in a sense, become a way of life among many groups, such as Israelis living under a continuous threat of terrorist attack. This can lead to "emergency routine" (Zahava Solomon, personal communication, May 7, 2002) that combines conducting necessary daily tasks with an ever-present sense of danger, characterized by tension, apprehension, and distress. Psychiatric casualties, typically suffering from acute stress disorder, are referred to in the media as anxiety or shock casualties. Hyperarousal during the postattack period is seen not only as normal but also as a desirable functional behavior. Avoidance that reduces the chance of becoming a casualty is interpreted as functional coping.

In a sample of 50 Israeli bus commuters, Gidron, Gal, and Zahavi (1999) examined the relationship between anxiety from terrorism and the use of three coping strategies: (a) emotion-focused coping (calming-distraction); (b) problem-focused coping (checking-behavior); and (c) denial (reduced perceived vulnerability). Commuting frequency was negatively correlated and problem-focused coping was positively correlated with anxiety from terrorism. Ratios of problem-focused coping/denial and of problem-focused/emotion-focused coping were each positively correlated with anxiety from terrorism. Coping ratios accounted for 15% of the variance in anxiety from terrorism, after considering commuting frequency. Combining minimal problem-focused preventive acts with distraction and reduced perceived vulnerability may be beneficial.

Seventeen years after Palestinian guerrillas took 120 high school children hostage, killed 22 and wounded many more, the survivors were still experiencing many PTSD symptoms, particularly those who were physically injured (Desivilya, Gal, & Ayalon, 1996). Nuttman-Shwartz and Lauer (2002) explained the difficulties that arose in group intervention with terror-injured people in Israel as paralleling and interacting with the unconscious difficulties of Israeli society as a whole in coming to terms with terror. Group cohesion and a sense of empowerment developed, but the members remained unable to cope with their terror-related emotions such as fear, humiliation, and helplessness stemming from their injuries, and they remained unable to mourn their losses. They clung to their shared identity as terror victims, as helpless and isolated from others. The authors likened the inability of the group members to go beyond this identity to the same inability that permeates Israeli society as a whole. Their analysis may have implications for other societies where terror is multidimensional, in that it is not only a personal but also a national trauma, and in that it is a constant, ever-present source of threat and tragedy.

REVIEW OF U.S. EMPIRICAL STUDIES
OF RESPONSES TO TERRORISM

The two events in the United States that have been studied empirically are the 1995 bombing of the Murrah Federal Building in Oklahoma City and the September 11, 2001, terrorist attacks. Curiously, the February 26, 1993 terrorist attack on the World Trade Center seems to have received only meager attention.

Bombing of the Alfred P. Murrah Federal Building

On the morning of April 19, 1995, the blast from a homemade car bomb destroyed the Murrah Building. Among the 167 people killed, 19 were children; 684 others were injured. North et al. (1999) studied a sample of 261 adults drawn from a confidential registry of survivors created by the Oklahoma State Department of Health. The investigators interviewed this sample about 6 months following the event. Findings indicated that about one-third of this directly exposed sample reported symptom patterns that met the criteria for PTSD, and 30% met the criteria for some disorder other than PTSD. Other disorders that were relatively prevalent among survivors were major depression (22.5%) and alcohol use disorder (9.4%). With respect to PTSD, virtually all of the survivors met the intrusive recollections and hyperarousal criteria, so the difference between survivors who did and did not have PTSD involved the avoidance and numbing criterion. This suggested to the investigators that screening (e.g., by primary care providers) to identify those affected following acts of terrorism should focus on these symptoms.

Taking a somewhat different approach, D. W. Smith, Christianson, Vincent, and Hann (1999) conducted a community-based, case control (nonequivalent comparison group) study in which probability samples of adults in the Oklahoma City and Indianapolis metropolitan areas were interviewed by telephone about 3 months after the bombing (July–August 1995), and a second set of cross-sectional samples was interviewed about 18 months following the bombing (September–November 1996). Assessment focused on participants' exposure to the bombing and on psychological symptoms, substance use (drinking and smoking), and help seeking in the follow-up period. More than 60% of the population of the Oklahoma City metropolitan area reported at least one direct impact on their life from the bombing (e.g., knew someone who was killed or injured, attended a victim's funeral). Outcome findings indicated higher levels of psychological distress, a greater increase in substance use, and more help seeking in Oklahoma City compared with Indianapolis, although symptom levels dropped in both cities over time.

Pfefferbaum and her colleagues conducted a series of studies of the Murrah Building bombing, many focusing on the effects on children in the surrounding community. In one study, Pfefferbaum, Nixon, Krug, et al. (1999) recruited 3,218 middle and high school students in the Oklahoma City Public School District about 2 months after the bombing. Participants were described as "volunteers recruited from class-rooms of teachers agreeing to distribute the survey instrument" (p. 1070). About 9% reported that a relative (parent, sibling, or other relative) had been killed in the blast, and about 15% reported that a relative had been injured. Analyses indicated that posttraumatic stress symptom levels were related to gender (girls higher), knowing victims injured or killed, and exposure to bomb-related television coverage.

In a more detailed analysis of the middle school student sample, Pfefferbaum, Nixon, Tivis, et al. (2001) found that "television exposure accounted for more variance than physical or emotional exposure . . . although the effect of all three types of exposure was small" (p. 209). Subsequently, Pfefferbaum, Seale, et al. (2000) assessed a sample of sixth grade students who lived in a community within 100 miles of Oklahoma City. Again, reports of knowing someone injured or killed, and exposure to the bombing through television, were found to be related to posttraumatic stress symptom levels.

Additionally, Pfefferbaum, Call, Lensgraf, Miller, Flynn, Doughty, et al. (2001) assessed traumatic grief in a convenience sample of people who suffered losses in the Murrah Building explosion. The investigators found a strong association between grief and PTSD symptoms, and they found that PTSD symptom levels moderated the relationship between grief and functioning. (The relationship between grief and functioning is higher for those with higher levels of PTSD symptoms.) They also noted the importance of these findings for the training of mental health (and other) professionals who serve victims.

More recently, North and her colleagues reported findings from retrospective assessments of a volunteer sample of firefighters, 97% of whom were male, who served as rescue and/or recovery workers at the Murrah Building after the bombing. Assessments were conducted over a long period, on average nearly 3 years after the event. North, Tivis, McMillen, Pfefferbaum, Spitznagel, et al. (2002) found that 13% of the firefighters reported symptoms consistent with a diagnosis of PTSD, compared with a rate of 23% of men directly exposed to the explosion. PTSD prevalence was higher among those firefighters who spent more time working at the site. As with other rescue worker studies, North et al. observed relatively high prevalence of substance use disorders, particularly alcohol abuse/dependence.

September 11, 2001

Initial empirical information about the psychological effects of the September 11 attacks, based on epidemiological surveys of the nation and of the areas most affected, became available relatively quickly. The following re-view presents the studies in chronological order.

A poll of 1,200 American adults (Pew Research Center, 2001) found that the percentage of Americans who reported feelings of depression as a result of the attacks peaked at 71% in mid-September and declined steadily to 24% by November 8. At about the same time, based on a random-digit dialing survey of 560 American adults conducted 3 to 5 days after September 11, Schuster et al. (2001) reported that 44% of their national sample were bothered "quite a bit" or "extremely" by at least one of five selected PTSD symptoms. Results varied by gender, race/ethnicity, and distance from the World Trade Center, and 35% of the adults surveyed said that their children had one or more of such symptoms. In a subsequent follow-up of this sample, Schuster et al. reported a substantial reduction in the reporting of the five selected PTSD symptoms, from 44% to 16% 2 months later.

Similarly, T. W. Smith, Rasinski, and Toce (2001) conducted telephone interviews of 2,126 American adults between September 13 and September 27, asking about physical and emotional responses to the September 11 attacks. The most common symptoms reported by more than half of respondents were crying, feeling nervous and tense, or having trouble getting to sleep. Investigators noted, however, that although levels of reported "negative affect" were somewhat elevated in New York City, levels for the U. S. population as a whole were close to normal levels.

The American Psychological Association (Bossolo, Bergantino, Lichtenstein, & Gutman, 2002) commissioned a random digit dialing survey of 1,900 Americans nationwide, including oversamples in New York and Washington, in the 4th month after the attacks. Findings indicated that about one quarter of Americans reported "feeling more depressed than at any other time" (p. 1) in their lives, and that levels of PTSD symptoms were much higher in New York than elsewhere in the country. Additionally, people who reported exposure to other traumatic events prior to the September 11 attacks were significantly more likely to report higher levels of symptoms of depression, anxiety, and PTSD compared with those who had not.

Bossolo et al. (2002) also noted that "Residents in the Washington, D.C. area are far less likely than New Yorkers—and even those elsewhere in the nation—to report feeling depressed or anxious. Washingtonians seem less introspective and personally affected by the attacks than the rest of the nation" (p. 3). Considering that it is in Washington that the decisions are made about the rest of the nation, these findings are worrisome. These initial studies share several strengths, including assessment in the immediate aftermath of the attacks and nationally representative samples. They also have some common problems, including use of mental health symptom measures whose relationship to clinical diagnosis is unknown, incomplete coverage of the sites that were directly attacked, and lack of quasi-experimental comparisons.

The next wave of studies addressed more directly the issue of clinically significant symptomatology. Galea et al. (2002) studied the prevalence of PTSD and of depression among adults living south of 110th Street in Manhattan. Using random digit dialing techniques, they conducted telephone interviews with a sample of more than 1,000 adults, focusing on September 11 exposures and the symptoms of PTSD and major depression, using mental health screening measures whose relationship with clinical diagnosis had been empirically established. Findings indicated that 7.5% of the adults living in the portion of Manhattan covered were likely cases of PTSD, and 9.7% were likely cases of major depression. Additionally, those living south of Canal Street—that is, closest to the World Trade Center site—were nearly three times as likely to have PTSD as those living farther away, and those who report two or more life stressors (from a checklist of eight) in the year before the attacks were more than five times as likely to have PTSD as those who reported having experienced none of the listed stressors.

In addition to studying PTSD and depression, these investigators also studied alcohol, tobacco, and marijuana use among their sample (Vlahov et al., 2002). Findings indicated that significant percentages reported increased use of each of these substances after September 11 and that the prevalence of PTSD was significantly higher among those whose use of cigarettes and marijuana increased, and the prevalence of depression was significantly higher for those who increased use of all three of the substances assessed.

Galea and his colleagues (2002) subsequently conducted a second cross-sectional survey of New York in the 4th month following the attacks, to gather information about the course of symptomatic responses. Using the same methods applied to the earlier survey, they found the prevalence of September 11-related PTSD to be 7.0% in the 4th month after the attacks.

Schlenger et al. (2002) surveyed a probability sample of 2,273 adults across the country, including oversamples of the New York City and Washington, DC, metropolitan areas, in the 2nd month after the attacks. The sample was selected from the Knowledge Networks Web-enabled Panel, a standing research panel that had recruited nearly 60,000 households nationwide at the time the study was conducted. The survey focused on specific exposures to the September 11 attacks and on mental health symptoms, assessed using well-validated measures of PTSD symptoms (the PTSD Checklist; Weathers, Litz, Herman, Huska, & Keane, 1993) and of clinically significant psychological distress (the Brief Symptom Inventory 18 global symptom index; Derogatis, 1994). Findings indicated that the prevalence of probable PTSD in the New York metropolitan area was 11.2%, compared with 2.7% in the Washington, DC, metropolitan area, 3.6% in other major metropolitan areas (that were not attacked), and 4.0% in the rest of the country (overall U.S. prevalence 4.3%). No significant differences were found, however, in the prevalence of clinically significant but nonspecific distress, which was found to be generally within normal limits in New York (16.6%),

Washington (14.9%), other major metropolitan areas (12.3%), and the rest of the country (11.1%; overall U.S. prevalence 11.6%).

Model-based comparisons of the prevalence of PTSD in the New York metropolitan area versus the remainder of the country, adjusted for sociodemographic characteristics, suggest that there are more than 500,000 "excess" cases of probable PTSD in the New York metropolitan area in the wake of the attacks. Additionally, multivariate analyses of the New York sample that included both exposure measures and sociodemographic characteristics showed that age, gender, direct exposure to the attacks, and number of hours of television coverage of the attacks watched were independently associated with PTSD symptom levels but that only gender, hours of television watched, and the television content index were independently associated with nonspecific distress. Schlenger et al. interpreted these findings as indicating that direct exposure to the attacks was closely related to PTSD symptomatology but not to nonspecific distress and that extended watching of television coverage of the attacks was better interpreted as a coping mechanism for people who were already distressed than as an exposure that caused distress.

Subsequently, Silver, Holman, McIntosh, Poulin, and Gil-Rivas (2002) reported findings from a three-wave, longitudinal study that began with a national sample of more than 2,700 adults. Assessment included direct and indirect exposures, psychological symptoms, and coping mechanisms. Descriptive findings indicated that acute stress and PTSD symptom levels decreased over time, and longitudinal models indicated that exposure and losses associated with the attacks, pre-attack mental health status, exposure to other traumas, and six specific coping styles were independently associated with PTSD symptom levels. Only active coping was associated with symptom reduction—the five others (behavioral disengagement, denial, support-seeking, self-blame, and self-distraction) were associated with increased symptom levels.

Finally, studies of September 11 published to date have focused on reactions of adults, for a variety of ethical and logistical reasons. Both Schuster et al. and Schlenger et al. asked adults in households with children about the reactions of the children, and in both studies substantial proportions of adults (35% nationwide in Schuster et al. and 49% nationwide and 61% in the New York metropolitan area in Schlenger et al.) indicated that one or more children were "upset." Although not definitive, these findings suggest the need for studies focusing specifically on the reactions of children. Hoven and her colleagues (2002) at Columbia University have conducted an as-yet unpublished epidemiological study of a probability sample of students in grades 4–12 in New York City schools, on behalf of the New York City Board of Education. The findings indicate that 10.5% of children in grades 4–12 report symptoms consistent with a diagnosis of PTSD, which represents about 75,000 public schoolchildren. Additionally, findings indicated that report of exposure to one or more traumatic events prior to September 11 was a significant risk factor for the development of PTSD post-September 11.

Thus, empirical information about reactions to the events of September 11 based on probability samples of the U.S. population became available surprisingly quickly following the attacks. Initial cross-sectional findings showed that many in the United States were deeply disturbed by the attacks, but subsequent longitudinal findings have been consistent with the stress evaporation hypothesis, suggesting that at least one component of the distress documented in the initial assessments is self limiting. Later studies that focused on clinically significant symptoms and disorder prevalence generally showed that PTSD prevalence was strongly associated with direct exposure (or "connection") to the attacks and that the PTSD problem following the attacks was concentrated in the New York metropolitan area. Additionally, the studies that (retrospectively) assessed pre-September 11 exposure to trauma found such exposure to be an important risk factor for the development of PTSD following the attacks.

The strengths of this body of literature include the speed with which preliminary information about reactions to the attacks has been made available, the use of probability samples, documentation of both direct and indirect exposures, and inclusion in some studies of well-validated screening measures of clinically significant symptomatology. As a result, policy makers and others have a much clearer early picture of the aftermath of the September 11 attacks than has previously been possible. Nevertheless, it is important that these initial findings be confirmed as extensively as possible with longitudinal studies that use comprehensive clinical assessments rather than screening instruments and that use methods that maximize sample member participation (i.e., minimize nonresponse). Additionally, the studies that assessed prior exposure to trauma, though assessed retrospectively, have shown that such exposure is a risk factor for developing PTSD to the September 11 attacks.

North and Pfefferbaum (2002) made comprehensive methodological comments on the September 11 studies. They raise the important question of indirect exposure, given the massive (and repetitive) media coverage of the events. They point out that the *DSM–IV* criteria mention "witnessing" as an exposure, but also note that "No provision is made, however, for classification of indirect witnessing through viewing media images of the event" (p. 635). It is also important to note that witnessing is included in the official United Nations definition of "victim" (UN General Assembly, 1985).

Although not in the published manuscript, Schlenger et al. (2002) found that more than 10 million adults in the United States reported that they had a family member, friend, or coworker killed or injured in the attacks, including about 7.5 million outside of the New York and Washington, DC, metropolitan areas. It seems likely that the subcommittee that developed the *DSM–IV* criteria for PTSD did not envision an event in which millions of Americans would watch on television the destruction of buildings where their family members, friends, and co-workers were working. This is an issue that will receive much more attention in the months and years ahead.

It is also not clear that the PTSD syndrome, as defined in *DSM–IV*, adequately captures the range of mental health consequences of terrorism, particularly for long exposures to it. As mentioned earlier, additional diagnostic categories have been and continue to be developed in attempts to do full justice to these complex phenomena.

Neria and his colleagues (Neria, Bromet, & R. Marshall, 2002) have pointed to an important limitation of standard community epidemiologic assessment methods. Those methods ask respondents to make a link only between traumatic exposures and PTSD symptoms but not the symptoms of other psychiatric disorders and may thus mask the relationship of other psychiatric disorders (e.g., depression) with trauma. If so, the current body of epidemiologic research may underestimate substantially the full impact of trauma on the lives of those exposed. Given the emphasis in recent (and presumably future) versions of the *Diagnostic and Statistical Manuals of Mental Disorder* on the empirical bases for diagnostic criteria, this masking may have found its way into the diagnostic nomenclature as well. These issues should be high on the agenda for researchers and clinicians interested in documenting and treating the symptomatic responses of people exposed to terrorism and related events.

INTERVENTIONS

Interventions following exposure to terrorist attacks may include (a) secondary prevention efforts targeted at all of the victims, followed by (b) treatment for those who develop clinically significant symptoms. Public safety is usually a first priority in the wake of terrorism, followed by a variety of basic relief services (food, water, health, shelter, etc.). (Re)establishing and maintaining safety in an area subject to terrorism is a complex problem (United Nations, 2000b) that must be viewed from the community-at-large perspective. Whereas preparedness is critical to efforts at prevention in general, it is particularly challenging in the case of terrorism because we do not know what to prepare for. *Mental Health and Mass Violence* (National Institute of Mental Health, 2002) is one attempt at summarizing consensus on best practices for early psychological intervention for victim/survivors of mass violence, reached shortly following September 11, 2001 (see also Ruzek & Watson, 2001).

Secondary Prevention

The most frequently used early intervention is *psychological debriefing*, a general term applied to efforts that involve helping those affected by trauma to "process" their experiences. Its primary purpose is to reduce the likelihood that immediate distress develops into acute stress disorder or PTSD. Debriefing implies a capacity to relinquish what has been experienced, what has happened, or what is known. It is customary to apply one or another of its forms (e.g., critical incident debriefing) immediately after exposure to trauma, including terror attacks.

Despite its frequent use, there is little evidence of its efficacy in preventing PTSD (Litz, Gray, Bryant, & Adler, 2002). Rather, there is a growing body of evidence across diverse populations that its utility is limited, and that, in fact, it may be inappropriate for a great many individuals. Although it is frequently perceived by participants as helpful, there is no correlation between such perceived helpfulness and better outcomes. Indeed, it may be perceived as most helpful by those who appear to need it least (Raphael & Ursano, 2002).

The Federal Emergency Management Agency (FEMA) has undertaken many initiatives to support the mental health and social service systems in their response to the terrorist attacks. Most notable are FEMA's crisis counseling programs, which are based on a public health outreach model of strengthening the affected communities at the grass roots level. Crisis counseling programs have been implemented in New York, New Jersey, Massachusetts, Connecticut, and Pennsylvania.

Project Liberty crisis counseling services have been delivered through New York's State Office of Mental Health and New York City's Department of Health and Mental Hygiene with the cooperation of 160 participating agencies with more than 2,600 outreach workers. Early in the disaster, FEMA dispatched Community Relations Teams to distribute information in 22 different languages to heavily impacted populations. The information discussed normal reactions to and self-care after a disaster, provided crisis counseling hotline numbers, and listed agencies that provide assistance. This was made possible through the combined efforts of New York State, New York City, and numerous voluntary agencies. Project Liberty offers public education groups and both individual and group crisis interventions. Following their participation in the outreach and psychoeducation effort, those who appear to need more intensive treatment are referred to mental health providers. As of August 2002, Project Liberty has served approximately 168,000 people, in more than two dozen languages. (The total number served in all affected areas is 223,000.)

Most experienced clinicians agree that a first requirement in working with terrorism victims is to establish a safe and supportive environment, which may be challenging in the immediate postterror situation. Danieli (2001) recommended empathic listening; reassuring people that they are experiencing normal reactions to abnormal and malevolent reality, and helping them examine how it influences their lives and their way of being in a world that for them has changed forever. She also emphasized focusing on what they can do despite overwhelming feelings of helplessness. Shear et al. (2001) described a pilot study of the effects of treatment of survivors suffering traumatic grief following the unexpected death of a loved one from a variety of causes. The 4-month treatment protocol included imaginal reliving of the death and interpersonal (reengagement) therapy, which led to significant reduction in grief symptoms and associated anxiety and depression (see also S. C. Jacobs & Prigerson, 2000).

Treatment

Many therapeutic approaches have been used in treating terrorism victims, in all existing modalities (see, e.g., Friedman, 2000). The evidence base concerning treatment for PTSD has grown substantially in recent years. At least two sets of practice guidelines (Foa, Davidson, & Frances, 1999; Foa, Keane, & Friedman, 2000) have been published that translate the empirical findings of treatment efficacy into specific algorithms that clinicians can follow in practice. Efficacy has been demonstrated empirically for a variety of psychotherapeutic approaches (e.g., exposure therapy, cognitive therapy) with victims exposed to specific traumatic events (e.g., sexual assault). Additionally, the Food and Drug Administration has approved two pharmacologic agents (sertraline and paroxetine) for the treatment of PTSD. Although more evidence is needed with respect to which interventions work best for which victims—and under what circumstances—the current evidence represents an excellent foundation on which future work can build.

There are several important aspects in the design of meaningful and cost-effective psychosocial interventions with victims of trauma. First, local treatment providers should be used whenever possible and further trained by consulting experts when needed. These trainees may in turn train other providers, thus extending their reach. The success of treatment efforts, however, depends on the existence of a well-trained, experienced, and accessible cadre of therapists to whom those in need of treatment can be referred.

Culturally competent intervention approaches that rely on the full range of indigenous resources and that the victims find acceptable and meaningful should be used. A comprehensive approach should incorporate a variety of interventions aimed at social and community re-integration for exposed individuals and others (Danieli, Rodley, & Weisaeth, 1996; Marsella, 1998; Weine et al., 2002). However, the principle remains that the interventions should address the broad set of dimensions that may be affected, as noted in the trauma framework described above. Finally, effectiveness should be monitored as a routine part of all outreach and treatment efforts.

In the words of one writer, America has

an infrastructure, mindset, and collection of values that appear unable to respond well to the behavioral health needs of the nation in times of wide-scale trauma resulting from war and national tragedies. . . . (we must) reinforce our message to Congress and the nation that mental health truly matters now more than ever before. . . . The United States cannot afford another generation of citizens or soldiers left permanently damaged by the neglect of their behavioral healthcare needs in the wake of great tragedy or trauma. (Ray, 2001, pp. 13–15)

Indeed, a conspiracy of silence has shrouded the experiences of the victims of, and whatever lesson may have been learned from, the 1993 precursor of the September 11 terrorist attacks on the World Trade Center.

During his visit to Ground Zero in New York City, Oklahoma City Mayor Kirk Humphreys predicted that the emotional response would be the most difficult effect of September 11. He advised New Yorkers to focus on hearts and minds, not wallets, and emphasized the need to make long-term counseling available. "The physical is the easiest part," he said, "and right when you think it is over, you realize that you need to address those other needs. You are going to have many people struggling for a long time. More substance abuse. More divorce. More emotional burnout. More suicides" (Blair, 2002, p. A14). His remarks emphasize the need to overcome the stigma surrounding mental health related issues through public education and other means.

Thus, although the importance of mental health has finally been more widely acknowledged, debates continue about community-based counseling and psychoeducational group versus treatment approaches, fueled in part by fear of the higher cost of treatment. This is a shortsighted view that does not take into account the untold multidimensional long-term and intergenerational costs of lack of treatment. In general, when such debates are couched in unidimensional terms, they are of limited value.

Recognizing the needs of people affected by September 11 "wherever the victims are and whenever they realized they needed it" (Goode, 2002, p. A1), the American Red Cross and the September 11th Fund (both charities) designed a program that would pay for their treatment. Part of the challenge in implementing these efforts is reaching the people who need them. As noted above (Kilpatrick et al., 2002), this may involve training all those who come into contact with victims in (the importance of) trauma mental health treatment (see, e.g., Danieli & Krystal, 1989; United Nations, 2000a), including the media, law enforcement, clergy, educators, and primary care physicians (Yehuda, 2002). This, in turn, will improve their ability to contribute to the healing process and reduce the likelihood of their inflicting the second wound (Symonds, 1980) or their participation in the conspiracy of silence (Danieli, 1984).

Participation by therapists and other care givers in the conspiracy of silence is often an indication of vicarious traumatization (Pearlman & Saakvitne, 1995), secondary traumatic stress (Hudnall Stamm, 1995), burnout (Maslach, 1982), or compassion fatigue (Figley, 1995). A recent book, *Sharing the Front Line and the Back Hills* (Danieli, 2002), addressed the costs to protectors and providers and the responsibilities of their organizations to train and support them before, during, and after their missions. Exposure to trauma has been shown to affect the interveners in multiple ways, both directly (sharing the same environment with the victims) and indirectly (listening to victims' accounts of their experiences in the context of attempting to help them or taking their testimonies). Thus, all those who help victims on the front lines are at high risk for double exposure.

In addition to the countertransference issues present in any psychotherapeutic interaction, working with trauma victims involves event countertransference (Danieli, 1982, 1988); that is, the therapists' reactions to patients' stories of their traumatic events rather than to the patients' behavior. "Our work calls on us to confront, with our patients and within ourselves, extraordinary human experience. This confrontation is profoundly humbling in that at all times these experiences challenge our view of the world and test the limits of our humanity" (Danieli, 1994a, p. 371). Following the September 11 terrorist attacks, therapists heard stories and images that they had never heard before. Those who suffered two (or more) exposures have their patients' images in addition to their own to cope with. In supervision, a therapist asked, "Whose September 11th is it?" The ubiquity of countertransference reactions has moved to the forefront of concern in the preparation and training of professionals who work with victims and trauma survivors.

In the context of training, it is important to emphasize that event countertransference reactions may inhibit professionals from studying and certainly from correctly diagnosing and treating the effects of trauma. They may also perpetuate the heretofore pervasive absence of traditional training for working with massive trauma and its long-term effects. Processing and working through event countertransference in the context of self-care are thus essential elements in training as well as during trauma work (Danieli, 1994a).

As mentioned earlier, many professional organizations assembled materials relevant to the aftermath of and recovery from trauma. The International Society for Traumatic Stress Studies Task Force on International Trauma Training has recommended the development of public information and civic education materials and the use of the most effective channels for their timely dissemination (Weine et al., 2002). Ruzek (2002) recommended that mental health training for post-terrorism interventions be accomplished (to the extent possible) before such events take place as part of ongoing professional education and community disaster planning. In the aftermath of such events, mental health professionals, paraprofessionals, and primary care providers will be called upon to apply new skills to an unfamiliar situation. He noted that although face-to-face training of these providers is important, it is unlikely to be sufficient to meet the training needs and must be augmented by written materials and other forms of dissemination, including the Internet.

Use of the Internet is likely to increase in importance given relatively low development costs, its ability to reach large numbers of people, the potential to "customize" content to particular disasters and audiences, and the ability to exert quality control over content. Groups of survivors can also use the Internet to access virtual support—facilitated by discussion forums—that may provide them with a tool to articulate their collective concerns and needs. Whenever possible, indigenous practitioners should be trained and used in psychosocial interventions. Community elders, tribal chiefs and informal indigenous leaders, and organizations such as the media, churches, and formal and informal community groups should be trained appropriately and involved in rehabilitation efforts. In most instances, leaders spontaneously step forward to help. Witness the "compassionate articulation" (Spratt, 2002) exhibited by New York City Mayor Rudolph Giuliani in the aftermath of September 11. All leaders should be encouraged to become involved in psychosocial recovery efforts.

Finally, the threat of bioterrorism raises additional complications because bioterrorism is likely to create casualties presenting a mix of symptoms related both to the biologic agent itself and the terror experienced. Thus, the broader health care system must be prepared to recognize and serve individuals with this mixed symptomatology. In particular, the system must avoid dismissing the distress associated with the attack and be as forthcoming as possible about its known and unknown effects. During a simulated bioterrorism exercise in Milwaukee, services were found not to be ready to manage large-scale anxiety reactions or family issues (Tyre, 2001). C. Engel (2001) noted that

> Polarized public discussion over science, policy, and media evidence following such incidents may reinforce the notion of cover-ups, create mutual doctor-patient mistrust, amplify symptom-related psychosocial distress and disability, and lead to unnecessary use of services. Under these circumstances, the clinician must always show respect, empathy and validation for a patient's concerns. (p. 48)

CONCLUSIONS AND RECOMMENDATIONS

In this chapter, we described and summarized international as well as U.S. national findings of some of the major effects of terrorism, their treatment and prevention, within a multidimensional, multidisciplinary integrative framework. At present, the empirical basis of our understanding of both the short- and long-term psychological effects of terrorism is limited, for logistical, scientific, and ethical reasons. Nevertheless, overcoming the obstacles to improving our understanding of these phenomena must be a high priority. Ideally, this research should be fully informed by both the conceptual and empirical literatures and conducted by empathic individuals who understand the phenomena and can either provide help or refer to those who can (see also Murray, 2002).

More systematic study of the sequelae of terrorism, designed to support more definitive causal inferences, is needed. This research should (a) clarify the full range of psychological responses to terrorism; (b) identify the most malignant aspects of terrorism and their specific pathogenic mechanisms; either of which may refine existing diagnostic constructs and/or lead to the development of new ones; and (c) identify effective early interventions and treatment interventions that combine to improve comprehensively victims' functioning. This work is best done in the context of the multidimensional framework outlined above that identifies the broad range of potential effects, including the psychological, social, economic, and political effects, on victims, their families, their helpers, and the societies and the world in which they live. Specific attention should be paid to the effects of terrorism on children (especially young children up to age 8) and adolescents and the effects of indirect exposures, particularly exposure through the media. Planning for children should not be limited to interventions in schools and in the community, but must involve the family. In all cases, the studies must be longitudinal.

The combination of the FEMA community outreach model and the September 11th Fund for mental health services for victims mentioned above holds promise. Careful evaluation of FEMA's efforts on the community level and of the training of treatment providers and its effectiveness is critical to integrating these systems to work optimally in serving affected individuals and communities. If successful, one of the legacies of September 11 would be a renewed and improved, multidimensional model for (mental) health care that may help reduce the prevailing stigmas associated with seeking and receiving mental health services.

Furthermore, preventive preparedness, based on comprehensive training of all professionals and others who interface with the various aspects of massive trauma—including their own reactions—is necessary. A critical challenge in designing such training is to tailor it to professionals who are at differing levels of training in trauma work. All interventions, even short-term, should be thought through from a long-term perspective, and each specific intervention component should be considered in its multidimensional context. Coordination, cooperation, and local involvement in its full contextual complexity (multicultural, ethnic, racial, religious, lingual) are important to success.

Clearly, there is no "quick fix" for these problems. Although the time dimension is sometimes implied in the trauma literature, it has generally been under-emphasized. Conceptualizing the aftermath of and the timeline of recovery from terrorism as adaptation underscores the centrality of the time dimension and provides a useful comparative framework within victim/survivor populations and across different traumata.

As stated at the beginning of this chapter, the individual and collective challenge following terrorism is creating a new normality whose central question—for which there is neither a single nor a simple answer—is, How do we live with growing levels of threat, anxiety, fear, uncertainty, and loss? We have attempted to meet several of the demands of this grave and formidable challenge.

12

TERRORISM AND THE MENTAL HEALTH AND WELL-BEING OF REFUGEES AND DISPLACED PEOPLE

MICHAEL G. WESSELLS

In contemporary armed conflicts, most of which are fought within state borders, terrorism plays a prominent role as a means of achieving political aims. The prevalence of terrorism is evident in the form of bombings in Northern Ireland; suicide bombings in Palestine; arm amputations of villagers in Sierra Leone by the opposition group Revolutionary United Front; and scorched earth policies by repressive regimes in Guatemala, Indonesia, and other countries.

Globally, terrorism and armed conflicts produce mass displacement of people because most casualties are civilians, and fighting occurs predominantly in and around communities. Worldwide, there are over 21 million refugees (United Nations High Commissioner for Refugees, 2002), people who have left their country out of well-founded fear of persecution and in hopes of obtaining safety and political asylum elsewhere. In addition, an estimated 20–25 million are internally displaced people (IDPs), that is, they have been uprooted from their homes and moved to other locations within their country. Often, they face grave security situations, because they remain in areas of active fighting and are mostly invisible and difficult to reach. A third vulnerable group consists of asylum seekers who need refuge but have not obtained refugee status. Many asylum seekers get shuttled from country to country (United Nations High Commissioner for Refugees, 2001) and are at risk of being returned to situations in which they may be persecuted.

All of these groups—refugees, IDPs, and asylum seekers—face significant mental health issues (cf. Marsella, Bornemann, Ekblad, & Orley, 1994). Refugees, for example, may bear the emotional burden of multiple losses, attack, or political persecution. In the host country, they typically experience great stress associated with exile, loss of cultural identity, stigmatization, separation from family, joblessness, and difficulties negotiating an unfamiliar cultural and social system. As a result, refugee populations often experience high rates of mental health problems, including trauma, anxiety, and depression. These reactions further compound the difficulty of adjusting to the new situation. The mental health effects interweave with the wider array of economic, cultural, social, and political problems. For example, war-affected refugees may seek revenge or attempt to return to political power, and they may use terrorism as a means of achieving their goals. Furthermore, discrimination and poverty in exile may place greater emotional burdens on them than do the wounds of war. These facts caution against narrow focus on mental illness and call for a holistic, prevention-oriented approach to the psychosocial well-being of displaced people (Ahearn, 2000).

My purpose in this chapter is to analyze the linkages between terrorism and the psychosocial impacts on displaced people by drawing on the extant literature and my field experience in various war zones. In the first section, I examine the psychosocial impact on refugees and displaced people as understood within the frameworks of mental illness and social well-being. In the second section, I analyze the kinds of psychosocial interventions that help to support refugee and displaced peoples. Using an ecological framework, I highlight the value of community-based, culturally grounded supports. In the third section, I analyze how powerlessness, difficult life conditions, and social injustice can lead displaced people toward terrorism. I suggest that prevention requires meeting the basic needs and improving the well-being of displaced people.

IMPACT ON MENTAL HEALTH AND WELL-BEING

The mental health and well-being of displaced people are placed at risk in different phases of their displacement. In their homes and communities, they may have been exposed to attack, fear of death, torture, and genocidal practices such as ethnic cleansing. In flight, they may have experienced loss, gender-based violence, attack, exposure to landmines, separation from loved ones, and uncertainty about their future. In resettlement, they may have experienced discrimination, poverty, loss of social status and means of livelihood, separation from family and cultural supports, and difficult living conditions in camps or resettlement areas, some of which may be controlled by hostile groups. The return home, too, is saturated with risks. In East Timor, following the attacks and mass displacements of September 1999, returnees from West Timor were often discriminated against and regarded with suspicion as having been possible supporters of Indonesian paramilitaries. In Guatemala, the returning opposition groups who had spent 25 years in the mountains reported feeling out of place, discriminated against, and ill-prepared to meet basic challenges such as earning a living and meeting basic needs for their families.

Because significant risks occur at different phases, it is an oversimplification to focus solely on preflight experiences as the primary source of the challenges to displaced people's mental health and well-being. The multiplicity of stressors and stages also impedes efforts to parse out the effects of specific terrorist incidents, which are typically embedded in difficult life circumstances and chronic stress.

Mental Health

Epidemiological evidence, although difficult to obtain, indicates rather high rates of posttraumatic stress disorder (PTSD) and depression among displaced people who have experienced terrorist attacks and torture (Girolamo & McFarlane, 1996). In a clinical sample of Vietnamese refugee men who had experienced detention and torture, Mollica et al. (1998) observed a 90% prevalence of PTSD and 49% prevalence of major depressive disorder. In a study of Central American refugees, Michultka, Blanchard, and Kalous (1998) reported a PTSD prevalence rate of 68%. Allden, Poole, Chantavinich, and Khin (1996) reported lower rates for PTSD and depression—23% and 38%, respectively—among Burmese refugees living in Thailand.

Traumatic stress reactions may also occur in response to life-threatening events in a host country, making it misleading to think of refugees as being in a posttraumatic situation (Richman, 1998). Following the 1994 Rwandan genocide, refugees in camps in Goma, Zaire told humanitarian workers that they were not safe in the camps and found the refugee situation nearly as stressful as that which they had fled. Furthermore, preflight and postflight stresses interact in complex ways. Following the September 11 attacks, traumatic stress reactions occurred among Arab refugees living in the United States and Arab Americans who had fled from repressive societies in which they had experienced losses, detention, and torture. For these already vulnerable people, the attacks awakened traumatic memories and shattered their sense of safety, which was undermined even further by the attacks and threats made against Arabs, Arab Americans, and Muslims in the United States in the weeks following September 11.

Despite the high incidence rates of PTSD and depression among refugees, one should not assume that these diagnostic categories universally describe the primary mental health impacts of terrorism and armed conflict on refugees. In fact, the categories PTSD and depression are products of Western psychiatry and psychology and do not map well onto indigenous concepts of mental health and well-being in non-Western cultures (Honwana, 1999; for reviews, see Lopez & Guarnaccia, 2000; Marsella, Friedman, Gerrity, & Scurfield, 1996; Nader, Dubrow, & Stamm, 1999). In many developing countries, somatic symptoms are idioms of distress that signal and communicate a wide array of personal and social concerns. Similarly, much distress and suffering in sub-Saharan Africa, where spirituality is regarded as the center of well-being, is regarded as spiritual. In Angola, which has been torn by 40 years of war, displaced people show high rates of PTSD (Eyber, 2002; McIntyre & Ventura, 2003). When asked about it, however, most Angolans from rural areas report that their stresses stem mostly from spiritual sources. For example, one 11-year-old girl who had seen her home destroyed and her parents killed had to run away in order to avoid death herself. She reported that her greatest distress stemmed from the fact that she had run away without having completed the culturally appropriate burial rituals for her parents. According to local beliefs, her parents' spirits were unable to make the transition to the world of the ancestors, and they lingered and caused problems for the girl and the living community. For this displaced girl, trauma was less the issue than spiritual distress (Wessells & Monteiro, in press). This example serves as a poignant reminder that one's response to traumatic events is mediated by the meanings one ascribes to them, and these meanings are culturally scripted. To focus on PTSD or depression in such contexts is to overlook locally constructed idioms and meanings. Furthermore, the imposition of outsider categories can marginalize local views and make psychology a tool of imperialism (Wessells, 1999).

The limits on Western concepts of mental health also become conspicuous in regard to the effects of state terrorism, which in the 1980s wars in Latin America aimed to end political opposition to entrenched states through the use of torture, "disappearances," and other human rights abuses. States often used their perceived legitimacy and power to control communications to construct a social reality in which opponents were "terrorists" who had to be controlled through use of violence. Whereas PTSD and depression diagnoses emphasize individual problems and pathology, the effects of state terrorism are best described in terms of a social relational framework that emphasizes the shattering of social relations, intergroup polarization, and state-guided definition of what counts as normal, acceptable behavior (Martin-Baro, 1996). In discussing the effects on displaced campesinos in El Salvador, Martin-Baro (1996) noted the prevalence of hypervigilance, distrust of outsiders, and paranoid thinking. He noted that these were not symptoms of mental illness but rather "a realistic response to their life situation" (p.

111) and a manifestation of damaged social relationships. Furthermore, the impacts were collective as well as individual. In Guatemala, the government conducted terror campaigns against Mayan communities, defined the social world as consisting of "Us" versus "Them," and demonized the resistance movement. In such cases, the torture used consists of more than traumatic experiences; it is an organized assault designed to destroy meaning (Sveaass, 1994), to fracture the social relations of the society by splitting off one group as the "enemy" (Martin-Baro, 1996), and to define social reality in a manner that leads citizens to perceive anyone picked up by the police as a "terrorist." For survivors of state-sponsored terrorism, issues of trust, identity, and social relations are as prominent as those of trauma and depression. This emphasis on social relations is consistent with a wider reframing of the issues in terms of social ecologies.

Social Ecologies, Well-Being, and Resilience

Refugee mental health and well-being is best understood within a conceptual framework that integrates the social ecologies of the refugee experience with a holistic conception of well-being. Multiple social ecologies include the premigration environment, flight-related environments, and the social contexts of exile and resettlement. Each of these contexts presents a mixture of social stressors and risks, social roles, and social supports that influence psychological responses and well-being. For example, extensive family and social networks in the exile context support effective adjustment and adaptation, whereas mental health issues might arise if the exile context entailed isolation and alienation. How a particular individual responds to displacement depends not only on the current situation but also on the history of previously encountered stressors, supports, and reactions. For example, someone who was feeling overwhelmed by preflight experiences such as killings and rape might be affected more strongly by a subsequent attack on a refugee camp than someone who had no such experiences. A key feature of this conception is that how one responds to an event depends on the amount and quality of social support one has at various stages. Although individual factors such as temperament and pre-existing problems are important (cf. Marsella et al., 1994), this framework emphasizes the importance of the social contexts and the social supports for and challenges to successful adaptation at different stages.

Within the framework of multiple social ecologies, it is valuable to think about refugee well-being rather than mental illness. Whereas the mental illness idiom emphasizes deficits, the well-being idiom emphasizes that refugees have a sense of agency and different capacities for coping. Ascriptions of mental illness can stigmatize refugees or cast them into victim roles that impede self-reliance and effective functioning in the new social context. Refugees often face circumstances that can overwhelm them, and it can be damaging to attribute their behavior to mental illness rather than to their difficult circumstances. In addition, oversimplified generalizations about "traumatized populations" do not fit with the considerable resilience exhibited by many refugees and displaced people. In a deeper sense, refugees are survivors who have significant capacities and whose behavior reflects their circumstances. On a recent assessment visit to Afghanistan, which has been torn by decades of war, I observed that most people functioned reasonably well under very difficult circumstances and as defined by local cultural and social norms. When asked what had enabled them to cope with their circumstances, most replied that their faith (Islam), family support, and community solidarity had been key factors.

By definition, refugees and displaced people experience multiple risks such as loss of home and normal routines, separation from stable supports, and fear for the safety of themselves and their families. This does not mean that mental illness will inevitably develop because a variety of coping responses and protective factors such as family support may mitigate or ameliorate the effects of the risks and facilitate resilience and effective adaptation in the current context. As risks accumulate, however, there is increased likelihood that individuals' coping resources and social supports will be overwhelmed, leading to ineffective adaptation and negative outcomes such as social alienation, isolation, and depression. A refugee who already has accumulated multiple risks in preflight experiences will be at greater risk of negative outcomes resulting from exposure to risks in the flight or exile contexts. This dynamic conception of risk accumulation and amelioration is richer than are static conceptions of mental illness.

A holistic conception of well-being has roots in many traditions ranging from Western theories such as that of Maslow (1954) to traditional, indigenous systems of healing (Adler & Mukherji, 1995). With regard to refugees, a well-being perspective conceptualizes refugees' psychological situation in terms of physical health, economic, social, spiritual, and political considerations (Ahearn, 2000). Refugees' losses of home and means of earning a living, for example, are emotional losses, but their psychological impact is integrally connected with their economic and social implications. For a rural farmer, loss of home and farm often produces an immediate descent into poverty, which itself is a major risk factor. With poverty comes an inability to meet basic needs, poor health and nutrition, and heightened susceptibility to disease and psychological disorders associated with health and nutritional problems (Westermayer & Wahmanholm, 1996). Loss of home and livelihood typically entail loss of status and of meaningful social roles. Furthermore, being uprooted from one's land can be spiritually distressing for people who view the land as the repository of ancestral spirits and their connection with previous generations. Refugees I interviewed from countries such as Guatemala, Kosovo, Angola, and East Timor have often said that for them, the worst part was not their preflight experiences but the losses associated with flight, namely, the stigma of being poor and a refugee and the difficulty in adjusting to an unfamiliar cultural and social system. Many also reported that racism and discrimination in housing, education, and health care were major issues that hampered adjustment and impaired the quality of life.

The political dimensions of suffering are also crucial. A person who lives in a repressive society and seeks political asylum in another country may experience powerful fear about the political repercussions of his or her application for asylum. Furthermore, in relation to social identity, one may experience attacks on one's own ethnic group as wrongs directed toward oneself (Volkan, 1997). In this respect, suffering is best regarded as collective as well as individual.

INTERVENTION

Western psychology and psychiatry offer a variety of intervention tools for assisting refugees and displaced people (Marsella et al., 1994). Counseling, critical incident debriefing, and related clinical tools have been used widely. In northern host countries with extensive professional psychological resources, these tools are also used in acute, emergency contexts. In large-scale emergencies, teams of professional psychologists provide direct counseling to displaced people, often operating out of a tent or a health post.

Clinical, individualized approaches, which are steeped in a medical model constructed by Western psychiatry and psychology, are valuable but have a host of powerful limitations. Excessive reliance on outsiders can create dependency and can be damaging in other ways. In many cultures, it is inappropriate for individuals to tell their problems to someone they do not know, and there is no basis for professionalized counseling. Nonformal counseling often occurs in local communities through networks of religious leaders, family members, and friends. In addition, it can be stigmatizing to visit a psychologist because that could imply that one is "crazy" or could signal to the community that one is a victim of rape or some other crime that changes one's status in the community. As the international community learned in Bosnia, when a woman in a highly traditional culture admits or signals indirectly that she is a rape victim, this can mark her as a family dishonor, as being "damaged goods" and can lead to her rejection or even assault by the community. In some situations, talking and expressive modes of therapy may be regarded by local people as dangerous because they are viewed as inviting the return of harmful spirits (Honwana, 1999). Counseling and professional interventions are often unsustainable because in many situations of mass displacement, few psychologists are available, and those who are may be quite unaffordable for impoverished refugees. Furthermore, clinical approaches are in some cases imposed on local people without regard to the indigenous systems of healing and coping. When this occurs, outsider approaches can marginalize and weaken local healing systems, resulting in damage to valuable local psychosocial supports (Wessells, 1999).

Perhaps the greatest limit of traditional clinical approaches is that they do not address the wider array of issues outlined above that affect refugees' well-being. In many cases, they are not comprehensive because they focus narrowly on clients' emotional needs without addressing economic, social, or cultural issues that impede adjustment and well-being in the exile or resettlement context.

An Ecological Approach

An ecological approach to refugee mental health provides a useful corrective for this problem (K. Miller, 1999). Because this approach addresses the social ecologies of preflight, flight, exile, and resettlement contexts that create risk, resilience, and need of intervention, it focuses on the stresses of exile or resettlement in addition to those associated with attack and flight. Emphasizing the social dimensions of refugee experience, this psychosocial approach analyzes the impact of social processes such as loss of meaningful social and personal roles, loss of social and cultural identity, and social isolation resulting from the loss of supportive social networks. It also takes a holistic approach that extends the intervention process to include elements such as job training, increasing employment opportunities, helping parents understand and deal with the new social rules their children encounter, building language and cultural competencies that enable mastery of the new environment, teaching basic life skills that make it possible to use public transport or health facilities, expanding access to meaningful social activities and roles, and developing effective social support networks in the exile or resettlement context.

An ecological approach fits with the cultural and political dimensions of refugee experience. Refugees often go through an extended process of cultural bereavement (Eisenbruch, 1991) in which they mourn the collective loss of social meaning, status, and views of self in relation to society. From this standpoint, the provision of psychosocial support includes the strengthening of contacts between refugees and other members of their culture in the exile context. It may also include the use of local cultural resources such as traditional healers who are from the refugees' country of origin. An ecological approach also recognizes the importance of political solidarity and construction of meaning in the exile context. Because many refugees have been political activists whose commitments had given meaning to their suffering, political activism and expressions of solidarity in the exile context can have a positive effect on refugee well-being (Gorst-Unsworth & Goldenberg, 1998). Similarly, communal testimony that provides a collective validation of people's suffering and torture has proven to be very useful in assisting survivors of torture (e.g., Agger & Jensen, 1990; Herman, 1992; Tutu, 1999). In many respects, then, an ecological approach moves beyond the traditional therapeutic context toward a community-based, culturally grounded approach. This same kind of approach is indicated in emergency contexts involving masses of displaced people.

Emergency Psychosocial Assistance

When terrorism or armed conflict creates mass displacement and an acute emergency, psychosocial assistance is a valuable component of a comprehensive effort to alleviate suffering and promote well-being. Although the provision of emergency psychosocial assistance on a large scale is a relatively recent endeavor, experience in different refugee emergencies has brought forward numerous lessons learned. Two main lessons concern vulnerable groups and holistic, community-based support.

Vulnerable People

In situations of armed conflict, all displaced people experience the shattering of social trust and multiple losses associated with the fighting, loss of homes and property, and displacement. This being the case, everyone needs support. It can be damaging to single out some people for support while excluding others. Nevertheless, particular individuals tend to be at greater risk, need more support than others, and warrant additional steps toward protection. Which people are most vulnerable varies according to the situation. In the case of the former Yugoslavia, where mass rape was used an instrument of terrorism, victims of sexual violence were highly vulnerable. In other situations, other forms of violence may have been used to terrorize and control civilian populations, and the categories of vulnerable people change accordingly. The following list of vulnerable people applies to many emergencies, although clearly not everyone within a group is equally at risk.

- Separated Children. Amidst emergency population movements, children often become separated from their parents or extended family. In any armed conflict, significant numbers of children become orphans as a result of the fighting. Particularly if they have no adult accompaniment, separated children are at risk of abduction, sexual victimization, military recruitment, and poor health.
- Single Women. Wars tend to create large numbers of widows, who may live in abject poverty and have in their care five or more children. In many developing countries, women lack property rights, and the loss of a husband begins a spiral into increased poverty, homelessness, and poor health. Single women therefore may be at increased risk of gender-based violence and

may have little protection from the gender discrimination that is prevalent in traditional, patriarchal societies.

- Disabled People. In war zones such as Afghanistan, Angola, Bosnia, and Cambodia, military forces use landmines in part to terrorize civilian populations. Population movements typically trigger many landmine incidents, which can result in death or injury and disability. Disabled people often suffer stigma, poor access to services, and psychological wounds associated with loss of limb, disfigurement, and changed social and economic status, among others.
- The Elderly. Adaptation to rapidly changing circumstances is usually easier for young people than for elderly people, who often have difficulty negotiating the complexities of new situations, including those involving differences of language, culture, and social norms. As a result, elderly refugees may experience depression and alienation, and their situation may be worsened by a wide generation gap.
- Torture Victims. People who have been subjected to torture frequently experience health-related problems, anxiety, trauma, depression, and loss of meaning. In the flight and exile contexts, they may experience high levels of fear, anxiety, and distrust that can make it difficult to achieve asylum or adapt to the new situation.
- People Who Have Experienced Gender-Based Violence. Rape is often used as an instrument of war and terror. In displacement settings such as camps, sexual exploitation is a large issue and not uncommonly is associated with actions by peacekeepers and national staff of international relief agencies. Peacekeepers' arrival often spawns a cottage industry of prostitution by girls and women who are desperate to feed their families.

One should resist the temptation to regard people at risk as victims or alternatively as passive program beneficiaries. In fact, members of these groups are survivors and have capacities and knowledge that they can use to improve their situation and well-being. In many situations, outside assistance and support is needed to enable a process of self-healing and of social reconstruction. Outside support is best provided through community-based assistance designed to empower local people and meet needs in a holistic manner.

Community-Based Assistance

Community-based psychosocial assistance aims to strengthen holistic, nonprofessionalized, local supports for people affected by terrorism and war. The approach is holistic in that it links emotional and social support with steps to meet basic needs for shelter, food, and physical reconstruction. It is holistic also in that it provides assistance to the entire community. This is achieved not by bringing in outside counselors and therapists but by mobilizing community resources and awareness, strengthening processes of collective planning and action, and providing additional, nonstigmatizing aid to vulnerable groups as part of a wider process of community support (Boothby, 1996; Gibbs, 1997; Reichenberg & Friedman, 1996; Wessells & Monteiro, 2001).

Community-based assistance recognizes that refugee communities do not exist in a vacuum but have a variety of supports such as women's groups, youth groups, religious leaders, and traditional healers, who can be mobilized to build wider, collective processes of healing and adaptation to difficult circumstances. For example, women's groups can reach out to vulnerable women in a community, thereby providing emotional and social support in a sustainable manner. With outside funding and appropriate preparation, the women's groups can help to create income-generating activities for single women. In this approach, local communities and groups own and guide the programs. Outside psychologists play roles of facilitation, training, technical assistance, and other processes of capacity building (Wessells, 1999). Local communities, however, take primary responsibility for their own rebuilding and healing, using local, culturally grounded idioms and tools in the process. Thus, empowerment is at the heart of community-based approaches. Following terrorism, war, and displacement, one of the most fundamental needs is to reestablish systems of collective planning and action. Through planning and acting, people regain the sense of control and self-efficacy and cultivate a sense of hope about the future. In a war zone, the strengthening of collective planning and action can enable displaced people to resist political manipulation and to make group decisions about how to protect their collective well-being.

One recent example (Wessells & Monteiro, in press) serves to illustrate a community-based approach to psychosocial assistance for displaced people. In Angola, torn by 40 years of war, nearly one-third of the population has been displaced internally, and many had suffered terror at the hands of UNITA, the opposition group, which used Maoist methods of control and persecution. To aid displaced groups on a large scale and in areas that afforded weak security and poor access, Christian Children's Fund (CCF)/ Angola established a mobile team of two experienced, Angola trainers who understood local idioms of distress and had through previous work (Wessells & Monteiro, 2001) acquired skill in interweaving Western and traditional approaches to assisting war-affected children. During the period 1999–2001, the mobile team trained local staff people including from the IDPs themselves to conduct normalizing activities for children that help to restore a sense of safety; enable emotional expression and social integration; and build basic cognitive, social, and cultural competencies.

To implement a holistic approach, the mobile team used a strategy of integrating psychosocial activities for children into the work of national staff of nongovernmental organizations (NGOs) that provided health, water, and other basic services. Having selected key NGO staff and also community leaders who were respected for their work on behalf of children, the mobile team conducted a week-long, highly interactive training concerning children's healthy development, the impact of violence on children, cultural practices on mourning and healing, activities for assisting children, and peace education. Following the training, the participants organized activities for children such as recreation, soccer games, story-telling, and singing. Twice monthly, the mobile team made follow-up visits to provide ongoing support and to advise on how to address difficult situations. Among the adults, they organized dialogues about how to assist and support children. They also facilitated the construction of playgrounds and *jangos*, traditional huts where community meetings occur and without which communities reported feeling disconnected from the ancestors.

The project engaged more than 17,000 children in normalizing activities. This had immediate benefits in increasing children's safety and providing adult structure and supervision. Preliminary evaluation identified the following psychosocial outcomes for children: reduced fighting, increased play and cooperation, decreased social isolation, and more positive attitude toward the future. NGO staff reported that they had become more sensitive to the needs of displaced people, treated their clients with greater respect, and had organized activities for children and families that increased satisfaction with services such as therapeutic feeding. Adult members of IDP groups also reported positive outcomes such as improved relations between adults and children and increased organization and community planning. Many adults, including elders, said that as a result of having constructed a jango and having initiated planning dialogues, they felt more hopeful, less anxious and pessimistic, and in a better position to improve their circumstances and support children. Adults also reported that they had benefited collectively from the strengthening of traditional patterns of leadership and organization. In a modest way, this served to decrease the sense of inferiority that resulted from hundreds of years of colonial domination and that, left unaddressed, undermines local people's belief that they have the capacity to build a positive future.

Although promising, community-based psychosocial interventions face multiple challenges, one of which concerns impact assessment. There is a lack of widely agreed upon outcome indicators and methods for assessing impact, and few careful impact evaluation studies have been conducted. As a result, it is difficult to judge the comparative efficacy of intervention approaches or to construct "gold standards" for quality interventions. In addition, significant gaps often arise in the application of community-based interventions. In many emergencies such as those in Kosovo and East Timor, international agencies usually focus excessively on predominantly urban areas that have large populations and are accessible. Too often, rural areas that have greater needs receive little support. Furthermore, powerful ethical issues arise in connection with populations affected by terrorism. Refugees from the Rwandan genocide, for example, included genocidaires who had committed atrocities and sought to use humanitarian aid in the camps in Goma to strengthen their power (Human Rights Watch, 1999). Humanitarian workers faced difficult choices about whether and how to provide assistance to the refugees. For psychologists, tension exists between the desire not to support terrorism and the humanitarian principle of aiding everyone equally. These challenges admit no easy answers, and they continue to stimulate dialogue, research, and maturation of community-based approaches.

REFUGEE WELL-BEING AND TERRORISM PREVENTION

As suggested earlier, displacement and terrorism are intimately connected. Before the Rwandan genocide, the Hutu-dominated regime of Juvenal Habyarimana had created difficult life circumstances for Tutsis, many of whom became refugees in Uganda. Many of these Rwandan refugees became soldiers with the Rwandan Patriotic Front (RPF), which launched repeated attacks against the Rwandan government. This phenomenon of refugees becoming fighters is unsurprising in light of the passions created by political persecution, forced exile, and the desire to liberate one's homeland. The linkage between terrorism and refugees is also conspicuous in Afghanistan, where al-Qaeda and Taliban supporters were often recruited from refugee camps in Pakistan (Rashid, 2000). In East Timor, people displaced by Indonesian military operations fought for liberation and were labeled "terrorists" by the government (J. Taylor, 1999). In the Israeli–Palestinian conflict, refugees have been a severely contentious issue (F. Khouri, 1985), and Palestinian refugee camps are widely believed to be incubators for radicalism and terrorism.

Analysis of this linkage provides useful insights into the causes of terrorism and can enable us to take steps toward prevention. It is important to note, however, that there are different kinds of terrorism that may have different causes (Laquer, 1987). Furthermore, psychological factors are only one source of terrorism, which requires multidisciplinary analysis. As Cairns (1996) noted, some psychological analyses have been oversimplified quests to find the "terrorist personality" or have portrayed terrorists as mentally ill. These analyses have failed and have been superceded by analyses of psycho–political situation, group processes, and cognitive influences (e.g., Bandura, 1990; Reich, 1998). This section complements these analyses by emphasizing two key features of the refugee situation: powerlessness and the failure to meet basic needs in milieus saturated with real or perceived victimization and social injustice.

Powerlessness

Displacement is typically the result of attack, oppression, and political persecution, all of which leave deep wounds and invite retaliation and efforts to recover one's homeland. Refugees view themselves as victims of political oppression and typically interpret their current difficult situation as a form of social injustice meted out by the dominating Other. Making this sense of domination and injustice worse is their perceived or real inability to change the situation using nonviolent means such as petitions to the UN and other international authorities.

The loss of personal and collective power is a pervasive feature of displaced people's experience. The situation is particularly bleak in refugee and IDP camps, where people typically live in difficult conditions, have very limited ability to control their circumstances, and depend on external aid. In addition, camp residents often report that they feel invisible—the world does not take notice of their plight unless they happen to be part of the crisis that currently occupies global attention. Residents feel they have no one to turn to for additional assistance. Feeling invisible and voiceless, camp residents experience a sense of depersonalization and loss of dignity that amplifies their feelings of powerlessness and accompanying frustration. If the camps are located near areas of active fighting, the sense of powerlessness is usually heightened by fear and the inability to protect oneself and one's family. Furthermore, people in camps often report feeling as if they are pawns in a struggle they cannot control, and they may feel that neither government nor opposition groups regard the well-being of civilians as a high priority.

Outside camps and conflict zones, too, powerlessness is a major issue. Refugees who have fled from oppressive regimes have in a very real sense been overpowered and disempowered. That they had to flee is itself testimony to their failure of resistance and lack of power to change conditions in their home country. In applying for asylum, they often face significant bureaucratic obstacles, especially because immigration and refugee policies have become more restrictive in many countries. Dealing with authorities in an alien system can itself be a strongly humiliating, disempowering experience. Even following a grant of refugee status, the experience of living in forced exile is harsh. Refugees typically report feeling that they have no home, no nationality, and no positive status or cultural and social ties to the country or countries they have entered (Kushner & Knox, 1999). Lacking a job or living in poverty, feeling stigmatized, and having little understanding of the new social system, refugees typically feel alienated and powerless.

That significant numbers of displaced people are victims of torture should also be taken into account. Torture is a powerful instrument through which people in authority exercise control over the oppressed (Fanon, 1963; Foucault, 1995), and the aim of the torturer is often to destroy the victim's sense of control, meaning, and personhood (Sveaass, 1994).

Although the vast majority of refugees are not terrorists and disavow the use of violence as a means of obtaining their objectives, it is widely recognized that terrorism is a tool often used by the relatively weak against a much more powerful opponent. Terrorism enables people to call attention to their cause, to retaliate for the bad things that have been done to them, or to try to achieve their political objectives through violence but without the benefits of large armies. For example, many Palestinians during the second intifada and the current fighting with invading Israeli Defense Forces view terrorism as a necessary response to social injustice and the only means at hand to fight Israeli domination. This is not to endorse terrorism but to point out that terrorism is not typically the irrational act that it is often made out to be by advocates of the "madman" view of terrorism (Rubenstein, in press).

The Failure to Meet Basic Needs

Conspicuous features of most refugee camps are the horrible living conditions: overcrowding, squalor, inadequate sanitation, poor shelter, no privacy, and inadequate access to food, clean water, and health care. Difficult life conditions for displaced people are by no means restricted to camps. In the tiny Gaza Strip, a Palestinian area roughly 6 by 20 miles bordered by Egypt and mainly by Israel, there are 853,000 registered refugees. Just over half live in camps, but nearly all live in overcrowded, impoverished conditions that do not meet basic human needs. These difficult life conditions constitute a form of structural violence and may serve as instigators of violence as a means of meeting basic needs (Staub, 1996). As political analysts point out, people who do not have their basic needs met are likely to organize politically to meet their needs, and hungry people are susceptible to political manipulation.

Key among the difficult life conditions are perceptions of injustice and oppression, both of which create a sense of relative deprivation and fuel destructive conflict (Rubin, Pruitt, & Kim, 1994). Palestinian refugees, for example, have real grievances associated with their uprooting in the 1948 war, the denial of their right to return, and their difficult living conditions. However, it is often the perception of comparative injustice that weighs most heavily on Palestinians. Many Palestinians, for example, ask why the world gave so much attention and assistance to the Kosovar refugees and insured their right to return when so little attention and support has been given to Palestinian refugees.

Perceived injustices are often extensions of a more basic sense of collective victimization at the hands of the Other. Because refugees see themselves as having been forced out under imminent threat, they attribute their life in forced exile to the wrongdoings of the political regime they were forced to escape. Living in exile and feeling victimized, they construct collectively "chosen traumas" brought on them by the hostile Other (Volkan, 1997).

Through communal discussions and remembrances, these negative memories and hostile attributions become part of the collective memory of the group, which typically feels a strong sense of "Us versus Them." As polarization between groups continues and as new perceived wrongdoings are attributed to the hostile Other, both sides may harbor intense enemy images of the Other (Silverstein, 1989). Over time, societal beliefs arise that depict the Other as intractable, unwilling to build peace, and best dealt with through violence (Rouhana & Bar-Tal, 1998). These beliefs and the accompanying sense of victimization become integrated into one's social identity and worldview. As a result, Israelis define themselves in part by virtue of opposition to the Palestinian Other, and vice versa.

Furthermore, young people are socialized into this system of oppositional social identities, hostile worldviews, and shared sense of victimization. For young Israelis who have the most powerful military in the Middle East by far, military service may seem not only an obligation but as a necessary step because it fits in with the dominant, societal ideology and with their own sense of social identity. For Palestinian youth, serving and fighting in the ranks of an army is not an option for addressing the challenges of what they perceive as the much stronger Israeli enemy. Seeing little way of meeting even their basic need for security and regarding Israelis as the implacable enemy, Palestinian youth tend to view terrorism as an acceptable instrument for fighting back. The recent increase in young suicide bombers cannot reasonably be attributed to mental illness among young Palestinians; by many reports on the ground, it is the best and brightest who volunteer as suicide bombers. More likely, this terrorism stems from the combination of powerlessness and desperation mixed with perceptions of injustice and humiliation at the hands of the Israeli oppressor. These perceptions, which are associated closely with the failure to meet basic human needs, need not be accurate to influence behavior. Ultimately, perceptions guide behavior.

This analysis of how refugee experience can shape negative perceptions and feelings of powerlessness in ways that enable terrorism has important implications. First, it suggests that comprehensive terrorism prevention should include steps to meet basic human needs in a more equitable manner. Psychologists can do their share in this regard by working to assist refugees in various parts of the world, urging greater equity in the provision of psychosocial assistance, and helping to build systems of nonviolence that correct injustices and enhance peace (D. Christie, Wagner, & Winter, 2001). Continuing the theme of the need for a holistic approach, it is necessary to coordinate psychosocial assistance with political and economic reforms so as to decrease powerlessness and desperation, increase power-sharing, and meet basic needs.

Second, it suggests that with regard to terrorism, the work of psychologists alone is not curative. As pointed out by Martin-Baro (1996), the liberation psychologist who was murdered in El Salvador in 1989 as part of state-sponsored terror, "The curative work of the psychologist is necessary, but if psychology's work is limited to curing, it can become simply a palliative that contributes to prolonging a situation which generates and multiplies the very ills it strives to remedy" (p. 122). For psychologists, as for all professions, a key task is to help prevent terrorism.

13

PSYCHOLOGY'S RESPONSE
TO TERRORISM

RONALD F. LEVANT, LAURA BARBANEL, AND PATRICK H. DeLEON

President George W. Bush has said that the United States is at war with terrorism. The nature of this war is fundamentally psychological. The aim of the terrorists is to create crippling fear and psychological debilitation in the populace in order to force the United States to submit to their demands.

The psychological impact has been very significant. We all felt and still feel to some extent the shock and grief that came in the immediate aftermath of the attacks on September 11, 2001. Months after the attack we began to experience the worst of the trauma responses to the attacks. In addition, there are continuing fears resulting from the spate of anthrax incidents and the specter of biological and chemical terrorism. We also have the copycats, hoax perpetrators, and domestic terrorists (e.g., the mailing to family planning clinics of suspicious-looking envelopes). More recently we have been warned that suicide bombings in public places such as those that occur

Some of the material in this chapter has been adapted from "Psychology Responds to Terrorism," by R. F. Levant, 2002, *Professional Psychology: Research and Practice, 33*, pp. 507–509. Copyright 2002 by the American Psychological Association. Adapted with permission.

in Israel will occur here and that our national landmarks, nuclear power plants, hazardous chemical plants, and the water and food supply may be attacked. In May 2002, Vice President Dick Cheney warned that we will be attacked again—the question is not if, but when. In addition to these very serious threats or predictions of dangers, the fabric of our life is being disrupted; the terrorists are putting sand into the gears of everyday life. American citizens now have to cope with increased difficulties and disruptions in air travel, postal deliveries, airport and building evacuations, and the like. Clearly, the psychological toll of this war is likely to considerable.

We have long argued for a role for psychology in informing public policy on the grounds that psychology has much to offer on a range of social matters, including terrorism (e.g., DeLeon, 1988, 2002; DeLeon, Eckert & Wilkins, 2001; Lorion, Iscoe, DeLeon, & VandenBos, 1996; Martinez, Ryan, & DeLeon, 1995). Given the psychological nature of terrorism, it is clear that psychology has a major role to play in the national effort to counteract it. The American Psychological Association (APA) has been very active in responding to the terrorist attacks of September 11, 2001. In this chapter we discuss APA's efforts to address the threat and the impact of terrorism. We also consider a response to disaster, and we review what the literature has to say about promoting resilience in response to terrorism.

On September 19, 2001, the APA Board of Directors held a conference call to discuss the terrorist attacks of September 11, and this resulted in the establishment of a Board Subcommittee on Psychology's Response to Terrorism. The mission of the Subcommittee was to explore what psychologists can contribute to the efforts to address the threat as well as the impact of terrorism. The members of the Subcommittee were APA Recording Secretary Ronald F. Levant (chairperson), Past members of the APA Board of Directors Laura Barbanel and Nate Perry, Past Chairperson of the American Psychological Association of Graduate Students Derek Snyder, Executive Director of the Science Directorate Kurt Salzinger, Executive Director of the Education Directorate Cynthia Belar, Executive Director of Affairs Rhea Farberman, Executive Director of the Practice Directorate Russ Newman, Executive Director of the Public Interest Directorate Henry Tomes, and Executive Director of the Publications and Communications Directorate Gary VandenBos.

ADDRESSING THE THREAT OF TERRORISM

Psychology played a significant role in the war efforts during both world wars of the last century, contributing scientific knowledge and expertise in such areas as officer-candidate selection, visual perception, and ergonomics. Similarly, psychology can contribute scientific knowledge and expertise to the goal of ending terrorism. Contributions can be found in the foundational areas of the discipline such as social psychology and its work on malignant attitude formation, such as prejudice and fanaticism. Contributions can also be found in the more applied areas such as international psychology, peace psychology, conflict resolution, multicultural psychology, the psychology of religion, military psychology, and the psychology of criminal justice.

The Subcommittee on Psychology's Response to Terrorism assembled lists of potential contributors and queried the presidents of APA divisions about who might be conducting research that has relevance to combating terrorism. Dozens of colleagues wrote back with offers of help or suggestions of who might be able to help. The subcommittee members also decided to find out what might be of genuine assistance to key policy- and decision-makers. Accordingly, we networked with psychologists working in mission-critical governmental departments (e.g., Department of Defense, Department of State, the FBI) and have had requests for assistance from several of these agencies. On February 28, 2002, an invitational conference titled Countering Terrorism: Integration of Practice and Theory was held at the FBI academy in Quantico, Virginia, with 70 participants; about half were APA member psychologists, and the other half were law enforcement personnel. On March 1, 2002, APA staff arranged for a day of informal meetings between psychological scientists and senior staff of the Senate and House Science committees, to raise awareness of the relevance of psychological science to countering terrorism. The APA Council of Representatives approved funding for additional congressional science briefings on terrorism in 2002, and so these efforts will continue.

ADDRESSING THE IMPACT OF TERRORISM

With regard to addressing the impact of terrorism, the APA Practice Directorate's Disaster Response Network has been working hand in glove with the American Red Cross in responding to the needs at the World Trade Center, the Pentagon, Pennsylvania, California, and elsewhere. This effort is discussed in more detail in the section titled "Disaster Response: A First-Person Account," which was written from the perspective of one of the authors (Laura Barbanel), who participated as a member of the Disaster Response Network in New York. The APA staff have also posted on APA's Web site a host of helpful materials on coping with trauma, stress, anxiety, and grief, as well as on helping children to cope. There was also information about psychologist self-care, which stressed the need for members to monitor themselves for signs of caretaker trauma. In addition, the APA Committee on Colleague Assistance developed a document for the Web site titled "Tapping your resilience in the wake of terrorism," which offers guidance to practitioners on coping with the challenges of working with patients in the aftermath of the terrorist attacks. We have also looked at what psychologists might contribute to addressing the rising number of anti-Islamic and anti-Middle Eastern hate crime incidents, racial profiling, and the erosion of civil liberties. The anthrax attacks took on the character of workplace violence, and we looked at what psychologists might contribute to address that as well. We are aware that these events have different impacts on different segments of our pluralistic society (e.g., postal and mail-room employees are often ethnic minorities; older adults often have a higher degree of resilience).

The subcommittee also looked at the possibilities of insuring that psychological services are included in Senator Edward Kennedy's Bioterrorism Preparedness Act and of seeking to include psychologists as major participants in the new Homeland Security office.

To provide authorization for these activities, the APA Board of Directors took emergency action at its December 2001 meeting and adopted a resolution on terrorism (Levant, 2002, p. 507).

DISASTER RESPONSE: A FIRST-PERSON ACCOUNT

This section provides a first-person account of the disaster response effort in New York, written by the second author (Laura Barbanel).

APA's Disaster Relief Network and the New York State Psychological Association's Disaster Relief Network activated hundreds of psychologists who volunteered to work on-site and in the aftermath of the disaster, counseling families of victims, rescue workers, those who lost homes, and those who lost jobs. APA, the National Mental Health Association, and the Ad Council put together a series of public service advertisements such as "Talk With Your Kids," which advised parents that children might be frightened and what to do about it.

When the tragedy hit, individual psychologists sought to figure out where they could be of use. There was so much confusion in the days following the attack, which, coupled with difficulties in communication, made it difficult to determine where one could be of use. Depending on the proximity to the World Trade Center, phone lines, e-mail, and TV reception were affected in varying degrees. I was first asked to go to a police academy in lower Manhattan where there was a need for psychologists, but I could not get there. Bridges, tunnels, and subways to Manhattan were closed except to rescue workers. As a person who had been certified by the Red Cross, I was initially called to register at the Red Cross for this disaster and then was told, "No, the need is somewhere else." When my e-mail started to function, I received hundreds of e-mail messages from psychologists wanting to help. Some were able to get through the confusion and to help. Many were frustrated because they could not get through or had been turned down by the Red Cross. Others were looking for colleague assistance or were writing of their experiences at the various settings in which they were deployed.

Psychologists ended up working in shelters for displaced people; the Compassion Center (which had been set up for the families of individuals who were "lost"); Service Centers for people who were working at the World Trade Center and who needed economic and other help, as well as for people who were displaced from their homes because of the disaster; and the Missing Person's Hotline, where thousands of people called to find out how to locate people and services.

The breadth of these experiences suggests the breadth of this disaster. The Compassion Center, which had been set up in an Armory, was where families of victims came to look through hospital lists to see whether their loved ones could be found. Rarely was anyone located. The hospitals in New York City had been on alert for emergency care; the doctors waited in vain. There weren't many admissions because so many had died.

Psychologists have been involved in providing psychological services during disasters for some time. Some consider themselves traumatologists, and there is a movement to have a new division of APA that is made up of psychologists who study and work in the field of trauma. However, the full range of psychology's contribution to this disaster and its aftermath, to the recovery and to the healing, has yet to be recorded.

What did psychologists do? Not therapy as we know it, but *emotional first-aid* as it came to be named. Some families were very contained and did not ask for any emotional help. Others sat down and wept and wanted contact. In the Compassion Center, a man from India asked me to speak to his young, pregnant wife about the loss of her brother. A worker asked me to speak to a young African-American man who was looking for a woman who had at the time of the attack fallen down on the ground in front of him, told him she was not going to make it, and given him her student ID card and her keys. Weeping, he told me that he felt he hadn't helped her enough. He was hoping to find that she had survived.

In the Armory, the walls were totally filled with pictures of people who were lost (a euphemism for those who had died), put up by family members who held out the hope that perhaps their loved ones had been seen by someone else. The pictures were all of happy occasions, a wedding, a boating trip, a father holding a child. They all seemed to be 28 years old. Many of the people looking were the parents of the victims; some were wives, husbands, girlfriends, and boyfriends. There were the representatives of various governments who were looking for their citizens who had been working in one of the towers. It would be their job to inform the families of the deaths.

For psychologists, working in this disaster was different from any work in previous disasters. The scale was larger than anyone had experienced before, and more city, state, and federal agencies and governmental bodies were involved. In some places, services overlapped; in places there were gaps. All of the services were strained. Most important, it was clear that the psychologists working in it were affected in a very different way than other kinds of disasters. It was their disaster just as it was the disaster of the people they sought to help. Rescue workers began to feel the emotional strain of seeing the gruesome and the macabre. There were bodies falling or jumping out of windows, the smell of incinerated flesh. It was difficult to work on-site because communication broke down. Running water was not available at the beginning, and there were threats of gas main explosions. The air was thick with smoke and debris. Chaos reigned.

In the midst of all of the chaos and what was described as evil were great acts of kindness and generosity. Food was sent in for rescue workers from all of the finest restaurants in New York City. A Red Cross worker who was at ground zero the day of the disaster described her role, which included passing out chocolate-covered strawberries on a tray to rescue workers. She felt a bit odd about that aspect of her role. Clothing was donated by individuals and by shops. Money poured in for the families of the victims.

The headlines told of the large brokerage firms having "lost" thousands of people. Talking to immigrant parents of an only son who was lost, to the man whose wife had perished and left three small children all under age 5, to the man whose brother-in-law was lost and whose sister could not bear to come to this place, gave yet another picture of this tragedy. Blue-collar workers also suffered. The Central Labor Council began to report that they were getting anxious calls from members—the cleaners, security guards, data clerks, secretaries, repair people, limousine drivers—who were out of work as a result of the disaster. People of all classes, ethnicities, and racial groups were represented; so too were foreign nationals from at least 91 countries ("9/11 Toll," 2002).

Responding to this disaster was different than the responses psychologists have been typically trained to make. First of all, one needed to know whether a response was required or wanted. Some people wanted help and could ask for it. Others wanted to be left alone to rely on their own resources. Many, however, wanted help and could not reach out. To distinguish between the latter two types of people required sensitivity that psychologists are rarely asked to have.

A young couple I met in the Service Center is illustrative. The young man approached to ask me whether a psychologist could talk to his girlfriend, who had been sleeping poorly and having nightmares since the disaster. She did not eat and was not "getting on with her life." She was glued to the TV and watched all of the reports. He thought that TV was retraumatizing her. I sat down next to the couple on folding chairs to talk. Although they had no real privacy, everybody in the room respected the island that the three of us had created. The young woman was from South America and a recent medical school graduate. The two of them met in New York and had been living together since May. They had just moved into an apartment in the area of the World Trade Center. On the morning of September 11, the woman was walking out of her apartment when the planes struck. She was frozen to the spot as she watched what transpired. She saw people running and the buildings topple, and she began to run also. The scene that kept repeating in her mind and that she described was of a firefighter falling down in front of her. She could not help him but waited with him until the Emergency Medical Service staff picked him up. She kept saying to herself, "I am a doctor and I cannot help him." It was this fact that was the most disturbing to her, the feeling of helplessness. She went over the scene several times. I pointed out to her that she had indeed helped him by staying with him. She visibly relaxed. Although this was not therapy, it was certainly therapeutic.

Eventually, one large Service Center was set up at Pier 94 on the West side of Manhattan. Here a comprehensive set of services was made available for categories of people: for families of victims, people who lost their homes, and people who lost their jobs. There was a special room for children, with soft animals and mental health personnel to talk to them. There were chaplains, massage therapists, and therapy dogs. As a psychologist on "the floor," the job was to do what somebody characterized as "active lurking." The trick is to be able to talk to somebody and know how to be interested without being intrusive. Not always easy for psychologists who typically have people come to their offices with a clearly defined task on hand.

Family members of the "lost" were taken on a ferry down to the site where a staging area was set up for viewing the devastation. There were flowers and teddy bears available as well as cards for family members to write notes to leave in the memorial area. As a "worker," the task was to hand these items out to the family members and to stop to chat as you did. On the boat one was asked to put on a hard hat and given goggles and a mask should one need it in the area.

At the special platform built at the site to see the devastation, many began to weep. A view of the site made it clear that nobody in there could survive. For families that had not found bodies, this brought both great pain and some kind of closure. There was also a memorial area where the flowers and other items could be left. Pictures, notes, flowers, and teddy bears were left there. The National Guardsmen who were in the footpath stood at attention and saluted. It was very moving.

Many of the families that were on the boat were extended families or relations from out of town—parents, aunts, uncles, cousins, friends—who had come in for memorials. It was suggested that one "adopt" a family. I spent time with a family that consisted of two male cousins of a young man who was "lost" at ground zero. The three "boys" (as the wives referred to them) had grown up together and were like brothers. They spoke about many things, from the skyline of New York City to the importance that this trip had for them. When they parted, they hugged me, saying that it had been a great "comfort" to them. Not the kind of work psychologists usually do, but definitely therapeutic.

I was impressed by the sensitivity and care with which these boat trips were designed and by the people who arranged and executed them. There were boat trips from New Jersey with the families of Port Authority employees who had died and from the Brooklyn Navy Yard with the families of first responders who had perished. A woman who lost her husband of 17 years said after the experience at Pier 94 and the trip to the site that this place and the kindness that she experienced "restored her faith in humanity."

Many heroes emerged. The group that seemed to achieve the greatest reputation for heroism was firefighters. Firefighters, hardly noticed in ordinary times by most people, became the symbol of romantic heroism in this tragedy. Dressed in all their gear, they did what they always do: Serve the public by putting out fires and protecting people. They also displayed support and loyalty to their comrades in a way that is particularly characteristic of firefighters. The dashing figure of the stockbroker or lawyer gave way to the figure of the firefighter who protected and rescued others. Police officers, who, over the last few years, have not been seen favorably, were admired for their bravery and the challenges of their work.

Less mentioned but certainly no less worthy are other heroes such as the teachers and school personnel who responded to the need immediately and in the postcrisis phase. Teachers in the schools closest to the World Trade Center had to lead their children to safety. In a cloud of smoke and debris the teachers of children as young as 4 and 5 linked hands with their students and led them the many blocks to safety. The principal and faculty of Stuyvesant High School, located near the site of the World Trade Center, evacuated all of the 3,000 students from the school. Teachers walked students across the Brooklyn Bridge, the 59th St. Bridge, to Queens, uptown (A. Deutsch, 2001). The younger students, who had just started high school that week, some from other boroughs of the city, were organized into groups to be helped to find their way. There were 8,000 students in eight Manhattan schools that are in that area of the city. All of the children reached physical safety ("A Time to Mourn," 2001). The New York City Schools were closed the next day, but school psychologists and other staff attended special sessions on handling the emotional fallout for children, parents, and staff. Psychologists in the schools were indeed in the forefront in offering children and their parents needed help. The threat of bioterrorism and the need to develop resilience in children are issues that continue to need to be confronted.

One of the most touching experiences that I had was when I left the Red Cross headquarters late one night and was stopped by a police officer who asked me if I wanted a free taxi ride home. I told him that I was heading for Brooklyn. He said that was fine. In front of the Red Cross headquarters was a line of taxis standing, prepared to take people involved in this effort home. This was their volunteer service. I entered a cab driven by a Sikh driver. His English was broken, but he wanted to tell his story and to hear mine. The Red Cross had debriefed me before that, but this was my real debriefing for the day.

Local universities set up special counseling units and hotlines for students who were displaced from their houses or their classrooms or who could not get to classes because of transportation difficulties. Faculty at universities were asked to develop programs to help students, both in and outside of the classroom. Student trainees needed to know how to deal with children affected by the trauma. Trauma and grief experts were called in to schools, colleges, and universities and to businesses as they reopened. Programs were developed, assistance given, responses improvised. Workshops were developed and provided for students and faculty at colleges. Psychologists who had not been previously trained to deal with trauma asked for training to cope with the trauma around them as well as with their own secondary trauma.

Caretaker trauma began to be discussed. Psychologists started to set up "training" for themselves within weeks. Within days, the New York State Psychological Association set up an impromptu meeting of psychologists working with the disaster. A panel was formed of a number of senior members (myself included) of the Disaster Relief Network, and people had an opportunity to speak and to listen.

Reactions to the attacks varied widely. Ayalon (1983), in a description of the Israeli experience of coping with terrorism, pointed to the dichotomization of response in victims between those who took on an attitude of resentment bordering on paranoid suspicions and those who took an altruistic, self-sacrificing attitude. Here, also, for some the response was anger and the wish for revenge; others exhibited an attitude of self–sacrifice and almost spiritual coping. The latter seemed to be the more common attitude immediately after September 11. New York City seemed to become a kinder, gentler place. New Yorkers, known for their toughness and almost rudeness to strangers, were observed to be more considerate of each other. On a ride home on a crowded "F" train, the only one going to Brooklyn in those first days, I saw people make room for one another and give directions to passengers who were unfamiliar with this subway line with an attitude of concern rarely demonstrated in the city. In being helpful, the individual feels less like a victim and more like a rescuer. Helplessness is transformed into hopefulness.

One of the defining characteristics of all disasters is their unpredictability. Floods, tornados, and forest fires do not announce themselves. The randomness leaves people surprised, helpless, and frequently hopeless. Technological disasters add another dimension of unpredictability, threat, terror, and horror (L. Austin, 1992). The disaster of September 11 has no precedent in U.S. history. Victims and others, who might not be at first described as victims, reported classic symptoms of expectable reactions after a terrorist attack. Recurring thoughts of the incident, fears, particularly of leaving home, and inability to maintain usual routines were all reported. A young woman who presented herself for help about a week after the event is an example. She described herself as being unable to resume her activities. She had arrived late to work that day and was still in the lobby of the World Trade Center when the attack occurred. As debris began to fly around and people around her could not figure out what had happened or what to do, the security guards told them all to stay in the building rather than to leave. She did not feel that these instructions were sound, so she slipped out of the building and managed to make her way to her home in Brooklyn through a series of circuitous routes. Although physically safe, she could not shake off her fears and apprehension, symptoms of acute stress reaction. I pointed out her resourcefulness in saving herself. She stared at me in silence and after a moment said, "Thank you." This simple recognition of her own active engagement in her flight to safety diminished her sense of helplessness and helped to reduce her symptoms.

In addition to the usual complaints of sleeping and eating problems, grief, emotional numbing, and depression, survivors experience this trauma as a persistent one (LeDoux & Gorman, 2001). The magnitude of the event, which has an enormous ripple effect, followed by continued threat of terrorism (including biological terrorism and war) and the continual admonishment by the authorities to "be on alert" have led to the experience of chronic anxiety for many.

The psychological devastation may not be known for months, perhaps years (Everly & Mitchell, 2001). Psychologists and other mental health providers have continued to offer counseling services to the victims, their families, and others affected by the disaster. All kinds of pro bono and low cost services were set up and continue to operate. The Federal Emergency Management Agency, the Red Cross, and the September 11 Fund all set up funds and referral networks for victims to access mental health services. The psychological community organized pro bono and low-cost referral networks. Nonetheless, 6 months after the disaster, there was a newspaper report (S. Marshall, 2002) of thousands of New Yorkers struggling with the psychological aftermath of the trauma and having difficulty accessing mental health services. Six months after the disaster, all New Yorkers (and perhaps all Americans) were still experiencing a heightened state of alertness.

We have gone from disaster to anxieties and fears, some clearly identifiable but others nagging and below the surface. Although there is some semblance of normalcy, the following clinical vignettes illustrate the unsettled state of mind of many people:

- A firefighter with 15 years experience reports that he is uneasy crossing bridges, wondering what large trucks may be carrying. He also worries about his wife and children. Asked if this affects his work of fighting fires, he states that it does not.
- A 7-year-old girl being seen for psychotherapy in New York City reports that there was a fire drill in her school and that she

was scared, as were many of her classmates. This, however, is not the reason that she began therapy.

- A parent brings a child in to see a psychologist in California because he gets extremely anxious and cannot sleep when he hears planes overhead, thinking that this might be an attack.
- Five months after the attack, a young lawyer who was working near the site of the disaster started to have difficulty sleeping and nightmares when he fell asleep. He has started a new relationship with a woman who has asked him to tell her his story of September 11. He is meeting a lot of new people through her and has to retell his story many times.

This anxiety cuts across all levels of society, from the young stockbrokers and lawyers who ran from their offices, to the security officers in the schools nearby who had to evacuate, to the dishwashers in the restaurants in the area. Undocumented aliens worry about getting deported, as do foreign students, some of whom have the added anxiety of belonging to the national or religious group from which the terrorists came and who are therefore the object of rage. The same Muslim and Sikh cabdrivers who were offering free rides are worried that people will hold them responsible for the attacks (Pratt & Lefkowitz, 2001).

Ads in New York City subways read: "It's normal to be anxious since Sept 11—lots of people are"; a telephone number is provided for a referral to talk to someone. There are also tips for people, like, "Heroes talk" or "Speaking to family and friends can be helpful."

As many people continue to experience chronic anxiety, psychologists must figure out how to respond to this need and to consider how the aftermath may affect their work. We must respond to the chronic anxiety and fear in a way that is different than our more traditional work. Our work with this population and on these issues involves developing greater understanding of resilience and how to foster its development.

PROMOTING RESILIENCE IN RESPONSE TO TERRORISM

Like the schoolyard bully, terrorism depends for its effect on being able to induce fear in its intended victims. To the extent that psychology can contribute to enhancing the resilience of citizens so that we react with less fear when terrorism strikes, we reduce not only the impact of terrorism but also the incentives for terrorists to engage in violent acts. Hence, there is a need for good information on psychological resilience, coping with disasters, and programs designed to help citizens deal with the continuing threat of terrorism.

The psychology we offer the public must be based on sound psychological research and good clinical judgment. Our current situation is unprecedented; we do not expect to find any studies addressing it directly. We have been advised by our science colleagues to look at the literature on psychological resilience, as well as the literature on terrorism in other countries (e.g., Northern Ireland, Israel) and on the response to natural disasters like hurricanes and earthquakes. In addition, stress inoculation programs and programs for dealing with acute and chronic stress and anxiety are likely to help in coping with threat of terrorist attacks. We are also aware that different segments of our diverse society have different methods of coping with and managing stress. Hence, we need to keep the diverse needs of our pluralistic society uppermost in our mind as we develop information on programs.

Funding was recently approved for collaboration between APA and the American Psychological Foundation on an Integrated Science–Practice Task Force on Promoting Resilience in Response to Terrorism. The Task Force would develop information for psychologists and graduate students, State Psychological Associations, and external groups such as the National Mental Health Association on psychological resilience, coping with disasters, and programs that are most likely to help our citizens deal with the stress, anxiety, and fear caused by terrorism. The work product would present a range of approaches, materials, and information, leaving it up to the clinician to determine what fits best under specific circumstances. The focus would be on programs aimed at building strengths and promoting resilience and health.

To provide a scientific foundation for this effort, we conducted a literature search using APA's online search services in January 2002, using the keywords *terrorism*, *ethnopolitical warfare*, *ethnic or religious conflict or war*, *disasters*, *defining and measuring resilience and hardiness*, *resilience*, *hardiness*, *promoting or enhancing resilience or hardiness*, *preventing PTSD* [posttraumatic stress disorder], *stress inoculation programs*, and the *efficacy of stress management programs*. We briefly summarize the salient findings.

Terrorism, Ethnopolitical Warfare, Ethnic or Religious Conflict or War

The psychological literature on terrorism, ethnopolitical warfare, ethnic or religious conflict or war is sparse. In addition to the recent volume published by APA on ethnopolitical warfare (Chirot & Seligman, 2001), we were able to identify only a handful of articles and very little empirical research. We could only find several studies, and these were on the Oklahoma City bombing (e.g., Pfefferbaum, Gurwitch, et al., 2000; Pfefferbaum, Nixon, Tivis, Doughty, Pynoos, Gurwitch, & Foy, 2001). Most of them were review or conceptual articles dealing with such matters as the Holocaust (Suedfeld, 2000), the conflict in Northern Ireland (Cairns & Darby, 1998), the Israeli–Palestinian conflict (Rouhana & Bar-Tal, 1998), terrorism in Guatemala and Peru (Comas-Diaz, Lykes, & Alarcon, 1998), ethnic conflict in Sri Lanka (Rogers, Spencer, & Uyangoda, 1998), and global psychology (Mays, Bullock, Rosenzweig, & Wessells, 1998; Mays, Rubin, Sabourin, & Walker, 1996). Needless to say, this is an area in great need of research and development.

Disasters

The psychological literature on disasters is much larger than the literature on terrorism. The psychological sequellae of natural disasters have been studied with regard to hurricanes (Anthony, Lonigan, & Hecht, 1999; Barnard & Rothgeb, 2000; Dudley-Grant, Mendez, & Zinn, 2000; Jones, Frary, Cunningham, Weddle, & Kaiser, 2001; La Greca, Silverman, Vernberg, & Prinstein, 1996; La Greca, Silverman, & Wasserstein, 1998; Norris & Kaniasty, 1996; Thompson, Norris, & Hanacek, 1993; Vernberg, La Greca, Silverman, & Prinstein, 1996); tornadoes (McMillen, Smith, & Fischer, 1997); earthquakes (Knight, Gatz, Heller, & Bengtson, 2000; Nolen-Hoeksema & Morrow, 1991; Weiss, Marmar, Metzler, & Ronfeldt, 1995; Wood et al., 1992); and floods (Phifer, 1990). In addition, human-made disasters have also been the subject of psychological study, including airline disasters (Butcher & Hatcher, 1988; Dougall, Herberman, Delahanty, Inslicht, & Baum, 2000; Jacobs, Quevillon, & Stricherz, 1990; McMillen et al., 1997; C. Williams, Solomon, & Bartone, 1988), bus accidents (A. Turner, 2000), ship sinkings (Lindeman, Saari, Verkasalo, & Prytz, 1996; Rosen, 1995), and mass killings (McMillen et al., 1997). Technological disasters and toxic accidents have also been the subject of study (Baum & Fleming, 1993; Baum, Gatchel, & Schaeffer, 1983; Kronik, Akhmerov, & Speckhard, 1999). For an excellent overview of the development of the field of disaster mental health, see G. A. Jacobs (1995).

Among the findings most relevant to our subject, namely promoting resilience in the face of terrorism, a number of variables have been identified as predictors of postdisaster symptoms. Weiss et al. (1995) found that postdisaster symptoms in adults (emergency service personnel) can be predicted by exposure to trauma, social support, experience (years on the job), locus of control, and dissociative tendencies. Dougall et al. (2000) found that prior exposure to trauma that was dissimilar to the current trauma resulted in greater postdisaster symptoms in a sample of disaster personnel. Nolen-Hoeksema and Morrow (1991) found that postdisaster symptoms in college students could be predicted by exposure, prior symptoms, and a tendency toward rumination. Norris and Kaniasty (1996) found evidence for their social support deterioration deterrence model, which stipulates that postdisaster mobilization of support counteracts the deterioration in expectations of support often experienced by disaster victims. McMillen et al. (1997) found that perceived benefit 4–6 weeks following exposure to disaster predicted posttraumatic stress disorder 3 years later and moderated the effect of severity of disaster exposure. With regard to children, La Greca et al. (1996) found that postdisaster symptoms can be predicted by a model that includes five factors: Exposure to traumatic events during and after the disaster, Demographic characteristics, Occurrence of major life stressors, Availability of social support, and Coping strategies. Although a range of predictive factors have been identified, the literature suggests that degree of exposure to the disaster, prior symptoms, and occurrence of major stressors in the aftermath of the disaster, tend to be related to greater postdisaster symptoms and that personality resources and social support tend to ameliorate postdisaster symptoms.

For the most part, the literature on demographic differences in the response to disasters is contradictory and inconclusive. For example, Lindeman et al. (1996) found that women experience more postdisaster symptoms than men; however, in an older adult sample. Phifer (1990) found men experience more postdisaster symptoms than women. Clearly the relationship between gender and postdisaster symptoms is quite complicated, reflecting the complexity of the larger relationship between gender and mental health (cf. Levant & Kopecky, 1995). Jones et al. (2001) examined levels of self-reported postdisaster symptoms among African American, Hispanic, and Caucasian elementary and middle school children and found no differences on the basis of race–ethnicity. On the other hand, La Greca et al. (1998) found that race predicted self-reported postdisaster symptoms 7 months after the disaster; African Americans fared worse than other children. Thus, it appears that the relationship between race–ethnicity and postdisaster symptoms is a complicated one. Focusing on adults over 60 years of age (who have been found to exhibit fewer postdisaster symptoms than adults of less than 60 years), Knight et al. (2000) found that older adults' greater resilience is more likely the result of inoculation as a result of prior experience with disasters than the result of maturation.

Risk and Protective Factors in a Stage Model of Disasters

Building on the work of Zinner and Williams (1999), Pann (2001) identified the unique risk and protective factors at both the individual and community levels across a series of stages from the pretrauma period to the posttrauma period.

Pretrauma Period

In addition to factors already noted, several personality traits are associated with resilience to traumatic stress. One such variable is *coping styles*, which can be emotion-focused or problem-focused or oriented toward approach or avoidance. These different coping styles can have different outcomes depending on the situation. For example, emotion-focused coping can be helpful if the individual focuses on managing distressing emotional reactions, but it can be maladaptive if the individual engages in excessive rumination. So too, problem-focused coping can aid in the adjustment process, but if used excessively relative to emotion-focussed coping or denial it may lead to greater anxiety levels. Hence, people may be better served by learning a range of coping responses and being flexible in their use. Another variable is *cognitive appraisal of stress or threat*. A tendency to appraise events as unpredictable and threatening can increase vulnerability to traumatic events. *Attributional style* is a related variable, which has three dimensions: *locus* (the tendency to assume an internal vs. an external chain of causality of a traumatic event), *stability* (the tendency to assume that the traumatic event will continue vs. viewing it as temporary), and *globality* (the degree to which events are seen as affecting one's entire life or only specific aspects of it). An attribution style consisting of an internal locus, stability, and globality would increase one's vulnerability, whereas *self-efficacy*, or the view that one can cope with stressful events, is a protective factor, as is *psychological stability* (in contrast to *neuroticism*). In addition to personality variables, several community-level variables are important risk and protective factors during the pretrauma period. Risk factors include past unresolved traumas and previous losses. Protective factors include a psychological sense of community, belonging and cohesion, levels of support structures in place, and the ability to mobilize for emergencies.

Trauma Period

Individual risk factors include sense of threat (to life, limb or family member), sense of helplessness, loss of significant others, bereavement, injury to self or family member, loss of possessions, significant property damage, dislocation, displacement, sense of personal responsibility, sense of inescapable horror, sense of human malevolence, panic during the disaster, exposure to media coverage of the disaster, and severity of symptoms exhibited during the early phases of disaster recovery (especially avoidance and numbing symptoms). Risk factors at the level of the community include human-caused disasters, extreme destruction, great injury and death, serious financial loss, and degree of dislocation of community functions.

Primary Intervention Period

The primary intervention period can be described as a "heroic period," in which large amounts of time and energy are directed toward rescue operations and stabilizing the situation. In the acute phase of recovery, individual risk and protective factors include social support, availability of information about the disaster, presence of other stressors, presence of resources (higher income and education, recovery services), and successful mastery of past traumatic events. Community factors include leadership, communication, and the provision of trauma resources to victims.

Secondary Adjustment Period

Key individual factors include the restoration of normality and a sense of security. At the community level, large-scale devastation can impair the quality of life for a considerable time. Rituals and memorials can assist communities in coping with losses.

Posttrauma Period

Most individuals return to their predisaster level of functioning in 6 months to 3 years after the event. Those most directly exposed to life threat are at greatest risk for adverse effects. Hard hit communities may struggle for quite some time to regain a sense of normalcy.

Preventing PTSD, Stress Inoculation, and Stress Management Programs

Preventing PTSD

Bryant and Harvey (2000) have suggested that Acute Stress Disorder (ASD) is a precursor of PTSD. Hence, they argued, PTSD can be prevented by identifying and treating (with cognitive behavioral therapy) trauma victims who suffer from ASD. Bryant, Harvey, Dang, Sackville, and Basten (1998) found that brief cognitive behavioral therapy of ASD resulted in significantly fewer cases of PTSD at posttreatment and 6-month follow-up, as compared with a supportive counseling condition. Foa, Hearst-Ikeda, and Perry (1995) found that a brief (4-session) cognitive behavioral program aimed at arresting the development of PTSD in female victims of assault significantly reduced the severity of PTSD symptoms as compared to an assessment control group 2 months postassault.

Stress Inoculation Training

Stress inoculation training (SIT), according to Meichenbaum (1993), is a "flexible, individually-tailored, multifaceted form of cognitive behavioral therapy" (p. 378). The concept of inoculation is borrowed from both medicine and social psychological research on attitude change. The underlying concept is that by enhancing a person's coping responses to mild stressors through skills training and development, one can reduce the likelihood of developing symptoms in the face of severe stress. Meichenbaum described three phases to SIT. SIT begins with a conceptualization phase through which the problem is assessed and clients are taught that their appraisal of stressful events mediates their reaction to them. The second phase focuses on coping skill acquisition and rehearsal. The final phase, application and follow through, involves exposure, in which the client is encouraged to apply their coping skills to gradually increasing levels of stressful situations. SIT has been applied to a wide range of stressful situations: medical problems such as preparation for surgery or other stressful medical procedures; reducing the stress associated with mental illness; treatment of performance anxiety; adjustment to life transitions such as unemployment or entering military service; helping those in high-stress occupations, such as first responders to disaster; and helping victims of trauma.

Stress Management Programs

We searched the literature on the outcomes of stress management programs and found studies demonstrating efficacy in several areas: workplace and job stress (Adams, 1981; Bunce, 1997; Bunce & West, 1996; Murphy, 1986; Stensrud & Stensrud, 1983), medical illness (Baum, Herberman, & Cohen, 1995; Heinrich & Schag, 1985; Ludwick-Rosenthal & Neufeld, 1988), life transitions (Schinke, Schilling, & Snow, 1987), and family stress (Falloon, 1985; Schinke, Barth, Gilchrist, & Maxwell, 1986; Weinberg, 1999).

Summary

Several variables are associated with postdisaster psychological status. Predisaster psychological vulnerability (e.g., prior episodes of PTSD), degree of exposure to the traumatic event during and immediately after the disaster, and the occurrence of major life stressors (e.g., loss of home, unemployment) are associated with poorer postdisaster adjustment. On the other hand, personality resources such as resilience or hardiness and social support are associated with better postdisaster psychological status. SIT and stress management programs might be of considerable help in preparing some individuals to cope with the threat of terrorist attack. Very little is known about how different demographic groups respond to disasters; more research is needed in this area. One challenge for the future is to design and evaluate psychoeducational programs aimed at enhancing the factors of resilience (Confident Optimism, Productive and Autonomous Activity, Interpersonal Warmth and Insight, and Skilled Expressiveness) and hardiness (Sense of Control Over One's Life, Commitment as a Result of Finding Meaning in One's Existence, and Viewing Change as Challenge).

CONCLUSION

Psychology has always possessed the potential to contribute meaningfully to society. As active participants within the APA governance for over a quarter of a century, we have collectively been very pleased with the extent to which our profession has gradually accepted this important societal responsibility in an increasingly wide range of areas. The tragic events of September 11 have brought psychology's unique expertise to the forefront, and

we are proud of how APA and our colleagues across the nation spontaneously responded to this crisis. This is truly the mark of a maturing profession.

The essence of the War On Terrorism is, above all else, one of psychology. Immediately following the unprecedented attack, our clinical colleagues
reached out to provide high quality health care—fully realizing that individuals are different, that children are not merely little adults, and that those
closest to the horror would most likely respond differently than those farther
away. An impressive range of psychological expertise was demonstrated, including informing the media and developing data-based responses to real-life
psychological experiences. At both the national and state association level,
psychologists were critical force in shaping our nation's response. We really
do know a tremendous amount about the underlying experiences our citizens
underwent, and fortunately our voice was heard. The behavioral sciences are
the key to survival and flourishing in the 21st century.

Our nation is now entering another phase in this war: how to deal with
continual vague and often unsubstantiated threats. To many, this strikes at
the essence of the American dream. Once again, psychology's calm and
thoughtful voice is being heard—in the media and at the highest levels of
public policy making. From a public policy perspective, we must soon expect
the emergence of yet another phase: how to aggressively address the underlying causes of a seemingly irrational hatred and violence that is being directed
at our citizens and our fundamental way of life. Fortunately, our discipline
has a long and rich history of scientifically addressing closely related issues.

We fully expect that throughout these challenges, we shall once again
see the best and brightest of our nation's behavioral scientists unselfishly
contributing to the ongoing national (and international) debate as it un-
folds. In time, we further expect that our profession's educators will become
meaningfully involved in crafting creative solutions. In our judgment, this is
as it should be. The key to the future is quality education for all individuals
and this simply cannot be accomplished without the active engagement of
our world's educational institutions. Our planet is becoming increasingly interdependent, with physical distances having increasingly little significance.
Daily we are faced with a virtual explosion in technological advances; international, if not instant, communications; and virtually unforeseen transportation capabilities that we have now almost come to expect. As we enter the
21st century, all nations and their enlightened citizenry must come to appreciate the inexorable march to globalization. Our world is becoming smaller
and smaller, forcing an intimacy on disparate societies. This is a challenge
that psychology is destined to play an important part in meeting.

REFERENCES

Abenhaim, L., Dab, W., & Salmi, L. (1992). Study of civilian victims of terrorist attacks (France 1982–1987). *Journal of Clinical Epidemiology, 45*, 103–109.

Abi-Hashem, N. (1992). The impact of the Gulf War on the churches in the Middle East: A socio-cultural and spiritual analysis. *Pastoral Psychology, 41*(1), 4–26.

Abi-Hashem, N. (1997). Reflections on international perspectives in psychology. *American Psychologist, 52*, 569–570.

Abi-Hashem, N. (1999, Fall–Winter). Ethnopolitical conflicts: A Lebanese perspective. *International Psychology Reporter: APA Division 52 Newsletter, 3*(2, 3), 29–31.

Abi-Hashem, N. (2000). Psychology, time, and culture. *American Psychologist, 55*, 342–343.

Abi-Hashem, N. (2001a, August). *Peace in the Middle East: Political reality or psychological illusion?* Paper presented at the 109th Annual Convention of the American Psychological Association, San Francisco, CA.

Abi-Hashem, N. (2001b). Rediscovering hope in American psychology. *American Psychologist, 56*, 85–86.

Abu Fadel, H. (2002, May 29). Ulbatu el-Asraar [Mystery box]. *An-Nahar Newspaper*, p. 17.

Abu-Nimer, M. (2000). Peace building in postsettlement: Challenges for Israeli and Palestinian peace educators. *Peace and Conflict: Journal of Peace Psychology, 6*, 1–21.

Abu-Rabbi', I. M. (1996). *Intellectual origins of Islamic resurgence in the modern Arab world.* Albany: State University of New York Press.

Ackerman, P., & Kruegler, C. (1994). *Strategic nonviolent conflict: The dynamics of people power in the twentieth century.* Westport, CT: Praeger.

Adams, J. D. (1981). Health, stress, and manager's life style. *Group & Organization Studies, 6*, 291–301.

Adler, L., & Mukherji, B. (Eds.). (1995). *Spirit versus scalpel: Traditional healing and modern psychotherapy*. Westport, CT: Bergin & Garvey.

Adorno, T., Frenkel-Brunswik, E., Levinson, D., & Sanford, R. (1950). *The authoritarian personality*. New York: Harper Press.

Afemann, E. (1997). *Internet for the third world—Chance or threat?* Retrieved from http://www.uni–muenster.de/EthnologieHeute/eh1/ afe.htm#CultureClash.

Agger, I., & Jensen, S. (1990). Testimony as ritual and evidence in psychotherapy for political refugees. *Journal of Traumatic Stress, 3*, 115–130.

Agger, I., & Jensen, S. (1996). *Trauma and recovery under state terrorism*. London: Zed.

Agha, H., & Malley, R. (2002, May/June). The last negotiation: How to end the Middle East peace process. *Foreign Affairs, 81*(3), 10–18.

Ahearn, F. (2000). Psychosocial wellness: Methodological approaches to the study of refugees. In F. Ahearn (Ed.), *Psychosocial wellness of refugees* (pp. 3–23). New York: Berghahn.

Ahmad, K. (Ed.). (1999). Islam: The essentials. In K. Ahmad (Ed.), *Islam: Its meaning and message* (3rd ed.). Leicester, UK: The Islamic Foundation.

Ahmed, R., & Gielen, U. (1998). *Psychology in the Arab countries*. Cairo, Egypt: Menoufia University Press.

Akbar, S. A. (1999). *Islam today: A short introduction to the Muslim world*. New York: St. Martin's Press.

Allden, K., Poole, C., Chantavanich, S., & Khin, O. (1996). Burmese political dissidents in Thailand: Trauma and survival among young adults in exile. *American Journal of Public Health, 86*, 1561–1569.

Allport, G. (1954). *The nature of prejudice*. Reading, MA: Addison-Wesley.

American Psychiatric Association. (1994). *Diagnostic and statistical manual of mental disorders* (4th ed.). Washington, DC: Author.

Anderson, S., & Sloan, S. (1995). *Historical dictionary of terrorism*. Metuchen, NJ: Scarecrow Press.

Andrus, B. C. (1969). *The infamous of Nuremberg*. London: Fravin.

Anthony, J. L., Lonigan, C. J., & Hecht, S. A. (1999). Dimensionality of posttraumatic stress disorder symptoms in children exposed to disaster: Results from confirmatory factor analyses. *Journal of Abnormal Psychology, 108*, 326–336.

Aristotle. (1947). *Politics* (Trans. W. Ellis). London: Dent Dutton.

Armstrong, K. (2000). *The battle for God: Fundamentalism in Judaism, Christianity, and Islam*. New York: Knopf.

Aronson, E. (2000). *Nobody left to hate: Teaching compassion after Columbine*. New York: Worth.

Asch, S. E. (1956). Studies of independence and conformity: A minority of one against a unamimous majority. *Psychological Monographs, 70*, 1–70.

A time to mourn. (2001, November). *American Teacher*, p. 10.

Atran, S. (2003). Genesis of suicide terrorism. *Science, 299*, 1534–1539.

Austin, L. (1992). *Responding to disaster: A guide for mental health professionals.* Washington, DC: American Psychiatric Press.

Austin, W. (1989). Living on the edge: The impact of terrorism upon Philippine villagers. *International Journal of Offender Therapy and Comparative Criminology, 33,* 103–119.

Awwad, J. (2001). The kingdom of God and the state. *Theological Review, 12*(1), 35–60.

Ayalon, O. (1983). Coping with terrorism: The Israeli case. In D. Meichenbaum & M. E. Jarenko (Eds.), *Stress reduction and prevention* (pp. 293–337). New York: Plenum Press.

Ball-Rokeach, S. J. (1972). The legitimation of violence. In J. F. Short, Jr. & M. E. Wolfgang (Eds.), *Collective violence* (pp. 100–111). Chicago: Aldine-Atherton.

Bandura, A. (1973). *Aggression: A social learning analysis.* Englewood Cliffs, NJ: Prentice Hall.

Bandura, A. (1982). The psychology of chance encounters and life paths. *American Psychologist, 37,* 747–755.

Bandura, A. (1986). *Social foundations of thought and action: A social cognitive theory.* Englewood Cliffs, NJ: Prentice Hall.

Bandura, A. (1990). Mechanisms of moral disengagement. In W. Reich (Ed.), *Origins of terrorism: Psychologies, ideologies, theologies, states of mind* (pp. 161–191). Cambridge, England: Cambridge University Press.

Bandura, A. (1992). Social cognitive theory of social referencing. In S. Feinman (Ed.), *Social referencing and the social construction of reality in infancy* (pp. 175–208). New York: Plenum Press.

Bandura, A. (1999). Moral disengagement in the perpetration of inhumanities [Special issue]. *Personality and Social Psychology Review, 3,* 193–209.

Bandura, A., Underwood, B., & Fromson, M. E. (1975). Disinhibition of aggression through diffusion of responsibility and dehumanization of victims. *Journal of Research in Personality, 9,* 253–269.

Barakat, H. (1993). *The Arab world: Society, culture, and states.* Los Angeles: University of California Press.

Barber, B. (1996). *Jihad vs. McWorld.* New York: Random House.

Barber, F. (2001). Political violence, social integration and youth functioning: Palestinian youth from the Intifada. *Journal of Community Psychology, 29,* 259–280.

Barnard, A. G., & Rothgeb, I. V. (2000). Rebuilding a private practice in psychology following a hurricane: The experiences of two psychologists. *Professional Psychology: Research and Practice, 31,* 393–397.

Barron, J., & Paul, A. (1977). *Murder of a gentle land: The untold story of communist genocide in Cambodia.* New York: Readers Digest Press.

Barnett, V. J. (1999). *Bystanders: Conscience and complicity during the Holocaust.* Westport, CT: Greenwood Press.

Bassiouni, M. C. (1981). Terrorism, law enforcement, and the mass media: Perspectives, problems, proposals. *The Journal of Criminal Law & Criminology, 72,* 1–51.

Baum, A., & Fleming, I. (1993). Implications of psychological research on stress and technological accidents. *American Psychologist, 48,* 665–672.

Baum, A., Gatchel, R. J., & Schaeffer, M. A. (1983). Emotional, behavioral, and physiological effects of chronic stress at Three Mile Island. *Journal of Consulting and Clinical Psychology, 51,* 565–572.

Baum, A., Herberman, H., & Cohen, L. (1995). Managing stress and managing illness: Survival and quality of life in chronic disease. *Journal of Clinical Psychology in Medical Settings, 2,* 309–333.

Baumeister, R. F. (1997). Identity, self-concept, and self-esteem: The self lost and found. In R. Hogan, J. A. Johnson, & S. Briggs (Eds.), *Handbook of personality psychology* (pp. 681–710). San Diego, CA: Academic Press.

Baumeister, R. F. (Ed.). (1999). *The self in social psychology.* Philadelphia: Psychology Press.

Baumeister, R. F., Boden, J. M., & Smart, L. (1996). Relation of threatened egotism to violence and aggression: The dark side of high self–esteem. *Psychological Review, 103,* 5–33.

Becker, J. B. (1996). *The news media, terrorism, and democracy: The symbiotic relationship between freedom of the press and acts of terror.* Los Angeles: Emergency Operations Bureau, Los Angeles County Sheriff Department.

Benedict, R. (1934). *Patterns of culture.* Boston and New York: Houghton Mifflin.

Berke, J. (1988). *The tyranny of malice: Exploring the dark side of culture and character.* New York: Summit Books.

Bernstein, R., & Weisman, S. R. (February 17, 2003). NATO settles rift over aid to Turks in case of a war. *The New York Times,* p. A8.

The Bhagavad Gita. (1968). (E. Deutsch, Trans.). New York: Holt, Rinehart and Winston.

Billig, O. (1984). Case history of a German terrorist. *Terrorism: An international journal, 7,* 1–10.

Billig, O. (1985). The lawyer terrorist and his comrades. *Political Psychology, 6,* 29–46.

Billington, J. (1980). *Fire in the minds of men: Origins of revolutionary faith.* London: Temple, Smith.

Blair, J. (2002, March 25). Advice on the task of rebuilding, from a mayor who knows terror's toll. *The New York Times,* p. A14.

Blake, R. R., & Mouton, J. S. (1964). *The managerial grid.* Houston, TX: Gulf.

Blazak, R. (2001). White boys to terrorist men: Target recruitment of Nazi skinheads. *American Behavioral Scientist, 44,* 982–1000.

Blight, J. G. (1987). Toward a policy-relevant psychology of avoiding nuclear war: Lessons for psychologists from the Cuban missile crisis. *American Psychologist, 42,* 12–29.

Blumenfeld, L. (2002). *Revenge: A story of hope.* New York: Simon & Schuster.

Boas, F. (1928). *Anthropology and modern life.* New York: Norton.

Bodansky, Y. (2001). *Bin Laden: The man who declared war on America.* New York: Random House/Forum.

Bollinger, D. (1982). *Language: The loaded weapon.* London: Longman.

Boothby, N. (1996). Mobilizing communities to meet the psychosocial needs of children in war and refugee crises. In R. J. Apfel & B. Simon (Eds.), *Minefields in their hearts: The mental health of children in war and communal violence* (pp. 149–164). New Haven, CT: Yale University Press.

Borger, J. (2001). Rhetoric to arouse the Islamic world [Electronic version]. *The Guardian.* Retrieved October 8, 2001, from http://www.guardian.co.uk/Print/0,3858,4272496,00.html

Bossolo, L., Bergantino, D., Lichtenstein, B., & Gutman, M. (2002). Many Americans still feeling effects of September 11th; are reexamining their priorities in life. Retrieved February 22, 2002, from APA Online: http://www.apa.org/practice/poll_911.html

Brehm, J. (1966). *A theory of psychological reactance.* New York: Academic Press.

Britt, L., & Heise, D. (2000). From shame to pride in identity politics. In S. Stryker, T. J. Owens, & R. W. White (Eds.), *Self, identity, and social movements* (pp. 252–268). Minneapolis: University of Minnesota Press.

Bruner, J. S. (1991). The narrative construction of reality. *Critical Inquiry, 18*(1), 1–21.

Bryant, R., & Harvey, A. (2000). *Acute stress disorder: A handbook of theory, assessment, and treatment.* Washington, DC: American Psychological Association.

Bryant, R., Harvey, A., Dang, S., Sackville, T., & Basten, C. (1998). Treatment of acute stress disorder: A comparison of cognitive–behavioral therapy and supportive counseling. *Journal of Consulting & Clinical Psychology, 66,* 862–866.

Bunce, D. (1997). What factors are associated with the outcome of individual-focused worksite stress management interventions? *Journal of Occupational & Organizational Psychology, 70,* 1–17.

Bunce, D., & West, M. A. (1996). Stress management and innovation interventions at work. *Human Relations, 46,* 209–232.

Burkle, F. S. (1999). *Combined humanitarian assistance response training course.* Honolulu, HI: Center of Excellence in Disaster Management and Humanitarian Assistance.

Burrows, R. J. (1996). *The strategy of nonviolent defense.* Albany: State University of New York Press.

Burton, J. (Ed.). (1990). *Conflict: Human needs theory.* New York: St. Martin's Press.

Burton, J. W. (1987). *Resolving deep-rooted conflict: A handbook.* Lanham, MD: University Press of America.

Butcher, J., & Hatcher, C. (1988). The neglected entity in air disaster planning: Psychological services. *American Psychologist, 43,* 724–729.

Bynner, J., & Ashford, S. (1994). Politics and participation: Some antecedents of young people's attitudes to the political system and political activity. *European Journal of Social Psychology, 24,* 223–236.

Cairns, E. (1996). *Children and political violence*. Cambridge, England: Blackwell.

Cairns, E., & Darby, J. (1998). The conflict in Northern Ireland: Causes, consequences, and controls. *American Psychologist, 53*, 754–760.

Cairns, E., & Toner, I. (1993). Children and political violence in Northern Ireland: From riots to reconciliation. In L. Leavitt & N. Fox (Eds.), *The psychological effects of war and violence on children* (pp. 215–229). Hillsdale, NJ: Erlbaum.

Carmichael, D. J. C. (1982). Of beasts, gods, and civilized men: The justification of terrorism and of counterterrorist measures. *Terrorism, 6*, 1–26.

Carnegie Commission on the Prevention of Deadly Conflict. (1997). *Preventing deadly conflict: Final report*. New York: Carnegie Corporation.

Carr, C. (2002). *The lessons of terror: A history of warfare against civilians, why it has always failed and why it will fail again*. New York: Random House.

CBS reportedly paid 2 fugitives. (1983, September 22). *San Francisco Chronicle*.

Charny, I. W. (Ed.). (1999). *Encyclopedia of genocide* (Vols. 1–2). Santa Barbara, CA: ABC-CLIO, Inc.

Chirot, D., & Seligman, M. E. P. (2001). *Ethnopolitical warfare: Causes, consequences, and possible solutions*. Washington, DC: American Psychological Association.

Chomsky, N. (2001). *9–11*. New York: Seven Stories Press.

Chong, D. (2000). *The girl in the picture: The story of Kim Phuc and the photograph that changed the course of the Vietnam War*. New York: Viking.

Choueiri, Y. M. (1990). *Islamic fundamentalism*. Boston: Twayne.

Christie, D. J. (1997). Reducing direct and structural violence: The human needs theory. *Peace and Conflict: Journal of Peace Psychology, 3*, 315–332.

Christie, D. J., Wagner, R. V., & Winter, D. D. (2001). *Peace, conflict, and violence: Peace psychology for the 21st century*. Upper Saddle River, NJ: Prentice Hall.

Cicourel, A. V. (1976). *The social organization of juvenile justice*. London: Heinemann.

Clay, R. (2002, September). Research on 9/11: What psychologists have learned so far. *Monitor on Psychology, 33*, 28–31.

Clymer, A. (2002, December 5). World survey says negative views of U.S. are rising. *The New York Times*, p. A11.

Coille, Z. (2002, January 13). Smart bombs put U.S. strikes under greater scrutiny. *San Francisco Chronicle*, p. A6.

Cole, M. (1998). *Cultural psychology: A once and future discipline*. Cambridge, MA: Harvard University Press.

Comas-Diaz, L., Lykes, M. B., & Alarcon, R. D. (1998). Ethnic conflict and the psychology of liberation in Guatemala, Peru, and Puerto Rico. *American Psychologist, 53*, 778–792.

Cooper, H. H. A. (1978). Terrorism: The problem of the problem of definition. *Chitty's Law Journal, 26*, 105–108.

Cooper, H. H. A. (2001). Terrorism: The problem of definition revisited. *American Behavioral Scientist, 44*, 881–893.

Cooper, J., Nettler, R., & Mahmoud, M. (Eds.). (2000). *Islam and modernity: Muslim intellectuals respond.* New York: Palgrave.

Coser, L. A. (1974). *Greedy institutions: Patterns of undivided commitment.* New York: Free Press.

Cote, J., & Levine, C. (2002). *Identity, formation, agency, and culture: A social psychological synthesis.* Mahwah, NJ: Erlbaum.

Council on Foreign Relations. (2003). *What is Aum Shinrikyo?* Retrieved April 21, 2003, from http://www.terrorismanswers.com/groups/aumshinrikyo.html

Courbage, Y., & Fargues, P. (1998). *Christians and Jews under Islam.* New York: St. Martin's Press.

Crawshaw, S. R. A. (1988). Averting a terrorist attack: A case study. In R. H. Ward & H. E. Smith (Eds.), *International terrorism: Operational issues* (pp. 47–59). Chicago: University of Illinois at Chicago Press.

Crenshaw, M. (1986). The subjective reality of the terrorist: Ideological and psychological factors in terrorism. In R. O. Slater & M. Stohl (Eds.), *Current perspectives on international terrorism.* New York: St. Martin's Press.

Crenshaw, M. (1998). The logic of terrorism. In W. Reich (Ed.), *Origins of terrorism: Psychologies, ideologies, theologies, and states of mind.* Washington, DC: Woodrow Wilson Center Press.

Crenshaw, M. (2000). The psychology of terrorism: An agenda for the 21st century. *Political Psychology, 21,* 405–420.

Crenshaw, M. (2002). Terrorism. *Encyclopedia Americana On-line.* Retrieved April 20, 2002, from http://216.74.27.40/cgi–bin/webFeat.Dll?Command =Search&Databases.

Crocker, J., & Major, B. (1989). Social stigma and self-esteem: The self-protective properties of stigma. *Psychological Review, 96,* 608–630.

Crossette, B. (2002, July 2). Study warns of stagnation in Arab societies. *The New York Times,* p. A7.

Curran, P., Bell, P., Murray, A., Loughrey, G., Roddy, R., & Rocke, L. (1990). Psychological consequences of the Enniskillen bombing. *British Journal of Psychiatry, 156,* 479–482.

Dalacoura, K. (1998). *Islam, liberalism and human rights.* New York: St. Martin's Press.

Danieli, Y. (1982). Therapists' difficulties in treating survivors of the Nazi Holocaust and their children. *Dissertation Abstracts International, 42*(12-B, Pt 1), 4927. (UMI No. 949–904)

Danieli, Y. (1984). Psychotherapists' participation in the conspiracy of silence about the Holocaust. *Psychoanalytic Psychology, 1*(1), 23–42.

Danieli, Y. (1985). The treatment and prevention of long-term effects and intergenerational transmission of victimization: A lesson from Holocaust survivors and their children. In C. R. Figley (Ed.), *Trauma and its wake* (pp. 295–313). New York: Brunner/Mazel.

Danieli, Y. (1988). Confronting the unimaginable: Psychotherapists' reactions to victims of the Nazi Holocaust. In J. P. Wilson, Z. Harel, & B. Kahana (Eds.), *Human adaptation to extreme stress* (pp. 219–238). New York: Plenum.

Danieli, Y. (1994a). Countertransference, trauma and training. In J. P. Wilson & J. Lindy (Eds.), *Countertransference in the treatment of post-traumatic stress disorder* (pp. 368–388). New York: Guilford Press.

Danieli, Y. (1994b). Resilience and hope. In G. Lejeune (Ed.), *Children worldwide* (pp. 47–49). Geneva: International Catholic Child Bureau.

Danieli, Y. (1997). As survivors age: An overview. *Journal of Geriatric Psychiatry, 30*(1), 9–26.

Danieli, Y. (Ed.). (1998). *International handbook of multigenerational legacies of trauma.* New York: Kluwer Academic/Plenum Press.

Danieli, Y. (2001). ISTSS members participate in recovery efforts in New York and Washington, DC. *Traumatic Stress Points, 15*(4), 4.

Danieli, Y. (Ed.). (2002). *Sharing the front line and the back hills: International protectors and providers, peacekeepers, humanitarian aid workers and the media in the midst of crisis.* Amityville, NY: Baywood Publishing.

Danieli, Y., & Krystal, J. H. (1989). *The initial report of the Presidential Task Force on Curriculum, Education and Training of the Society for Traumatic Stress Studies.* Chicago: The Society for Traumatic Stress Studies.

Danieli, Y., Rodley, N. S., & Weisaeth, L. (Eds.). (1996). *International responses to traumatic stress: Humanitarian, human rights, justice, peace and development contributions, collaborative actions and future initiatives.* Amityville, NY: Baywood Publishing.

de la Rey, C. (2001). Reconciliation in divided societies. In D. J. Christie, R. V. Wagner, & D. D. Winter (Eds.), *Peace, conflict, and violence: Peace psychology for the 21st century* (pp. 251–261). Upper Saddle River, NJ: Prentice Hall.

DeLeon, P. H. (1988). Public policy and public service: Our professional duty. *American Psychologist, 43,* 309–315.

DeLeon, P. H. (2002). Presidential reflections—Past and future. *American Psychologist, 57*(6/7), 425–430.

DeLeon, P. H., Eckert, P. A., & Wilkins, L. R. (2001). Public policy formulation: A front line perspective. *The Psychologist Manager Journal, 5*(2), 73–81.

Demaris, O. (1977). *Brothers in blood.* New York: Scribner.

Derogatis, L. R. (1994). *The Brief Symptom Inventory (BSI): Administration, scoring, and procedures manual* (3rd ed.). Minneapolis, MN: National Computer Systems.

des Forges, A. (1999). *Leave none to tell the story: Genocide in Rwanda.* New York: Human Rights Watch.

Desivilya, H., Gal, R., & Ayalon, O. (1996). Extent of victimization, traumatic stress symptoms and adjustment of terrorist assault survivors: A long-term follow-up. *Journal of Traumatic Stress, 9,* 88–89.

Deutsch, A. (2001, Fall). An administration in crisis. *The spectator: The Stuyvesant high school paper*, pp. 4–5.

Deutsch, M. (1983). The prevention of World War III: A psychological perspective. *Political Psychology, 4*, 3–31.

Dickens, C. (1963). *A tale of two cities.* New York: Airmont Books. (Original work published 1859)

Diener, E. (1977). Deindividuation: Causes and consequences. *Social Behavior and Personality, 5*, 143–156.

Diener, E., Dineen, J., Endresen, K., Beaman, A. L., & Fraser, S. C. (1975). Effects of altered responsibility, cognitive set, and modeling on physical aggression and deindividuation. *Journal of Personality and Social Psychology, 31*, 328–337.

Dougall, A., Herberman, H., Delahanty, D., Inslicht, S., & Baum, A. (2000). Similarity of prior trauma exposure as a determinant of chronic stress responding to an airline disaster. *Journal of Consulting & Clinical Psychology, 68*, 290–295.

Dudley-Grant, G. R., Mendez, G. I., & Zinn, J. (2000). Strategies for anticipating and preventing psychological trauma of hurricanes through community action. *Professional Psychology: Research and Practice, 31*, 387–392.

Dwairy, M. (1998). *Cross-cultural counseling: The Arab–Palestinian case.* New York: Haworth Press.

Ehrlich, P. R. (2000). *Human natures: Genes, cultures, and the human prospect.* Washington, DC: Shearwater.

Eisenbruch, M. (1991). From post traumatic stress disorder to cultural bereavement: Diagnosis of Southeast Asian refugees. *Social Science and Medicine, 30*, 673–680.

El-Nawawy, M., & Iskandar, A. (2002). *Al-Jazeera: How the free Arab news network scooped the world and changed the Middle East.* Cambridge, MA: Westview Press.

Eltahawy, M. (2002, September 3). Keeping faith with Islam in a new world. *The New York Times*, p. A19.

Engdahl, B., Jaranson, J., Kastrup, M., & Danieli, Y. (1999). Traumatic human rights violations: Their psychological impact and treatment. In Y. Danieli, E. C. Stamatapoulou, & J. Dias (Eds.), *The universal declaration of human rights fifty years and beyond* (pp. 337–356). Amityville, NY: Baywood Publishing.

Engel, C. (2001). Outbreaks of medically unexplained physical symptoms after military action, terrorist threat, or technological disaster. *Military Medicine, 166*(Suppl. 2), 47–48.

Engel, S. (2000). *The context is everything: The nature of memory.* New York: Freeman.

Erikson, E. H. (1963). *Childhood and society* (2nd ed.). New York: Norton.

Esposito, J. L. (1996). *The Islamic threat: Myth or reality?* (2nd ed.). New York: Oxford University Press.

Esposito, J. L. (Ed.). (1997). *Political Islam: Revolution, radicalism, or reformation?* Boulder, CO: Lynne Rienner.

Everly, G. S., Jr., & Mitchell, J. T. (2001). America under attack: The "10 commandments" of responding to mass terrorist attacks. *International Journal of Emergency Mental Health, 3*(3), 133–135.

Eyber, C. (2002). *Alleviating psychosocial suffering: An analysis of approaches to coping with war-related distress in Angola.* Unpublished doctoral dissertation, Queen Margaret University College, Edinburgh.

Ezekiel, R. S. (1995). *The racist mind.* New York: Penguin Books.

Falloon, I. R. (1985). Family management in the prevention of morbidity of schizophrenia: Clinical outcome of a two-year longitudinal study. *Archives of General Psychiatry, 42,* 887–896.

Fanon, F. (1963). *The wretched of the earth.* New York: Grove Wheatland.

Feather, N. T. (1995). National identification and ingroup bias in majority and minority groups: A field study. *Australian Journal of Psychology, 47*(3), 129–136.

Federal Bureau of Investigation. (1999). *Terrorism in the United States, 1999.* Washington, DC: U.S. Government Printing Office. Available at http://www.fbi.gov/publications/terror/terror99.pdf

Fein, H. (1993). Accounting for genocide after 1945: Theories and some findings. *International Journal of Group Rights, 1,* 79–106.

Figley, C. R. (Ed.). (1995). *Compassion fatigue: Coping with secondary traumatic stress disorder in those who treat the traumatized.* New York: Brunner/Mazel.

Finkel, N. (1995). *Commonsense justice: Jurors' notions of the law.* Cambridge, MA: Harvard University Press.

Firestone, R. (1999). *Jihad: The origin of the holy war in Islam.* New York: Oxford University Press.

Flynn, B. (1996, April). *Psychological aspects of terrorism.* Presented at the First Harvard Symposium on the Medical Consequences of Terrorism, Boston, MA.

Foa, E. B., Davidson, J. R. T., & Frances, A. (1999). The Expert Consensus Guidelines Series: Treatment of posttraumatic stress disorder. *Journal of Clinical Psychiatry, 60*(Suppl. 16), 1–76.

Foa, E. B., Hearst-Ikeda, D., & Perry, K. J. (1995). Evaluation of a brief cognitive–behavioral program for the prevention of chronic PTSD in recent assault victims. *Journal of Consulting & Clinical Psychology, 63,* 948–955.

Foa, E. B., Keane, T. M., & Friedman, M. J. (2000). *Effective treatments for PTSD: Practice guidelines from the International Society for Traumatic Stress Studies.* New York: Guilford Press.

Foucault, M. (1995). *Discipline and punish* (2nd ed.). New York: Vintage.

Franks, L., & Powers, T. (1970, September 17). Profile of a terrorist. *Palo Alto Times,* pp. 26–28.

Freedland, J. (2002, August 29–September 4). Israel set on tragic path–Chief rabbi. *The Guardian Weekly, 167*(10), p. 1.

Friedman, M. (2000). *Post traumatic stress disorder: The latest assessment and treatment strategies.* Kansas City, MO: Compact Clinicals.

Friedman, M. J., Charney, D. S., & Deutch, A. Y. (1995). *Neurobiological and clinical consequences of stress: From normal adaptation to PTSD.* Philadelphia: Lippincott-Raven.

Friedman, T. L. (2002, January 27). The two domes of Belgium. *The New York Times*, p. 13.

Fromm, E. (1941). *Escape from freedom*. New York: Holt, Rinehardt, & Winston.

Fromm, E. (1973). *The anatomy of human destructiveness*. Greenwich, CT: Fawcett Publications.

Fuller, G., & Pitts, F. R. (1990). Youth cohorts and political unrest in South Korea. *Political Geography Quarterly, 9*(1), 9–22.

Galdi, T. (1995, December 11). Revolution in military affairs? Competing concepts, organizational responses, outstanding issues. *CRS Report for Congress*.

Galea, S., Ahern, J., Resnick, H., Kilpatrick, D., Bucuvalas, M., Gold, J., et al. (2002). Psychological sequelae of the September 11 terrorist attacks in New York City. *New England Journal of Medicine, 346*, 982–987.

Galtung, J. (1996). *Peace by peaceful means: Peace and conflict, development and civilization*. London: Sage.

Gambino, R. (1973, November–December). Watergate lingo: A language of non-responsibility. *Freedom at Issue, 22*, 7–9, 15–17.

Gautam, S., Gupta, I., Batra, L., Sharma, H., Khandelwal, R., & Pant, A. (1998). Psychiatric morbidity among victims of bomb blast. *Indian Journal of Psychiatry, 40*, 41–45.

Geertz, C. (1973). *The interpretation of cultures*. London: Hutchinson.

George, A. (Ed.). (1991). *Western state terrorism*. New York: Routledge.

Gibbs, S. (1997). Postwar social reconstruction in Mozambique: Reframing children's experiences of trauma and healing. In K. Kumar (Ed.), *Rebuilding war-torn societies: Critical areas for international assistance* (pp. 227–238). Boulder, CO: Lynne Rienner.

Gidron, Y., Gal, R., & Zahavi, S. (1999). Bus commuters' coping strategies and anxiety from terrorism: An example of the Israeli experience. *Journal of Traumatic Stress, 12*(1), 185–191.

Gilovich, T. (1981). Seeing the past in the present: The effect of associations to familiar events on judgments and decisions. *Journal of Personality and Social Psychology, 40*, 797–808.

Girolamo, G., & McFarlane, A. (1996). The epidemiology of PTSD: A comprehensive review of the international literature. In A. Marsella, M. Friedman, E. Gerrity, & R. Scurfield (Eds.), *Ethnocultural aspects of posttraumatic stress disorder* (pp. 33–85). Washington, DC: American Psychological Association.

Goode, E. (2002, August 21). Program to cover psychiatric help for 9/11 families: Joint offer by charities. *The New York Times*, pp. A1–A14.

Goodwin, J. (1998). Buried alive: Afghan women under the Taliban. *OTI Online*. Available at http://mosaic.echonyc.com/~onissues/su98goodwin.html

Gorst-Unsworth, C., & Goldenberg, E. (1998). Psychologial sequelae of torture and organized violence suffered by refugees from Iraq. *British Journal of Psychiatry, 172*, 90–94.

Green, B., Friedman, M., de Jong, J., Solomon, S., Keane, T., Fairbank, J., et al. (Eds.). (2002). *Trauma interventions in war and peace: Prevention, practice, and policy.* New York: Kluwer Academic/Plenum Press.

Greenberg, J., Arndt, J., Simon, L., Pyszczynski, T., & Solomon, S. (2000). Proximal and distal defenses in response to reminders of one's mortality: Evidence of a temporal sequence. *Personality and Social Psychology Bulletin, 26,* 91–99.

Grosscup, B. (2002). *The newest explosions of terrorism: From the cold war to the World Trade Center/Pentagon attacks.* Far Hills, NJ: New Horizon Press.

Gurr, T. R. (1970). *Why men rebel.* Princeton, NJ: Princeton University Press.

Gurwitch, R. H., Sullivan, M. A., & Long, P. J. (1998). The impact of trauma and disaster on young children. *Child & Adolescent Psychiatric Clinics of North America, 7,* 19–32.

Halliday, F. (1996). *Islam and the myth of confrontation: Religion and politics in the Middle East.* New York: Tauris.

Hamada, L. B. (1990). *Understanding the Arab world.* Nashville, TN: Thomas Nelson.

Hamady, S. (1960). *Temperament and character of the Arabs.* New York: Twayne.

Han, H. (Ed.). (1993). *Terrorism and political violence: Limits and possibilities of legal control.* New York: Oceana.

Haney, C., Banks, W. C., & Zimbardo, P. G. (1973). Interpersonal dynamics in a simulated prison. *International Journal of Criminology & Penology, 1,* 69–97.

Harff, B. (1996). Early warning of potential genocide: The cases of Rwanda, Burundi, Bosnia, and Abkhazia. In T. R. Gurr & B. Harff (Eds.), *Early warning of communal conflicts and genocide: Linking empirical research to international responses.* Tokyo: United Nations Press.

Haritos-Fatouros, M. (2002). *The psychological origins of institutionalized torture.* London: Routledge.

Harmon, C. C. (2000). *Terrorism today.* London: Frank Cass.

Hedges, C. (2003). *War is a force that gives us meaning.* New York: Public Affairs Books.

Hefner, R. W. (2000). *Civil Islam.* Princeton, NJ: Princeton University Press.

Heilman, M. E. (1976). Oppositional behavior as a function of influence attempt intensity and retaliation threat. *Journal of Personality and Social Psychology, 33,* 574–578.

Heinrich, R. L., & Schag, C. C. (1985). Stress and activity management: Group treatment for cancer patients and spouses. *Journal of Consulting & Clinical Psychology, 53,* 439–446.

Helm, C., & Morelli, M. (1979). Stanley Milgram and the obedience experiment: Authority, legitimacy, and human action. *Political Theory, 7,* 321–346.

Helmreich, W. B. (1992). *Against all odds: Holocaust survivors and the successful lives they made in America.* New York: Simon & Schuster.

Herlinger, C. (2002, May 22–29). Reckoning with Israel: Thorny issue for mainline churches. *Christian Century, 119*(11), 6–7.

Herman, J. L. (1992). *Trauma and recovery*. New York: Basic Books.

Hilberg, R. (1961). *The destruction of the European Jews*. New York: Harper & Row.

Hitchcock, J. (2001, November). The essence & power of evil. *Touchstone, 14*(9), 3.

Hitchcock, R. K., & Twedt, T. M. (1997). Physical and cultural genocide of various indigenous peoples. In S. Totten, W. S. Parsons, & I. W. Charny (Eds.), *Century of genocide: Eyewitness accounts and critical views*. New York: Garland Publishing.

Hoffer, E. (1951). *The true believer*. New York: Time, Inc.

Hoffman, B. (1993). *"Holy terror": The implications of terrorism motivated by a religious imperative* (RAND Research Paper P–7834). Santa Monica, CA: RAND.

Hoffman, B. (1998). *Inside terrorism*. New York: Columbia University Press.

Holmes, G. (Ed.). (1992). *The Oxford history of medieval Europe*. Oxford, England: Oxford University Press.

Honwana, A. (1999). Non-western concepts of mental health. In M. Loughry & A. Ager (Eds.), *The refugee experience* (Vol. 1, pp. 103–119). Oxford, England: Oxford University, Refugee Studies Programme.

Horowitz, M. J. (1976). *Stress response syndrome*. New York: Aronson.

Hostetler, J. A. (1980). *Amish society* (3rd.ed.). Baltimore: Johns Hopkins University Press.

Hourani, A. (1991). *A history of the Arab peoples*. New York: Warner Books.

Hoven, C. W., Duarte, C. S., Lucas, C. P., Mandell, D. J., Cohen, M., Rosen, C., et al. (2002). *Effects of the World Trade Center attack on NYC public school students—Initial report to the New York City Board of Education*. New York: Columbia University Mailman School of Public Health–New York State Psychiatric Institute and Applied Research and Consulting, LLC.

Hoveyda, F. (1998). *The broken crescent: The "threat" of militant Islamic fundamentalism*. Westport, CT: Praeger.

Hudnall Stamm, B. (Ed.). (1995). *Secondary traumatic stress: Self-care issues for clinicians, researchers, & educators*. Lutherville, MD: Sidran Press.

Human Rights Watch. (1999). *Leave none to tell the story: Genocide in Rwanda*. New York: Author.

Hunter, S. T. (1998). *The future of Islam and the West: Clash of civilizations or peaceful coexistence?* Westport, CT: Praeger.

Huntington, S. (1993). The clash of civilizations. *Foreign Affairs, 72*, 22–49.

Huntington, S. (1999). The lonely superpower. *Foreign Affairs, 78*, 35–49.

Ignatieff, M. (1997). *The warrior's honor: Ethnic war and the modern conscience*. New York: Metropolitan Books.

Injury Protection Service, Oklahoma State Department of Health. (1996). *Investigation of physical injuries directly associated with the Oklahoma City bombing*. Retrieved February 20, 2003, at http://www.health.state.ok.us/program/injury/okcbom.html

Interagency OPSEC Support Staff. (1996). *Intelligence threat handbook*. Washington, DC: Author.

IRA 'regrets' bombing, blames British for civilian toll. (1987, November 10). *San Francisco Chronicle*, p. A11.

Jackson, F., & Perkins, R. (1997). *Cosmic suicide: The tragedy and transcendence of Heavan's Gate*. Dallas, TX: Pentaradial Press.

Jacobs, G. A. (1995). The development of a national plan for disaster mental health. *Professional Psychology: Research & Practice, 26*, 543–549.

Jacobs, G. A., Quevillon, R. P., & Stricherz, M. (1990). Lessons from the aftermath of Flight 232: Practical considerations for the mental health profession's response to air disasters. *American Psychologist, 45*, 1329–1335.

Jacobs, S. C., & Prigerson, H. (2000). Psychotherapy of traumatic grief: A review of evidence for psychotherapeutic treatments. *Death Studies, 24*, 479–495.

Jenkins, B. M. (1985). *International terrorism: The other world war* (November 1985 R–3302–AF). Santa Monica, CA: Rand.

Johnson, D. R., Lubin, H., Rosenheck, R., Fontana, A., Southwick, S., & Charney, D. (1997). The impact of the homecoming reception on the development of posttraumatic stress disorder: The West Haven Homecoming Stress Scale (WHHSS). *Journal of Traumatic Stress, 10*(2), 259–277.

Johnson, D. W., & Johnson, R. T. (1989). *Cooperation and competition: Theory and research*. Edina, MN: Interaction.

Johnson, J. T. (2002, June/July). Jihad and just war. *First Things, 124*, 12–14.

Jones, R. T., Frary, R., Cunningham, P., Weddle, J., & Kaiser, L. (2001). The psychological effects of Hurricane Andrew on ethnic minority and Caucasian children and adolescents: A case study. *Cultural Diversity and Ethnic Minority Psychology, 7*, 103–108.

Kahana, B., Harel, Z., & Kahana, E. (1989). Clinical and gerontological issues facing survivors of the Nazi Holocaust. In P. Marcus & A. Rosenberg (Eds.), *Healing their wounds: Psychotherapy with Holocaust survivors and their families* (pp. 197–211). New York: Praeger.

Kaplan, D. E., & Marshall, A. (1996). *The cult at the end of the world: The terrifying story of the Aum doomsday cult, from the subways of Tokyo to the nuclear arsenals of Russia*. New York: Crown.

Kaplan, H. P., & Liu, X. (2000). Social movements as collective coping with spoiled personal identities: Intimations from a panel study of changes in the life course between adolescence and adulthood. In S. Stryker, T. J. Owens, & R. W. White (Eds.), *Self, identity, and social movements* (pp. 215–238). Minneapolis: University of Minnesota Press.

Karon, T. (2002, March 20). *Despite signs of truce, Israel's dilemma remains*. Retrieved from http://www.time.com/time/world/article/0,8599,219113,00.html

Kawana, N., Ishimatsu, S., & Kanda, K. (2001). Psycho-physiological effects of the terrorist sarin gas attack on the Tokyo subway system. *Military Medicine, 166*(Suppl. 2), 23–26.

Kaysen, C., Miller, S. E., Malin, M. B., Nordhaus, W. D., & Steinbruner, J. D. (Eds.). (2002). *War with Iraq: Costs, consequences, and alternatives*. Cambridge, MA: American Academy of Arts and Sciences.

"Keep faith and be clean," hijackers told. (2001, September 28). *Honolulu Advertiser*, p. A5.

Kelman, H. C. (1973). Violence without moral restraint: Reflections on the dehumanization of victims and victimizers. *Journal of Social Issues, 29*, 25–61.

Kelman, H. C. (1986). An interaction approach to conflict resolution. In R. K. White (Ed.), *Psychology and the prevention of nuclear war* (pp. 171–193). New York: New York University Press.

Kelman, H. C. (1990). Applying a human needs perspective to the practice of conflict resolution: The Israeli-Palestinian Case. In J. Burton (Ed.), *Conflict: Human needs theory*. New York: St. Martin's Press.

Kelman, H. C., & Hamilton, V. L. (1989). *Crimes of obedience: Toward a social psychology of authority and responsibility*. New Haven, CT: Yale University Press.

Kennedy, M. (1998). The 21st-century conditions likely to inspire terrorism. In H. Kushner (Ed.), *The future of terrorism: Violence in the new millennium* (pp. 185–194). Thousand Oaks, CA: Sage.

Key points of loan program for Israel outlined. (1991, September 18). *The Orange County Register*, p. 15.

Khouri, F. (1985). *The Arab–Israeli dilemma* (3rd ed.). New York: Syracuse University Press.

Khouri, R. (1991, January–March). The post-war Middle East. *The Link: Americans for Middle East Understanding, 24*, pp. 1, 3, 7.

Kilham, W., & Mann, L. (1974). Level of destructive obedience as a function of transmitter and executant roles in the Milgram obedience paradigm. *Journal of Personality and Social Psychology, 29*, 696–702.

Kilpatrick, D. G., Best, C. L., Smith, D. W., & Falsetti, S. A. (2002). Lessons from Lockerbie: Service utilization and victim satisfaction after the Pan Am 103 terrorist bombing. *The Behavior Therapist, 25*(2), 40–42.

King, M. L., Jr. (1967). *Where do we go from here: Chaos or community?* New York: Harper & Row.

Kinzie, J. D., Boehnlein, J., Riley, C., & Sparr, L. (2002). The effects of September 11 on traumatized refugees: Reactivation of posttraumatic stress disorder. *Journal of Nervous and Mental Disease, 190*, 437–441.

Kipnis, D. (1974). The powerholders. In J. T. Tedeschi (Ed.), *Perspectives on social power* (pp. 82–122). Chicago: Aldine.

Klein, M. E. (1987). Transmission of trauma: The defensive styles of children of Holocaust survivors. *Dissertation Abstracts International, 48*(12-B, Pt 1), 3682–3683. (UMI No. 8802441)

Klein-Parker, F. (1988). Dominant attitudes of adult children of Holocaust survivors toward their parents. In J. P. Wilson, Z. Harel, & B. Kahana (Eds.), *Human adaptation to extreme stress* (pp. 193–218). New York: Plenum Press.

Knight, B., Gatz, M., Heller, K., & Bengtson, V. (2000). Age and emotional response to the Northridge earthquake: A longitudinal analysis. *Psychology & Aging, 15*, 627–634.

Korostelina, K. V. (2002). *Identity based training to reduce ethnic conflict in the Crimea.* Unpublished manuscript.

Kramer, M. (1990). The moral logic of Hizballah. In W. Reich (Ed.), *Origins of terrorism: Psychologies, ideologies, theologies, states of mind* (pp. 131–157). Cambridge, England: Cambridge University Press.

Kristof, N. D. (2002, December 10). The next Africa? *The New York Times*, p. A31.

Kronik, A., Akhmerov, R., & Speckhard, A. (1999). Trauma and disaster as life disrupters: A model of computer-assisted psychotherapy applied to adolescent victims of the Chernobyl disaster. *Professional Psychology: Research & Practice*, 30, 586–599.

Kuhr, S., & Hauer, J. M. (2001). The threat of biological terrorism in the new millennium. *American Behavioral Scientist*, 44, 1032–1041.

Kurzman, C. (1998). *Liberal Islam.* New York: Oxford University Press.

Kushner, T., & Knox, K. (1999). *Refugees in an age of genocide.* London: Frank Cass.

La Greca, A., Silverman, W., Vernberg, E., & Prinstein, M. (1996). Symptoms of posttraumatic stress in children after hurricane Andrew: A prospective study. *Journal of Consulting & Clinical Psychology*, 64, 712–723.

La Greca, A., Silverman, W., Vernberg, E., & Roberts, M. (Eds.). (2002). *Helping children cope with disasters.* Washington, DC: American Psychological Association.

La Greca, A., Silverman, W., & Wasserstein, S. (1998). Children's predisaster functioning as a predictor of posttraumatic stress following hurricane Andrew. *Journal of Consulting & Clinical Psychology*, 66, 883–892.

Langholtz, H. (2002). Comments on Jerald Post's article: Differentiating the threat of chemical and biological terrorism: Motivations and constraints. *Peace and Conflict: Journal of Peace Psychology*, 8, 219–221.

Laquer, W. (1987). Reflections on terrorism. In W. Laquer & Y. Alexander (Eds.), *The terrorism reader* (pp. 378–392). New York: Penguin.

Laquer, W. (1999). *The new terrorism: Fanaticism and the arms of mass destruction.* New York: Oxford University Press.

Laquer, W. (2001). *A history of terrorism.* New Brunswik, NJ: Transaction.

Larsen, K. S., Coleman, D., Forbes, J., & Johnson, R. (1972). Is the subject's personality or the experimental situation a better predictor of a subject's willingness to administer shock to a victim? *Journal of Personality and Social Psychology*, 22, 287–295.

The last word: Why hate America? (2002, September 9). *Newsweek* [International edition], p. 56.

Lawrence, B. B. (1998). *Shattering the myth: Islam beyond violence.* Princeton, NJ: Princeton University Press.

Lederach, J. P. (1997). *Building peace: Sustainable reconciliation in divided societies.* Washington, DC: United States Institute of Peace Press.

LeDoux, J., & Gorman, J. (2001). A call to action: Overcoming anxiety through active coping. *American Journal of Psychiatry*, 158, 1953–1955.

Lelyveld, J. (2001, October 28). All suicide bombers are not alike. *The New York Times Magazine*, p. 49.

Lerner, M. J. (1971). Justified self-interest and the responsibility for suffering: A replication and extension. *Journal of Human Relations, 19*, 550–559.

Lerner, M. J. (1980). *The belief in a just world: A fundamental delusion*. New York: Plenum Press.

Lerner, M. J., & Miller, D. T. (1978). Just world research and the attribution process: Looking back and ahead. *Psychological Bulletin, 85*, 1030–1051.

Lerner, M. (2001). Healing after terror. *Tikkun: A Bimonthly Jewish Critique of Politics, Culture, and Society, 16*, 6–10.

Levant, R. (2002). Psychology responds to terrorism. *Professional Psychology: Research and Practice, 33*, 507–509.

Levant, R. F., & Kopecky, G. (1995). *Masculinity reconstructed: Changing the rules of manhood—at work, in relationships, and in family life*. New York: Dutton.

LeVine, R. A., & Campbell, D. T. (1972). *Ethnocentrism: Theories of conflict, ethnic studies and group behavior*. New York: Wiley.

Levinger, G., & Rubin, J. Z. (1994). Bridges and barriers to a more general theory of conflict. *Negotiation Journal, 10*, 201–215.

Lifton, R. J. (1999). *Destroying the world to save it: Aum Shinrikyo, apocalyptic violence, and the new global terrorism* [hardcover ed.]. New York: Holt.

Lifton, R. J. (2000). *Destroying the world to save it: Aum Shinrikyo, apocalyptic violence, and the new global terrorism* [paperback ed.]. New York: Holt.

Lindeman, M., Saari, S., Verkasalo, M., & Prytz, H. (1996). Traumatic stress and its risk factors among peripheral victims of the M/S Estonia disaster. *European Psychologist, 1*, 255–270.

Lindner, E. G. (2002). Healing the cycles of humiliation: How to attend to the emotional aspects of "unsolvable" conflicts and the use of "humiliation entrepreneurship." *Peace and Conflict: Journal of Peace Psychology, 8*, 125–138.

Linenthal, E. T. (2001). *The unfinished bombing: Oklahoma City in American memory*. New York: Oxford University Press.

Lira, E. (2001). Violence, fear, and impunity: Reflections on subjective and political obstacles for peace. *Peace and Conflict: Journal of Peace Psychology, 7*, 109–118.

Litz, B. T., Gray, M. J., Bryant, R. A., & Adler, A. B. (2002). Early intervention for trauma: Current status and future directions. *Clinical Psychology: Science and Practice, 9*(2), 112–134.

Lopez, S., & Guarnaccia, P. (2000). Cultural psychopathology: Uncovering the social world of mental illness. *Annual Review of Psychology, 51*, 571–598.

Lorion, R. P., Iscoe, I., DeLeon, P. H., & VandenBos, G. R. (Eds.). (1996). *Psychology and public policy: Balancing public service and professional need*. Washington, DC: American Psychological Association.

Louis, W. R., & Taylor, D. M. (2002). Understanding the September 11th terrorist attack on America: The role of intergroup theories of normative influence. *Analyses of Social Issues and Public Policy, 2*(1), 87–100.

Ludlow, L. (2001, October 7). Osama speaks: Inside the mind of a terrorist. *San Francisco Chronicle*, p. D1.

Ludwick-Rosenthal, R., & Neufeld, R.W. (1988). Stress management during noxious medical procedures: An evaluative review of outcome studies. *Psychological Bulletin, 104*, 326–342.

Lupsha, P. A. (1987). The role of drugs and drug trafficking in the invisible wars. In R. H. Ward & H. E. Smith (Eds.), *International terrorism: Operational issues* (pp. 177–190). Chicago: University of Illinois at Chicago.

Lutz, W. D. (1987). Language, appearance, and reality: Doublespeak in 1984. In P. C. Boardman (Ed.), *The legacy of language—A tribute to Charlton Laird* (pp. 103–119). Reno: University of Nevada Press.

Lykes, M. B. (2001). Human rights violations as structural violence. In D. J. Christie, R. V. Wagner, & D. D. Winter (Eds.), *Peace, conflict, and violence: Peace psychology for the 21st century* (pp. 158–167). Upper Saddle River, NJ: Prentice Hall.

Malik, H. C. (2000). *Between Damascus and Jerusalem: Lebanon and Middle East peace* (2nd ed.). Washington, DC: The Washington Institute for Near Eastern Policy.

Mandel, D. R. (2002). Evil and the instigation of collective violence. *Analysis of Social Issues and Public Policy, 2*, 101–108.

Mandelstam, P. (2001, December 29). IRA aims make them freedom fighters, says Mandelstam. *The London Times*, p. 2.

Mantell, D. M., & Panzarella, R. (1976). Obedience and responsibility. *The British Journal of Social and Clinical Psychology, 15*, 239–246.

Manwaring, M. (2001) Thinking about contemporary conflict. Retrieved from http://carlisle–www.army.mil/usassi/welcome.html

Marsella, A., Bornemann, T., Ekblad, S., & Orley, J. (Eds.). (1994). *Amidst peril and pain: The mental health and well-being of the world's refugees*. Washington, DC: American Psychological Association.

Marsella, A., Friedman, M., Gerrity, E., & Scurfield, R. (Eds.). (1996). *Ethnocultural aspects of posttraumatic stress disorder*. Washington, DC: American Psychological Association.

Marsella, A. J. (1998). Toward a "global-community psychology": Meeting the needs of a changing world. *American Psychologist, 53*, 1282–1291.

Marsella, A. J. (1999). In search of meaning: Some thoughts on belief, doubt, and well-being. *The International Journal of Transpersonal Studies, 18*, 41–52.

Marsella, A. J. (2000). Internationalizing the psychology curriculum. *International Psychology Reporter, 4*, 1–3.

Marshall, S. (2002, March 4). Mental health system failing 9/11 victims. *Crain's New York*, p. 4.

Martin, S. (2002, January). Thwarting terrorism. *Monitor on Psychology*, 28–29.

Martin-Baro, I. (1996). *Writings for a liberation psychology*. Cambridge, MA: Harvard University Press.

Martinez, R., Ryan, S. D., & DeLeon, P. H. (1995). Responding to trauma—Extraordinarily meaningful. *Professional Psychology: Research and Practice, 26*, 541–542.

Maslach, C. (1982). *Burnout: The cost of caring.* Englewood Cliffs, NJ: Prentice Hall.

Maslow, A. (1954). *Motivation and personality.* New York: Harper.

Mays, V., Bullock, M., Rosenzweig, M., & Wessells, M. (1998). Ethnic conflict: Global challenges and psychological perspectives. *American Psychologist, 53,* 771–777.

Mays, V., Rubin, J., Sabourin, M., & Walker, L. (1996). Moving towards a global psychology: Changing theories and practice to meet the needs of a changing world. *American Psychologist, 51,* 485–487.

McAlister, A., & Bandura, A., Morrison, T., & Grussendorf, J. (2003). *Mechanisms of moral disengagement in support of military force: The impact of 9/11.* Manuscript submitted for publication.

McCauley, C. (1991). *Terrorism research and public policy.* London: Frank Cass.

McCauley, C. (in press). Making sense of terrorism after 9/11. In R. Moser (Ed.), *Shocking violence II: Violent disaster, war, and terrorism affecting our youth.* Springfield, IL: Thomas.

McCauley, C. R., & Segal, M. D. (1989). Terrorist individuals and terrorist groups: The normal psychology of extreme behavior. In J. Groebel, & J. F. Goldstein (Eds.), *Terrorism* (pp. 39–64). Seville, Spain: Publicaciones de la Universidad de Sevilla.

McGarty, C. (1999). *Categorization in social psychology.* Thousand Oaks, CA: Sage.

McIntyre, T., & Ventura, M. (2003). Children of war: Psychosocial sequelae of war trauma in Angolan adolescents. In. T. McIntyre & S. Krippner (Eds.), *The impact of war trauma on civilian populations: An international perspective.* New York: Greenwood.

McMillen, J., Smith, E., & Fisher, R. (1997). Perceived benefit and mental health after three types of disaster. *Journal of Consulting & Clinical Psychology, 65,* 733–739.

Medved, M. (2001, October 15). Can Hollywood change its ugly version of USA? *USA Today,* p. A17.

Medved, M. (2002, June 24). Admit terrorism's Islamic link. *USA Today,* p. A13.

Meeus, W. H. J., & Raaijmakers, Q. A. W. (1986). Administrative obedience: Carrying out orders to use psychological–administrative violence. *European Journal of Social Psychology, 16,* 311–324.

Meichenbaum, D. (1993). Stress inoculation training: A 20-year update. In P. M. Lehrer & R. L. Woolfolk (Eds.), *Principles and practice of stress management* (2nd ed.; pp. 373–406). New York: Guilford Press.

Melson, R. (1992). *Revolution and genocide.* Chicago: University of Chicago Press.

Michultka, D., Blanchard, E., & Kalous, T. (1998). Responses to civilian war experiences: Predictors of psychological functioning and coping. *Journal of Traumatic Stress, 11,* 571–577.

Milgram, S. (1963). Behavioral study of obedience. *Journal of Abnormal and Social Psychology, 67,* 371–378.

Milgram, S. (1965). Some conditions of obedience and disobedience to authority. *Human Relations, 18*, 57–76.

Milgram, S. (1974). *Obedience to authority: An experimental view.* New York: Harper & Row.

Miller, K. (1999). Rethinking a familiar model: Psychotherapy and the mental health of refugees. *Journal of Contemporary Psychotherapy, 29*, 283–305.

Miller, M., & File, J. (2001). *Terrorism factbook.* Peoria, IL: Bollix Press.

Mir, H. (2001, November 15–21). Hamid Mir's interview, *Guardian Weekly*, p. 3.

Mitchell, J. (1990). *Working paper for Critical Incident Stress Debriefing: Basic, Executive and Team Development Training.* Honolulu, HI: Fire Department Training Center.

Mittleman, J. (2000). *The globalization syndrome: Transformation and resistance.* Princeton, NJ: Princeton University Press.

Moen, D. G. (1993). *Arming dictators* [Center for Defense Information, Japan]. Retrieved September 10, 2002, from http://tsujiru.net/moen/video_trams/003.html

Moerk, E. (2002). Scripting war-entry to make it appear unavoidable. *Peace and Conflict: Journal of Peace Psychology, 8*, 229–248.

Moghaddam, F. M. (1998). *Social psychology: Exploring universals across cultures.* New York: Freeman.

Moghaddam, F. M. (2002). *The individual and society: A cultural integration.* New York: Worth.

Mollica, R., McInnes, K., Pham, T., Fawzi, M., Smith, C., Murphy, E., & Lin, L. (1998). The dose–effect relationships between torture and psychiatric symptoms in Vietnamese expolitical detainees and a comparison group. *Journal of Nervous & Mental Disease, 186*, 543–553.

Montiel, C. J., & Anuar, M. K. (2002). Other terrorisms, psychology and media. *Peace and Conflict: Journal of Peace Psychology, 8*, 201–206.

Morgan, J., O'Neill, C., & Harré, R. (1977). *Nicknames.* London: Routledge and Kegan Paul.

Morgan, J. N. (2002, January 21). Try little humility [Letter to editor]. *The New York Times*, p. A19.

Morris, N., & Demick, B. (2000, October 8). "The peace is dead. This is a war." *Seattle Times*, p. A23.

Mortimer, E. (1982). *Faith and power: The politics of Islam.* New York: Random House.

Moscovici, S. (1985). Social influence and conformity. In G. Lindzey & E. Aronson (Eds.), *The handbook of social psychology* (3rd ed., pp. 347–412). Hillsdale, NJ: Erlbaum.

Moscovici, S. (1994). Three concepts: Minority, conflict, and behavioural style. In S. Moscovici, A. Mucchi-Faina, & A. Maas (Eds.), *Minority influence* (pp. 233–251). Chicago: Nelson-Hall

Moscrop, A. (2001). Mass hysteria is seen as main threat from bioweapons. *British Medical Journal, 323*, 1023.

Moussalli, A. S. (1998). Introduction to Islamic fundamentalism: Realities, ideologies, and international politics. In A. S. Moussalli (Ed.), *Islamic fundamentalism: Myths and realities.* Reading, United Kingdom: Ithaca Press.

Murphy, L. R. (1986). A review of organizational stress management research: Methodolgical considerations. *Journal of Organizational Behavior Management, 8*, 215–227.

Murray, B. (2002, February). What a recovering nation needs from behavioral science. *Monitor on Psychology, 33*(2), 30–32.

Nader, K., Dubrow, N., & Stamm, B. (Eds.). (1999). *Honoring differences: Cultural issues in the treatment of trauma and loss.* New York: Taylor & Francis.

Nail, P. R., MacDonald, G., & Levy, D. A. (2000). Proposal of a four-dimensional model of social response. *Psychological Bulletin, 126*, 454–470.

Nash, J. (1998). *Terrorism in the 20th century: A narrative encyclopedia from anarchists, through the Weathermen, to the Unabomber.* New York: Evans.

A nation challenged. (2001, October 8). *The New York Times,* pp. B6–B7.

National Institute of Mental Health. (2002). *Mental health and mass violence: Evidence-based early psychological intervention for victims/survivors of mass violence. A workshop to reach consensus on best practices* (NIH Publication No. 02–5138). Washington, DC: U.S. Government Printing Office. Available online at http://www.nimh.nih.gov/research/massviolence.pdf

Neria, Y., Bromet, E., & Marshall, R. (2002). The relationship between trauma exposure, post-traumatic stress disorder (PTSD) and depression. *Psychological Medicine, 32*, 1479–1480.

9/11 toll includes 500 foreigners. (2002, April 6). *New York Post,* p. 8.

Nisbett, R., & Ross, L. (1980). *Human inference: Strategies and shortcomings of social judgment.* Englewood Cliffs, NJ: Prentice Hall.

Nolen-Hoeksema, S., & Morrow, J. (1991). A prospective study of depression and posttraumatic stress symptoms after a natural disaster: The 1989 Loma Prieta earthquake. *Journal of Personality & Social Psychology, 61*, 115–121.

Norris, F., & Kaniasty, K. (1996). Received and perceived social support in times of stress: A test of the social support deterioration deterrence model. *Journal of Personality & Social Psychology, 71*, 498–511.

Norris, F. H. (2002). Psychological consequences of disasters. *PTSD Research Quarterly, 13*(2), 1–7.

North, C., Nixon, S. J., Shariat, S., Mallonee, S., Curtis McMillen, J., Spitznagel, E., et al. (1999). Psychiatric disorders among survivors of the Oklahoma City Bombing. *Journal of the American Medical Association, 282*, 755–762.

North, C., & Pfefferbaum, B. (2002). Research on the mental health effects of terrorism. *Journal of the American Medical Association, 288*, 633–636.

North, C., Tivis, L., McMillen, J., Pfefferbaum, B., Spitznagel, E., Cox, J., et al. (2002). Psychiatric disorders in rescue workers after the Oklahoma City bombing. *American Journal of Psychiatry, 159*, 857–859.

Nuttman-Shwartz, O., & Lauer, E. K. (2002). Group therapy with terror injured persons in Israel: Societal impediments to successful working through. *Group, 6*(1), 5–16.

Oakes, P. J., Haslam, A., & Turner, J. C. (1994). *Stereotyping and social reality*. Oxford, England: Blackwell.

Oberschall, A. (2001). From ethnic cooperation to violence and war in Yugoslavia. In D. Chirot & M.E. P. Seligman (Eds.), *Ethnopolitical warfare: Causes, consequences, and possible solutions* (pp. 119–150). Washington, DC: American Psychological Association.

Ogden, C., Kaminer, D., Van Kradenburg, J., Seedat, S., & Stein, D. (2000). Narrative themes in response to trauma in a religious community. *Central African Medical Journal, 46*, 178–184.

Ohanyan, A., & Lewis, J. (2002). *Interethnic peace camps as a conflict resolution strategy*. Unpublished manuscript.

Osgood, C. E. (1962). *An alternative to war or surrender*. Urbana, IL: University of Illinois Press.

Packer, G. (2002, December 8). The liberal quandary over Iraq. *The New York Times Magazine*, p. 104.

Palmer, D. L., & Taylor, D. M. (2000). *A proposed alternative policy for the granting of asylum within Canada's borders*. Unpublished manuscript.

Pann, J. G. (2001). *Managing with uncertainty*. Unpublished report, Practice Directorate, American Psychological Association, Washington, DC.

Pareto, V. (1935). *The mind and society: A treatise in general sociology* (4 vols.). New York: Dover.

Pasagic, I. (2000, November). Obstacles to reconciliation in the post-conflict situation in Bosnia and Herzegovina. In Y. Danieli (Chair), *Promoting a dialogue: The case of Bosnia and Herzegovina, and beyond: "Democracy cannot be built with the hands of broken souls."* Symposium conducted at the meeting of the International Society for Traumatic Stress Studies, San Antonio, TX.

Pastel, R. (2001). Collective behaviors: Mass panic and outbreaks of multiple unexplained symptoms. *Military Medicine, 166*(Suppl. 2), 44–46.

Pearlman, L. A., & Saakvitne, K. W. (1995). *Trauma and the therapist: Countertransference and vicarious traumatization and psychotherapy with incest survivors*. New York: Norton.

Pearlstein, R. (1991). *The mind of the political terrorist*. Wilmington, DE: Scholarly Resources Books.

Peristiany, J. G. (Ed.). (1965). *Honor and shame: The values of Mediterranean society*. London: Weidenfeld & Nicolson.

Peterson, C. (2002, August). Character strengths before and after September 11. In R. G. Tedeschi (Chair), *Posttraumatic growth in the aftermath of terrorism*. Symposium conducted at the meeting of the American Psychological Association, Chicago, IL.

PEW Research Center. (2001, January 11). *Worries about terrorism subside in Mid-America*. Retrieved January 18, 2002, from http://www.people–press.org/110801rpt.htm

Pfefferbaum, B., Call, J. A., Lensgraf, S. J., Miller, P. D., Flynn, B. W., Doughty, D. E., Tucker, P., et al. (2001). Traumatic grief in a convenience sample of victims seeking support services after a terrorist incident. *Annals of Clinical Psychology, 13*(1), 19–24.

Pfefferbaum, B., Gurwitch, R., McDonald, N., Leftwich, M., Sconzo, G., Messenbaugh, A., & Schultz, R. (2000). Posttraumatic stress among young children after the death of a friend or acquaintance in a terrorist bombing. *Psychiatric Services, 51,* 386–388.

Pfefferbaum B., Nixon, S. J., Krug, R. S., Tivis, R.D., Moore, V. L., Brown, J. M., et al. (1999). Clinical needs assessment of middle and high school students following the 1995 Oklahoma City Bombing. *American Journal of Psychiatry, 156,* 1069–1074.

Pfefferbaum, B., Nixon, S. J., Tivis, R. D., Doughty, D. E., Pynoos, R. S., Gurwitch, R. H., & Foy, D. (2001). Television exposure in children after a terrorist incident. *Psychiatry, 64,* 202–211.

Pfefferbaum, B., Seale, T. W., McDonald, N. B., Brandt, Jr., E. N., Rainwater, S. M., Maynard, B. T., et al. (2000). Posttraumatic stress two years after the Oklahoma City Bombing in youths geographically distant from the explosion. *Psychiatry, 64,* 358–370.

Phifer, J. F. (1990). Psychological distress and somatic symptoms after natural disaster: Differential vulnerability among older adults. *Psychology and Aging, 5,* 412–420.

Pick, T. M. (2001). The myth of the trauma/The trauma of the myth: Myths as mediators of some long-term effects of war trauma. *Peace and Conflict: Journal of Peace Psychology, 7,* 201–226.

Plato. (1987). *The republic* (Trans. Desmond Lee). Harmondsworth, United Kingdom: Penguin.

Pearlstein, R. M. (1991). *The mind of the political terrorist.* Wilmington, DE: Scholarly Resources.

Pilisuk, M., & Wong, A. (2002). State terrorism: When the perpetrator is the government. In C. Stout (Ed.), *Psychology of terrorism.* Praeger Publication.

Post, J. (1990). Terrorist psycho-logic: Terrorist behavior as a product of psychological forces. In W. Reich (Ed.), *Origins of terrorism: Psychologies, ideologies, theologies, states of mind* (pp. 25–40). Cambridge, England: Cambridge University Press.

Post, J. M. (2001, November 15). *The mind of the terrorist: Individual and group psychology of terrorist behavior.* Testimony prepared for Sub-Committee on Emerging Threats and Capabilities, Senate Armed Services Committee.

Post, J. M. (2002a). Differentiating the threat of chemical and biological terrorism: Motivations and constraints. *Peace and Conflict: Journal of Peace Psychology, 8,* 187–200.

Post, J. M. (2002b). Response. *Peace and Conflict: Journal of Peace Psychology, 8,* 223–227.

Powers, P. C., & Geen, R. G. (1972). Effects of the behavior and the perceived arousal of a model on instrumental aggression. *Journal of Personality and Social Psychology, 23,* 175–183.

Powers, S. (2002). *A problem from hell: America and the age of genocide*. New York: Basic Books.

Pratt, C., & Lefkowitz, M. (2001, September 16). Arab, Sihk cabbies offer free rides. *Newsday* [online]. Retrieved March 18, 2003, from http://www.newsday.com/ny-2368900sep16,0,3996843.story

Prigerson, H., & Jacobs, S. C. (2001). Traumatic grief as a distinct disorder: A rationale, consensus criteria, and a preliminary empirical test. In M. S. Stroebe, R. O. Hansson, W. Stroebe, & H. A. W. Schut (Eds.), *Handbook of bereavement research: Consequences, coping, and care* (pp. 613–645). Washington, DC: American Psychological Association.

Pyszcznski, T., Solomon, S., & Greenberg, J. (2002). *In the wake of 9/11: The psychology of terror*. Washington, DC: American Psychological Association.

Radcliffe-Brown, A. R. (1952). *Structure and function in primitive society*. London: Cohen and West.

Radical Islamic group Hamas' history began with conflict. (2002, August 2). *The Seattle Times*, p. A14.

Raphael, B., & Ursano, R. J. (2002). Psychological debriefing. In Y. Danieli (Ed.), *Sharing the front line and the back hills: International protectors and providers, peacekeepers, humanitarian aid workers and the media in the midst of crisis* (pp. 343–352). Amityville, NY: Baywood Publishing.

Rapoport, D. C. (Ed.). (2001). *Inside terrorist organizations* (2nd ed.). London: Frank Cass & Co.

Rapoport, D. C., & Alexander, Y. (Eds.). (1982). *The morality of terrorism: Religious and secular justification*. Elmsford, NY: Pergamon Press.

Rashid, A. (2000). *Taliban*. New Haven, CT: Yale University Press.

Ray, C. (2001). Don't run roughshod over behavioral healthcare. *Behavioral Healthcare Tomorrow, 10*, 12–15.

Reich, W. (Ed.). (1998). *Origins of terrorism*. Washington, DC: Woodrow Wilson Center Press. (Original work published 1990)

Reichenberg, D., & Friedman, S. (1996). Traumatized children. Healing the invisible wounds of war: A rights approach. In Y. Daniele, N. S. Rodley, & L. Weisaeth (Eds.), *International responses to traumatic stress* (pp. 307–326). Amityville, NY: Baywood Publishing.

Rich, M. S. (1982). *Children of Holocaust survivors: A concurrent validity study of a survivor family typology*. Unpublished doctoral dissertation, California School of Professional Psychology, Berkeley.

Richman, N. (1998). Looking before and after: Refugees and asylum seekers in the West. In P. Bracken & C. Petty (Eds.), *Rethinking the trauma of war* (pp. 170–186). London: Free Association Books.

Roberts, A. (2002, November 6). Can we define terrorism? *Oxford Today: The University magazine*. Retrieved from http://www.oxfordtoday.ox.ac.uk/archive/0102/14_2/04.shtml

Rodman, J., & Engdahl, B. (2002, August). Posttraumatic growth and PTSD in WWII and Korean War veterans. In R. G. Tedeschi (Chair), *Posttraumatic growth in the* aftermath of terrorism. Symposium conducted at the meeting of the American Psychological Association, Chicago, IL.

Rogers, D., Spencer, J., & Uyangoda, J. (1998). Sri Lanka: Political violence and ethnic conflict. *American Psychologist, 53,* 771–777.

Rosen, G. M. (1995). The Aleutian Enterprise sinking and posttraumatic stress disorder: Misdiagnosis in clinical and forensic settings. *Professional Psychology: Research & Practice, 26,* 82–87.

Roth, S., Newman, E., Pelcovitz, D., Van der Kolk, B., & Mandel, F. (1997). Complex PTSD in victims exposed to sexual and physical abuse: Results from the DSM–IV Field Trial for Posttraumatic Stress Disorder. *Journal of Traumatic Stress, 10,* 539–555.

Rothman, J. (1992). *From confrontation to cooperation: Resolving ethnic and regional conflict.* Newbury Park, CA: Sage.

Rothman, J. (1997). *Resolving identity-based conflict.* San Francisco: Jossey-Bass.

Rouhana, N. N., & Bar-Tal, D. (1998). Psychological dynamics of intractable ethnonational conflicts: The Israeli–Palestinian case. *American Psychologist, 53,* 761–770.

Rubenstein, R. (in press). The psycho-political sources of terrorism. In C. Kegley (Ed.), *The new global terrorism.* Westport, CT: Praeger.

Rubin, J., Pruitt, D. G., & Kim, S. H. (1994). *Social conflict: Escalation, stalemate, and settlement* (2nd ed.). New York: McGraw-Hill.

Rummel, R. J. (1992). *Democide: Nazi genocide and mass murder.* New Brunswick, NJ: Transaction Publishers.

Rummel, R. J. (1994). *Death by government.* New Brunswick, NJ: Transaction.

Ruzek, J. (2002). Dissemination of information and early intervention practices in the context of mass violence or large-scale disaster. *The Behavior Therapist, 25,* 32–36.

Ruzek, J., & Watson, P. (2001). Early intervention to prevent PTSD and other trauma-related problems. *PTSD Research Quarterly, 12*(4), 1–7.

Sabat, S. R., Fath, H., Moghaddam, F. M., & Harré, R. (1999). The maintenance of self-esteem: Lessons from the culture of Alzheimer's sufferers. *Culture & Psychology, 5,* 5–31.

Salem, P. (1993). A critique of Western conflict resolution from a non-Western perspective. *Negotiation Journal, 9,* 361–369.

Schinke, S. P., Barth, R. P., Gilchrist, L. D., & Maxwell, J. S. (1986). Adolescent mothers, stress, and prevention. *Journal of Human Stress, 12,* 162–167.

Schinke, S. P., Schilling, R. F., & Snow, W. H. (1987). Stress management with adolescents at the junior high transition: An outcome evaluation of coping skills intervention. *Journal of Human Stress, 13,* 16–22.

Schlenger, W., Caddell, J., Ebert, L., Jordan, B., Rourke, K., Wilson, D., et al. (2002). Psychological reactions to terrorist attacks: Findings from the national study of Americans' reactions to September 11. *Journal of the American Medical Association, 288,* 581–588.

Schuster, M. A., Stein, B. D., Jaycox, L. H., Collins, R. L., Marshall, G. N., Elliott, M., et al. (2001). A national survey of stress reactions after the September 11, 2001, terrorist attacks. *New England Journal of Medicine, 345*, 1507–1512.

Schwebel, M. (Ed.). (2001). Promoting the culture of peace in children [Whole issue]. *Peace and Conflict: Journal of Peace Psychology, 7*(1).

Scott, S. (2001). *Islam: Looking at history helps to understand.* Available at http://www.chron.com/cs/CDA/story.hts/side.1076475

Seale, P. (2002, May 24). Sharon, the old warrior, still dominates Israeli politics. *The Daily Star,* p. 5.

Seligman, M. E. P. (1975). *Helplessness: On depression, development, and death.* San Francisco: Freeman.

Shahak, I., & Mezvinski, N. (1999). *Jewish fundamentalism in Israel.* Herndon, VA: Stylus.

Shanker, T. (2002, July 23). Rumsfeld called civilian deaths relatively low. *The New York Times,* p. A9.

Sharp, G. (1973). *Methods of nonviolent action.* Boston: Porter Sargent.

Shawcross, W. (1998). *Deliver us from evil.* New York: Simon & Schuster.

Shear, K. M., Frank, E., Foa, E., Cherry, C., Reynolds, C. F., Vader Bilt, J., & Masters, S. (2001). Traumatic grief treatment: A pilot study. *American Journal of Psychiatry, 158,* 1506–1508.

Sherif, M. (1936). *The psychology of social norms.* New York: Harper.

Sigal, J. J., & Weinfeld, M. (1989). *Trauma and rebirth: Intergenerational effects of the Holocaust.* New York: Praeger.

Silver, R. C., Holman, E. A., McIntosh, D. N., Poulin, M., & Gil-Rivas, V. (2002). Nationwide longitudinal study of psychological responses to September 11. *Journal of the American Medical Association, 288,* 1235–1244.

Silverstein, B. (1989). Enemy images: The psychology of U.S. attitudes and cognitions regarding the Soviet Union. *American Psychologist, 44,* 903–913.

Sivan, E. (1985). *Radical Islam: Medieval theology and modern politics.* New Haven, CT: Yale University Press.

Skeyhill, T. (Ed.). (1928). *Sergeant York: His own life story and war diary.* Garden City, NY: Doubleday, Doran.

Slim, R. M. (1992). Small-state mediation in international relations: The Algerian mediation of the Iranian hostage crisis. In J. Bercovitch & J. Z. Rubin (Eds.), *Mediation in international relations* (pp. 206–231). New York: St. Martin's Press.

Slouka, M. (2002, September). A year later: Notes on America's intimations of mortality. *Harper's Magazine, 305,* 35–46.

Smith, D. W., Christianson, E. H., Vincent, R., & Hann, N. E. (1999). Population effects of the bombing of Oklahoma City. *Journal of Oklahoma State Medical Association, 92,* 193–198.

Smith, M. B. (2002). The metaphor (and fact) of war. *Peace and Conflict: Journal of Peace Psychology, 8,* 249–258.

Smith, T. W., Rasinski, K. A., & Toce, M. (2001). *America rebounds: A national study of public response to the September 11th terrorist attacks: Preliminary findings*. Chicago: National Opinion Research Center, University of Chicago.

Southern Poverty Law Center. (1997a). *Active hate groups in the U.S. in 2000*. Retrieved February 20, 2003, from http://www.splcenter.org/cgi-bin/goframe.pl?dirname=/intelligenceproject&pagename+ip-2.html

Southern Poverty Law Center. (1997b). *False patriots: The threat of antigovernment extremists*. Montgomery, AL: Author.

Spratt, M. (2002, August 28). *9/11 Media may comfort, terrify*. Retrieved on August 29, 2002, from http://www.dartcenter.org

Sprinzak, E. (1986, September). *Fundamentalism, terrorism, and democracy: The case of the Gush Emunim underground*. Paper presented at the Woodrow Wilson Center, Washington, DC.

Sprinzak, E. (1990). The psychopolitical formation of extreme left terrorism in a democracy: The case of the Weathermen. In W. Reich (Ed.), *Origins of terrorism: Psychologies, ideologies, theologies, states of mind* (pp. 65–85). Cambridge, England: Cambridge University Press.

Staub, E. (1989). *The roots of evil: The origins of genocide and other group violence*. New York: Cambridge University Press.

Staub, E. (1996). The cultural–societal roots of violence: The example of genocidal violence and of contemporary youth violence in the United States. *American Psychologist, 51*, 117–132.

Staub, E. (1998). Breaking the cycle of genocidal violence: Healing and reconciliation. In J. Harvey (Ed.), *Perspectives on loss: A source book*. Washington, DC: Taylor & Francis.

Staub, E. (1999). The origins and prevention of genocide and other group violence. *Peace and Conflict: Journal of Peace Psychology, 5*, 303–336.

Staub, E. (2001). Genocide and mass killing: Their roots and prevention. In D. J. Christie, R. V. Wagner, & D. D. Winter (Eds.), *Peace, conflict, and violence: Peace psychology for the 21st century* (pp. 76–86). Upper Saddle River, NJ: Prentice Hall.

Staub, E. (2002). Preventing terrorism: Raising "inclusively" caring children in the complex world of the 21st century. In C. Stout (Ed.), *Psychology of terrorism*. New York: Praeger.

Staub, E. (in press). *The psychology of good and evil: Why children, adults and groups help and harm others*. New York: Cambridge University Press.

Staub, E., & Bar-Tal, D. (in press). Genocide and intractable conflict: Roots, evolution, prevention and reconciliation. In D. Sears, L. Huddy, & R. Jervis (Eds.), *Handbook of political psychology*. New York: Oxford University Press.

Staub, E., & Pearlman, L. (2001). Healing, reconciliation and forgiving after genocide and other collective violence. In S. J. Helmick & R. L. Petersen (Eds.), *Forgiveness and reconciliation: Religion, public policy, and conflict transformation* (pp. 205–229). Radnor, PA: Templeton Foundation Press.

Staub, E., & Pearlman, L. A. (2002, August). *Preventing renewed violence* [A workshop for leaders in Rwanda]. Kigali, Rwanda.

Staub, E., Pearlman, A. L., Hagengimana, A., & Gubin, A. (2002). *Healing, forgiving and reconciliation: An intervention and its experimental evaluation in Rwanda*. Manuscript in preparation.

Steele, J. (2002a, August 29–September 4). Dare to dream in Jerusalem. *The Guardian Weekly*, p. 14.

Steele, J. (2002b, June 13–19). U.S. claims right to pre-emptive strikes. *The Guardian Weekly*, p. 12.

Stensrud, R., & Stensrud, K. (1983). Coping skills training: A systematic approach to stress management counseling. *Personal & Guidance Journal, 62,* 214–218.

Stephenson, C. (2002). Peacekeeping and peacemaking. In M. Snarr & D. Snarr (Eds.), *Global issues* (pp. 71–87). Boulder, CO: Lynne Rienner.

Storey, J. W., & Utter, G. H. (2002). *Religion and politics: A reference handbook*. Santa Barbara, CA: ABC Clio.

Suedfeld, P. (2000). Reverberations of the Holocaust fifty years later: Psychology's contributions to understanding persecution and genocide. *Canadian Psychology, 41,* 1–9.

Sullivan, A. (2001, October 7). This is a religious war. *The New York Times Magazine*, pp. 44–47.

Sveaass, N. (1994). The organized destruction of meaning. In N. Lavik, M. Nygard, N. Sveaass, & E. Fannemel (Eds.), *Pain and survival: Human rights violations and mental health* (pp. 43–64). Oslo: Scandanavian University Press.

Symonds, M. (1980). The "second injury" to victims [Special issue]. *Evaluation and Change,* 36–38.

Taggart, S. (1994). *Living as if*. San Francisco: Jossey-Bass.

Tajfel, H. (1978). Social categorization, social identity and social comparison. In H. Tajfel (Ed.), *Differentiation between social groups* (pp. 61–76). London: Academic Press.

Tajfel, H., & Turner, J. C. (1979). An integrative theory of intergroup conflict. In W. G. Austin & S. Worchel (Eds.), *The social psychology of intergroup relations* (pp. 33–47). Monterey, CA: Brooks/Cole.

Tajfel, H., & Turner, J. C. (1986). The social identity theory of intergroup behavior. In S. Worchel & G. Austin (Eds.), *Psychology of intergroup relations* (pp. 7–24). Chicago: Nelson-Hall.

Tamimi, A., & Esposito, J. L. (2000). *Islam and secularism in the Middle East*. New York: New York University Press.

Taylor, D. M. (1991). The social psychology of racial and cultural diversity: Issues of assimilation and multiculturalism. In A. G. Reynolds (Ed.), *Bilingualism, multiculturalism, and second language learning* (pp. 1–19). Hillsdale, NJ: Erlbaum.

Taylor, D. M. (1997). The quest for collective identity: The plight of disadvantaged ethnic minorities. *Canadian Psychology, 38*(3), 174–190.

Taylor, D. M. (2002). *The quest for identity: From minority groups to generation Xers.* Westport, CT: Praeger.

Taylor, D. M., & Bougie, E. (2002). *Knowing the enemy: The psychology of the terrorist.* Unpublished manuscript.

Taylor, D. M., & McKirnan, D. J. (1984). A five-stage model of intergroup relations. *British Journal of Social Psychology, 23,* 291–300.

Taylor, D. M., & Moghaddam, F. M. (1994). *Theories of intergroup relations: International social psychological perspectives* (2nd. ed.). Westport, CT: Praeger.

Taylor, J. (1999). *East Timor: The price of freedom.* London: Zed Books.

Taylor, M. (1988). *The terrorist.* London: Brassey's Defense.

Tedeschi, R. G., & Calhoun, L. G. (1996). The posttraumatic growth inventory: Measuring the positive legacy of trauma. *Journal of Traumatic Stress, 9,* 455–471.

Terrorism Research Center. (1997). *The basics: Combating terrorism.* Alexandria, VA: Author. Retrieved from http://www.terrorism.com/modules.php?op=modload&name=News&file=article&sid=5671

Terry, D. J., & Hogg, M. A. (1996). Group norms and the attitude–behavior relationship: A role for group identification. *Personality and Social Psychology Bulletin, 22,* 776–793.

Terry, D. J., Hogg, M. A., & White, K. M. (2000). Attitude–behavior relations: Social identity and group membership. In D. J. Terry & M. A. Hogg (Eds.), *Attitudes, behavior, and social context* (pp. 67–93). London: Lawrence Erlbaum.

Tetlock, P. E. (1998). Social psychology and world politics. In D. T. Gilbert, S. T. Fiske, & G. Lindzey (Eds.), *The handbook of social psychology* (Vol. 2, 4th ed., pp. 868–912). Boston: McGraw-Hill.

Thomas, A. (1982). *Frank Terpil: Confessions of a dangerous man* [Film]. New York: Studio Film & Tape.

Thompson, M., Norris, F., & Hanacek, B. (1993). Age difference in the psychological consequences of hurricane Hugo. *Psychology and Aging, 8,* 606–616.

Tilker, H. A. (1970). Socially responsible behavior as a function of observer responsibility and victim feedback. *Journal of Personality and Social Psychology, 14,* 95–100.

Totten, S., Parsons, W. S., & Charny, I. W. (Eds.). (1997). *Century of genocide: Eyewitness accounts and critical views.* New York: Garland Publishing.

Turnbull, C. M. (1972). *The mountain people.* New York: Simon & Schuster.

Turner, A. L. (2000). Group treatment of trauma survivors following a fatal bus accident: Integrating theory and practice. *Group Dynamics, 4,* 139–149.

Turner, J. C., Hogg, M. A., Oakes, P. J., Reicher, S. D., & Wetherell, M. S. (1987). *Rediscovering the social group: A self-categorization theory.* Oxford, England: Blackwell.

Tutu, D. (1999). *No future without forgiveness.* New York: Random House.

Tyre, T. (2001). Wake-up call: A bioterrorism exercise. *Military Medicine, 166*(Suppl. 2), 90–91.

Undercurrent of hostility toward U.S. in Arab world. (2002, September 12). *The Seattle Times*, p. A10.

Understanding terrorism. (2002, January–February). *Harvard Magazine*, pp. 36–49, 99–103.

Unger, R. (Ed.). (2002). Terrorism and its consequences [Special issue]. *Analyses of Social Issues and Public Policy, 2*(2).

United Nations. (2000a). *Handbook on justice for victims: On the use and application of the United Nations declaration of basic principles of justice for victims of crime and abuse of power.* Retrieved September 10, 2002, from http://www.victimology.nl

United Nations. (2000b). *The role of United Nations peacekeeping in disarmament, de-mobilization and reintegration: Report of the Secretary General.* New York: UN Security Council.

United Nations General Assembly. (1985). *United Nations declaration of basic principles of justice for victims of crime and abuse of power* [GA Resolution 40/34].

United Nations High Commissioner for Refugees. (2001). *State of the world's refugees 2000: 50 years of humanitarian action.* New York: Oxford University Press.

United Nations High Commissioner for Refugees. (2002). *Basic facts.* Available at http://www.unhcr.ch/cgibin/texis/vtx/home?page=basics

Uranium Information Centre. (2001). *Three Mile Island: 1979* (Nuclear Issues Briefing Paper 48). Melbourne, Australia: Author.

Urfaan shaheed: El-Nasaara el-Arab [The Christian Arabs] [Editorial]. (2002, May 29). *An-Nahar*, p. 19.

U.S. Air Force Special Operations School. (1996). *Dynamics of international terrorism* [PowerPoint presentation]. Hurlbert Field, FL: Author.

U.S. Department of State. (2000). *Patterns of global terrorism, 2000* [online]. Available at http://www.state.gov/s/ct/rls/pgtrpt/2000/

van Langenhove, L., & Harré, R. (1999). *Positioning theory.* Oxford, England: Blackwell.

Vernberg, E., La Greca, A., Silverman, W., & Prinstein, M. (1996). Prediction of posttraumatic stress symptoms in children after hurricane Andrew. *Journal of Abnormal Psychology, 105,* 237–248.

Vlahov, D., Galea, S., Resnick, H., Ahern, J., Boscarino, J., Bucuvalas, M., et al. (2002). Increased use of cigarettes, alcohol, and marijuana among Manhattan, New York, residents after the September 11th terrorist attacks. *American Journal of Epidemiology, 155,* 988–996.

Volkan, V. (1997). *Bloodlines: From ethnic pride to ethnic terrorism* [hardcover ed.]. New York: Farrar, Straus and Giroux.

Voll, J. (1982). *Islam: Continuity and change in the modern world.* Boulder, CO: Westview Press.

Wagner, R. V. (1988). Distinguishing between positive and negative approaches to peace. *Journal of Social Issues, 44*(2), 1–15.

Wagner, R. V., & Wray, N. (1995). Promoción de la resolución indígena de conflictos en el Ecuador [Promoting indigenous conflict resolution in Ecuador]. *Psicología Política, 11,* 7–14.

Walzer, W. (1992). *Just and unjust wars: A moral argument with historical illustrations* (2nd ed.). New York: Basic Books.

Walzer, W. (2003, March 7). What a little war in Iraq could do. *The New York Times*, p. A27.

Watzlawick, P., Weakland, J. H., & Fisch, R. (1974). *Change: Principles of problem formation and problem resolution.* New York: Norton.

Weathers, F. W., Litz, B. T., Herman, D. S., Huska, J. A., & Keane, T. M. (1993, October 25). *The PTSD Checklist (PCL): Reliability, validity, and diagnostic utility.* Paper presented at the meeting of the International Society of Traumatic Stress Studies, San Antonio, TX.

Weber, T. (1997). *On the Salt March: The historiography of Gandhi's march to Dandi.* New Delhi, India: HarperCollins.

Weinberg, H. A. (1999). Parenting training for attention-deficit hyperactivity disorder: Parental and child outcome. *Journal of Clinical Psychology, 55*, 907–913.

Weine, S., Danieli, Y., Silove, D., Van Ommeren, M., Fairbank, J. A., & Saul, J. (2002). Guidelines for international training in mental health and psychosocial interventions for trauma exposed populations in clinical and community settings. *Psychiatry, 65*(2), 156–164.

Weiner, B. (1986). *An attributional theory of motivation and emotion.* New York: Springer-Verlag.

Weiss, D., Marmar, C., Metzler, T., & Ronfeldt, H. (1995). Predicting symptomatic distress in emergency services personnel. *Journal of Consulting & Clinical Psychology, 63*, 361–368.

Wessells, M. G. (1999). Culture, power, and community: Intercultural approaches to psychosocial assistance and healing. In K. Nader, N. Dubrow, & B. Stamm (Eds.), *Honoring differences: Cultural issues in the treatment of trauma and loss* (pp. 276–282). New York: Taylor & Francis.

Wessells, M. G., & Monteiro, C. (2001). Psychosocial interventions and post-war reconstruction in Angola: Interweaving Western and traditional approaches. In D. Christie, R. V. Wagner, & D. Winter (Eds.), *Peace, conflict, and violence: Peace psychology for the 21st century* (pp. 262–275). Upper Saddle River, NJ: Prentice Hall.

Wessells, M. G., & Monteiro, C. (in press). Psychosocial assistance to internally displaced people in Angola: A child focused, community-based approach. In K. Miller & L. Rasco (Eds.), *From clinic to community: Ecological approaches to refugee mental health.* Upper Saddle River, NJ: Erlbaum.

Wessely, S., Hyams, K., & Bartholomew, R. (2001). Psychological implications of chemical and biological weapons. *British Medical Journal, 323*, 878–879.

Westermeyer, J., & Wahmanholm, K. (1996). Refugee children. In R. Apfel & B. Simon (Eds.), *Minefields in their hearts* (pp. 75–103). New Haven, CT: Yale University Press.

White, J. R. (2002). Political eschatology: A theory of antigovernment extremism. *American Behavioral Scientist, 44*, 937–956.

White, R. K. (1984). *Fearful warriors: A psychological profile of U.S.–Soviet relations*. New York: Free Press.

White, R. K. (1986). Empathizing with the Soviet government. In R. K. White (Ed.), *Psychology and the prevention of nuclear war* (pp. 82–97). New York: New York University Press.

Whittaker, D. (2001). *The terrorism reader*. New York: Routledge.

Williams, C., Solomon, S., & Bartone, P. (1988). Primary prevention in aircraft disasters: Integrating research and practice. *American Psychologist, 43*, 730–739.

Williams, P. (2002). *Al Qaeda: Brotherhood of terror*. New York: Alpha Press.

Wood, J., Bootzin, R., Rosenhan, D., Nolen-Hoeksema, S., & Jourden, F. (1992). Effects of the 1989 San Francisco earthquake on frequency of content of nightmares. *Journal of Abnormal Psychology, 101*, 219–224.

Woodberry, J. D. (2002, Spring). Reflections on Islamist terrorism. *Fuller Focus, 10*(1), 4–6.

World Health Organization. (1992). *International classification of diseases* (10th ed.). Geneva: Author.

Yeats, W. B. (1983). "Easter, 1916." In R. J. Finneran (Ed.), *The poems: A new edition* (pp. 180–182). New York: Macmillian.

Yehuda, R. (2002). Post-traumatic stress disorders. *New England Journal of Medicine, 346*(2), 108–114.

Youssef, M. (1991). *America, oil, & the Islamic mind: The real crisis is the gulf between our ways of thinking*. Grand Rapids, MI: Zondervan.

Zakaria, F. (2001, October 15). Why do they hate us? The politics of rage. *Newsweek*, pp. 22–40.

Zakaria, F. (2003, March 24). Why America scares the world and what to do about it. *Newsweek*, pp. 18–33.

Zganjar, L. (1998, March 5). Forgotten hero of Mai Lai to be honored after 30 years. *San Francisco Chronicle*, p. A9.

Zimbardo, P. G. (1969). The human choice: Individuation, reason, and order versus deindividuation, impulse, and chaos. In W. J. Arnold & D. Levine (Eds.), *Nebraska symposium on motivation, 1969* (pp. 237–309). Lincoln: University of Nebraska Press.

Zimbardo, P. G. (2001, November). Opposing terrorism by understanding the human capacity for evil. *Monitor on Psychology*, 48–50.

Zinner, E. S., & Williams, M. B. (1999). Summary and incorporation: A reference frame for community recovery and restoration. In E. S. Zinner & M. B. Williams (Eds.), *When a community weeps: Case studies in group survivorship*. Philadelphia: Brunner/Mazel.

Zoroya, G. (2002, August 6). Fear, rage fester inside for West Bank children: Curfew, occupation push generation toward radicalism. *USA Today*, pp. A1–A2.

AUTHOR INDEX

Mandel, D. R., 138
Mandelstam, P., 95
Mann, L., 134
Mantell, D. M., 132
Manwaring, M., 12
Marmar, C., 277
Marsella, A. J., 42, 45, 46, 241, 248, 250, 251, 253
Marshall, A., 104
Marshall, R., 239
Marshall, S., 274
Martin, S., 209
Martin-Baro, I., 250, 251, 262
Martinez, R., 266
Maslach, C., 242
Maslow, A., 252
Maxwell, J. S., 281
Mays, V., 277
McAlister, A., 144
McCauley, C., 152, 153, 155, 157, 159, 160, 208
McFarlane, A., 249
McGarty, C., 108
McIntosh, D. N., 237
McIntyre, T., 250
McKirnan, D. J., 177
McMillen, J., 234, 277
Medved, M., 81, 84
Meeus, W. H. J., 132
Meichenbaum, D., 280
Melson, R., 164
Mendez, G. I., 277
Metzler, T., 277
Mezvinski, N., 77, 85
Michultka, D., 249
Milgram, S., 28, 42, 105, 130, 131, 132, 133, 170
Miller, D. T., 135
Miller, K., 254
Miller, M., 15, 16
Miller, P. D., 234
Miller, S. E., 149
Mir, H., 62
Mitchell, J., 192
Mitchell, J. T., 274
Mittleman, J., 30
Moen, D. G., 83
Moerk, E., 33
Moghaddam, F. M., 104, 106, 108, 110, 111, 112, 115, 116, 176, 177
Mollica, R., 249
Monteiro, C., 212, 217, 250, 255

Montiel, C. J., 17, 219
Morelli, M., 137
Morgan, J., 98
Morgan, J. N., 82, 83
Morris, N., 77
Morrison, T., 144
Morrow, J., 277
Mortimer, E., 77
Moscovici, S., 180
Moscrop, A., 228
Moussalli, A. S., 77, 79, 84
Mouton, J. S., 217
Mukherji, B., 252
Murphy, L. R., 281
Murray, B., 245

Nader, K., 250
Nail, P. R., 183
Nash, J., 18, 19, 21
National Institute of Mental Health, 239
Neria, Y., 239
Nettler, R., 85
Neufeld, R. W., 281
Nisbett, R., 129
Nixon, S. J., 234, 276
Nolen-Hoeksema, S., 277
Nordhaus, W. D., 149
Norris, F. H., 228, 277
North, C., 233, 234, 238
Nuttman-Shwartz, O., 232

Oakes, P. J., 108, 180
Oberschall, A., 213
Ogden, C., 231
Ohanyan, A., 217
O'Neil, C., 98
Orley, J., 248
Osgood, C. E., 181

Packer, G., 146
Palmer, D. L., 178
Pann, J. G., 278
Panzarella, R., 132
Pareto, V., 111
Parsons, W. S., 153
Pasagic, I., 227
Pastel, R., 228
Paul, A., 155
Pearlman, L. A., 151, 162, 165, 166, 167, 242
Pearlstein, R., 23, 104
Peristiany, J. G., 77

SUBJECT INDEX

Carlos the Jackal (terrorist), 57, 93
Carter, Jimmy, and Three Mile Island incident, 193
Central American refugees, mental health problems of, 249
Central Asia, Muslims in, 74
"Change of change," 110
Charismatic leadership, 160, 202
    of bin Laden, 214
Chechnya
    bandits vs. patriots in, 100
    in bin Laden's message, 40
    guerrilla groups seeking autonomy in, 212
    oppression and persecution in, 22, 163
Chemical terrorism, 19, 196, 265
    See also Aum Shinrikyo
Cheney, Dick, 266
Children
    effects of terrorism on, 245
    exposed to large-scale traumatic events, 230
    postdisaster symptoms in, 278
    separated, 255
    and September 11 tragedy, 272, 274–275
    socialization of, 167
Chile
    state terrorism in, 212
    "Dirty War," 64
    "Truth and Reconciliation" commissions in, 217
China, 22, 163
China Syndrome, The (movie), 193
"Chosen traumas," 261–262
Christian Children's Fund (CCF)/Angola, 257
Christians and Christianity
    in Arabic world, 74
    violence perpetrated by, 156
CIA-directed covert operations, advantageous comparisons with, 128
Cicourel, Aaron, 98
Civil rights movement
    adaptation to needed, 153
    extremists succeeded by moderates in, 181
Clash of Civilizations, The (Huntington), 40
Clausewitz, Carl von, 12
Cognitive appraisal of stress or threat, and resilience to traumatic stress, 279
Cognitive dissonance

in terrorism scholarship, 56–60
in terrorists' explanations, 52
Cognitive redefinition, moral justification as, 124, 126
Cold War
    and ethnic antagonisms, 213
    mentality of, 83
    and psychologists' role, 219
"Collateral damage," 134, 146, 147
Collective action, as diffusion of responsibility, 133
Collective identity. See Identity, collective
Collective violence. See Group violence
Colombia
    assault on institutions of, 194
    and connection of terrorism with drug trafficking, 112
    FARC in, 63, 211
    guerrillas and violence in, 153
    political/criminal terrorism in, 17
Communications workshop format, for promotion of empathy, 217
Community-based assistance, for refugees or displaced persons, 256–259
Comparative injustice
    Palestinians' perception of, 261
    See also Relative deprivation
"Compassionate articulation," 244
Compassion Center, for September 11 attack, 269
Complex humanitarian emergencies (CHEs), 188–189
    terrorist acts as, 187, 189
Conflict
    changed sources of, 205
    as source of terrorism, 211
    wide scope of, 12
Conformity
    Fromm on, 24
    and terrorists, 170
Consciousness raising, through terrorist acts, 113
Conspiracy of silence, 226, 242
Constructed world, 3–4
Contemporary world, political/economic order of, 12–13
Coping styles or strategies
    of Israeli bus commuters, 232
    and resilience to traumatic stress, 278–279
Countering Terrorism: Integration of Practice and Theory (conference), 267

Counterterrorist measures, 142–143
 military force as, 144–147
 and war on Iraq, 147–149
Countertransference, with trauma victims, 243
Creveld, Martin van, 86
Crime, and terrorism, 38, 49–50, 56, 57, 64, 112
 theatrical crime, 50, 51–52, 53, 59–60, 62, 64–65
Criminal terrorism, 16–17, 21
Crusades, 40, 43, 83, 99, 125, 156, 204
Cuba, 22
Cuban missile crisis, Iraq disarmament likened to, 146
Cultural bereavement, by refugees, 254
Cultural conflict, 29–30
 from change and Westernization, 30–31
 and ethnic identity, 31–32
 Huntington on, 40
 and Israeli–Palestinian conflict, 32–33
 over Kosovo, 43
Cultural devaluation, as contributing to violence, 158–159
Cultural facilitators, of group violence, 158–162
Cultural identity. See Identity, cultural
Culturally motivated terrorist, 201, 203–205
Cultural and moral invasion
 of Arab Islamic world by West, 81, 82, 214
 U.S. scapegoated for, 155
Cultural perspectives, on terrorism issues, 219
Cultural preconditions, 105–106
 for terrorist groups, 103–104, 106–107, 116–117
 belief in acts of terrorism to destabilize society, 113–114
 belief that ideal society justifies any means, 112–113
 belief that societal change improves group situation, 114–115
 categorical "good vs. evil" view of world, 108–109
 existence in isolation, 107–108, 110, 112, 115, 117
 perception of difficulty in leaving group, 115–116
 perception that group can bring about societal change, 114
 perception of lack of legal means of achieving change, 111–112

perception of need for radical social change, 110–111, 117
perception of present society as illegitimate and unjust, 109–110
protected, unstable, and inflated view of self, 115
and Western tradition of self-sacrifice, 115, 117
Cultural psychology, as analytical scheme, 100–102
Cyberterrorism, 18–19, 29
Cyprus, 75, 96, 209
Czechoslovakia, breakup of, 214
Czolgosz, Leon, 20

Dar Es Salaam, attack on embassy in, 194
Decision making, group, 133
Defense mechanisms, 24, 28
Dehumanization, 135–137
 of Muslims (Pope Urban II), 125
Delusion, of true believer, 41
Democide, 63, 63n
Democracies, terrorism within, 161
Democratization, in prevention of mass violence, 166
Demographic differences, in response to disasters, 278, 281
Department of Homeland Security, 189
 psychologists proposed for, 268
Department of State, U.S. See State Department, U.S.
Depersonalized death technologies, 133
Depression
 among displaced people, 249
 within Middle East communities, 89
 among terrorism victims, 230–231
"Depressive realism," in potential terrorist groups, 113
Destabilization of society, acts of terror for, 113–114
Destroying the World to Save It (Lofton), 23
Destructiveness, evolution of, 156–158
Developing countries, and somatic symptoms, 250
Diagnostic and Statistical Manual of Mental Disorders, 4th edition (DSM–IV), 228, 229, 239
Dickens, Charles, A Tale of Two Cities, 115
Diffusion of responsibility, 131–133
 in international weapons sales, 141–142
Direct violence, 209
Disabled people, as vulnerable, 256

Fire in the Minds of Men: Origins of Revolutionary Faith (Billington), 23

First Harvard Symposium on the Medical Consequences of Terrorism, 190

Fixity, 226–227

Francis Ferdinand (archduke of Austria), assassination of, 20

"Freedom fighters," terrorists as, 63, 210, 219
    in Mandelstam's distinction, 95, 96

French Maquis, 64

French Revolution, 20

Freud, Sigmund, 24, 116

Friedman, Thomas L., 154

Fromm, Erich, 24

Fundamentalism, 84
    as collective identity, 176–177
    destructive power of, 204
    fundamentalist groups, 16

Fundamentalism, Islamic (Islamism), 4, 79, 84–85, 204
    and collective identity, 176
    conditions behind, 32
    and conditions giving rise to terrorism, 34
    and cultural invasion by West, 81
    fundamentalist Muslim communities, 76
    and fundamentalist religious schools (*madrassas*), 31, 43
    and politicization of religion, 150
    and secularism, 81
    and war on terrorism as "Infinite Justice," 147

Fundamentalism, Jewish, 85–86

Future of terrorism, 205–206

Gama'a al-Islamiyya, 18

Gandhi, Mohandas, 39, 52, 53–54, 54n, 55, 58, 60, 61, 67, 88

Gangsters, 64

Gaza Strip, 261

Gender-based violence, vulnerability from, 256

Gender differences, in response to disasters, 278

Geneva Convention, 50, 52, 64

Genocidal terrorism, 21

Genocide
    and democracies, 161
    of indigenous peoples, 153
    of Jews and Armenians, 164
    See also Holocaust

Giuliani, Rudolph, 244

Globality, and resilience to traumatic stress, 279

Globalization
    and consequences of terrorism, 45
    in Muslim view, 34
    need to appreciate, 282
    social change from, 13
    and terrorists' feelings, 29
    as threat to cultural identity, 204–205

Global poverty, as condition of terrorism, 19

Global-structured violence, 17

Goals of terrorists, 197–198
    as increasingly nonachievable, 202
    See also Motivation of terrorism

Goeth (Nazi labor commandant), 136

"Good vs. evil" view of world, as precondition for terrorist groups, 108–109

Gradualistic moral disengagement, 139–140

"Grave threat" criterion, 129

Great Britain
    Indonesia supported by, 161
    and international court, 45
    and Israel, 86
    as "rogue nation," 22

Greedy groups, 115–116

Group decision making, 133

Groups, terrorist. *See* Terrorist groups

Group violence
    and bystanders, 162–163
    cultural facilitators of, 158–162 (*see also* Enabling history and leadership)
    evolution of destructiveness in, 156–158
    halting of, 164–165
    instigating factors in, 152–153
        processes in turning against other, 153–156
    leaders' role in, 163–164
    need to predict, 167

Gruesome or grotesque situations, exposure to, 191–192

Guatemala, 247, 249, 251, 252, 276–277

Guerrilla warfare, 57, 59, 64

Gulf War, 77, 83, 86–87

Guzman, Abimael, 160

Habyarimana, Juvenal, 163, 259

Hamas, 15, 17, 18, 73, 176

Harvard Symposium on the Medical Consequences of Terrorism, First, 190

Hate crime incidents, 268

Hate groups, 197
Havel, Vàclav, 61
Health status, of terrorist attack victims, 192–193
Heaven's Gate cult, 171
Helplessness
    learned, 190
    and September 11 survivors, 271, 273, 274
Hierarchical models in psychology, 116
Hierarchical system
    intermediaries as disengaged in,133–134
    in terrorist groups, 160
Hill, Paul, 126
Hirohito (emperor of Japan), 21
Hiroshima, bombing of, 207, 211n
Hispanics, and response to disasters, 278
History
    enabling, 66–67
    and memory of Kosovo, 43
    need to study, 46
Hitler, Adolf, 63
Hizballah, 15, 18
Hoffer, Eric, 41
Holistic conception of well-being, 252, 257–258
Hollywood, in Western cultural invasion of Arab Islamic world, 81
Holocaust, 21, 151, 204
    articles on, 276
    and Israel's moral position, 33
    and Israel's sense of vulnerability, 162
    and ongoing war, 164
    and September 11 attacks, 224
Homeland Security, Department of, 189
    psychologists proposed for, 268
Homeland Security Act, 45
Hostage taking, 142
    displacement of responsibility in, 132
Humanization, transformative power of, 138–139
Human rights, increased interest in, 163
Humphreys, Kirk, 242
Huntington, Samuel, 35, 40
Hussein, Saddam, 19, 148, 155, 213

Ideal society, as justifying any means, 112–113
Identity, 171
    and cultural clash, 31, 40
    ethnic, 31–32
    and group conflict, 152
    multiple systems involved in, 225–226
    and relative deprivation, 153
    and September 11 terrorists in Europe, 154
Identity, collective, 169, 172–173
    culture and religion in, 174–175
    and terrorism, 175–178, 184
        and Afghans, 185
        and bin Laden, 178
        normative structure of, 180–181
        outgroup role in,181–184
        and recruitment process, 178–180
        and Russians, 185
Identity, cultural, 31, 174
    increasing importance of, 213
    loss of from displacement, 248
    and terrorist motivation, 203–205
Ideology(ies)
    of antagonism, 158
    as instigating mass violence, 155–156
    in Northern Ireland "Troubles," 231
Ik group or people, 105
Illegitimacy of present society, terrorist groups' perception of, 109
Imitation, terrorism accepted through, 25
Impact assessment, for community-based psychosocial intervention, 258
Imperialistic manipulation, of Arab Islamic world by West, 82–83
Impression management, through terrorists' target selection, 194–197
India
    Hindu–Muslim conflict in, 39
    Muslims in, 74
Indonesia
    ethnic struggles in (Aceh Indonesia), 4
    Muslims in, 74
    oppression in, 22
    scorched-earth policies in, 247
Inequality, as contributing to violence, 159–160
Inferiority feelings, Adler on, 24
Injustice in present society
    as contributing to violence, 159–160
    terrorist groups' perception of, 109
Inside Terrorist Organizations (Rapoport), 23
Instrumental terrorism, 62, 63, 64
    Gandhi and followers reject, 58
Integrated Science-Practice Task Force on Promoting Resilience in Response to Terrorism, 276
Internally displaced people (IDP), 247

See also Refugees or displaced people

International Classification of Diseases (ICD-10), 228

International Monetary Fund, 29

International Society for Traumatic Stress Studies Task Force on International Trauma Training, 243

International terrorism, 15–16
    challenge of, 29
    substate, 21
    See also at Terrorism; Terrorist

International Terrorism: The Other World War (Jenkins), 56

Internet
    and globalization, 204–205
    terrorism web sites on, 23
    in treatment of terrorism victims, 244

Intervention period, primary, 279

Interventions
    for refugees or displaced people, 253–254
        ecological approach to, 254–255
        emergency psychosocial assistance, 255–259
    following terrorist attacks, 239
        recommendations on, 245
        secondary prevention, 239–241
        treatment, 241–244

IRA (Irish Republican Army), 16, 65, 93
    and base community, 163
    British reluctant to meet with, 216
    and Enniskillen bombing, 135
    Provisional, 201
    and society as unjust, 109
    U.S. support for, 94
    as wannabe "soldiers," 63

Iran, 22, 111
    as non-Arab, 74, 75
    and secular collective identity, 177
    toppling of Shah in, 115, 176, 213

Iran–Iraq War, and chemical weapons, 196

Iraq, 22, 40, 78, 86–87
    and Arab-Islamic anger toward U.S., 82–83, 155
    U.S. support of, 161
    war against, 86–87, 147–149
        reporters with combat forces in, 134

Iraqi Kurdish population, and chemical weapons, 196

Islam
    basic beliefs and tenets of, 80
    defenders of, 85

growth of, 74
liberal, 85
periods of dominance of, 31, 79
as sociopolitical, 79–80
and suicide or terror, 131
Wahabbism, 15, 45

Islamic fundamentalism. See Fundamentalism, Islamic

Islamic jihad, 109

Islamic resurgence, and modernity, 78

Islamic terrorism, 35, 44–45, 149–150, 215
    See also Terrorism

Islamism. See Fundamentalism, Islamic

Isolation, as precondition for terrorist groups, 107–108, 110, 112, 115, 117

Israel
    in advantageous comparisons, 128
    bus commuters in, 232
    and Hamas, 17
    political assassinations by, 18
    as "terrorist state," 72
    U.S. support of, 19

Israeli–Palestinian conflict, 13, 22, 32–33, 37, 77–78, 85–88
    Al-Jazeera images of carnage from, 147
    and anger toward U.S., 82
    and Arabs' view of U.S., 155
    articles on, 276
    attack by Jewish settler on Palestinians, 73
    in bin Laden's message, 40
    and definition of "terrorism," 71, 72–73
    evolution of destructiveness in, 156–158
    identical mental/emotional dynamics in, 87
    as intractable, 152
    and Israel's sense of vulnerability, 162
    and Jerusalem, 211
    and language of peace, 89
    moderates vs. radicals in, 72
    and nonviolence, 88
    and Palestinians' perceptions, 261–262
    and peacemaking, 216
    polarization in, 262
    and realistic empathy, 217
    refugee issue in, 259
    and significance of land, 86
    and slow or small negotiations, 77–78
    suicide bombings in, 18, 158, 247, 262 (see also Suicide bombers and terrorism)

"survival" as justification for, 13
and terrorism as retaliation or defense, 261

Japan
    bioterrorism by, (1930s), 19
    nuclear bombing of, 125
    Tokyo subway sarin attack, 195, 196–197, 209, 214, 228, 231
Japanese Red Army, 18, 175
Jealousy, Berke on, 25
Jenkins, Brian M., 56–57
Jewish communities, throughout Middle East, 74
Jewish fundamentalism, 85–86
Jihad, 80, 84, 87, 125
    in bin Laden speeches, 99, 125
Jones, Jim, 171
Jordan, regime of, 34
Journal of Terrorism and Political Violence, 56
Justification of terrorism, 200–205
    vs. explanation, 50, 55
    by Shiite clerics, 131
Just war principles, 144
Just world thinking, 156

Kaczynski, Ted, 63, 66
Kahane Chai, 18
Kashmir, rebels in, 212
Kelman, Herbert, 217
Kemeny, John G., 193
Kennedy, Edward, 268
Khatib, Nabil, 77
Khmer Rouge, 63, 155
    See also Cambodian killing fields
King, Martin Luther, Jr., 54n, 55, 61, 67, 88
Kohlberg, Lawrence, 116
Kosovo, 43, 146–147, 212–213, 252, 258, 261
Ku Klux Klan, 204
Kurdistan Workers' Party, 18
Kuwait, Iraq's invasion of, 155
Kyoto Treaty, 36

Labeling theory, 98
Language, euphemistic, 129–130
Leaders and leadership
    as crucial in hierarchical groups, 160
    enabling, 67
    and group violence, 163–164
Learned helplessness, 190
Leaving terrorist group, perceived difficulty of, 115–116

Lebanon, 22, 75
Legal means of achieving change, perception of, 111–112
Lerner, Michael, 36–37
Levant, Ronald F., 266
Liberation Tigers of Tamil Elam (Tamil Tigers), 18, 212
Liberia, 64
Libya, 22
Lifton, Jay, 23
Lockerbie, Scotland, airplane crash. *See* Pan American 103 terrorist bombing
London School of Health and Tropical Medicine, on complex emergencies, 189
Lone wolf operator, 203
Lost Art of Declaring War, The (Hallett), 5

Madrassas (fundamentalist religious schools), 31, 43
Mafia, 64
Mandela, Nelson, 55, 139
Mandelstam, Peter, 95–96
Manwaring, Max, 12
Mao Zedong, 14, 57, 59, 64, 67
Martyrs and martyrdom, 53
    and bin Laden on jihad, 125
    glorification of, 114–115
    and motivation for terrorism, 44
    al-Qaeda's use of, 145
    from suicide bombing, 150
        and Palestinian suicide bombers, 18, 73, 84
        (*see also* Suicide bombers and terrorism)
    and terror management theory, 112–113
    as Western value, 117
        in *A Tale of Two Cities*, 115
Marxist theory, 110, 111
Maslow, Abraham, 116
Mass executions, socially sanctioned, 130
Mass media
    battlefield death and destruction in, 134
    and moral justifications, 127
    public exposure to terrorist acts through, 194
        indirect exposure, 238
    in Western cultural invasion of Arab Islamic world, 81
Mass suicide, 171
Mass violence
    and democracies, 161

and U.S. as target, 198–199, 205
Mountain People, The (Turnbull), 105
Movies, in Western cultural invasion of Arab Islamic world, 81
Mujahedin-e Khalq Organization, 18
Munich appeasement, as analogy to hypothetical crisis, 145
Munich Olympics (1972), attack on Israeli athletes at, 195
Murrah Federal Building bombing. *See* Oklahoma City bombing
Muslims
    antiterrorism seen as intercultural wars by, 145
    and Arabs, 74–75
    and jihad, 125 (*see also* Jihad)
    psychosocial understanding of, 28
    and racism, 19
    social-cultural and political-ideological, 79
    Urban II's dehumanization of, 125
My Lai massacres, 130, 138–139

Nagasaki, bombing of, 211n
Nairobi, Kenya, attack on embassy in, 194
Nakosteen, Mehdi, quoted, 103
Narrative conventions, in positioning theory, 98
Narratives, in terrorist groups, 114
Nasreddin, Mulla, 103
Nationalist separatist groups, 16
National Mental Health Association, 276
National Muslim communities, 76
Nation-building, 22
    case studies of needed, 46
Nations, unstable, 22
Natural disasters, 188, 189
    psychological literature on, 277
Nazi Germany, 21
    and belief in authority, 41
    as democidal, 64
    displacement of responsibility in, 130
    and evolution of destructiveness, 156
    heterogeneous support for, 159
    ideology in, 155
    Jews devalued in, 158
    labor commandant's compassion and cruelty, 136
    life problems as reason for rise of, 211
    Munich appeasement of, 145
Negotiation
    and extremists vs. moderates, 181

and Israeli–Palestinian conflict, 77–78
    in Mandelstam's distinction, 95
    and peacemaking, 215–216
    with rationally motivated terrorists, 201
Neo-Nazis, 16
Newman, Russ, 266
"New normality," 224, 246
New York State Psychological Association Disaster Relief Network of, 268
    meeting of psychologists arranged by, 273
Nidal, Abu, 18
Nonviolence, 39
    and Palestinian resistance, 88
Normative construction, 102
Normative structure, of terrorist collective identity, 180–181
Northern Ireland, 4, 65, 163, 247
    articles on, 276
    Enniskillen bombing in, 135, 231
    lives lost to "troubles" in, 94
    origin of conflicts in, 213
    See also IRA
North Korea, 22
Nuclear arms race, and psychologists' role, 219
Nuclear terrorism, 19
Nuremberg Accords, 130

Obedience to Authority (Milgram), 105
Obedience experiments of Milgram, 42, 105–106, 131, 137, 170
Obedient aggression, 137–138
Ocalan, Abdullah, 160
Oil
    Middle East disputes over, 70
    as Muslim blessing, 79
Oklahoma City bombing, 4, 195, 197, 230
    psychosocial aftermath of, 233–234
    as revolutionary spark, 113
    studies on, 276
    victims' injuries in, 192
    See also McVeigh, Timothy
Olympic Games at Munich (1972), attack on Israeli athletes at, 195
Omar (Palestinian militant), 139
Oppression, and terrorism, 19, 22, 60–61
Origins of Terrorism, The (Reich), 23
Oslo Accords, 216
Ottoman empire, 31
    and Kosovo (1389), 43

Psychological stability, and resilience to traumatic stress, 279
Psychologists, and troubled places, 89
  Middle East troubles, 70
Psychology
  challenges to, 45–47
  discursive, 91
  and public policy, 266
  and terrorism, 23, 29, 208–210, 282
    in addressing impact, 267–268, 282
    in addressing threat, 266–267
    in first-person account of September 11 aftermath, 268–275
    literature on, 276
    in promoting resilience, 275–281
    questions for psychologists, 39
  See also Social psychology
Psychopathological terrorism, 21
Psychopathologists, on terrorism, 26
Psychosocial aftermath of terrorism
  international research findings on, 230–232
  and interventions, 239–244, 245
  and Oklahoma City bombing, 233–234
  research needed on, 244–245
  and September 11 attacks, 223–225, 228, 229–230, 234–239
Psychosocial approach to terrorism, 3, 11, 16
Psychosocial emergency assistance, for refugees or displaced people, 255–259
Psychosocial well-being of displaced people, 248
PTSD (posttraumatic stress disorder), 229
  among displaced people, 249, 250
  and locally constructed idioms or meanings, 250
  preventing of, 280
  and psychological debriefing, 240
  and range of mental health consequences of terrorism, 239
  in terrorism victims, 228, 230, 231, 232, 233, 234, 235, 236–238
  treatment for, 241
  See also Trauma
PTSD-related distress, among former POWs (2002), 225
Public policy, and psychology, 266

al-Qaeda network, 39
  as abandoning focus on positive outcomes, 183
  attraction of, 211–212, 214
  and collective identity, 175, 176
  and concept of terrorist, 93, 94, 95
  as fundamentalist (Post), 16
  heroin money supporting, 17
  Islamic fundamentalism of, 204
  as new type of enemy, 145
  organization of, 160
  Palestinian vs. U.S. view of, 15
  and recruitment from refugees, 259
  religious identity of, 214
  and September 11 attacks, 21, 143, 144
  U.S. efforts against, 33
    Afghanistan campaign, 33, 146, 147
  and Westerners or West-leaning leaders, 215
Quebec separatism, extremists succeeded by moderates in, 181

Rabin, Yitzhak, assassination of, 125
Race, and response to disasters, 278
Racism, as condition of terrorism, 19
Radiation leak at Three Mile Island, 193
Radicalization, 157
Radical societal change, perception of need for, 110–111, 117
al-Rahman, Omar Abri, 21
Rationally motivated terrorist, 200–202, 219
Reactance, 183
Realistic empathy, 216–218
Reconciliation, 217, 231
Red Cross, American, 242, 267, 268, 274
Refugee camps, terrorist recruitment from, 178–179, 182
Refugees or displaced people, 178–179, 247
  mental health problems of, 248–251
    interventions for, 253–259
    and social ecologies, 251–253
    and terrorism, 248, 259–262
Reign of Terror, 20
Reinforcement, Skinner on, 25
Relative deprivation
  as contributing to violence, 153, 159–160
  See also Comparative injustice
Religion
  in cultural identity, 203, 205
  politicization of, 125
  See also Fundamentalism; Fundamentalism, Islamic; Islam
Religious extremist terrorism, 16, 21
Religious identity, 174
  increasing importance of, 213

Religious militancy, 84–85

Reoccurrence, perception of potential for, 191

Republic (Plato), 111

Resilience, 7
  promoting of, 272, 275–281

Responsibility
  diffusion of, 132–133
    in international weapons sales, 141–142
  displacement of, 130–132
  two levels of, 132

Revenge, in Mandelstam's distinction, 95

Revere, Paul, 100

Revolutionary Armed Forces of Colombia (FARC), 18, 63, 211

Revolutionary United Front, Sierra Leone, 64, 247

Rights, in positioning theory, 97

Risk, consequences of exposure to, 191

Risk factors, in disaster model, 278–280

Road rage, terrorism contrasted with, 92, 93

Robespierre, Maximilien de, 20

Rogue nations, as condition of terrorism, 22

Roman Empire, 20

Ruby Ridge, Idaho, confrontation, 203

Russia (pre-Soviet), 20

Russian citizens (post-Soviet), collective identity absent for, 184–185

Rwanda
  and complex humanitarian emergencies, 189
  French support of regime in, 163
  genocidaires among refugees from, 259
  genocide in, 151
    and international community, 164
    as respect for authority, 160
  "Hutu power" in, 155
  and messianic terrorists, 63
  opportunities lacking in, 159–160
  professionals' feeling of helpfulness in, 224
  refugees from, 249
  and refugees becoming fighters, 259
  Tutsis as victims in, 158
  and understanding of violence, 165, 166

Rwanda-Congo, 4

Sa, Khun, 64

Salzinger, Kurt, 266

Sanctioning by indirection, 131

Sanitized language, 129–130

Sanko, Foday, 64

Satyagraha, 52–54

Saudi Arabia, 33, 109, 111, 159

Scapegoating, 154, 164, 212

Secondary adjustment period, 280

Secondary prevention, 239–241

Secularism
  and Islamic fundamentalism, 81
  and traditionalism (Middle East), 78

Secularization, in perception of society as illegitimate, 109

Secular Muslim communities, 76

Security, need for, 212

Self, 171
  personal vs. collective, 171–172
  protected, unstable and inflated view of, 115

Self-censure, evasion of. *See* Moral disengagement

Self-concept, 171–173

Self-determination
  as absent in Middle East, 214
  need for, 212–213

Self-efficacy, and resilience to traumatic stress, 279

Self-esteem, of terrorists, 115
  and psychologically motivated terrorist, 202

Self-interest, and mass violence, 153

Self-sanctions, 121

Self-vindication, through legitimate grievances, 135

Sendero Luminoso (Shining Path), Peru, 16, 18, 109, 160, 211, 214

Separated children, as vulnerable, 255

Separatist terrorism, 16

September 11th Fund, 242, 245, 274

September 11 terrorist attacks, 13–14, 21, 29, 39–40, 223–224
  absence of explanation for, 51
  as air raids if war declared (quote), 91
  and Arab stereotypes, 76
  background of terrorists in, 154
  consequences (aftermath) of, 143, 224–225, 265–266
    for Arab Americans including refugees, 249
    changed sources of conflict, 205
    moral disengagement, 144
    persecutions accepted, 163
    polarizing rhetoric, 138

psychosocial, 223–225, 228, 229–230, 234–239

stronger respect for authority, 160

and time dimension, 227, 245

and worldwide empathy, 167

cultural symbolism of, 194

as direct violence, 209

and distinction between national war and war on terrorism, 94

first-person account of response to, 268–275

motivation of, 43–44

psychological derangement not factor in, 169

and psychological expertise, 281–282

psychologists' response to, 266, 267–268

special salience of, 207–208

U.S. response to, 33–34

Serbian Black Hand Society, 20

Shadow lives, 116

Shan Liberation Army, Burma, 64

Shari'a, 80

Sharing the Front Line and the Back Hills (Danieli), 242–243

Sherif, M., 105

Shiite clerics, moral justification by, 131

Shiite Muslims, assassins among, 20

Shining Path (*Sendero Luminoso*), Peru, 16, 18, 109, 160, 211, 214

Sierra Leone, 22

Revolutionary United Front in, 64, 247

Single-issue groups, 16

Single women, as vulnerable, 255–256

Sinn Fein, 181

60 Minutes, *and Terpil*, 142

Skinner, B. F., 25

Snyder, Derek, 266

Social activism, and cognitive restructuring, 126

Social comparison, 128

Social conditions, vs. personal attributes as conditions for atrocities, 137

Social constructionist approach, 102

Social constructions, 92

Social ecologies, and refugees, 251–253

Socialization of children, 167

Socially constructed categories, 95–96, 100–101

Social psychology

and terrorism, 26, 170–171, 266–267

and world politics, 218

Social respect, need for, 213

Societal change

as improving terrorist-group situation, 114–115

terrorist groups' perception of accomplishing, 114

Societies, monolithic and autocratic vs. pluralistic and democratic, 160–161

Solomon Asch Center, University of Pennsylvania, 23

South Africa

after apartheid, 177

church massacre in, 231

"Truth and Reconciliation" commissions in, 217

Southern Africa, factions seeking self-determination in, 212

Southern Poverty Law Center, Militia Task Force of, 197

Soviet Union

breakup of, 214

See also Russian citizens

Sri Lanka, 4, 212, 277

Stability, and resilience to traumatic stress, 279

Stage model of disasters, risk and protective factors in, 278–280

Stalin, Joseph, 14, 21, 212

State Department, U.S.

on source nations for terrorism, 22

on terrorism, 15, 58–59

"State failure," 164

State or regime terrorism, 16

and fear of losing power, 212

under Hirohito in Japan, 21

in Latin America, 250–251 (see also Argentina; Chile; El Salvador; Guatemala)

State-related terrorism, 16, 94, 205

and categorical thinking, 108

and cultural preconditions, 104

functionaries in as patriots, 130

and isolation of groups, 108, 110

as morally disengaged, 131

and Palestinian/Arab view of Israel, 71

and stability of society, 113

State security services, 64

State-sponsored terrorism. *See* State-related terrorism

State-supported terrorism. *See* State-related terrorism

Stern gang, 93

Stress evaporation hypothesis, 238

Stress inoculation training (SIT), 276, 280–281

Stress management programs, 281

Structural violence, 209

Stuyvesant High School, and September 11 attack, 272

Substance use, by NYC residents (after September 11), 236, 242

Substate terrorism, 16, 21
See also Terrorism

Suffering
in Middle East, 89
of refugees, 261–262
unhealed wounds of, 161–162
See also Poverty; Refugees or displaced people; Victims

Suicide bombers and terrorism, 53, 95, 158
and cultural context, 117
as direct violence, 209
Palestinian, 18, 158, 247, 262
and poverty-stricken conditions, 212
as al-Qaeda weapon, 145
social approval of, 150
target selection of, 194
and terrorist approach to death, 112
warnings of, 265–266

Supporters, of terrorist groups, 201

Survival, emphasis on, 12–13

Symbolic acts, terrorism as, 210

Symbolism of target selection, in terrorist acts, 193–194

Symptoms, postdisaster, 277–278

Syria, 22

Tale of Two Cities, A (Dickens), 115

Taliban
Buddhist statues destroyed by, 194
collective identity provided by, 176
as government of Afghanistan, 94
and recruitment from refugees, 259
Pakistani support for, 199
as structuring Afghan society, 185, 203
tyranny of, 147
U.S. attack on, 33, 146

Tamil Tigers, 18, 212

Target selection
and impression management, 194–197
symbolism of, 193–194

Taylor, Charles, 64

Taylor, D. M., 172

Technologic emergencies or disasters, 188, 189, 273

psychological literature on, 277

Teleology, 187
See also Motivation of terrorism

Television
battlefield death and destruction in, 134
and moral justifications, 127
See also Mass media

Terpil, Frank, 141, 142

Terror, 61, 71

Terrorism, 14, 122–123
and agents of terror, 62–64
bin Laden's interpretation of, 125
books and Web sites on, 23, 28–29
causes of, 33–39, 211–215
formative and precipitating, 37, 38
hatred and revenge behind, 4
ideologies' role in, 155
and oppression, 60–61
and refugees or displaced people, 248, 259–262
and U.S. foreign policy, 155
as challenge to inquiry, 46–47
and collective identity, 175–178, 184
and Afghans, 185
normative structure of, 180–181
outgroup role in,181–184
and recruitment process, 178–180
and Russians, 185
concepts in explanation of, 23–29
conditions conducing to, 19, 22
consequences of, 45
psychosocial, 228 (see also Psychosocial aftermath of terrorism)
countermeasures against, 142–149
violent, 128
and crime, 38, 49–50, 56, 57, 64, 112
as theatrical crime, 50, 51–52, 53, 56, 59–60, 62, 64–65
definition(s) of, 15–16, 17, 58–60, 71–72, 73–74, 152, 210–211, 228
and bombing of Hiroshima, Nagasaki and Dresden, 211n
and Israeli–Palestinian conflict, 71, 72–73
from 1993 bombing of World Trade Center, 196
in United States Code, 170
within democracies, 161
ecology of (anti-American), 36
ends and means of, 13, 200
and explanation vs. justification, 50, 55

and lack of imagination, 55–56, 61
propositions governing, 54–55
vs. *satygagraha*, 52–54
goals of, 197–198, 247 (*see also* Motivation of terrorism)
group process and influence in, 44–45
history of, 19, 20–21
hostage taking, 132, 142
Islamic, 35, 44–45, 149–150, 215
justification of, 200
vs. explanation, 50, 55
by Shiite clerics, 131
and mass media,127
methods of, 18–19
and moral disengagement, 123–124
motivation of, 16, 17, 43–44, 201–205 (*see also* Motivation of terrorism)
as murder vs. as warfare, 49–50, 56, 57
patterns of, 16–17
peace psychological perspective on, 207, 209, 211, 219–220 (*see also* Peace psychology and peace psychological perspective)
prevention of, 166–167, 219–220
through meeting basic human needs, 262
and psychologists' work, 262–263
and psychology, 23, 29, 208–210, 282
in addressing impact, 267–268, 282
in addressing threat, 266–267
in first-person account of September 11 aftermath, 268–275
literature on, 276
in promoting resilience, 275–281
questions for psychologists, 39
social psychology, 26, 170–171, 266-267
psychosocial approach to, 3, 11, 16
psychosocial roots of, 14–15
reactions and responses to, 215–218, 219–220
psychosocial, 228–230
social construction of, 94
social milieu of, 60, 65–67
state or state-related, 16, 94, 113, 131, 205, 212, 250–251 (*see also* State or regime terrorism; State-related terrorism)
as threat to U.S., 83
and traditional repressive societies, 161
and true believers, 40, 41–43, 51, 55, 58, 64

victims of, 60, 190–193 (*see also under* Victims)
war distinguished from, 59, 94
and war on Iraq, 148, 149
Western analysis of, 114
Terrorism Reader, The (Whittaker), 23
Terrorism Research Center, 23
Terrorism scholarship, cognitive dissonance of, 56–60
Terrorist acts, 92–93, 187
as complex humanitarian emergencies, 187, 189
as destabilizing society,113–114
interventions following, 239
recommendations on, 245
secondary prevention, 239–241
treatment, 241–244
psychological impact of (factors influencing), 189–193
as symbolic, 210
target selection for
and impression management, 194–197
symbolism of, 193–194
and worldview of actors, 187–188
Terrorist attacks of September 11, 2001. *See* September 11 terrorist attacks
Terrorist entrepreneurs, 140–141
Terrorist groups, 16
and bystanders, 163
collective identity from, 180–181
cultural preconditions for, 103–104, 106–107, 116–117
belief in acts of terrorism to destabilize society, 113–114
belief that ideal society justifies any means, 112–113
belief that societal change improves group situation, 114–115
categorical "good vs. evil" view of world, 108–109
existence in isolation, 107–108, 110, 112, 115, 117
perception of difficulty in leaving group, 115–116
perception that group can bring about societal change, 114
perception of lack of legal means of achieving change, 111–112
perception of need for radical social change, 110–111, 117
perception of present society as illegitimate and unjust, 109–110

protected, unstable and inflated view of self, 115

and Western tradition of self-sacrifice, 115, 117

evolution of destructiveness in, 157

as fighting wars, 152

membership in as important, 202

and "Patriot" organizations or hate groups, 197

social rewards in, 140

support structure of, 201

Terrorists, 64–65, 71, 92–94, 188

advantageous comparisons made by, 128

vs. freedom fighters, 210

and cultural bias, 219

in Mandelstam's distinction, 95–96

gradualistic moral disengagement of, 140

justification by, 200–205

vs. explanation, 50, 55

self-vindication by, 135

Terror management theory, 112, 114, 230

Theatrical crime, terrorism as, 50, 51–52, 53, 56, 59–60, 62, 64–65

"Third World War," 57

Thompson (helicopter pilot at My Lai), 139

Threats, gravity of, 129

Three Mile Island Nuclear Station radiation leak, 193

"Time bomb" medical malady, 193

Tokyo subway sarin attack, 195, 196–197, 209, 214, 228, 231

Tolerance, principle of, 101, 102

Tomes, Henry, 266

Torture victims

displaced people as, 260

as vulnerable, 256

Toyama, Mitsuru, 21

Traditionalism

and Middle East tensions, 70

vs. modernity (Arab Islamic world), 81

and secularism (Middle East), 78

Traditional Muslim communities, 76

Traditional societies, 31

and terrorism, 161

Trauma

APA division on proposed, 269

and culturally scripted meanings, 250

and event countertransference reactions, 243

and fixity, 226–227

impact of underestimated, 239

multidimensional multidisciplinary integrative framework for study of, 225–226

self-reevaluation from, 229

See also PTSD

Trauma period, 279

Traumatic grief, 228

Treatment

for terrorism victims, 241–244

See also Interventions

"Tribute of lights" (September 11 site), 224

True Believer, The (Hoffer), 41

True believers, 40, 41–43, 51, 55, 58, 64

"Truth and Reconciliation" commissions, 217

Turkey, 32, 34, 36, 74, 75

Turkish Workers and Peasants Liberation Party, comments of leader of, 199

Turnbull, Colin, 105

Ulster Defense Force, 63, 65

Unabomber, 4

Unilateral expansion, by U.S., 83

United Nations (UN)

and consequences of terrorism, 45

Cyprus peacekeeping by, 209

and halting of violence, 164

and human rights, 163

and Israel, 33

190 member states of, 199

United States

cultural enlightenment needed by, 83

foreign policy of, 150

isolationism, 34–35

Indonesia supported by, 161

and international court, 45

and Israel, 32, 33, 86

Muslim view of, 34

national spirit of, 205

negotiation stance of, 215

"Patriot" organizations and hate groups in, 197

reasons for Arab-Islamic anger toward, 80, 155

cultural-moral invasion, 81

economic-financial exploitation, 81–82

military unilateralist expansion, 83

political and imperialistic manipulation, 82–83

relations of with Southern hemisphere, 211

right wing, racist movements in, 161
as "rogue nation," 22
school integration in (1950s), 209
and September 11 attacks, 33–34, 207–208 (*see also* September 11 terrorist attacks)
strengths of, 35
as target, 198–199, 205
terrorism as revenge against (Berke), 25
as terrorist nation, 4, 17
terrorists' feelings toward, 29–30, 31, 45
Urban II (pope), 125
Utilitarian justification
and countermeasures, 128
and preemptive war on Iraq, 148–149

VandenBos, Gary, 266
"Velvet Revolution," 61
Victimization, unhealed wounds of, 161–162
Victims
blaming of,134–135
as culturally devalued, 158–159
of terrorist attack, 60, 190–193
dichotomization of response in, 273
international research findings on, 230–232
interventions with, 239–244
and PTSD, 228, 230, 231, 232, 233, 234, 235, 236–238, 241
of school bus hostage taking in Israel, 232
of September 11 attack, 273–274
U.S. studies on, 233–239
of torture, 256, 260
"Victory," need to redefine, 12
Viet Cong, 64
Vietnamese refugees, mental health problems of, 249
Vietnam War
as analogy to hypothetical crisis, 145
Israeli–Palestinian conflict compared with, 86
My Lai massacre, 130, 138–139
photo of napalmed girl in, 134
as resulting in low tolerance for war, 147
Vietnam War protests, 17–18
Violence
on behalf of just causes, 126–127
belief in justification of, 13
cultural conflict as cause of, 31
direct, 209

forms of, 167 (*see also* Group violence; Mass violence)
gender-based, 256
moral appeals against, 127
nonviolent responses to, 215, 219
political, 56, 57n, 61
structural, 209
Voltaire, on absurdities and atrocities, 125
Vulnerable people, psychosocial assistance for, 255–256

Wahhabism, 15, 45
Walesa, Lech, 61
Wannabe "soldiers," 63, 64
War
as addiction, 27–28
new vision of, 12
preemption (U.S.), 83
terrorism distinguished from, 59, 94
terrorist attacks as, 83
War against Iraq, 86–87, 147–149
reporters with combat forces in, 134
War metaphors, 145–146
Warning, absence of in terrorist attack, 190–191
Wars of identity, 29, 40
reporters with combat forces in, 134
"War on terrorism," 13, 265, 282
critique of concept of, 145
"Infinite Justice" as code name for, 147
Israel's version of, 87
labeling of, 94
and moderates within Islamic societies, 150
vs. wars of past, 29
Washington, D.C. area residents, September 11 reactions of, 235
Water, Middle East disputes over, 70
Weapons of mass destruction, 149
Weapons sales
moral disengagement in, 140–142
terrorists' greater destructive capacity from, 208
Weathermen Underground Organizations, 18
Web sites, on terrorism, 23
Western concepts of mental health, limits on, 250, 253
Westernization
anger felt toward, 13
in perception of society as illegitimate, 109

ABOUT THE EDITORS

Fathali M. Moghaddam, PhD, was born in Iran and educated from an early age in England. He returned to work in Iranian universities after the 1979 revolution, then took up posts with the United Nations and McGill University before moving to his present position as a professor of psychology at Georgetown University. His main research interest is in the area of culture and justice. His most recent books are *The Individual and Society: A Cultural Integration* (2002) and *The Self and Others* (2003, with Rom Harré).

Anthony J. Marsella, PhD, DHC, is a professor of psychology at the University of Hawaii in Honolulu, where he has been a member of the faculty for 33 years. Dr. Marsella specializes in international and cross-cultural psychology and psychopathology. He has published 10 books and more than 130 book chapters, journal articles, and technical reports. He has also been a principal editor for two different encyclopedias of psychology. He has been a visiting professor in Australia, China, India, the Philippines, and South Korea and an invited lecturer at more than 25 national and international universities. Dr. Marsella has received the American Psychological Association Award for Distinguished Contributions to the International Advancement of Psychology, and he was awarded an honorary doctorate degree by the University of Copenhagen for his contributions to international peace and understanding.